Music in *The Girl's Own Paper*:
An Annotated Catalogue, 1880–1910

Nineteenth-century British periodicals for girls and women offer a wealth of material for understanding how girls and women fit into their social and cultural worlds in which music making was an important part. *The Girl's Own Paper*, first published in 1880, stands out because of its rich musical content. Keeping practical usefulness as a research tool and as a guide to further reading in mind, Judith Barger has catalogued the musical content found in the weekly and later monthly issues during the magazine's first thirty years in music scores, instalments of serialized fiction about musicians, music-related nonfiction, poetry with a musical title or theme, illustrations depicting music making, and replies to musical correspondents. The book's introductory chapter reveals how content in *The Girl's Own Paper* changed over time to reflect a shift in women's music making from a female accomplishment to an increasingly professional role within the discipline, using 'the piano girl' as a case study. A comparison with musical content found in *The Boy's Own Paper* over the same time span offers additional insight into musical content chosen for the girls' magazine. A user's guide precedes the chronological annotated catalogue; the indexes that follow reveal the magazine's diversity of approach to the subject of music.

Judith Barger is an independent scholar who holds PhDs in musicology (Indiana University) and nursing (The University of Texas at Austin). After a career as a United States Air Force nurse, she turned her attention to music, concentrating on music history and the organ. She is the author of *Elizabeth Stirling and the Musical Life of Female Organists in Nineteenth-Century England* (Ashgate 2007) and *Beyond the Call of Duty: Army Flight Nursing in World War II* (2013). Dr Barger lives in Little Rock, Arkansas, USA.

Music in Nineteenth-Century Britain
Series Editor: Bennett Zon
Durham University, UK

So much of our 'common' knowledge of music in nineteenth-century Britain is bound up with received ideas. This series readdresses both the work of the nineteenth century and works about the period and reassesses our perceptions of it, as well as encouraging scholarly research into aspects of the topic which hitherto remain unexplored. Volumes in the series cover areas such as music criticism, composers, concert venues and promoters, church music, women and music, reception history and domestic music making.

Recent titles in the series:

Music and Institutions in Nineteenth-Century Britain
Paul Rodmell

Our Ancient National Airs: Scottish Song Collecting from the Enlightenment to the Romantic Era
Karen McAulay

Hamish MacCunn (1868–1916): A Musical Life
Jennifer L. Oates

Music and Academia in Victorian Britain
Rosemary Golding

Opera in the British Isles, 1875–1918
Paul Rodmell

Michael Costa: England's First Conductor: The Revolution in Musical Performance in England, 1830–1880
John Goulden

The Musical Life of Nineteenth-Century Belfast
Roy Johnston with Declan Plummer

Music in *The Girl's Own Paper*: An Annotated Catalogue, 1880–1910

Judith Barger

LONDON AND NEW YORK

First published 2017
by Routledge
2 Park Square, Milton Park, Abingdon, Oxon OX14 4RN

and by Routledge
711 Third Avenue, New York, NY 10017

Routledge is an imprint of the Taylor & Francis Group, an informa business

© 2017 Judith Barger

The right of Judith Barger to be identified as author of this work has been asserted by her in accordance with sections 77 and 78 of the Copyright, Designs and Patents Act 1988.

All rights reserved. No part of this book may be reprinted or reproduced or utilised in any form or by any electronic, mechanical, or other means, now known or hereafter invented, including photocopying and recording, or in any information storage or retrieval system, without permission in writing from the publishers.

Trademark notice: Product or corporate names may be trademarks or registered trademarks, and are used only for identification and explanation without intent to infringe.

British Library Cataloguing in Publication Data
A catalogue record for this book is available from the British Library

Library of Congress Cataloging-in-Publication Data
Names: Barger, Judith, 1948– author.
Title: Music in *The Girl's Own Paper*: an annotated catalogue, 1880–1910 / Judith Barger.
Description: New York, NY : Routledge, 2017. | Series: Music in nineteenth-century Britain | Includes bibliographical references and indexes.
Identifiers: LCCN 2016006601 | ISBN 9781472454539 (hardback : alk. paper) | ISBN 9781315534930 (ebook)
Subjects: LCSH: Girl's own paper—Indexes. | Music—Periodicals—Indexes. | Teenage girls—England—Indexes. | Teenage girls—England—Indexes.
Classification: LCC ML5 .G527 | DDC 780.83/420941—dc23
LC record available at http://lccn.loc.gov/2016006601

ISBN: 9781472454539 (hbk)
ISBN: 9781315534930 (ebk)

Typeset in Times New Roman
by Apex CoVantage, LLC

Printed and bound by CPI Group (UK) Ltd, Croydon, CR0 4YY

Contents

List of figures — vii
Acknowledgements — ix
General editor's series preface — x

Introduction: music lessons in *The Girl's Own Paper* — 1
    The passing of 'the piano girl' 4
    The new magazine and its editors 18
    Inside *The Girl's Own Paper* 21
    Music in *The Boy's Own Paper* 45

User guide to the annotated catalogue — 54
    Chronological listing 54
    Indexes 57
    Exceptions 59

Chronological listing of musical content:
The Girl's Own Paper — 60

Topical listing of musical content:
The Girl's Own Paper — 288

Index to fiction — 288
    Musical heroines and heroes 288
    Music in cameo appearances 289
    Stories about music compositions 294

Index to nonfiction — 296
    Biography 296
    Business 297
    Church 297
    Competitions 297

Concerts 298
Crafts and needlework 298
Entertainments 299
Fashion 299
Fidelio Club 300
Hints 300
Instrument purchase, maintenance and construction 300
Music education 300
Music history and appreciation 300
Music mentioned in general nonfiction 301
Odds and Ends 304
Opinion pieces 304
Primers for performance and teaching 305
Repertoire 306
Reviews of printed music 307
Royalty 308
Self-improvement 308
Varieties 308

Index to poetry 314

Index to illustrations 320

Index to Answers to Correspondents 322
Music as a separate heading 322
Study and Studio heading with music replies 325
Music replies under other headings 327
Other replies to correspondents' musical questions 330

Index to music scores by instrument 331
Organ, harmonium 331
Pianoforte 331
Violin, cello 332
Voice, solo 333
Voice, ensemble 337

Index to music scores by composer 339

Works cited 350

Figures

1 First piano piece printed in *The Girl's Own Paper*, 'Le Dernier Papillon' (Edwin M. Lott), *The Girl's Own Paper* 3 (29 October 1881): 72–3   5
2 'Pianoforte Fronts: And How to Decorate Them' (Fred Miller), *The Girl's Own Paper* 6 (4 July 1885): 628   8
3 'Painted Canvas or Painted Sacking Hanging for Back of Piano', in 'A Pretty Pianoforte Back', *The Girl's Own Paper* 18 (7 August 1897): 708   9
4 'Trying over New Music', in 'New Music', *The Girl's Own Paper* 3 (8 July 1882): 652   10
5 'Dress for Evening Wear', in 'The Dress of the Month', *The Girl's Own Paper* 1 (27 March 1880): 201   12
6 'Practising', in 'Seasonable Dress, and How to Make It', *The Girl's Own Paper* 2 (26 March 1881): 401   13
7 'An excellent example of a wide grey and white striped material', in 'How a Girl Should Dress' (Norma), *The Girl's Own Paper* 28 (29 June 1907): 617   14
8 'Charles Peters, Editor', in 'Portrait Gallery of Contributors to "The Girl's Own Paper"', *The Girl's Own Paper* 20 (25 February 1899): foldout plate facing p. 344   19
9 'Miss Flora Klickmann', *The Girl's Own Paper* 29 (19 September 1908): plate facing p. 810   20
10 'Music', *The Girl's Own Paper* 2 (29 January 1881): 273   25
11 First-prize winner in first music composition competition in *The Girl's Own Paper*, 'The Rainy Day' (Ethel Harraden), *The Girl's Own Paper* 9 (7 April 1888): 436–40   27
12 Second-prize winner in first music composition competition in *The Girl's Own Paper*, 'The Rainy Day' (Amelia Corper), *The Girl's Own Paper* Extra Summer 9 (1888): 44–7   32
13 First-prize winner in second music composition competition in *The Girl's Own Paper*, 'Sorrow' – 'Joy' (Fannie Scholfield Petrie), *The Girl's Own Paper* 11 (30 August 1890): 763–5   37

14 'A Banjo Enthusiast', in 'Answers to Correspondents' with Music Heading, *The Girl's Own Paper* 13 (20 February 1892): 336   40

15 First music score printed in *The Girl's Own Paper*, 'Under the Snow' (John Farmer), *The Girl's Own Paper* 1 (31 January 1880): 71–2   43

Acknowledgements

Research for this book has been lengthy but rewarding because of many institutions and individuals that have facilitated my work in important ways. Staffs of libraries in the United States and in England have 'gone the extra mile' to help me find the annual volumes of *The Girl's Own Paper* and its extra holiday issues, as well as relevant supporting literature. Stateside, the interlibrary loan departments of the Indiana University Library in Bloomington and of the Central Arkansas Library System in Little Rock handled with dependable efficiency my numerous requests for materials not found within those libraries. Overseas, the staffs of the Rare Books and Music Reading Room at the British Library and of the Reference Department at the Birmingham Central Library provided access to annual volumes and holiday issues of *The Girl's Own Paper* not easily located elsewhere.

Colleagues at the Music in Nineteenth-Century Britain conferences in Birmingham 2007, Bristol 2009 and Cardiff 2013 offered support, encouragement and thoughtful critiques of my topic, as well as suggestions of additional facets to pursue. I am grateful for the help of those libraries and colleagues along the way.

Finally, a special thank you to Laura Macy, senior commissioning editor at Ashgate, for guiding me through the publication process with such patience and goodwill and to Bennett Zon, editor for the Music in Nineteenth-Century Britain series, in which the book appears. It has been a pleasure to work with them. Illustrations in the book are included with the kind permission of Lutterworth Press.

General editor's series preface

Music in nineteenth-century Britain has been studied as a topic of musicology for over two hundred years. It was explored widely in the nineteenth century itself and in the twentieth century grew into research with strong methodological and theoretical import. Today, the topic has burgeoned into a broad, yet incisive, cultural study with critical potential for scholars in a wide range of disciplines. Indeed, it is largely because of its interdisciplinary qualities that music in nineteenth-century Britain has become such a prominent part of the modern musicological landscape.

This series explores the wealth of music and musical culture of Britain in the nineteenth century and surrounding years. It does this by covering an extensive array of music-related topics and situating them within the most up-to-date interpretative frameworks. All books provide relevant contextual background and detailed source investigations, as well as considerable bibliographical material of use for further study. Areas included in the series reflect its widely interdisciplinary aims and, although principally designed for musicologists, the series is also intended to be accessible to scholars working outside of music in areas such as history, literature, science, philosophy, poetry and performing arts. Topics include criticism and aesthetics; musical genres; music and the church; music education; composers and performers; analysis; concert venues, promoters and organizations; the reception of foreign music in Britain; instrumental repertoire, manufacture and pedagogy; music hall and dance; gender studies; and music in literature, poetry and letters.

Although the nineteenth century has often been viewed as a fallow period in British musical culture, it is clear from the vast extent of current scholarship that this view is entirely erroneous. Far from being a 'land without music', nineteenth-century Britain abounded with musical activity. All society was affected by it, and everyone in that society recognised its importance in some way or another. It remains for us today to trace the significance of music and musical culture in that period and to bring it alive for scholars to study and interpret. This is the principal aim of the Music in Nineteenth-Century Britain series – to advance scholarship in the area and expand our understanding of its importance in the wider cultural context of the time.

Bennett Zon
Durham University, UK

Introduction
Music lessons in *The Girl's Own Paper*

When I first came across a few annual volumes from the 1880s of *The Girl's Own Paper* (*TGOP*) in the stacks of a major academic library, I was searching for information about female organists in nineteenth-century England.[1] My efforts were rewarded. Illustrations of young women on the organ bench in church lofts, fiction featuring young heroines who played the organ, replies to correspondents about organs and organ playing, reviews of organ books and occasional music scores composed for American organ or harmonium all suggested that organists were among the magazine's readers.

Perusal of these and additional volumes of *TGOP* revealed a rich musical content not limited to the organ in this weekly miscellany for girls published in London by the Religious Tract Society (RTS) beginning in 1880. Voice, piano, violin and their performers are well represented, and other instruments such as harp, harmonium, guitar and concertina also appear. Although not a music journal such as the concurrently published *Musical Standard*, *Musical Times* and *Musical World* that catered to professional and amateur musicians in concert and church settings, *TGOP* nevertheless clearly considered music a worthy topic for its readers. To place this worthiness in context, of the two so-called feminine accomplishments for which *TGOP* allotted the most space, musical content appeared more frequently than the numerous articles and prize competitions featuring plain and fancy needlework.

Music topics in a general interest periodical were not unique to *TGOP*. Publications such as *Atalanta*, *Girl's Realm*, *The Strand Magazine* and *The Windsor Magazine*, all begun in the 1890s, included music in fiction, nonfiction, illustrations, poetry and, in some, an occasional music score. What set *TGOP* apart was its greater amount of musical content. Of the 1,500 weekly issues of *TGOP* I reviewed spanning 3 January 1880 when the magazine began through 26 September 1908, after which publication was monthly, over 1,300 – approximately 88 per cent – include some type of musical content, whether a music score, an instalment of serialized fiction about a musician, music-related nonfiction, poetry with musical relevance, an illustration depicting music making or a reply to a musical correspondent. The numbers are even higher – over 1,400 issues, approximately 98 per cent – when all chapters of a story in which music makes only a cameo appearance are included. And all 47 extra issues of *TGOP* printed for the Christmas and, most years, summer holidays include music in topic or score as well.

2   Introduction

Although *TGOP* is the subject of at least two books and mentioned in others that chronicle the rise of publications targeting children and women readers, none focuses on music as one of the magazine's components. In *Great-Grandmama's Weekly: A Celebration of* The Girl's Own Paper *1880–1901*, Wendy Forrester provides an overview of the magazine's contents, which she categorizes as the Modern Woman, Health and Beauty, Fiction, Doing Good, Dress, Features, Domestic Arts, Competitions and Answers to Correspondents. Terri Doughty's *Selections from* The Girl's Own Paper, *1880–1907* reprints pages about Household Management, Conduct, Self-Culture, Education, Work, Independent Living and Health and Sports, each section introduced by the author. In *Constructing Girlhood through the Periodical Press, 1850–1915*, Kristine Moruzi, who examines five British girls' periodicals in print between 1850 and 1915 that 'reflect the shifting nature of girlhood during this period', devotes a chapter to coverage of health, fitness and beauty in *The Girl's Own Paper*.[2]

Ray Hindle's *Oh, No Dear! Advice to Girls a Century Ago* and June Grace's *Advice to Young Ladies from the Nineteenth-Century Correspondence Pages of* The Girl's Own Paper are edited collections of replies selected from Answers to Correspondents columns in *TGOP*. Few of Hindle's 500 selections from 1880 to 1882 and none of Grace's 32 selections from the nineteenth century are music related, and neither author gives a rationale for choosing those particular answers.[3]

Honor Ward's online The Girl's Own Paper Index, currently accessed at http://maths.dur.ac.uk/~tpcc68/GOP/welcome.html, provides links to fiction and non-fiction content, some of it music related, in the weekly – later monthly – magazine and its extra holiday issues from 1880 through 1941 by author and by subject, as well as background information about *TGOP*.

The important role that music played in the lives of young women, fictional and actual, in England during the long nineteenth century as reflected in novels and periodicals has been the focus of essay collections and monographs in the late twentieth and early twenty-first centuries. For example, in her essay 'Heroines at the Piano: Women and Music in Nineteenth-Century Fiction' in *The Lost Chord* edited by Nicholas Temperley, Mary Burgan found that over the course of that century, the piano served as a social prop, symbol of confinement and instrument of rebellion in women's lives. In *The Idea of Music in Victorian Fiction*, a collection of essays edited by Sophie Fuller and Nicky Losseff, Jodi Lustig's 'The Piano's Progress: The Piano in Play in the Victorian Novel' considers how what the piano signifies as an instrument of domestic music making and cultural capital in one novel could suggest its antithesis in another.[4]

For Phyllis Weliver, in *Women Musicians in Victorian Fiction, 1860–1900*, the discrepancies between fiction's portrayal of musical women and actual trends of music making reveal how literature dialogued with real life, either encouraging or condemning music's traditional place in women's lives. Paula Gillett's *Musical Women in England, 1870–1914* uses fiction, poetry, music journals and girls' and women's magazines – including *TGOP* – to understand highly contested perceptions of female musicians in late-Victorian culture.[5]

Situated within the broader context of music and literature, my book offers readers and scholars in both fields an easily accessible database for a single periodical, which circulation figures, self-reported praise and reader response suggest was widely read and popular among Britain's female readers of all ages. By the editor's acquired information, as he told correspondents Grey Hairs in 1880, A Scot in 1881 and A. M. in 1893, *TGOP* readers were from all walks of life and nearly all nationalities.[6] Correspondents' ages ranged from 6 to 80, and readership stretched to the Continent, the British colonies and beyond. Circulation figures support the editor's claims of early success: Patrick Dunae cites an initial weekly circulation of 250,000 copies, declining to 189,000 in 1889.[7] James Mason pictured the number of *TGOP* copies sold prior to its thousandth issue as the height of 56 Mount Blancs or the length of the equator's circumference with a bit of overlap.[8]

In its first year, *TGOP* already had caught the favourable attention of contemporary publications as 'a storehouse of amusement and instruction of the best kind' (*The Queen*), a paper 'we should like to see placed in the hands of our sisters and daughters' (*School Newspaper*), 'one of the best family magazines now publishing' (*Peterboro' Advertiser*) and was recommended 'to the attention of every parent in the land' (*South Wales Press*). Singled out specifically was 'How to Play the Piano' by Arabella Goddard, which was

> so full of good sense and so rich in practical suggestions, that some of the "girls" who already pride themselves on their powers as executants will find it worth their while carefully to study the advice here given and act upon it (*Rock*).[9]

After exploring the inclusion of material related to women organists in *TGOP*, I returned to the magazine to examine how it treated music as an accomplishment for young gentlewomen in late Victorian and Edwardian England. Over time, I located and perused every issue in every annual volume of *TGOP* and all but one of the extra holiday issues from 1880 through the end of 1910 and compiled an index of all their music-related material.[10] What I found regarding musical accomplishments supported other scholarship about women's music making in the long nineteenth century – that the musically accomplished young lady was expected to live her life so that she did not lose as an ideally feminine woman what she gained in proficiency as a musician.

Of more interest as I studied the musical content in *TGOP* was the shift in women's music making from a feminine accomplishment to an increasingly professional role within the discipline. Over its first 30 years, *TGOP* content was designed to appeal to novice, practising and committed musicians, since the magazine had readers at all three levels. For example, musical novices could learn about the instruments of the orchestra so they could enjoy concerts. Notices and reviews of new music, as well as music scores, assured musical practitioners of suitable repertoire. Committed musicians found detailed analyses of piano compositions, especially by Beethoven, and explanations of musical forms. All readers could learn about performers, composers and their music, as well as apply their skills to occasional competitions in music composition. But that content changed over time in response to the changing role of music in women's lives. The three-tier focus on music making that appeared *within* each volume characterized the magazine's musical content *across* the three decades as well.

The first decade of publication focused on the novice musician. All of the 'how-to' primers on playing musical instruments were printed between 1880 and 1889,

4 Introduction

from singing a song in Volume 1 to playing the zither in Volume 10. Music making, centred in the home, had much to do with setting a solid foundation, not only for musical competence but also for musical courtesy – a young gentlewoman *never* made her practice a nuisance to others. A good musical ear could lead to a musical calling if one had the right temperament and approached that calling with selflessness, truth and purity.

In the second decade, *TGOP* content began to reflect a shift in young ladies' musical accomplishment from avocation to vocation, from amateur to professional. The magazine was raising its musical bar higher in part as a reflection of higher societal expectations for music making in general. Singing and playing were no longer a mere pastime, and no one without decided musical talent should labour over music lessons and daily practice. Informative articles of the 1890s built on the primers of the 1880s.

By the third decade of the magazine's publication, the transition from music as pastime to music as profession was more complete, especially beginning in 1908 with the change in the magazine's editorship. *TGOP* now directed its content at committed musicians whose exceptional talent for music would lead them to careers as vocalists or instrumentalists. Piano playing received the most focus and offers a case study.

The passing of 'the piano girl'

'Here is a pretty paradox', wrote James Huneker in his essay 'The Eternal Feminine' in *Overtones: A Book of Temperaments* first published in 1904: 'the piano is passing and with it the piano girl, – there really was a piano girl, – and more music was never made before in the land!' The author was reflecting on an era during which the young woman and the piano had been linked closely in nineteenth-century Europe and America. 'Every girl played the piano', he continued. Not to play it 'was a stigma of poverty'.[11] Piano manufacturers, music teachers, composers and music publishers all had benefitted from the steady rate at which the piano took root in homes, aided in part by the hire-purchase system described in Cyril Ehrlich's book *The Piano* that enabled British families without sufficient funds on hand to buy a cottage piano for a down payment and monthly instalments over three years.[12]

The ubiquitous household instrument may have found its most ardent executants in England's middle-class maidens caught up in the piano mania that for a time seemed unabated, chronicled, for example, by Ehrlich and by Arthur Loesser.[13] 'Liszts in petticoats have been so numerous, as during the past twenty-five years to escape classification', Huneker continued. 'It was the girl who did not play that was singled out as an oddity.'[14]

The time span to which the author refers coincides with the first 30 years of *TGOP*. A close reading of its weekly – and later monthly – issues over the first three decades reveals the piano's influence not only in music scores but also in fiction, nonfiction, fashion, Varieties, poetry, Answers to Correspondents and, starting in 1901, the Fidelio Club, a monthly column offering analyses of pieces and replies to readers' questions. The musical journey of pianists through the pages of *TGOP* offers new insight into the changing role of music in the lives of young women in late Victorian and Edwardian England.

Like some other general interest magazines of the time, *TGOP* included music scores in its issues. Although most were for voice with piano accompaniment, piano solos appeared beginning in 1881. The first, 'Le Dernier Papillon' – The Last Butterfly – with its nod to Robert Schumann, is a two-page Intrada in G major by Edwin M. Lott (Figure 1). Thirty more piano solos appeared over the next three

Figure 1 First piano piece printed in *The Girl's Own Paper*, 'Le Dernier Papillon' (Edwin M. Lott), *The Girl's Own Paper* 3 (29 October 1881): 72–3

Figure 1 (Continued)

decades by little-known composers, regular contributors such as Clara Macirone and Myles Foster and composers of international stature such as Clara Schumann and Hubert Parry. An average of two pieces a year appeared through 1893; one appeared in 1895 – a three-page Mazurka in A minor by Lady Thompson (Kate Loder) – but ten years elapsed before another piano solo was forthcoming – a three-page Gavotte in D major with Musette in the parallel minor by Cécile Hartog.

The piano was heard in fiction as an instrument teaching some of life's important lessons. In 'Our Patty's Victory' of 1881, the victory is over the selfish desire, however well intended, to learn to play the piano. Patty's large farm family had neither a piano nor funds for lessons, but a young pianist who lived nearby offered to teach Patty for free. When the girl Patty hires to help her mother during lessons sets the chimney on fire, breaks the teapot and scalds the baby, a night of prayerful agonizing convinces the daughter that her duty clearly lies with her family's daily round in which the piano plays no part. 'The Mother and the Wonder-Child' by Ethel Turner, which ran in 1901, addresses the issue of child prodigies. While eight-year-old Challis and her mother are forging the young pianist's career overseas in Europe, the rest of the family remains home in Australia in financial difficulty kept from the world travelers. The eventual reunion is joyous for all but Challis, who no longer fits in – she had played concerts before royalty but had never learned to play like a normal child. The author's message is clear: Proud parents should weigh the benefits of nurturing genius in a talented child against the risks of separation and implied favouritism.

The piano appeared even more prominently in the magazine's nonfiction, with instructions on how to purchase and maintain it, drape it, select music for it and play it. An article in 1881 offered advice on 'How to Purchase a Piano and Keep It in Good Order'. By 1886, the importance of the right piano maintained in pristine condition merited a four-part series on that topic. The next year piano maintenance extended to its tuning – a skill that female pianists could learn for paid employment. Today's readers might consider making decorative drapes for the piano a trivial pursuit, but at a time when the piano was likened to an altar in the home, its accoutrements were important, and *TGOP* offered its readers designs to grace the piano front and back beginning in 1880 and still appearing as late as 1899 (Figure 2 and Figure 3).[15]

Music scores in *TGOP* must not have been sufficient to keep musical readers singing and playing contentedly. So many readers wrote to the magazine asking for advice on purchasing music that in 1881 the magazine began a monthly 'list of new music, with short descriptions of their character'; an illustrated page from Volume 3 is shown in Figure 4.[16] The regular column, which included piano music, vowed to review no compositions judged poor music or in bad taste. The column tapered off through 1894, lapsed for three years and then reappeared in 1898 in a new format more specific to voice type, instrument and style of music, written by composer Mary Augusta Salmond.

Arabella Goddard offered the first primer on piano playing in 1880. Her belief that it was never too late to learn must have pleased older readers eager to pursue this popular accomplishment. Her expectations for girls of any age were

PIANOFORTE FRONTS: AND HOW TO DECORATE THEM.

By FRED MILLER.

THERE are few places in a room that better repay the time spent upon beautifying them than pianoforte fronts, viz., that part which in many pianos is occupied by fretwork and pleated silk. It is a capital situation for putting in a little nice decoration, for whatever is placed there is seen to great advantage. The first thing to be done towards decorating this part of a piano is to carefully measure the opening that receives the fretwork, and it may be necessary to remove this fretwork to take the size accurately, though this is not often the case. The pleated silk is often stretched over a light framework of wood, and where this is the case the old silk can be removed and the painted silk tacked on to the existing framework. In some cases the silk is tacked on to the framework of the piano, and it is perhaps hardly necessary to have a framework made, as the silk to replace the old front can likewise be tacked on the framework when finished. There must be sufficient silk to allow of its being turned over and round. Some of the fine coloured satins, such as those used for embroidering, will be found to be a very suitable material for painting on if you decide to paint the design. The Adolfi medium mentioned in my hints on painting a mantel border is the vehicle I recommend for using with the ordinary oil colours in tubes. This medium dries quickly, and as it makes the colour elastic, there is little danger of the painting cracking or peeling off. You use the medium as you would turpentine to dilute the colours, and there is no necessity to use any other medium with the colours. The plan of painting the lights on thickly, and the darks on thinly, so that the material shows through, may be resorted to in the case of silk or satin. The colours need not in any case be painted on very thickly, as very little body of colour is

Figure 2 'Pianoforte Fronts: And How to Decorate Them' (Fred Miller), *The Girl's Own Paper* 6 (4 July 1885): 628

A PRETTY PIANOFORTE BACK.

It is a problem often taxing the ingenuity of the "angel of the house" what to do with the piano back, when the piano stands out in the room instead of being against the wall. I am going to give the readers of THE GIRL'S OWN PAPER a suggestion, and that is to paint a piece of canvas or similar material with liquid dyes or transparent colours so as to have the appearance of tapestry. In a former volume of THE GIRL'S OWN PAPER I wrote an article on tapestry painting, and it has often been a surprise to me that this painting of a textile with dyes and transparent colours has not been more practised, seeing that the effect is very pleasing, and the time taken in doing it brief in comparison with the effect produced. Stencilled ornamental friezes on coarse white canvas or sacking are largely used now in the decoration of rooms, and very charming are they as the dyes sinking into the fabric give a softness of colouring which is wanting in painted decoration.

Ordinary oil colours thinned with spirits of turpentine can be used, and here is the list of those which are most transparent and which therefore can be used like dyes.

Prussian blue, indigo, blueblack, burnt umber; raw sienna, burnt sienna, gamboge, lemon chrome; crimson lake, vermillion, cobalt green, viridian; aureolin, Indian yellow, cobnet.

In the design accompanying these hints the lower portion, which is divided into compartments, is occupied by conventional renderings of well-known flowers such as the daffodil, narcissus, pansy, zinnia and tulip, and it would be as well to draw these out the size they are to be painted. They should be then traced on tracing paper, and as they are repeated two or three times you might prick the designs with a coarse needle, having a piece of flannel under the tracing paper and make what are termed by decorators "pounces." In transferring a design, all you have to do is to place the pricked tracing on to the canvas and rub over it some broken up charcoal tied up in a piece of muslin. The charcoal will pass through the holes in the tracing and leave an impression on the canvas. This must be followed with a little thin colour, say, burnt sienna, using a red sable rigger, partly to

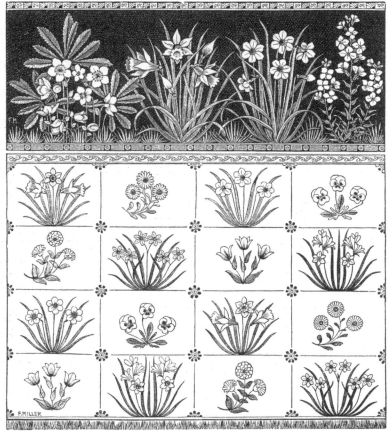

PAINTED CANVAS OR PAINTED SACKING HANGING FOR BACK OF PIANO.

10 Introduction

THE GIRL'S OWN PAPER.

she had yet learned all that she could learn by her own unaided exertions. The only expenditure she allowed herself was the hire of a piano, and the purchase of sundry drawing materials, additional to those she had already.

She laid out her plan and did not find many interruptions to it. She had spent several afternoons at the Murrays' house, but these, so far from being an interruption, were a help, as the Murray girls were as much interested in self-improvement as she was, and as each of them had her own hobby, and enjoyed all the advantages their father's position gave them of hearing of new methods and improved books, they could give her much valuable advice, while they, on their side, said to each other that her dainty taste and original way of looking at things were quite refreshing to them. Faith had also made acquaintance with several other young ladies, by meeting them at the Murrays' house—she had seen Miss Gordon again three or four times. But her acquaintanceship with these had ended there. Because Faith had very strong attachments and affections, therefore her longing was rather for a few friends, of whom one can hardly see too much, rather than for a wide circle, with whom one can never get far below the surface. Therefore the door-bell had very seldom any interest for Faith. So one afternoon when she heard it ring twice, rapidly and imperatively, though she wondered to herself who was in such an unreasonable hurry, it never occurred to her it could be anybody to call on her.

For once, she was mistaken. Miss Milne knocked rather sharply at the parlour door, and coming in with a somewhat pursed-up mouth, handed Faith a visiting-card, bearing the name of "Katherine Scott."

(*To be continued.*)

NEW MUSIC.

J. B. CRAMER AND Co.

Sing Again, ye Happy Children. Written by H. F. Duncan. Composed by Joseph L. Roeckel. In two keys: E flat for tenor or soprano, in C for baritone or contralto.—This is a particularly pleasing song, written in a happy and joyful strain, but partaking of a sacred character; thus, in the second verse—

"Heralded by radiant angels,
 Purer than the whitest snow,
Lo! the Lord of highest Heaven
 Came to us on earth below."

Both words and music are grand in conception and idea. We recommend this composition to our musical girls.

TRYING OVER NEW MUSIC.

Figure 4 'Trying over New Music', in 'New Music', *The Girl's Own Paper* 3 (8 July 1882): 652

exacting: lots of scales, sight-reading, memory work and avoiding all affected sentiment. Lady Benedict followed with 'How to Improve Your Pianoforte Playing' in the next volume. Authors assumed a beginning level of musical expertise and intended their instruction to supplement, not replace, formal lessons by a reputable music master.

Oliveria Prescott anthropomorphized the piano, which was not always pleased with the touch it felt on its keys and had no qualms making its views known. 'It behooves us, therefore, to be very careful what we say to the piano,' she warned, 'and if we do not want our hearers to think we are hard and unkind, or nervous, or unthinking of the music, we must not teach the piano that such is the case.'[17]

In the magazine's second decade, Fanny Davies, a Clara Schumann protégé, offered instruction 'On the Technique of the Pianoforte' to help earnest students lay a solid foundation for future success. Talent might be God-given, she said, but 'loving patience and long earnest study is necessary for its development, however great the gift'. Technique was a means to that end, 'but not the end itself'.[18] In 'Some Remarks on Modern Professional Pianoforte Playing', William Porteous offered Davies as an excellent example of the Classical Style.

Lady Benedict and Prescott guided pianists through Mendelssohn *Songs Without Words* and Beethoven sonatas. In 'On the Choice of Pianoforte Pieces', concert pianist Ernst Pauer, an advocate of the 'simpler is better' philosophy, stressed the prudence of playing an easier piece correctly rather than scrambling a more difficult one. His 'Impressions of Celebrated Pianoforte Pieces' followed. Other articles offered pianists lessons on practising and fingering.

In its third decade, beginning in 1901, *TGOP* offered pianists among its readers the Fidelio Club to guide them in their practice, conducted by Dublin-born concert pianist Eleonore d'Esterre-Keeling. Three months after its start, the club had over 100 members, suggesting it filled a need. At six months, that number had doubled, and by June 1903, it was up to 400.

When Charles Peters, the magazine's editor since its first issue, died at the end of 1907, new editor Flora Klickmann did not continue the Fidelio Club. But her interest in the piano led to articles by concert pianists such as Joseph Hofmann, who contributed five between 1908 and 1910.

Three other types of content mark pianists' musical journey through *TGOP*: fashion illustrations, the Varieties column and poetry. In a fashion article of 1880, 'Dress for Evening Wear' shows a young woman standing at an upright piano, her eyes focused on sheet music in her right hand, her left hand poised over the keyboard (Figure 5). A year later, the pianist sits at a grand piano (lid closed) 'Practising' (Figure 6). By 1907, a more assured-looking pianist sits at a grand piano (lid open), turning a page of music while accompanying a vocalist (Figure 7). Fashions changed, as did pianos, but the subliminal message remained the same: the best-dressed young women were also accomplished pianists.

Perhaps to inspire musical readers' efforts but not inflate their egos, in the Varieties column, silly tidbits share space with serious ones. Some of the former spoof the craze for piano playing, as in:

> MUSICAL PROGRESS. 'How are you getting on with the piano?' asked Alphonso of his best girl.
> 'Oh, very well; I can see great progress in my work'.
> 'How is that?'
> 'Well, the family that lived next door moved away within a week after I began to practise. The next people stayed a month, the next ten weeks, and the family there now have remained nearly six months'.[19]

THE DRESS OF THE MONTH.

A HOME-MADE JACKET.

Although reckoned amongst the months of spring, March certainly seems to belong, by its low temperature, rightly to winter; the winds are cold and piercing, the rain is even more chilly than the wind, and the sky is usually dull; while clouds of dust add to the general discomfort. The warm winter garments cannot be discarded without great danger to health and life, and numberless are the accounts of dangerous illness which accrue from this cause alone.

But on its few bright days how shabby we all feel, both in our houses and our apparel; and how we long for something new and fresh in our surroundings. The custom of wearing new dresses and bonnets at Eastertide has very much passed into oblivion, but most of our mothers can remember that their mothers thought that to wear a white bonnet and veil on Easter Sunday was absolutely necessary. So our winter costumes and dresses may be worn throughout March, unless the season be much altered this year from its usual type, although this fact must not make us the less busy, for we have many preparations to commence, and many stitches to set in, if we be our own dressmakers and needlewomen, as I trust many of us are.

In the first place there are the underclothing and the stockings to be kept in constant repair. And those girls who have to make the most of a modest allowance will find that the simplest and most economical way of replacing under-linen will be to have always a new garment in hand to work upon in spare moments. Thus the expense of purchasing a large number is avoided, and the addition of the new garment at intervals keeps the stock in fair and presentable order. The calico should be, without dress, 36 inches in width, and of a good quality, without uneven and large threads in it. An expenditure of from fivepence to sixpence a yard will ensure the acquisition of an excellent wearing quality. The amount required for a nightdress is four yards, for a chemise two yards and three quarters, for a pair of drawers two yards, while a yard is sufficient for a petticoat-bodice, and three yards of flannel for an ungored petticoat.

Scarlet has very much gone out of favour for flannel petticoats, as it is liable to be so spoilt in the hands of an incompetent laundress, and I do not know anything so ugly as badly-washed red flannel, with large discoloured blotches in it, and the original colour changed to an unhealthy hue of repulsive-looking red. Pink, blue, violet, and grey have been adopted in its stead, and the two latter are quite as pretty as the red when new, and wash and wear well. Of course, in the country, white can still be worn, but in our foggy London it has to be relinquished entirely.

The next thing, after the underclothes, which we should examine, is our stock of thinner dresses for the summer; for just at this moment there is plenty of time to make up our minds as to what we shall need, and to use our money when the spring goods come in to the best advantage. Last summer the cooler garments in our wardrobes had a rest, and perhaps will need but slight alteration. I hear that large quantities of our old friend, the "Galatea" stripes, and uni-coloured materials to wear with them as trimmings, are being prepared by the wholesale trade. This will be good news to many people, who had discovered the worth of this material, in its washing and wearing, especially for children and younger girls. It required such plain making-up, too, and neither flounces nor kiltings looked well, only flat bands to match the predominating colour of the stripe. We are fortunate, too, in the fact that polonaises and *princesse* dresses are both as much worn as they were, though the drapery at the back must be a little modified and rearranged, and perhaps some fulness taken out.

Those of our readers who have patronised velveteen this winter will find that the skirts will be most useful this spring, and will be much used with over-dresses and polonaises of the new "all-wool homespuns," which are beautifully light in texture and moderate in price. I have inspected some manufacturers' patterns, which will be sold in the shops at about a shilling a yard. The colours most worn in them will be the various shades of "old gold," a very pretty and becoming colour for girls. Velveteen will both dye and clean well, and if it were good when purchased, it will by and bye appear in the spring costume "quite as good as new."

White dresses of all materials will be very much in favour, and white serge is especially mentioned, as forming a charming spring costume. White cashmere is pretty, also a good white alpaca, both of which would answer for a best dress at any time.

The illustration below is a pretty evening dress, of a brocaded material of a grey colour. The trimmings are of grey or black linen-backed satin. Folds of satin are laid in front, and it has elbow-sleeves, with bows of satin at the sides. The necklace is of coral beads, and the hair is simply coiled and held up with a comb, the rose being worn or not, as required or liked. This dress is inexpensive, and might be made with long sleeves and closed at the neck, if preferred. The jacket is intended to show—what has been several times inquired for by our corre-

DRESS FOR EVENING WEAR.

VOL. II.—No. 65.   MARCH 26, 1881.   [PRICE ONE PENNY.

SEASONABLE DRESS, AND HOW TO MAKE IT.

WE FEAR that in the spring we shall all be obliged to make a stand, firm and bold, against the invasion of that most inconvenient and needless incumbrance, the crinoline. All through the winter at the extremely fashionable *modistes*, the "dress improver" has been dangling before our eyes, but very few even of the most *outré* dressers have adopted it. We hope the same right feeling will continue in the spring. It is the duty of us all as individuals to make a resolute stand, and prevent a foolish and atrociously ugly fashion from enslaving us again. So we shall look to the readers of THE GIRL'S OWN PAPER, as warm and hearty auxiliaries in the matter, as to them we are always endeavouring to show a duty in all things, small and great; so that, even in their dress, as well as in their demeanour, they may display to the world the highest possible ideal of a fair and Christian womanhood, and a girlhood so thoughtful in spirit and so beautiful in taste, that it could not stoop to extremes of dress or to the adoption of unseemly and monstrous fashions. Happily for us of late we English women have become much emancipated from the control of French fashions, and we are not so much afraid of displaying a little individuality in our dress. For this change we are indebted in a great measure to the high-art votaries or æsthetes, who, in spite of extrava-

[*All rights reserved.*]   PRACTISING.

Figure 6 'Practising', in 'Seasonable Dress, and How to Make It', *The Girl's Own Paper* 2 (26 March 1881): 401

An excellent example of a wide grey and white striped material. The bodice, with its modified kimono sleeves, is treated in the most becoming style. It should be noted that the front and back widths of the skirt are cut on the straight, while the side widths are on the cross. The figure at the piano has the little hanging kimono sleeves very perfectly cut, but much more difficult to copy than the ones on the striped gown.

Figure 7 'An excellent example of a wide grey and white striped material', in 'How a Girl Should Dress' (Norma), *The Girl's Own Paper* 28 (29 June 1907): 617

Poetry, too, has musical titles, text and illustrations. In 'The Piano and the Player' of 1892, for example, William Luff inspired readers: 'Alone we are mute and silent; / But if the great Master's hand / Is laid on the idle keyboard, / What music may cheer the land!'[20]

But in 1899, some keys remained idle, as noted in 'On a Very Old Piano: Lately Seen in a London Shop Window, and Labeled, "Cash Price, Two Guineas"'. 'Poor faded, long-neglected thing', the unnamed poet begins, 'Not worth a glance / From eyes disdainful as they pass, / While you stand there, the sport, alas! / Of circumstance'. The little maid no longer played quaint old tunes; the young woman no longer played to her lover. 'Your reign is over; here you wait, is your fate / In London Town.'[21] In 1891, 'A Use for Old Pianos', giving detailed instructions on how to turn an unused upright piano into a combination bookcase, writing desk and cabinet, hinted at the same fate.

One way to determine what *TGOP*'s pianists actually were doing musically is to examine the Answers to Correspondents column. Replies about music appeared in most issues. Although no questions were printed, the column offers insight into readers' participation in music. A common question apparently asked was how long to practise daily. The editor told over a dozen correspondents between 1880 and 1892 that daily practice should not exceed one-and-a-half hours. He warned Kitten against 'immoderate practice' that could become a nuisance and advised that 'half an hour's really good practice is preferable to any amount of indifferent careless work'.[22]

The editor was brusque with readers who likely tried to impress him with excessive practice. He hoped Topsey did not 'live in a row, square or semi-detached house, or we pity the neighbours who must listen to a five hours' practising, in one house alone, every day! It is well that THE GIRL'S OWN PAPER is not edited next door.'[23] Yet the editor told Red Riding Hood, whose hands ached from practice that obviously exceeded an hour and a half a day, 'We wish your complaint were more common.'[24] Faced with such contradictions, readers could become confused when using *TGOP* as their source of musical information. But the magazine did not deviate from two messages: One's music making should never be a nuisance to others, and only those readers with a good ear for music should pursue that accomplishment.

Social downgrading of the piano – Ehrlich's term – was evident in correspondent E. Litchy who wanted to practise on her mistress's piano when the mistress was away, an action that the editor said would betray her employer's trust, 'not to speak of the great annoyance to neighbours within hearing distance of your mistakes'.[25] And Kate Wren 'might as well "cry for the moon"' regarding piano practice in her current domestic position.[26]

As the magazine ended its first decade, A Templar writing about 'The Girls of To-day' noted the new standard of perfection detailed in Lady Catherine Milnes Gaskell's 'Women of To-day', an article published in the journal *Nineteenth Century* in 1889 that extended to musical accomplishments.[27] Mediocre was 'happily banished to limbo', A Templar wrote.[28] If a woman must live by her music, she would excel in it. Gaskell had raised the bar for musical women of *TGOP*'s second decade, but hers was not a new standard. The magazine had been preaching against mediocrity from its start, when Alice King, in 'What Our Girls May Do', urged readers in 1880 to break down the notion of respectable English families that all daughters should be taught to play the piano.

Young women of the 1890s were cultivating broader academic, occupational and recreational interests. Although they still pursued music as an accomplishment, it was not their only option for pleasure and profession. Like their sisters in wider society, *TGOP* readers were falling under the influence of the New Woman, and music soon would be viewed through her spectacles.

Little content in *TGOP* sympathized with or supported the New Woman, however. Some replies to correspondents revealed readers interested in pursuing musical examinations and degrees, including doctorates in music. Generally, the magazine charted a course similar to its previous ten years, though content began to reflect a shift from music as avocation to music as vocation, from amateur to professional.

In 1900, the editor suggested that Inca, short on time but long on desire to be a musician, learn singing instead of piano, which required more practice, but told her not to be distressed at not being a musician: 'The time has gone by when every woman is expected to play or sing.'[29] Nor did every woman *want* to play or sing.

Musical accomplishments seemed at risk of disappearing in clouds of dust raised by young women on their bicycles – a trend the *Musical Times* watched with concern in 1896, identifying the bicycle as a 'new and most formidable enemy' for luring its riders off the piano stool.[30] But not necessarily, as Mrs George de Horne Vaizey noted in *TGOP* of the fictional Rendell sisters in 'A Houseful of Girls', which ran in 1900. Young women were shunning 'promiscuous accomplishments' in order to do one thing well, which could be piano playing.[31] Yet musical accomplishment now extended from piano keys to business savvy and common sense, beyond the practice room out into the world.

By the end of the third decade of *TGOP*, the transition to music as a profession was more complete. Intelligent listening at orchestral concerts, the topic of a two-part article in 1884, had expanded to an 11-part series in 1903 with expectations for detailed study of individual instruments and ability to follow along with a full score. Musical content of the magazine had shifted primarily to piano playing.

In *Girl's Only?*, a book about gender and popular fiction in Britain, Kimberly Reynolds suggests that from 1880 to 1910 *TGOP* 'seems to have operated in a "prefigurative" way', making a

> bridge between the rapidly changing experience of being young and female in British society and the residual notion of what it *should* be like. New ideas about education, careers for women, health and exercise were made acceptable by being related to traditional values, behaviour, and occupations.[32]

TGOP reflected traditional values and was not concerned, Reynolds states, with providing a platform for women 'actively engaged in challenging conventional attitudes'.³³ The magazine accepted but did not encourage a career as a professional pianist, for example. This stance was reinforced in articles that offered aspiring professional musicians a reality check. In the multi-part 'Music as a Profession', beginning in 1903, for example, A. Foxton Ferguson offered the thousands of students studying music as a means to earn their livelihood – though often in a light-hearted manner – a sobering fact: only 1 per cent of them would succeed. In support of his thesis, the author addressed issues of superficial glamour, well-meaning friends, masters, agents and concert giving and wealth. Madame Nellie Melba's 1909 'Why So Many Students Fail in the Musical Profession' was aimed at the numerous young women who traveled abroad inadequately equipped with either money or talent to support their music studies.

Emil Reich's anachronistic view in 1908 that girls should leave the piano and violin alone and focus instead on the harp, which would aid them in singing beautiful music, likely had little influence on pianists who sought professional status. They had already crossed that bridge and were not looking back. In *A Magazine of Her Own?* Margaret Beetham notes the periodical's diversity that allows different viewpoints and empowers readers to choose what they want to read and how carefully, accepting or rejecting text at will.³⁴ Discerning readers thus could have taken Reich's 'The English Girls of To-morrow' with a grain of salt.

Huneker offers the last word concerning the 'piano girl'. The current generation of girls could thank their older sisters for 'immunity from useless piano practice', he said. Instead, today's young woman 'golfs, cycles, rows, runs, fences, dances, and pianolas! While she once wearied her heart playing Gottschalk, she now plays tennis, and she freely admits that tennis is greater than Thalberg.'³⁵ She goes to a piano recital if she wants to hear 'the "lilies and languours" of Chopin and the "roses and raptures" of Schumann' that she has forsaken by choice. The recitalist might be a woman, however, for 'new girls' who had a musical gift still *did* play the piano with 'consuming earnestness'. 'We listen to her', Huneker continues, 'for we know that this is an age of specialization when woman is coming into her own, be it nursing, electoral suffrage, or the writing of plays.'³⁶ Or, he might have added, in the musical journey to becoming a professional pianist.

This book catalogues the musical journey of 'the piano girl' and others through the first three decades of *TGOP*, from the magazine's start-up in 1880 through the first change in editorship. *TGOP*'s first editor, Charles Peters, died at the end of 1907, and the magazine changed from a weekly to a monthly issue under the new editor Flora Klickmann, beginning with the next annual volume. By 1910, the catalogue's cut-off, the magazine clearly reflected Klickmann's stamp. Choice of an annotated catalogue format allows a means to determine *what* musical content is found in *TGOP*, delineated in a chronological listing by volume. Further division of that content into topical indexes reveals the magazine's diversity of approach to the subject of music. The catalogue format does not reveal *why* the magazine included so much music, however. The answer may rest in large part on the publisher's view of the role music should serve in the lives of *TGOP* readers and the backgrounds of the magazine's first two editors who were themselves musicians.

The new magazine and its editors

Looking back from the thousandth, 25 February 1899, issue, James Mason, a frequent contributor to *TGOP*, recalled the day when he first heard about the new magazine over lunch with Charles Peters, who was 'full of a scheme' for a paper expected to 'appeal to and cater for those sensible girls who are always in fashion and who hitherto had possessed no magazine of their own'. Peters's confidence in the new venture was, as Mason remembered it, 'infectious'.[37]

Like most magazines with which it competed, *TGOP* included a wide variety of topics intended to engage readers' interests. But unlike other publishers, RTS imbued most topics with a sense of what was morally right or, at the very least, what was not in questionable or bad taste. RTS Editorial Secretary Samuel Green, writing about *TGOP* in 1899, elaborated on the magazine's noble purpose:

> The period of girlhood is short and perilous. While the young man is still at college, a girl is frequently a wife and mother. A young man of eighteen or twenty is very youthful compared with a girl of the same age. Between her schooldays and the serious commencement of her responsibilities, what can influence a girl for the better so much as a wise, Christian magazine? We earnestly and with thankfulness believe that the hopes expressed in our preliminary prospectus have been and are continuing to be fulfilled – that *The Girl's Own Paper* is to its readers a guardian, instructor, companion, and friend, and that it is preparing them for the responsibilities of womanhood and for a heavenly home.[38]

With its stated diverse readership of 'sisters of all ages and all nationalities', this was a tall order for *TGOP* to fill.[39] But its editor was not new to the packaging of moral lessons in magazine format.

Charles Peters (Figure 8) was 28 years old and a subeditor at *The Quiver*, a semi-religious Protestant penny weekly published by Cassell beginning in 1861 for family Sunday reading, when RTS recruited him as editor for the 1880 launch of *TGOP*. Given its evangelical and nonsectarian stance, *The Quiver* would have offered excellent preparation for Peters's new position with RTS.[40] He apparently had grown up in the church and was a musician as well. Charles Harrison, a contemporary at Cassell, remembered that Peters had been a choirboy who ladies thought looked angelic in his surplice – a resemblance that was less obvious in the more fleshy adult Peters.[41]

Who's Who 1907 lists music as one of Peters's recreations, an interest he pursued as a promoter and first secretary of Trinity College London, founded for the advancement of church music and choral singing.[42] Peters's name appears not only as 'Assistant Secretary' in the college's academic calendar for 1877–1878 but also as a Student in Music, having earned a Preliminary Certificate, and as a Student of Music of the college since the 1875 Michaelmas term, having passed the Choral Associate examination in sight-singing and management of the voice.[43] Although not mentioned in Harold Rutland's history of Trinity College, Peters likely made many valuable contacts while serving as college secretary. Some of the names associated with that college such as board members J. Gordon Saunders, J. W. Hinton and E. M. Lott, identified in the academic calendar for 1877–1878, were also contributors to *TGOP*.[44]

CHARLES PETERS,
Editor.

Figure 8 'Charles Peters, Editor', in 'Portrait Gallery of Contributors to "The Girl's Own Paper"', *The Girl's Own Paper* 20 (25 February 1899): foldout plate facing p. 344

A 'genial' bachelor and 'intensely creative' described in a *TGOP* memoriam as loving the beautiful in Art and Nature, Peters was a poet and enjoyed gardening at his country home in the Surrey village of Peaslake southwest of London.[45] Long suffering from 'weak health' and pain, Peters nonetheless fulfilled his editorial responsibilities for *TGOP* through Volume 28 and already had shaped the content of Volume 29 before his death at age 53 in December 1907.[46] His was a behind-the-scenes presence, rarely one as an identified author, though poems by 'C. P.' in the annual volumes and extra holiday issues during Peters's editorship likely were his, especially those with musical titles such as 'Come, Let Me Sing, Sweet Muse Sublime', 'The Piano-Player: A Life Picture', 'Mental Melodies' and 'A Singing Lesson'.

Verses that Charles Peters by name wrote, reminiscent of 'The Lost Chord', the well-known poem by Adelaide Anne Proctor set to music by Arthur Sullivan in 1877, were set to music in 1894 for *TGOP* by Polish pianist and composer Natalie Janotha in 'Tuning Up'. The similarity of the lyrics is striking; both poems focus on organ playing, discordant sound and a search for peace. Silence follows in each poem, but only death's angel in heaven might hear Procter's lost chord, while Peters hears a hymn of praise begin like angel's joy. Both pieces are centred in F major, with 'Tuning Up' beginning in the relative D minor. The 'weary souls adrift' trying to attune their lives with holiness and the organist seeking vainly for the lost chord stray from the tonic but return to it when their struggles lead them to angelic thoughts of heaven. Peters also wrote the lyrics for 'The Invitation' set to music for *TGOP* in 1900 by Myles B. Foster. The invitation is from the Lord to draw near to the Saviour and accept the promise of His mercy.

MISS FLORA KLICKMANN.

The New Editor of "THE GIRL'S OWN PAPER," who assumes control of the Magazine with the November issue.

Figure 9 'Miss Flora Klickmann', *The Girl's Own Paper* 29 (19 September 1908): plate facing p. 810

Peters edited *TGOP* from its first issue in 1880. After he died, the magazine continued under a new editor, Flora Klickmann (Figure 9), who was a musician before she was a journalist. Born in 1867, young Klickmann dreamed of becoming a concert pianist. She studied music at Trinity College and later at the Royal College of Organists, but ill health and a weak heart caused a change in plans.[47] In an interview with Klickmann for *TGOP* in 1908, Mary H. Melville described her as 'a musician of exceptional calibre' whose musical training 'was of a very thorough order' and included instruction in piano, organ and violin, counterpoint and orchestration.[48] As an organist, she had played on the great organs at the Crystal Palace, Portsmouth Town Hall, Royal Albert Hall, Saint Paul's Cathedral and Westminster Abbey. At age 21, Klickmann taught piano at the Chapel Royal, Saint James's Palace, and began writing short articles about music such as 'Moments with Modern Musicians: Famous Organists' published in *The Windsor Magazine* in 1896.[49]

Klickmann was raised Baptist, and she applied her Christian convictions to her work. After her start in music journalism, she joined the literary department of the British and Foreign Bible Society and became involved in the Wesleyan Methodist Missionary Society, transforming that society's rather stiff bulletin into a new magazine, *The Foreign Field*.[50] During her four years as editor, *The Foreign Field* became the top-selling missionary magazine in England.[51] It was from that post that Klickmann was recruited to take over the editorship of *TGOP* in 1908.

The difference between *TGOP* under Peters's guidance and under Klickmann's was apparent from page one of Volume 30 with its expanded *The Girl's Own Paper and Woman's Magazine* title targeting both girls and women on an equal basis. In her first 'The Editor's Page', a new department, Klickmann paid homage to Peters's leadership of the magazine. She knew his death had come as a personal loss to 'tens of thousands' of readers who had never met him but considered him an intimate friend.[52]

'From the very first Mr. Peters had but one aim in editing this magazine', Klickmann told readers,

> viz., to foster and develop that which was highest and noblest in the girlhood and womanhood of England, helping his readers to cherish their finest ideals, and teaching them to see the things of life in their proper perspective – putting the best things first, and vanishing the worthless from his pages.[53]

The new editor reassured her readers that 'the aim of the magazine will not be altered. Our motto will still be "The Best Things First." We want the paper to be of assistance to you when you are in perplexity and when you are confronted with life's difficult problems'.[54] Before turning to how musical content fit into Peters's and Klickmann's vision of 'The Best Things First' in their magazine, it is helpful to understand more about the magazine itself.

Inside *The Girl's Own Paper*

TGOP was a weekly quarto-sized miscellany magazine of 16 pages that sold for only a penny throughout its first 29 years of publication. Weekly issues were also available bound as a monthly volume. Annual volumes, which ran from the first of October until the end of September to take advantage of Christmas gift giving, also could be purchased from the publisher.

Extra holiday issues of 64 pages appeared beginning with the third volume of *TGOP* at the request of readers who may have read that type of issue in their brothers' magazine, *The Boy's Own Paper* (*TBOP*). Given titles such as 'Christmas Carillon' and 'Summer Songs', these special issues of *TGOP* were ready for purchase each year by the end of November and the end of June, respectively, and contained content similar to that of regular issues but with an obvious holiday theme and title appropriate to the season. Each extra issue was complete in itself, so readers could enjoy the fiction in its entirety. Beginning with Volume 22, the themed titles were dropped for the more generic 'Extra Christmas Part' and 'Extra Summer Part', and in the next volume the extra summer issue was dropped altogether. The special winter issue of *TGOP* was discontinued as well in Volume 30 when the new editor chose instead to offer a double December holiday issue for what was now a monthly publication.

The structure of *TGOP* varied little over the magazine's first two decades. Content was divided into short and serialized fiction, nonfiction features, poetry, abundant illustrations, music scores, filler such as the Varieties (Odds and Ends in later volumes) column and Useful (later Household) Hints, competitions and Answers to Correspondents. An occasional page of amateur contributions gave aspiring young authors a chance to appear in print, and subscription lists for charitable causes acknowledged contributors by name, as did published lists of competition prize-winners. A new masthead or heading appeared in Volume 16, the result of a competition for readers of *TGOP* that had been announced in the previous volume, and in Volume 22, format changed from a three-column layout to two.

Peters had gathered around him a staff of experienced writers, artists, poets and musicians, male and female, some who were already published authors and composers, others who became well known from their association with *TGOP*. Peters had undoubtedly known many of them from his days at Cassell, for they wrote for *The Quiver* as well as for *TGOP*.

Writers for *TGOP* came from diverse backgrounds and occupations, with the clergy well represented – no surprise given the magazine's publisher. Archbishops, artists, athletes, botanists, gardeners, homemakers, dressmakers, lawyers, journalists, nurses, physicians, musicians, students, spinsters, titled nobility – even royalty – contributed to the magazine, some by name, others anonymously. Writers crossed over between fiction and nonfiction and even poetry and art, but it was fiction that initially caught the readers' eyes as they glanced at the magazine's first page in most issues. In the first year, fiction opened all but one issue – an article about Saint Valentine's Day appeared on page one of the 14 February 1880 issue. And in many cases, the readers of *TGOP* were the first to experience what would become popular books published after serialization in *their* magazine.

Forrester notes that fiction was the mainstay of *TGOP*, as it was in other contemporary periodicals, and perusal of *TGOP* bears this out.[55] Each weekly issue included an instalment of at least one lengthy serialized story and one or more chapters from a shorter story. Fiction tended to focus on young gentlewomen the age of the target readership from about 15 to 25 years old who were out of school and awaiting the next step in life. Stories about factory workers and needlewomen, however, occasionally joined those about governesses and new brides. Stories featured several recurring themes that provided moral lessons in overcoming adversity as well as in reinforcing good character traits and weeding out bad ones such as foolishness, carelessness and selfishness.

If fiction was the mainstay of *TGOP*, the nonfiction features reinforced the magazine's relevance to a wide target readership throughout its long publication run. Although most fictional heroines are gentlewomen, nonfiction features served readers of the upper, middle and working classes in what Hilary Skelding terms a 'bewildering range' of features.[56] That articles from baby care to career advice, from poultry-keeping to presentation at court tend to obscure a precise demographic for whom the magazine was intended in favour of a miscellany with universal appeal was likely intentional. Some articles are decidedly class specific, however; the topic of servants provides one example. 'Wages of Domestic Servants' could be of interest to servants and mistresses alike, but 'How We Managed Without Servants' clearly targeted actual and would-be mistresses of the upper classes. Likewise, features such as 'Old Court Customs' and 'Curiosities of Court Receptions' might interest all readers, but 'How Girls Are Presented at Court' and 'How I Was Presented at Court' describe something about which most readers only could dream.

To Skelding the aforementioned articles provide an example of both a deliberate expectation of 'selective reading' and the promotion of 'cross education between the classes', giving working women and those of the upper classes a glimpse of their sister readers' lives.[57] To Peters, readers of the 'upper ten thousand' had an obligation to read everything in the magazine, because of 'their money, time, and superior intelligence', while readers of less high position could concentrate on features relevant to their current situation.[58] Articles covered the gamut of interests and employments – a young woman with no access to formal schooling conceivably could use *TGOP* as a textbook to learn how best to function in her particular life circumstances.

Topics of nonfiction can be divided loosely into ten categories, though much overlap exists:

- Character Building, including Charities, Growing Up and Role Models
- Domestic, including Childcare, Crafts, Entertainment, Etiquette, Fashion, Food, Hobbies, Home Decorating and Furnishing, Housekeeping, Needlework and Servants
- Education and Training
- Health, including Beauty, Medicine and Physical and Mental Well Being
- Humanities, including Art, Biography, Ethics, History, Language, Law, Literature, Music, Philosophy and Religion
- Recreation, including Exercise and Sports
- Royalty

- Sciences, including Animals, Archeology, Astronomy, Botany, Gardening, Geography and Meteorology
- Social Customs, including Culture, Girls of Other Lands and Travel
- Work, including Banking, Business, Economy, Government and Politics, Industry, Occupations and Professions and Technology

Some topics could fit easily into two categories, such as features about Gardening (Hobbies or Science) and Servants (Work or Domestic). All fit under the umbrella of self-improvement, evident in the many 'how to' articles that imparted information to develop knowledge and skills – how to read the Bible, how to recite a poem – and sought to influence a reader's outlook on life – how to have an easy mind, how to cope with schoolgirl troubles.

Of particular interest are the articles in *TGOP* on character building that were concerned as much with the hereafter as with the here and now. Its content was tucked into articles of all kinds to help girls navigate through the uncertainties of their adolescent and young adult years. In 'What Would You Like to Be?', for example, pampered only child Nellie Graham, who wants to be a great singer, must teach music instead to support her mother and herself after Mr Graham's death following an unfortunate financial speculation. The author adds a moral: 'And she is always happy, as all are who strive to do their duty in whatever position they may be placed.'[59]

Character building, overtly addressed in nonfiction content and found more subtly as a feature of fiction, is found also in the magazine's abundant poetry, prize competitions and Varieties column. Often illustrated, poems in *TGOP* offer a brief lesson in right living, frequently within a religious context, but almost always inspirational in tone.

Poetry was a regular feature of women's periodicals of the time, Kathryn Ledbetter points out, that 'taught noble attitudes and Christian values that prepared women readers for their important role of maternal saviors in the domestic plan for improving civilization'.[60] Readers may not have perceived these noble purposes – and may not even have read the poetry included in a magazine – but editors viewed poetry as essential content and, presumably, what readers wanted. Its sheer volume attests to the importance that RTS assigned to poetry in *TGOP*, as does its frequent appearance, often illustrated, on the first page of an issue. Like other content in the magazine, poems offer a snapshot of what the poets themselves, or the culture within which they wrote, considered important in their own lives and those of their readers.

Poetry with music in the title and / or text is common in *TGOP*. The poem 'Music' appearing in January 1881 (Figure 10) exalts music as the art best representing the bliss of heaven. In the accompanying illustration, eight young adults are at a musical party at which a female vocalist is singing. One of the two men is paying special attention to the pianist, while the other one turns her pages. In an illustrated poem of the same title in April 1897, a young woman at the piano accompanies a man playing the violin. The text with its biblical imagery bids music to 'breathe airs of Eden o'er my soul'.[61]

Illustrations in *TGOP*, many of them musical, are lavish and abundant, ranging from full-page plates and drawings to smaller illustrations used as filler. Fiction,

MUSIC.

Of all the arts beneath the heaven
That man has found, or God has given
None draws the soul so sweet away
As Music's melting, mystic lay;
Slight emblem of the bliss above,
It soothes the spirit all to love.

[All rights reserved.]

Figure 10 'Music', *The Girl's Own Paper* 2 (29 January 1881): 273

nonfiction and poetry all included drawings or later photographs relevant to their content. Beginning in Volume 5, some of the plates in the annual volumes were in colour. Photographs first appeared in Volume 16.

Varieties or Odds and Ends and Useful or Household Hints represent content that is practical, instructive and entertaining. Pearls of wisdom from the pens of famous authors and musicians predominate in the Varieties column, but content also mentions and even ridicules the accomplishments as in Coleridge's 'Swans sing before they die; 'twere no bad thing / Should certain persons die before they sing.'[62] The majority of the tidbits are of the character-building sort, such as 'We Want to Grow Better. – Small kindnesses, small courtesies, small considerations, habitually practised in our social intercourse, give a greater charm to the character than the display of great talents and accomplishments.'[63]

A quotation attributed to Saint Augustine found in the magazine's second Varieties column suggests the ideal woman that RTS envisioned:

> WOMAN'S POSITION. If God had designed woman as man's master, He would have taken her from his head; if as his slave, He would have taken her from his feet; but as He designed her for his companion and equal, He took her from his side.[64]

Whether in fact woman always was portrayed as man's equal in the pages of *TGOP*, however, is open to interpretation.

Useful or Household Hints were intended to ease the work of housewives or daughters learning domestic skills and house servants alike, with suggestions on cooking, storing and preparing food, cleaning, mending, stain removal and care of the teeth and hair. Household Hints in the 5 December 1896 issue gave 22 such tips, among them how best to light a kitchen fire, preserve mustard, store eggs, make lemonade, mend tears in dresses and umbrellas, hang meat and put off rats. Recipes were standard fare in the Hints columns.

Competitions required readers to use their hands as well as their heads. Essay writing, historical research, painting and later photography and even music were the objects of competitions during the years of *TGOP* under consideration, but needlework remained the focus of prize competitions. Writing in 1886 about 'What Girls Read', Edward Salmon considered the prize competitions 'probably the best feature' of *TGOP*, because of their charitable purpose. Once judging was finished, clothing, bags, dolls and paintings brightened the lives of children and adults in hospital, destitute and deserted girls, fatherless and board-school children, missionaries abroad and sailors at sea who were the deserving recipients of readers' philanthropy.[65]

In October 1887, the editor announced the magazine's first musical composition competition for the two best arrangements of Longfellow's poem 'The Rainy Day', printed in *TGOP*, for voice with piano accompaniment. Adjudicator John Stainer found the results, which exceeded his expectations, very satisfactory on the whole.[66] He judged two of the 288 entries excellent and awarded the prizes to Ethel Harraden and Amelia Corper, respectively.[67] Both compositions were printed in *TGOP* (Figure 11 and Figure 12).

Figure 11 First-prize winner in first music composition competition in *The Girl's Own Paper*, 'The Rainy Day' (Ethel Harraden), *The Girl's Own Paper* 9 (7 April 1888): 436–40

Figure 11 (Continued)

Figure 11 (Continued)

Figure 11 (Continued)

Figure 11 (Continued)

Figure 12 Second-prize winner in first music composition competition in *The Girl's Own Paper*, 'The Rainy Day' (Amelia Corper), *The Girl's Own Paper* Extra Summer 9 (1888): 44–7

Figure 12 (Continued)

Figure 12 (Continued)

Figure 12 (Continued)

Editor Peters immediately announced the next musical composition competition for 'a short pianoforte piece in two movements, descriptive of SORROW and JOY'.[68] Stainer, who again judged the competition, must not have been satisfied with the response, for he opened the report with an admonition that more readers should have tried their hand at composing. To be good musicians, he continued, they must recognize good music. And the best ways to do this were to unravel the works of others and to make their own attempts to compose music.

Stainer reported no bad manuscripts submitted. Some showed 'considerable facility' but lacked interest; others seemed 'spontaneous and pleasing' but lacked originality; and still others included 'charming ideas' poorly worked out. First prize went to Fanny Scholfield Petrie for a 'distinctly "Schumannesque"' piece that 'runs smoothly; is thoroughly and naturally expressive of joy and sorrow; and lies well under the hands of the performer'. Her piece (Figure 13) was printed in the next volume of the magazine. Amelia Corper again won second prize. Her setting, judged 'slightly uneven in character', had a melodious first movement (Sorrow) 'breathing the sweetness of Mendelssohn', but the second movement (Joy) did not offer adequate musical contrast.[69] Corper's piece did not appear in *TGOP*.

A competition for the three best musical settings of a 'Grace Before and After Meat' followed. Additional competitions in the magazine related to music but did not involve composition.

The Answers to Correspondents column appeared weekly beginning with the third issue of *TGOP*'s first volume, when the editor doled out advice and information about Dress, Needlework, Recreations, Cookery, Art and Housekeeping, as well as answers to Miscellaneous questions. New headings appeared over the years. By the seventh issue of *TGOP*, questions about music were answered in the Answers to Correspondence column in most issues, and the editor received enough music-related questions that in the last issue of Volume 1, Music was included as a separate heading. An illustrated Answers to Correspondents page from Volume 13 is shown in Figure 14.

For a time, the column was continued in *TGOP* supplements to accommodate the enormous number of correspondents, to whom Peters referred in some of his replies. Kirsten Drotner has observed that taken together, the categories of answers offer a microcosm of the nonfiction contents of the paper but also point to glaring contradictions with advice found in those articles.[70] Unknown context of the actual questions – since only replies were printed – might mediate what appears to be contradictory advice or information, however. The periodic inclusion of rules first printed in the 6 March 1880 issue and actual content of replies indicate that some readers were abusing the privilege of corresponding with the editor, asking far more questions than his limited time and the magazine's space allowed.

Fiction, nonfiction, poetry, varieties, hints and competitions all reveal what RTS *expected* readers to be and do, with religious teaching never far below the surface. The rules for a Socks or Stockings Competition in 1904, for example, exhorted readers to 'Do your best for God's poorest, dear girls.'[71] Answers to Correspondents offer a glimpse of what readers actually *wanted* to be and do, as well as a demographic of those readers. Some examples from the Miscellaneous

Figure 13 First-prize winner in second music composition competition in *The Girl's Own Paper*, 'Sorrow' – 'Joy' (Fannie Scholfield Petrie), *The Girl's Own Paper* 11 (30 August 1890): 763–5

Figure 13 (Continued)

Introduction 39

Figure 13 (Continued)

heading paint a picture of the many concerns the readers had and the many facets of Peters's personality in addressing those concerns. As much as he might have been tempted at times, the editor told Perseverance in 1897 that he did not throw most of the letters received 'unanswered into the wastepaper basket', but rather gave them 'conscientious care and attention'.[72] As he told A Well-Wisher, some

ANSWERS TO CORRESPONDENTS.

EDUCATIONAL.

IRISH KATIE (Dorset).—We can only recommend you to study our article, which recently appeared in this magazine, on "The Governess Difficulty." We endorse the opinion that if they wish to emigrate, and obtain assisted or free passages, they must offer themselves as "lady helps," as governesses are not eligible for them, nor is there any demand for them in the colonies. Your proficiency in needlework and cutting-out would be a great recommendation to you. You should have letters from your clergyman and as many persons holding good private or public positions as you can get, as introductions and certificates of character and connections. You write an excellent hand.

THISTLE.—The ancient inhabitants of Caledonia (as it is called by the Roman historian Tacitus), were probably Caledonians and Picts, tribes of the Celts who passed over from Gaul in the early part of the 4th century. They were invaded by the Scythians, since called Scots, who drove the Picts to the north, and settled in the lowlands, and gave their name to the whole country. The Venerable Bede says it was called Caledonia till A.D. 258, when it was invaded by an Irish tribe, and called Scotia. Kenneth II. was first king of Scotland, 838.

ROSY CHEEKS.—1. If "an assistant mistress" of a school, how is it that you spell "oblige," "oblidge," and "truely"? 2. The fees for the classes and lectures of the women's department of King's College, London, are a guinea a term for each class, excepting in two or three special subjects. For ladies engaged in teaching, these fees are reduced by one-third. Apply to Miss Schmitz, 13, Kensington Square (lady superintendent), for further particulars and prospectus. You can also obtain a syllabus of lectures from her, price fourpence.—2. When friends make you a present, thank them, of course; say all you can in praise of their gift, and say that you value their kind thought of you.

C. A.—The Holy Scriptures tell us "There is not a just man upon earth that doeth good and sinneth not" (Eccles. vii. 20). Again, "If we say that we have no sin, we deceive ourselves, and the truth is not in us" (I. St. John, i. 8). But we are also told that "we are complete in Him," whose "righteousness is unto all and upon all them that believe" (II. Cor. v. 21). As we are only finite beings, nothing can be perfect about us, although we are bound to strive after holiness by the aid of the Holy Spirit. But our blessed Lord is "made unto us . . . righteousness"; for it is "imputed unto us" by Him, who, though "He knew no sin," in reality, was "made sin for us," or, in other words, our sin was "imputed" to Him, and He bore its responsibility and punishment for us.

ART.

DESIGN.—1. To dispose of original designs for wallpaper, we think you should apply to the head manager of some great manufactory of such paper, and show what you have done. First write and state what you want, and, if possible, show your work in person, after making an appointment if you can, still better, get a gentleman friend to do so for you.—2. All specimens of work must be sent in to the Council of the Royal Academy, Burlington House, before June 28th, accompanied by a printed form duly filled in. You must get a member to write and ask for this form from the Registrar. If your specimens of work be approved, you will be admitted for a period of six months as a probationer. A further specimen showing proficiency will then be required; and if approved, you will be received as a student for a period of six years.

MUSIC.

AN INNOCENT.—1. The zither is a difficult instrument on which to acquire proficiency. You should have some lessons to begin with. The lowest price you should pay would be from 15s. to £1. The instrument would be but a child's toy at less than that.—2. For failure of sight from loss of nervepower, wearing glasses is not sufficient as a restorative. If on a clay soil, you should remove to a dry, sandy, or gravel one, and a bracing air on a hill, or by the sea. You should live well, and go to bed early; avoid eye light as much as possible, rest the eyes, and bathe them in cold water. A weak solution of vinegar and cold water, used at least twice a day, is strengthening. We know a lady suffering from the same trouble, and who was ordered to Brighton from a clay soil, who was able to read and work a little within a week of the change.

JENNY.—The Royal College of Music, Kensington Gore, S.W., gives scholarships to both sexes, tenable during three years, of which fifty-three are open and nine local. The fee for students is £40 per annum for tuition.

MISCELLANEOUS.

WINDY WEATHER.—Address a dean as "The Very Rev. the Dean of ——"; and a captain in the Army, as "Captain B——, 9th Regiment," etc.

OLIVE BURNHAM.—The brother's property would be divided equally between his sisters. The sister's son would have no rights if his mother were alive.

NETTIE WHITE.—1. Remain with your friend during the brief time she makes a few friendly remarks in her acquaintances en passant.—2. We are gratified by your letter.

A TURKISH LASSIE.—1. The 28th August, 1863, was a Friday, and the 1st May, 1852, a Saturday.—2. We do not think that you can need to go into a hospital for "weakness on the nerves and pain in the head." But there is one for nervous diseases, including paralysis and epilepsy, in Queen Square, Bloomsbury, W.C.—Secretary, Mr. B. Burford Rawlings; also at Portland Terrace, Regent's Park, N.W., and another at 73, Welbeck Street, W.

'A BANJO ENTHUSIAST.'

AN OLD SUBSCRIBER.—You should go to a surgical instrument maker, taking a letter of direction from your doctor, relative to your ears, and naming the sort of appliance that your form of deafness requires. Much depends on the cause of deafness. It might be from an accident, a fall, or an explosion; it might be hereditary, or from temporary depression of the general system.

AN ELEVEN YEARS' SUBSCRIBER.—1. We know of no way better than washing with soap and water to "fetch mould off your face."—2. You do not explain what sort of "marks" are to be "fetched off a light velvet dress." Are they "mould" marks also, or grease, ink, or ordinary dirt? We think you had better cover them with some lace or gimp trimming, or else alter the folds so as to hide them.

A READER.—The version of the Psalms in the Bible is that made by the translators of the Bible in the reign of James I. That in the Prayer Book was anterior to it, and made in 1539, chiefly from the Greek text. It is dear to many, and familiarised by custom; but that of the Bible is translated directly from the Hebrew, and probably of superior authority as regards a disputed reading of a text. The Latin headings are merely the repetition from the first words of the Psalm.

MARTHA.—Marriage with a deceased wife's sister is illegal in this country. Your going over to Canada, the United States, or to Australia, to have the ceremony performed would not avail you, nor your children, as an English woman, on your return to your own country. You could not be received into society, and your children would be illegitimate, and, excepting by will, could not inherit your own or family property, nor could they claim their father's surname, although he might give them leave to use it, as they might a nickname. It is a very serious thing to marry in defiance of the law. We thank you for your kind letter.

ONE IN DOUBT.—Our blessed Lord said, "Why take ye thought for the morrow?" "anxious or unnecessary thoughts. God inspired His holy prophets, and what they foretold in His Name and by His command is not to be compared to what any old woman may tell you in return for your "crossing her hand" with a sixpenny-piece. No; rather say, in humble faith, "My times are in Thy hand." It is enough.

A CONSTANT READER.—In taking photographs intended to represent the four seasons, "Spring" would be a fair young girl dressed in a flowing robe of pale green or white, with spring flowers—primroses, crocuses, and daffodils. "Summer" is also dressed in white, with summer flowers—principally roses. "Autumn" is generally robed in yellow, with red leaves and autumn flowers, such as the chrysanthemum. "Winter" wears white fur and holly berries, and a gown of some thick white material, such as cloth. You could have screens at the back to represent appropriate landscapes; and as they should be out of doors, there might be rocks and trees. Snow is represented by salt and cotton wool in such pictures.

ROSY MAY.—When you become naturalised you obtain all the rights of a native-born subject—protection from foreign interference and wrong, conscription if a man, the benefit of the laws for marriage, property, protection of good name, the right to vote, etc. We are much gratified by your kind letter, and your opinion that our paper grows "nicer than ever."

MAN wishes to know the meaning of "tit-bits." The term is derived from two Anglo-Saxon words, tit, tid, or tydder, which signify "nice" or "tender," and bita, a "bite," or "mouthful." Literally, it refers to things delicate and appetising which are edible; but the use of the term has been extended to bon mots and trifles of a piquant character in news, stories, etc.

PUPIL TEACHER.—1. The best English spoken in England, amongst the people in general, is that spoken in the east midland counties—in Essex, Lincolnshire, Norfolk, and Suffolk—all bordering on the ancient monastic regions. You will find our authority for this statement in French's work on English, Past and Present.—2. It is quite possible that the temporary failure, in a measure, of your sight is occasioned by biliousness. When the liver is out of order the whole nervous system is upset, and the most delicate of the nerves, such as those of the eye, become more or less disabled. And not only dimness of sight, but double vision, may be experienced. To "see double" is by no means peculiar to hard drinking.

H. D. P.—According to Hazell's last edition, the number of Wesleyan Methodists is 28,000,000 throughout the world. In the northern states of America there are 1,900,000 members; in the southern, 1,200,000. The total number of members of the Anglican communion is said to be 20,000,000. In the United States there are 1,250,000 members.

DUCHESS.—1. The name "duke" occurs in Gen. xxxvi., 15. It is not a title of nobility, but is considered only used to mean a leader or chief.—2. Perth was first an important place in the 11th century; but tradition ascribes its foundation to the Romans. It was the capital and residence of the Scottish kings till the ruthless murder of James I. by the wild clansmen of Grahame, 1437, showed it to be too near the Highlands for safety. The kings had no palace here, and the Court lived in the Cistercian abbey. Edward I. of England, wishing to annex Scotland to England in 1296, dethroned John Balliol, ravaged the country, destroyed the muniments of Scottish history, and carried the prophetic stone of Scone to Westminster, where the present chair was made to receive it. The history of this stone goes back to 513, when it was in the cathedral of Cashel, the capital of the kings of Munster. It was called the Lia Fail, or Fatal Stone. It was borrowed by Fergus I., a prince of the royal line, to be crowned on in 330, and never returned.

FATIMA.—You would have to advertise for the book, and get it second-hand.

Figure 14 'A Banjo Enthusiast', in 'Answers to Correspondents' with Music Heading, *The Girl's Own Paper* 13 (20 February 1892): 336

letters were 'very silly', others gave him 'needless trouble'; some of the letters required 'the severest rebukes', but others merited 'encouragement, sympathy, and praise'.[73] Some letters must have filled Peters with mirth. One can almost hear him chuckle as he told Edith, Gussie and Mabel in 1894, 'we hope this answer will come in time to prevent your eating too many halfpenny buns. We should say two each would be quite enough.'[74]

Religious counsel was not unusual in the Answers to Correspondents column, though it may be hard to believe that readers of *TGOP* actually were such deep thinkers to contemplate life's great mysteries. The replies speak volumes about the editor as well – or perhaps his designated respondent – who was willing to give such detailed, thoughtful replies. Whether Peters answered each question himself is not clear; he at least might have consulted an adviser or contributor before fashioning some of the lengthier, more complex answers.

Peters's answers were especially acerbic when letters had misspellings, especially from correspondents who sought work requiring command of the English language, as Anxious Applicant, who wanted to be a 'nersury' governess to teach three small 'gurls . . . reading, riting, and speling' discovered in 1884: 'Eight mistakes in spelling in a few lines do not, we think, entitle any honest woman to take a situation as nursery governess, and we hope you will think better of so dishonest a step.'[75] The Rush and the Flag was told simply, 'We think that a girl is not old enough, nor fit to have a sweetheart, if she cannot spell the word.'[76]

Silliness received the brunt of Peters's sarcasm. One can picture him, tongue-in-cheek, having a bit of fun at the correspondent's expense in many cases. His answer in 1880 to Eustachie, who asked 'up to what age a girl may climb a tree', is illustrative:

> If a pack of wolves were after you, we should advise you to climb a tree up to ninety or a hundred! Otherwise, why make yourself look so like one of Dr. Darwin's monkey-progenitors? Were there apples in the tree, we should excuse your so doing; but otherwise it is not so delightful to be up a tree, nor a suitable position for a girl.[77]

The vice of vanity was cause for scolding in 1889. Peters told Abrupt,

> We cannot give you any recipe for making your hair grow dark, nor any for 'getting rid of a double chin'. Be thankful that you have got any hair or chin at all, and that the hair you complain of does not grow on your chin.[78]

By Volume 18, Peters had decided that readers needed a mother figure as well as a father figure – perhaps also to take the pressure off of an ailing editor – and introduced 'The Twilight Circle', which began in 1896 as a series of articles by Ruth Lamb, whom readers confided in as their 'Mother Confessor'. In 1899, after its third series, Twilight Circle moved to the regular correspondence column to focus on the piles of letters that gradually had accumulated.

It appears that letters from musical readers asked questions in the categories of voice, piano, violin and other instruments; choosing an instrument and music; daily practice and practising societies; repertoire; composers and performers; music

42   *Introduction*

history and appreciation; musical terms and pronunciation; music examinations and colleges; and music theory and composition. Others concerned health – particularly vocal – and performance nerves and etiquette. Many replies were general, merely suggesting that the correspondent inquire at a music shop, for example.

One common question apparently concerned the age at which one could start voice lessons from girls still too young. Eager would-be singers, many between age 12 and 14, were told not to start lessons until age 15 or 16. The editor did not tell his young correspondents *why* they must wait until then, however, and they continued to ask the same question. Perhaps they were not reading answers given to other correspondents or thought the answer would not apply to them.

Beginning in Volume 4 the Answers to Correspondents column included in its replies information about Musical Practising Societies organized by readers of the magazine. One of the most mentioned was Miss Emily Hartland's Practising Society, which had 70 members in 1891 and was still mentioned in *TGOP* in 1894. Hartland gave details of her organization and offered rules to prospective readers who sent her a stamped envelope. Members who paid a yearly subscription fee of 1s, 6d were expected to practise five hours a week. At the end of the term, fines might be levied and prizes were given. But, as the editor told A Lover of Good Music in 1898, 'To join a practising society, as you suggest, is no guarantee that the practising is carefully done. Membership of such a body only serves as a kind of link of fellowship between musical people.'[79]

Many *TGOP* readers tried their hands at musical compositions, which they submitted to *TGOP* for the editor's critique. Piano, Organ, Violin's piece was 'Not quite up to our mark yet', bearing 'all the marks of having been composed (as you say it was) in five minutes'.[80] Submissions often contained consecutive fifths and octaves and, in Nydia's case, 'too many mistakes to specify'.[81] While occasional works earned Peters's praise and encouragement, he treated others with unusual tact: Fiddler's apparently unmusical composition of 1899 had no melody but was beautifully copied.

Although the Answers to Correspondents column continued throughout the second decade of *TGOP* publication, Music headings decreased beginning in 1895, and in 1896, in Volume 18, the column's format changed to incorporate music replies under the new Study and Studio heading. The 29 August 1908 reply in Volume 29 in which C.S.S.M. thanked correspondent M.F.P. for copying the hymn text about which she had inquired was the last music-related reply found under Peters's editorship. The next month readers were introduced to the new editor, Flora Klickmann, who did not continue the Answers to Correspondents column when she assumed control of *TGOP* for Volume 30.

In the music scores printed in *TGOP*, vocal pieces predominate, most for solo voice but occasionally for more singers. Hymns, carols, sacred songs and anthems are well represented, and texts offering heavenly prayers and blessings appear in songs not overtly religious. Extra issues include sacred cantatas and cantatinas. Of the secular songs, nature topics, lullabies and love lost and found are common themes. The first vocal piece, 'Under the Snow' composed by John Farmer in Volume 1 (Figure 15), gives some idea of the level of musical proficiency expected of readers.[82] A simple piano accompaniment joins an even simpler vocal line of just

Figure 15 First music score printed in *The Girl's Own Paper*, 'Under the Snow' (John Farmer), *The Girl's Own Paper* 1 (31 January 1880): 71–2

Figure 15 (Continued)

over an octave, peaking on high E, with some chromatics. The lyrics fall under the category of character building with their inspirational message to be patient, like the crocus under the snow, in today's gloomiest hour, for tomorrow will be brighter.

The first instrumental music, 'A Sister's Lullaby' for solo violin with piano accompaniment by Lady Lindsay of Balcarres, appears in Volume 2. The first piano solo, 'Le Dernier Papillon' by Lott, appears in Volume 3. Later volumes offer works for harmonium or American organ, and a single piece appears for violin and cello with piano accompaniment, 'On Richmond Hill' by C. A. Macirone, in Volume 14.

In February 1880, the editor told correspondent Mary Jane, 'We hope to publish a piece of music every month.'[83] The number of music scores peaked in the magazine's third and fourth volumes, with 13 scores in each, averaging 11 music scores in each of the first 10 volumes. Music scores tapered off during the second decade to about half those of the previous decade, and by the magazine's third decade, no volume had more than three music scores, with none in some volumes.

Titles of scores printed from 1900 suggest that younger readers were expected to perform the pieces. 'Two Little Tiny Wing*s*' for voice and piano composed by E. Markham Lee to words by Samuel Taylor Coleridge features a straightforward vocal line with few chromatics. The *Slowly and Calmly* tempo suggests the ease with which the piece could be performed by pianist and vocalist. The part song 'Chirp and Twitter' was the last new music score of the decade. Its subtitle 'Birds' Song' refers not only to the song text but also to the oft-repeated descriptions in *TGOP* fiction of vocalists who sing like birds. The lilting rhythm and *Allegro con grazia* tempo suggest the quick fluttering movements of birds. The farthest these winged creatures stray from the tonic is a brief flight into the harmonic minor before hopping back to rest on a lengthy concluding C-major chord.

The last music score of the third decade, for voice and piano by Princess Beatrice, youngest child of Queen Victoria, to words by Charlotte Elliot, was reprinted from an October 1896 issue. The song's title 'Retrospection' has resonance on many levels. Elliott's 'soul of feeling' that muses on absent friends evokes the unseen editor Peters who offered *TGOP* as a friend to girls and sought to build a community of readers.[84] The poet's conclusion, which points thoughts heavenward, alludes to the magazine's ongoing purpose to fit readers for a life on earth that will prepare them for their heavenly home.

To a solemn minim (half note) accompaniment in C minor, the voice sings the first verse in a more active recitative-like style, while the piano holds onto 'Memory's stores' not yet unsealed.[85] The harmonic rhythm quickens as these memories awaken from their sleep in the second verse, and the melody modulates to A-flat major. The vocalist is encouraged to soar to a high G as the soul is incited, with an optional, more comfortable, D for those less inspired, before coming to rest on the C-major tonic cadence in which the piano has the last word on an open C chord.

The editors' backgrounds offer some insight into choice of musical content for *TGOP*. British society's expectation for women's music making underlies how that content is presented in the magazine. Comparison of musical content in *TGOP* with that found in *TBOP*, published concurrently through the 30 years covered in the catalogue, offers additional insight into musical content chosen for the girls' magazine.

Music in *The Boy's Own Paper*

The importance that RTS attached to the musical content of its girls' magazine was apparent when the Society printed several advertisements, most of them full page, in *Musical Standard* and *Musical Times* in 1880 shortly after the magazine was launched and again when the first and second annual volumes were published. As printed in the advertisement copy, RTS expected the numerous papers, stories and songs to be of interest 'to all Amateur and Professional Musicians'.[86] In its December 1885 review, *Musical Times* gave the new volume of *The Girl's Own Annual* high marks. 'Musically', the article noted, 'it appeals to us with irresistible force' for its 'original compositions by eminent composers' and its 'papers on various subjects connected with the art.'[87]

RTS had been keeping track of press reactions to *TGOP* ever since the magazine's debut. Among the favourable press that the Society included in its Annual Report of 1880 was that of the *Court Circular*: 'The *Girl's Own Paper* does for girls what the *Boy's Own Paper* does for the other sex, and is proportionately quiet and domestic.'[88]

The *Court Circular* did not spell out just what *TGOP* did that was the same as found in *TBOP* but proportionately quieter and more domestic. Might it have been related in part to musical content? That possibility was addressed by reviewing the weekly issues in 25 volumes of *TBOP* published in late Victorian and early Edwardian England, as well as extra holiday issues, to determine how the boy's magazine differed from that of the girls', most specifically in musical content.

According to Editorial Secretary Green, RTS long had felt the need for wholesome periodicals for boys and girls to offset the pernicious effects of penny dreadfuls – the cheap sensational fiction circulating among the nation's mostly working-class youth. When no alternative seemed forthcoming, the Society, hesitant to embark on a publication not clearly within its scope of distributing evangelical tracts, undertook the project. Fears that such a publication would be a risky financial venture proved unfounded, and, in 1879, RTS unexpectedly found itself with a best-selling magazine in *TBOP*, targeted at readers age 12 to 16, under the leadership of Managing Editor George Hutchinson and Sub-Editor James Macaulay.[89] The success of *TBOP* – and the realization that boys' sisters were reading their brothers' magazines on a regular basis – led RTS to give girls their own publication a year later.[90] With missionary fervour, RTS sought to put these magazines into the hands of young boys and girls who would derive benefit from a judicious mix of morally upright entertainment and instruction. Musical content was part of the winning formula that RTS adopted for both magazines.

Although a companion to *TBOP*, as Forrester notes, *TGOP* 'was by no means a B.O.P. with the sexes changed'.[91] Close examination of the respective magazines reveals a disparity in musical offerings between them. The musical content that appears abundantly in *TGOP* not only in music scores but also as music making in fiction and nonfiction, in poems and illustrations, and in Answers to Correspondents, appears less frequently in the magazine for boys. That difference can be attributed at least in part to societal expectations about gender roles and manly behavior for British boys.

As a national pastime, music in Victorian England was class and gender specific. Both boys and girls of the upper classes learned music to some extent as an ornament to the more solid, useful subjects of their education. For girls, music making was confined largely to the home as a constructive activity to fill hours that might otherwise be given over to idleness and dissipation. For boys, music was more a recreational activity to offset the rigors of schoolwork outside the home.[92] Gifted young females were expected to settle for being appreciated as amateur musicians; career options were essentially nonexistent except that of a music governess, should life circumstances necessitate paid employment. Young males were not encouraged to embrace music to such an extent as their sisters, but those who showed exceptional talent could be placed on the fast track to virtuoso status, where they were applauded as professionals; societal loopholes also offered them careers as church organists and orchestra players.[93]

These expectations affected coverage of music in *TBOP* compared to that in *TGOP*, evident in less musical content and less diversity of that content in the boys' magazine when compared with the girls' magazine. While girl readers received primers on how to sing and how to play piano, violin, organ, harmonium, harp, guitar, concertina, mandolin, zither, banjo and xylophone in that order in *TGOP*, boys received only four primers on how to play the violin and the banjo – both of which they also were taught how to build in follow-on articles – the guitar, and drums and fifes in *TBOP*. The five-part 'Miss Mandoline and Her Sisters' gave hints on playing some of the popular plucked stringed instruments. Another article in *TBOP* instructed readers how to build a xylophone. In their magazine, girls were taught only how to make a metronome.

Choice of primers in the two magazines is noteworthy. While *TGOP* included a wide range of primers on keyboards, upper strings, concertina and xylophone as listed earlier, *TBOP* limited its scope to upper strings and fife and drums. Neither boys nor girls were encouraged to play brass, woodwind or lower stringed instruments such as violoncello and double bass, if the lack of primers for those instruments is an indication. Primers in *TGOP* did not extend to the flute, clarinet or violoncello, for example, although some young women played – or wanted to play – these instruments, as implicated in Answers to Correspondents columns. And unlike its sister publication, *TBOP* did not instruct its readers on singing or playing the piano. Notably, *TBOP* also lacked follow-on articles on how to improve one's music making that appeared in *TGOP* for singing and for playing the piano and the violin. The mechanics of music took precedence over its performance for boy readers.

Types of music scores differed between the two magazines. Excluding a piece in the series about the mandolin family, music scores in *TBOP* are all songs with lyrics focusing on character building, patriotism, school, sports and the sea. With few exceptions, music printed in *TBOP* is scored for chorus, not solo vocalists, with simple piano accompaniment, and many pieces in earlier volumes are scored for tonic sol-fa choral singing as well. *TGOP* offered its readers music scores not only for voice but also for piano and occasionally for violin as well as organ or harmonium.

TGOP has far more music-related fiction than *TBOP*. Fiction in *TGOP* is not limited to musical heroines; hero musicians are frequently in the wings, often performing with their female musical colleagues and then marrying them after having been their music master, accompanist or critic. Male musicians sometimes take center stage in the magazine's fiction, with female characters in the supporting roles. While not all stories have music making as the primary theme, in some fiction, the ubiquitous home piano suggests that at least one daughter is musical, and her playing and singing further the plot development. In some cases, these cameo appearances serve as the means to deliver life's lessons thinly veiled as entertainment.

Moral lessons embedded in *TGOP* fiction stress selflessness and duty to one's family, no matter how talented a musician might be. The magazine's first serialized story, 'Zara; or, My Granddaughter's Money', which ran in the first 23 weekly issues, stresses 'taking the high road'. Zara Meldicott Keith, a music-hall singer, and her 'saviour' Paul Tench are morally upright characters who have made some bad, though entirely reversible, decisions and are in need of redirection. The *deus ex machina* is a long-suffering clergyman's daughter whose future happiness with Paul depends on this successful redirection.

Zara's story contrasts sharply with that of 'Quite a Lady', in which Rose Everleigh, whose attempts to secure a public engagement as a singer in order to offset a financial crisis finally succeed, serves as a mouthpiece for *TGOP* in her distaste for appearance on stage. It is significant that Zara, a milliner's assistant by day, and Rose, the daughter of a lord, are from different social classes and that both women are 'rescued' by marriage from their financial reasons for singing in public.

Young male musicians make rare cameo appearances in *TBOP* fiction, as when Soady is heard practising scales, which he does not find very amusing, on an old upright piano after school, when he would rather be out on the playground. An older Reginald Cruden offers to play piano for a game of musical chairs, but his choice of a Weber waltz, a Corelli gavotte and a German air are not well suited to the game. Georgie Masterton, a cellist in a trio with violinist and pianist – both female – for a village concert, takes a tumble with his instrument when his chair leg tips off the improvised stage. He and the cello are unharmed, and with some assistance, the lad regains his position.[94] In a reflection of social expectations, musical girls and young women appear far more often in *TGOP* fiction than do musical boys and young men in *TBOP* fiction. Even in cameo appearances, music making in *TGOP* often offers readers a 'teachable moment' when poor musical choices have their consequences, while good musical choices often bring rewards. Boys' music making in *TBOP* fiction does not serve the same function.

In the category of musical composition competitions, however, the boys' magazine far exceeded its sister publication, with 18 such competitions compared with three in the girls' magazine. The first, in Volume 3 of *TBOP*, offered prizes for 'the best original musical setting of a sea-song, or hymn bearing on the sea' with words written before 1840.[95] One hundred thirty-one readers competed from which three winners were chosen. Two of these pieces were printed in the magazine's next annual volume. Later musical competitions were split into Senior and Junior Divisions. Beginning in Volume 11, one youthful repeat winner of the Junior Division was 14-year-old Gustav Holst, who was awarded a Certificate the first year but won the Junior Division prize the next three years. Five of the prize-winning music scores were printed in issues of *TBOP* – two in Volume 4, two in Volume 8 and one in the extra Christmas issue of Volume 8. Although Holst's name, age and address appear in lists of prize-winners printed in the magazine, neither his nor other competitors' pieces are mentioned by title, nor are any other winning competitions printed in *TBOP* during those years.

Both magazines had monthly columns of correspondence that printed answers to readers' questions. Girls continued to ask about piano practice and vocal training but apparently also were practising or at least were interested in concertina, guitar, harmonium, harp, violin and zither – all instruments found in their magazine's primers. By far most musical correspondents in *TBOP* were interested in violin, followed by military instruments such as fife and drums and high brass, banjo and concertina. Pianists as correspondents were rare in *TBOP*, and only one answer was addressed to a singer. Correspondent E.S.K. was put in his place for his atrocious spelling and unrealistic aspirations with the reply, 'If you have not sufficient time to play "a bango or a cordien or a concertina," your chance of musical proficiency is almost hopeless. Perhaps the tambourine or the bones might suit you, though it is not an easy thing to play the bones properly.'[96]

Unlike its abundance in *TGOP*, poetry is rare in the boys' magazine, and few of the poems in *TBOP* are music related. Musical illustrations are seen in both magazines, but with a difference. Illustrations in *TGOP* usually depict the ideal female musician in socially accepted music making, though in two drawings monkeys, not humans, are the musicians.[97] In contrast, a number of drawings in *TBOP* spoof music making by assigning it to diverse members of the animal kingdom.

Some general observations on musical diversity promoted on the pages of the two magazines are apt. Both magazines perpetuated the status quo concerning the role of music in their readers' lives. And that status quo, reflected in the goal of *TGOP* to fit its readers for their earthly home and their heavenly reward and in the motto for *TBOP*, 'Quicquid agunt pueri nostri est farrago libelli', translated 'Whatever boys do is the manifold subject of our little book', was linked in part to time, power and control.[98] It was proper – even encouraged – for women, who were essentially powerless in Victorian society, to spend their leisure hours practising and perfecting their skill in music, which was an ephemeral act with an intangible product to show for one's efforts.[99]

But masculine leisure, as well as masculine business, ought to produce tangible, measurable results. To spend too much time at music took away from the active pursuit of life's important goals.[100] Exceptions were made for military instruments, because of their masculine association, and for the violin, because its feminine associations of size and curvaceous shape necessitated metaphorical control by its male performer.[101] But unless a boy chose to become a professional musician in church, in orchestra pit or on stage, he was not to get too good at music making. Songs about cricket, sailing and school valued camaraderie over skilled singing, and the playing of fifes, drums and bugles in military bands practised one's patriotism. Both emphasized masculinity.

With perhaps the exception of the organ, the music making offered in *TGOP* kept its female readers safely in the home setting on instruments presenting a graceful appearance in performance. Young females were, in essence, biding their time between finishing their schooling and getting married. And music, which occupied hours of practice but whose performance seldom led to status or income, fit in nicely with society's expectations for these stay-at-home maidens.

Young males were in many cases still in boarding school where they were preparing for their life's occupation or vocation. Others were already out in the world of work, perhaps as apprentices. In both cases, music, which might divert them from these more important attainments, was slighted as unworthy of their time beyond the occasional singing of glee-like choruses often in conjunction with school or sports – and possibly participation in village bands – that reinforced masculine esprit de corps and taught some of life's important lessons about character building. With their simple melodies and low technical demands, these songs were sung to please the singers, not to entertain audiences, but they served a didactic purpose as well. For both girls and boys, music was thus an important way that gender and class diversity of larger Victorian society were inculcated in the minds and lives of its youngsters. It may have been a pleasant lesson for most, but a lesson nonetheless.

Notes

1 Judith Barger, *Elizabeth Stirling and the Musical Life of Female Organists in Nineteenth-Century England* (Aldershot and Burlington, VT: Ashgate, 2007).
2 Wendy Forrester, *Great-Grandmama's Weekly: A Celebration of* The Girl's Own Paper *1880–1901* (Guilford and London: Lutterworth, 1980); Terri Doughty, ed., *Selections from* The Girl's Own Paper, *1880–1907* (Peterborough, ON and Orchard Park, NY: Broadview, 2004); Kristine Moruzi, *Constructing Girlhood Through the Periodical Press, 1850–1915* (Farnham and Burlington, VT: Ashgate, 2012).
3 Roy Hindle, ed., *Oh, No Dear! Advice to Girls a Century Ago* (London: David and Charles, 1982); June Grace, ed., *Advice to Young Ladies from the Nineteenth-Century Correspondence Pages of* The Girl's Own Paper (N.p.: Author, 1997).
4 Mary Burgan, 'Heroines at the Piano: Women and Music in Nineteenth-Century Fiction', in *The Lost Chord: Essays on Victorian Music*, ed. Nicholas Temperley (Bloomington and Indianapolis: Indiana University Press, 1989), 42–66; Jodi Lustig, 'The Piano's Progress: The Piano in Play in the Victorian Novel', in *The Idea of Music in Victorian Fiction*, ed. Sophie Fuller and Nicky Losseff (Aldershot and Burlington, VT: Ashgate, 2004), 83–104.
5 Phyllis Weliver, *Women Musicians in Victorian Fiction, 1860–1900: Representations of Music, Science and Gender in the Leisured Home* (Aldershot and Burlington, VT: Ashgate, 2000); Paula Gillett, *Musical Women in England, 1870–1914: 'Encroaching on All Man's Privileges'* (New York: St Martin's, 2000).
6 'Answers to Correspondents: Grey Hairs', *TGOP* 2 (2 October 1880): 15; 'Answers to Correspondents: A Scot', *TGOP* 2 (17 September 1881): 816; 'Answers to Correspondents: A.M.', *TGOP* 15 (4 November 1883): 80.
7 Patrick Dunae, '*Boy's Own Paper*: Origin and Editorial Policies', *The Private Library* 2nd ser. 9/4 (1976): 211, 217.
8 James Mason, 'Looking Back: A Retrospect, with Some Surprising Figures and a Presentation to the Editor', *TGOP* 20 (25 February 1899): 341.
9 Samuel Green, *The Story of the Religious Tract Society for One Hundred Years* (London: Religious Tract Society, 1899), 288. *TGOP* content that may be found in the catalogue that follows is not cited unless a quotation.
10 I could not locate 'The Morning of the Year' Christmas and New Year's number for *TGOP* Volume 15, 1893.
11 James Huneker, *Overtones: A Book of Temperaments* (New York: Scribner, 1904), 286, 289–90.
12 Cyril Ehrlich, *The Piano: A History* (London: Dent, 1976), 98–104.

Introduction   51

13 See Ehrlich, *Piano;* and Arthur Loesser, *Men, Women and Pianos: A Social History* (New York: Simon and Schuster, 1954).
14 Huneker, *Overtones*, 291.
15 'Are We a Musical People?' *Chambers's Journal of Popular Literature, Science, and Art* 4th ser., 18 (2 July 1881): 418.
16 'New Music' *TGOP* 2 (29 January 1881): 287.
17 Oliveria Prescott, 'Touching the Pianoforte', *TGOP* 8 (12 March 1887): 378.
18 Fanny Davies, 'On the Technique of the Pianoforte: A Practical Talk to Earnest Students', *TGOP* 12 (25 October 1890): 53.
19 'Varieties: Musical Progress', *TGOP* 12 (15 November 1890): 107.
20 William Luff, 'The Piano and the Player', *TGOP* 14 (17 December 1892): 177.
21 'On a Very Old Piano: Lately Seen in a London Shop Window, and Labeled, "Cash Price, Two Guineas"', *TGOP* 20 (10 June 1899): 590.
22 'Answers to Correspondents: Kitten', *TGOP* 3 (28 January 1882): 286.
23 'Answers to Correspondents: Topsey', *TGOP* 3 (30 September 1882): 847.
24 'Answers to Correspondents: Red Riding Hood', *TGOP* 2 (9 April 1881): 448.
25 Ehrlich, *Piano*, 93; 'Answers to Correspondents: E. Litchy', *TGOP* 16 (7 September 1895): 784.
26 'Answers to Correspondents: Kate Wren', *TGOP* 12 (28 February 1891): 352.
27 Catherine Milnes Gaskell, 'The Women of To-day', *Nineteenth Century* 26 (November 1889): 776–84.
28 A Templar, 'The Girls of To-day', *TGOP* 11 (21 December 1889): 179.
29 'Answers to Correspondents: Inca', *TGOP* 21 (13 January 1900): 239.
30 'The Pianoforte and Its Enemies', *Musical Times* 37 (1 May 1896): 309.
31 Mrs George de Horne Vaizey, 'A Houseful of Girls', *TGOP* 22 (6 October 1900): 1.
32 Kimberly Reynolds, *Girls Only? Gender and Popular Children's Fiction in Britain, 1880–1910* (Philadelphia: Temple University Press, 1990), 145, 147.
33 Ibid., 147.
34 Margaret Beetham, *A Magazine of Her Own? Domesticity and Desire in the Woman's Magazine, 1800–1914* (London and New York: Routledge, 1996), 12–13.
35 New Orleans native Louis Moreau Gottschalk (1829–1869) and Swiss-born Sigismond Thalberg (1812–1871) were popular nineteenth-century composers and virtuoso pianists. See Irving Lowens and S. Frederick Starr, 'Gottschalk, Louis Moreau', and Robert Wangermée, 'Thalberg, Sigismond', *Grove Music Online*, ed. Deane Root, Oxford University Press, accessed 1 August 2015 at http://oxfordmusiconline.com.
36 Huneker, *Overtones*, 291–3. On the polemics of women as orchestral musicians and composers in America, see Judith Tick, 'Passed Away Is the Piano Girl: Changes in American Musical Life, 1870–1900', in *Women Making Music: The Western Art Tradition, 1150–1950*, ed. Jane Bowers and Judith Tick (Urbana: University of Illinois Press, 1986), 325–48.
37 Mason, "Looking Back", 341.
38 Green, *The Story of the Religious Tract Society*, 128. See also 'Your Valentine From the Editor', *TGOP* 2 (12 February 1881): 320.
39 'Answers to Correspondents: Charlton', *TGOP* 4 (14 July 1883): 655.
40 See 'Portrait Gallery of Contributors to "The Girl's Own Paper"', *The Girl's Own Paper* 20 (25 February 1899): foldout plate facing p. 344; *The Story of the House of Cassell* (London, New York, Toronto, Melbourne: Cassell, 1922), 120.
41 Ibid., 143.
42 *Who's Who 1907: An Annual Biographical Dictionary* (London: Adam and Charles Black; New York, Macmillan, 1907), 1389; 'Literary Gossip', *Athenaeum* no. 4184 (4 January 1908): 17.
43 *Trinity College, London: Calendar for the Academical Year 1877–1878* (London: Reeves, 1877), 18, 49–50.
44 Harold Rutland, *Trinity College of Music: The First Hundred Years* (London: Trinity College of Music, 1972); *Trinity College, London*, 19.

45 David Lazell, *Flora Klickmann and Her Flower Patch: The Story of 'The Girl's Own Paper' and The Flower Patch Among the Hills* (Warmley: Flower Patch Magazine, n.d.), 18, 28; 'Literary Gossip', 17; *Who's Who 1907*, 1389.
46 *Who's Who 1907*, 1389; A. R. B., 'In Memoriam: Charles Peters, Editor of "The Girl's Own Paper," 1880–1907', *TGOP* 29 (25 January 1908): 272.
47 Lazell, *Flora Klickmann and Her Flower Patch*, 16.
48 Mary H. Melville, 'The New Editor of the "G.O.P.": An Interview with Miss Flora Klickmann', *TGOP* 29 (19 September 1908): 813.
49 Ibid., 17; Flora Klickmann, 'Moments with Modern Musicians: Famous Organists', *The Windsor Magazine* 111 (January to June 1896): 665–78.
50 Lazell, *Flora Klickmann and Her Flower Patch*, 18.
51 Ibid., 19.
52 'The Editor's Page', *TGOP* 30 (November 1908): 1.
53 Ibid.
54 Ibid., 3.
55 Forrester, *Great-Grandmama's Weekly*, 13.
56 Hilary Skelding, 'Every Girl's Best Friend?: The *Girl's Own Paper* and its Readers', in *Feminist Readings of Victorian Popular Texts: Divergent Femininities*, ed. Emma Liggins and Daniel Duffey (Aldershot, Burlington, VT, Singapore, Sydney: Ashgate, 2001), 38.
57 Ibid., 42–3.
58 'Answers to Correspondents: Grey Hairs', 15.
59 M. R., 'What Would You Like to Be?' *TGOP* 3 (12 November 1891): 103.
60 Kathryn Ledbetter, *British Victorian Women's Periodicals: Beauty, Civilization, and Poetry* (New York: Palgrave Macmillan, 2009), 3.
61 G. K. M., 'Music', *TGOP* 18 (3 April 1897): 417.
62 'Varieties: For Those Who Sing Out of Tune', *TGOP* 2 (24 September 1881): 823.
63 'Varieties: We Want to Grow Better', *TGOP* 24 (18 April 1903): 476.
64 'Varieties: Woman's Position', *TGOP* 1 (10 January 1880): 32.
65 Edward Salmon, 'What Girls Read', *Nineteenth Century* o.s. 116, n.s. 20 (1886): 520.
66 John Stainer (1840–1901) was a British composer, organist of Saint Paul's Cathedral, London, and Professor of Music, Oxford. See Nicholas Temperley, 'Stainer, Sir John', *Grove Music Online*, ed. Deane Root, Oxford University Press, accessed 24 July 2015 at http://www.oxfordmusiconline.com.
67 Ethel Harraden, who had attended the Royal Academy of Music, came from a musical family and was a published composer of songs, instrumental works and at least four operettas. See Nigel Burton, 'Harraden, R. Ethel', *Grove Music Online*, ed. Deane Root, Oxford University Press, accessed 24 July 2015 at http://www.oxfordmusiconline.com. Her song *Was It?* with words by her brother Herbert was reviewed favourably in the New Music column in *TGOP* Volume 2, p. 673; *Severed the Tie*, a song by Herbert and Ethel Harraden with *ad lib* accompaniment for violin, concertina and violoncello was reviewed in a Volume 5, New Music column, p. 158.
68 'Our Next Musical Composition', *TGOP* 9 (24 March 1888): 405.
69 John Stainer, 'Report on the Musical Competition', *TGOP* 10 (15 December 1888): 173.
70 Kirsten Drotner, *English Children and Their Magazines, 1751–1945* (New Haven and London: Yale University Press, 1988), 156–7.
71 'Crochet Shawl Competition: A Labour of Love for the Christmas Holidays', *TGOP* 26 (26 November 1904): 134.
72 'Answers to Correspondents: Perseverance', *TGOP* 18 (3 June 1897): 639.
73 'Answers to Correspondents: A Well-Wisher', *TGOP* 3 (28 January 1882): 287.
74 'Answers to Correspondents: Edith, Gussie and Mabel', *TGOP* 16 (10 November 1894): 95.
75 'Answers to Correspondents: Anxious Applicant', *TGOP* 5 (17 May 1884): 528.

Introduction 53

76 'Answers to Correspondents: The Rush and the Flag', *TGOP* 15 (28 April 1894): 480.
77 'Answers to Correspondents: Eustacie', *TGOP* 1 (18 September 1880): 607.
78 'Answers to Correspondents: Abrupt', *TGOP* 10 (25 May 1889): 544.
79 'Answers to Correspondents: A Lover of Good Music', *TGOP* 19 (11 June 1898): 592.
80 'Answers to Correspondents: Piano, Organ, Violin', *TGOP* 12 (17 January 1891): 256.
81 'Answers to Correspondents: Nydia', *TGOP* 20 (19 August 1899): 751.
82 Composer John Farmer (1835–1901) was music master at Harrow School from 1862 until 1885, when he left to become organist at Balliol College, Oxford. He composed several books of school songs. See Bernarr Rainbow, 'Farmer, John (ii)', *Grove Music Online*, ed. Deane Root, Oxford University Press, accessed 24 July 2015 at http://www.oxfordmusiconline.com.
83 'Answers to Correspondents: Mary Jane', *TGOP* 1 (28 February 1880): 144.
84 H.R.H. the Princess Beatrice, 'Retrospection', *TGOP* 32 (December 1910): 178. Princess Beatrice had lost her husband, Prince Henry of Battenburg, in 1896 after 10 years of marriage, so her composition had resonance on a personal level as well.
85 Ibid.
86 'The Girl's Own Annual', *Musical Standard* 23 (17 September 1881): 192; 'The Girl's Own Annual', *Musical Times* 22 (1 October 1881): 536.
87 'No More Appropriate Christmas Present', *Musical Times* 26 (1 December 1883): 740.
88 *The Eighty-First Annual Report of the Religious Tract Society* (London: Religious Tract Society, 1880), 288.
89 Jack Cox, *Take a Cold Tub, Sir!: The Story of the* 'Boy's Own Paper' (Guildford: Lutterworth, 1982), 22, 23.
90 Green, *The Story of the Religious Tract Society*, 127.
91 Forrester, *Great-Grandmama's Weekly*, 13.
92 About the gendering of music making in England, see Gillett, *Musical Women in England*, esp. 1–31; and Richard Leppert, *Music and Image: Domesticity, Ideology and Socio-Cultural Formation in Eighteenth-Century England* (Cambridge: Cambridge University Press, 1988). About British society's penchant for singing, see Michael Turner and Antony Miall, eds., *The Parlour Song Book: A Casquet of Vocal Gems* (London: Michael Joseph, 1972).
93 See, for example, John Locke, *Some Thoughts Concerning Education* [1693] (Cambridge: At the University Press, 1895), 174; and Philip Dormer Stanhope, *Letters to His Son by the Earl of Chesterfield* [1749], vol. 1, ed. Oliver H. G. Leigh (Washington and London: Dunne, 1901), 170. About societal loopholes for male musicians, see Loesser, 214; and Cyril Ehrlich, *The Music Profession in Britain since the Eighteenth Century: A Social History* (Oxford: Clarendon, 1985), 111–12.
94 Paul Blake, 'School and the World: A Story of School and City Life', *TBOP* 7 (4 October 1884): 1–2; Talbot Baines Reed, 'Reginald Cruden: A Tale of City Life', *TBOP* 7 (30 May 1885): 545–8; A. N. Malan, 'The Silver Whistle: A Story of School and Home', *TBOP* 15 (29 April 1893): 483.
95 'Our Prize Competitions (New Subjects): III. – Music Competition', *TBOP* 3 (25 June 1881): 627.
96 'Correspondence: E.S.K.', *TBOP* 6 (12 July 1884): 656.
97 '"Serious" and "Sentimental"', *TGOP* 7 (17 October 1885): 48.
98 'Correspondence: Our Motto', *TBOP* 3 (8 January 1881): 248.
99 See, for example, Leppert, *Music and Image*, 28–9, 199–200.
100 Ibid.
101 Leppert, *Music and Image*, 58; Gillett, *Musical Women in England*, 85–7.

User guide to the annotated catalogue

My primary goal for compiling an annotated catalogue of music in *TGOP* is its practical usefulness as a research tool and as a guide to further reading for scholars and readers interested in musical content found in non-specialized periodical literature of late Victorian and Edwardian Britain. Nineteenth-century British periodicals for girls and women offer a wealth of material in which to understand not only what information and activities publishers considered important for their readers but also what readers themselves considered important in their lives. Taken together, these two perspectives give a revealing picture of how girls and women fit into their social and cultural worlds. One of these activities, music making, has been the focus of research that uses periodicals as source material, and *TGOP* is among the magazines consulted.

The catalogue is divided into two sections. The first is an issue-by-issue chronological listing of musical content in annual volumes and extra holiday issues of *TGOP*. The second lists that musical content by category under Fiction, Nonfiction, Poetry, Illustrations, Answers to Correspondents and Music scores.

Chronological listing

Each annual volume is identified by volume number and by span of dates covered, below which the volume's weekly issues are arranged chronologically, headed by issue number and date. Only entries with identified musical content are included for each issue; issues with no obvious musical content are not listed. Monthly issues that began in 1908 did not have issue numbers printed on first pages and in the catalogue are headed only by month and year, easily determined by the bound volume's layout.

Musical content in extra issues for Volumes 3 through 29 is listed following the entries for weekly issues in each volume. Each extra issue is identified by title, Christmas or Summer, volume of which it is a part, and year. Entries follow the same conventions for weekly issues. Volumes 3 through 22 include both Christmas and Summer extra issues; Volumes 23 through 29 include only Christmas extra issues.

User guide to the annotated catalogue 55

Many entries in the Chronological listing are annotated to identify the relevance of entries to the catalogue's users. Examples include plot summaries for fiction with musical heroines or heroes; explanation of cameo music appearances in otherwise nonmusical fiction; mention of music in general nonfiction; and description of musical illustrations. Annotations for serialized fiction appear under the first entry for that title.

Fiction and nonfiction
Fiction and nonfiction entries share a similar format that begins with title and subtitle, author in parentheses when known, chapter or part number(s) when relevant and page number(s). When lengthy serialized fiction includes only one or more chapters with musical content, all chapters are listed, with musical chapters indicated by an asterisk. A captioned musical illustration accompanying fiction and nonfiction is listed with its page number below the relevant chapter or part.

Title	(Author)	Chapter	Pages
Quite a Lady: In Four Chapters	(Anne Beale)	Ch. 3	pp. 504–5
Illustration 'By degrees the trembling voice stopped'			p. 505
Michaelmas Daisy	(Sarah Doudney)	Ch 5*	pp. 569–71

Title	(Author)	Pages
How to Play the Harmonium	(King Hall)	pp. 472–3

For musical entries in the Varieties column, the title follows in parentheses.

Poetry
Poems are identified as such in parentheses after the title; the name of the poet follows when known.

Title	(poem)	(Poet)	Page
The Gift of Song	(poem)	(Mrs G. Linnaeus Banks)	p. 844

I have included poems with music in title and/or text, even when the title is the only musical reference, and nonmusical poems with a musical illustration.

Illustrations

Full-page captioned illustrations not connected with other *TGOP* entries are listed separately by title, identified as an illustration in parentheses and followed by artist in parentheses when known. If an illustration is a plate, its facing page number is included.

Title	(illustration)	(Artist)	Page
An Old Song Ended	(illustration)	(from Frank Cox painting)	plate facing p. 352

I have included artists' names only when *TGOP* includes an attribution in an accompanying caption.

Answers to Correspondents

When the Answers to Correspondents column has a Music heading, this is indicated in parentheses after the column title, as is a Study and Studio heading with musical replies. When musical replies are under other headings, no parenthetical identifier is given. Each name or pseudonym to whom a musical reply is addressed is included below the entry, followed by the topic(s) of the reply in parentheses.

Title	(Heading)	Pages
Answers to Correspondents	(Music heading)	pp. 415–16
Barbiton (violin), Hauteur (performance etiquette), Edith A. W. (general), Terpsichore (harmonium), Flossy (voice), Irene, Helen M. and Ada (general), Marie (voice, performance etiquette)		

Music score

Entries for music scores list the title and then the music score designation in parentheses. Composer and text author for vocal music when known follow in parentheses.

Title	(music score)	(Composer,	Text Author)	Pages
Morning	(music score)	(Gordon Saunders,	Words Lewis Novra)	pp. 248–9

User guide to the annotated catalogue 57

Indexes

Indexes are organized under categories of Fiction, Nonfiction, Poetry, Illustrations, Answers to Correspondents, Music scores by instrument and Music scores by composer. The Fiction and Nonfiction categories are subdivided into headings as indicated in this section. Headings are not mutually exclusive, and some overlap exists. An example is the story 'Business *Versus* Art' that I include under Fiction but whose topic addresses the Business of music, which is a Nonfiction heading. In each case, I have included entries under the heading that I determined the best fit. Weekly, extra and monthly issues are incorporated under headings within each Index. Index entries are alphabetical with exceptions noted and give only enough information to guide the reader to a particular entry in the issue-by-issue Chronological listing where full details are found. All volume numbers are in bold type for easy identification, as are the Christmas or Summer designations for extra issues.

Fiction

Fiction is subdivided into Musical heroines and heroes in which music plays a major role in the plot and Music in cameo appearances in which music plays a minor role. Entries are listed by title, with volume number, total number of chapters and date range of print run indicated. The story about Zara, the music-hall singer that opens Volume 1, is the first type of fiction.

Title	Volume	(Total Chapters)	Date Range of Print Run
|	|	|	|
Zara; or, My Granddaughter's Money	1	(40 chs)	3 Jan–5 Jun 1880

'Three Years of a Girl's Life' in the same volume falls under the second type of fiction, for although Cora Forest is musical, her piano playing is heard only in 3 of the 17 chapters.

Nonfiction

Nonfiction entries are indexed under topical headings of Biography; Business; Church; Competitions; Concerts; Crafts and needlework; Entertainments; Fashion; Fidelio Club; Hints; Instrument purchase, maintenance and construction; Music education; Music history and appreciation; Music mentioned in general nonfiction; Odds and Ends; Opinion pieces; Primers for performance and teaching; Repertoire; Reviews of printed music; Royalty; Self-improvement; and Varieties. With two exceptions, all entries are listed by title within each heading followed by volume and date(s). Entries for the Fidelio Club and Reviews of printed music are organized chronologically with a separate entry for columns in

58 User guide to the annotated catalogue

each annual volume; the Reviews of printed music heading has separate entries for title variations within a volume.

Title	Volume	Dates of Column
Fidelio Club, The	23	12 Oct, 30 Nov, 28 Dec 1901; 25 Jan, 29 Mar, 26 Apr, 31 May, 28 Jun 1902

Title	Volume	Date of Column
New Music	9	22 Oct, 26 Nov 1887
Notices of New Music	9	17 Dec, 31 Dec 1887; 28 Jan, 25 Feb, 24 Mar, 12 May, 23 Jun, 15 Sep 1888

Poetry
Title, volume and date are given for poetry with music in title or text and for poems with a musical illustration.

Illustrations
Title, volume and date are given for full-page illustrations not connected with other *TGOP* material.

Answers to Correspondents
The Answers to Correspondents category is divided into Music as separate heading, Study and Studio heading with music replies, and Music replies under other headings. The category concludes with a section of Other replies to correspondents' musical questions found elsewhere in *TGOP*. Answers to Correspondents columns are listed chronologically by volume and dates found within that volume. Each volume entry includes an alphabetical list of topics of replies found in that volume.

 2   26 Mar, 28 May, 2 Jul, 16 Jul, 20 Aug, 27 Aug, 10 Sep, 24 Sep 1881

 Topics: concertina, copyright, general, harmonium, instrument maintenance, health, music copying, music as profession, music education, music history and appreciation, organ, page turning, performance etiquette, piano, pronunciation, repertoire, terms, violin, voice

Music scores by instrument
Music scores appear under the headings Organ, Harmonium; Pianoforte; Violin, Cello; Voice, solo; and Voice, ensemble. Titles are alphabetical within each heading. Entries include only the composer's name; the text author, when appropriate,

is found in the Chronological listing. Variations from the instrument heading are included in parentheses after the composer's name.

Title	(Composer)	(Instrument Variation)	Volume	Date
Adagio ma non Troppo	(Myles B. Foster)	(pianoforte or American organ)	**19**	10 Sep 1898

Music scores by composer
Composers are listed alphabetically with titles alphabetized under each composer, followed by volume and date.

Abt, Franz

All in Vain (Ballad) **4** 1 Sep 1883

Exceptions

With some exceptions, I have included in the catalogue all references to music that I discovered in my careful reading of *TGOP*; assiduous readers might find even more. My focus is on human music making, and for the most part, that excludes animals, mythical and spiritual beings and elements of Nature.

Space limitations dictated that I omit passing references to music in otherwise nonmusical material. Not every instance of music coming from birds, fairies, angels, bells, bands, churches, nurseries and nature is found in Music in general nonfiction and in Poetry. In Music in cameo appearances under Fiction, if music is mentioned only briefly and does not further overall plot or character development or give insight into music making of the time, those references do not appear in the catalogue. In Answers to Correspondents, I have omitted replies concerning musical plants and animals and how to make an Aeolian harp since that instrument is 'played' by the wind. The catalogue contains only those musical replies found in weekly issues of *TGOP*, not in the monthly supplements sometimes printed to accommodate a greater than usual volume of reader correspondence.

Chronological listing of musical content: *The Girl's Own Paper*

Volume 1 (3 January 1880–25 September 1880)

Number 1 (3 January 1880)
Zara; or, My Granddaughter's Money Chs 1, 2 pp. 1–4
> When Paul Tench finds Zara Meldicot Keith to give her the money left by her now deceased grandmother at his family's lodging house long ago, Zara is a music-hall singer. Significantly, he hands over the fortune only after she has left that line of work and married a responsible man.

Varieties (An Intelligent Musician – *Schumann*) p. 11
Our Cooking Class: Roasting (Phillis Browne) pp. 12–13
> Makes analogy between girls expecting to play piano without musical training and expecting to prepare dinner without cooking education.

A Winter Song (poem) p. 16

Number 2 (10 January 1880)
Zara Chs 3, 4 pp. 17–19

Number 3 (17 January 1880)
Varieties (How to Become an Intelligent Musician – *Schumann*) p. 32
Zara Chs 5, 6 pp. 33–5

Number 4 (24 January 1880)
Zara Chs 7, 8 pp. 49–51
Home Accomplishments I. How to Sing a Song (Madame Mudie-Bolingbroke) pp. 54–6
> Illustration 'Domestic Music' p. 56

Number 5 (31 January 1880)
Zara Chs 9, 10, 11 pp. 65–8
Under the Snow (music score) (John Farmer, Words Hannah F. Gould) pp. 70–1

Number 6 (7 February 1880)
Zara Ch. 12 pp. 82–3
Margaret: A Sketch on Board Ship pp. 94–5
> Margaret Carter's poignant singing of inspirational songs and hymns marks her last music making, for she dies from consumption at the end of her journey from England to Madeira to join her brother.

Varieties (Making Melodies – *Schumann*) p. 96

Number 7 (14 February 1880)
Zara Chs 13, 14 pp. 99–101
Answers to Correspondents p. 111
   First column to include music-related replies.
   Vixen (repertoire), Ella (practising)

Number 8 (21 February 1880)
Zara Ch. 15 pp. 113–15
Good Night (music score) (J. W. Hinton, Words Sarah Doudney) pp. 124–5
Answers to Correspondents p. 127
   Effie (piano, music potential)

Number 9 (28 February 1880)
Zara Chs 16, 17 pp. 129–31
The Song of the Sewing Machine (poem) p. 136
Ballad Stories, Suggested by Popular Songs: Twickenham Ferry pp. 138–9
Varieties (Singing – *Schumann*) p. 143
Answers to Correspondents p. 144
   Flora (repertoire), Mary Jones (repertoire), May (repertoire)

Number 10 (6 March 1880)
Zara Chs 18, 19 pp. 145–7

Number 11 (13 March 1880)
Zara Ch. 20 pp. 161–3
How to Play the Piano (Madame Arabella Goddard) pp. 164–6
   Illustration 'An Accompaniment' p. 165
Answers to Correspondents p. 176
   Fanciful Fan (voice, health), Rag Bag (repertoire)

Number 12 (20 March 1880)
Zara Chs 21, 22 pp. 177–9
The Blue Alsatian Mountains p. 183
Parting: A Trio for Female Voices (music score) (C. H. Purday) pp. 184–5
Answers to Correspondents pp. 191–2
   Bella (voice), A Scraper (violin)

Number 13 (27 March 1880)
Zara Chs 23, 24 pp. 193–6
The Dress of the Month pp. 201–2
   Illustration 'Dress for Evening Wear' shows young woman at an upright piano p. 201
Answers to Correspondents p. 208
   Mariquita (voice), Poppy (harmonium, guitar), Tot and Tiny (voice)

Number 14 (3 April 1880)
Zara Ch. 25 pp. 209–11
Answers to Correspondents p. 223
   M.M.G. (harp, piano, choosing instrument), G. E. (general)

Number 15 (10 April 1880)
Zara Chs 26, 27 pp. 225–7
How to Play the Violin (Lady Lindsay of Balcarres) pp. 232, 234–5

62 Catalogue of musical content

Answers to Correspondents p. 240
    Catherine Henrietta (music education), Madge (theory), A Village Organist (organ)

Number 16 (17 April 1880)
Zara Chs 28, 29 pp. 241–3
My Work Basket (M. L.) pp. 244–5
    Includes instructions for making a music ottoman.
    Illustration Fig. 5 Music Ottoman p. 244
Morning (music score) (Gordon Saunders, Words Lewis Novra) pp. 248–9
Answers to Correspondents p. 255
    Mahala (piano), Forget-Me-Not (voice, nuisance)
How to be Happy: A Poem for Girls (C. I. Pringle) p. 256

Number 17 (24 April 1880)
Zara Ch. 30 pp. 257–9
'Won't You Buy My Pretty Flowers?' pp. 266–7
Answers to Correspondents p. 272
    E. L. (piano, practising, nuisance)

Number 18 (1 May 1880)
Zara Ch. 31 pp. 273–5
Answers to Correspondents pp. 287–8
    Mouse (general), Wilhelmina and Bertha (repertoire, pronunciation), A North Country Lassie (voice, practising), E. A. (repertoire), Excelsior (general), Magie (repertoire), Mary (organ)

Number 19 (8 May 1880)
Zara Chs 32, 33 pp. 289–91
Musical Composers p. 291
    Describes composing habits of Haydn, Gluck and others.
Feeding the Deer (music score) (James Russell, Words John Huie) pp. 296–7
The Song of the Needle; or, The Girl's Own Compass (poem) p. 300
Answers to Correspondents p. 304
    Charlie (voice), Sally in Our Alley, Minnie, Jane S., S. E., etc. (voice), Eliza (general), Wild Cat (general)

Number 20 (15 May 1880)
Zara Chs 34, 35 pp. 305–7
The Dress of the Month pp. 316–17
    Illustration 'Indoor Costume' shows a young woman at an upright piano p. 316
Answers to Correspondents pp. 319–20
    Pussie (theory), Ruby (voice, health), Xena Rosckma (performance etiquette)

Number 21 (22 May 1880)
Zara Chs 36, 37 pp. 321–3
Outline Embroidery pp. 323–5
    Illustration 'Fig. 7', a musical design for a figure screen, shows a young woman playing a harp p. 325
How to Play the Organ (John Stainer) pp. 328–30
Varieties (Bridal Hymn) p. 334
Answers to Correspondents pp. 334–6
    Pattie (piano, performance nerves), Mabel (voice), Petite (terms)

Number 22 (29 May 1880)
Zara Chs 38, 39 pp. 337–9
Turnham Toll p. 343
Answers to Correspondents p. 352
    Rachel L. M. (voice), Bonn (voice)

Number 23 (5 June 1880)
Three Years of a Girl's Life Ch. 1 pp. 353–5
    For after-dinner music with friends, pianist Cora Forest plays a Schubert symphony and Cherubini overture, closing with an evening hymn. Clara Henderson's singing voice is like a peacock's pitched an octave too high; her sister Alice's contralto is reminiscent of a bird with a cough.
Zara Ch. 40 pp. 357–8
Birds of a Feather pp. 360–1
    Entranced by music she hears coming from a neighbour's Nuremberg apartment, Fräulein Hilda von Oertzen falls in love with a young physician who is also a flutist.
    Illustration 'It is that serenade of Schubert's he is playing' p. 360

Number 24 (12 June 1880)
Three Years of a Girl's Life Ch. 2 pp. 369–71
Whither? (music score) (Humphrey J. Stark, Words H. W. Longfellow from German of Muller) pp. 380–2
Answers to Correspondents p. 383
    Winifred (general), Theta (repertoire)

Number 25 (19 June 1880)
Three Years of a Girl's Life Ch. 3 pp. 385–6
Answers to Correspondents pp. 399–400
    Buttercup (voice)

Number 26 (26 June 1880)
Three Years of a Girl's Life Ch. 4 pp. 401–3
Etiquette for Ladies and Girls (Ardern Holt) Part 2 p. 407
    Proper etiquette for amateur afternoon musical parties dictates that guests not indulge in conversation while someone is singing.
The Lights of London Town: A Ballad Story p. 408
How to Improve the Voice (Mary Davies) pp. 409–10
    Illustration 'An Encore' p. 409
Answers to Correspondents pp. 415–16
    Lily of the Valley (repertoire), R. P. (general), M.A.B. (organ), Cheilonis (piano), Annis (piano, practising), Midge (repertoire)

Number 27 (3 July 1880)
Three Years of a Girl's Life Ch. 5* pp. 417–19
    Illustration 'She glided into the air of St. Gabriel' p. 417
A Hymn for the Girls (music score) (The Rev. Sir F. A. Gore Ouseley.) p. 424
Answers to Correspondents p. 431
    Ferry (voice, health), Joe Burton (repertoire)

Number 28 (10 July 1880)
Three Years of a Girl's Life Ch. 6 pp. 433–5
Quite a Lady: In Four Chapters (Anne Beale) Ch. 1 pp. 440–2

64 *Catalogue of musical content*

When Rose Everleigh's mother dies, she relies on her vocal talent for much-needed income. She finds her one paid engagement as a concert singer so distasteful that she vows to starve rather than reappear on stage.
Answers to Correspondents p. 447
F.E.R.N. (voice, health), Primrose (voice), Waterfall (flageolet, choosing instrument), Presto (practising, nuisance)

Number 29 (17 July 1880)
Three Years of a Girl's Life Ch. 7 pp. 449–50
Care of the Voice (Medicus) p. 454
Warns about dangers of straining the voice, singing at too high or too low a pitch and singing too loud when taking voice lessons.
The Children's Home: A Ballad Story p. 456
What Our Girls May Do (Alice King) pp. 462–3
Music is among the accomplishments that a girl should pursue only if she has a talent for it; otherwise, she had best leave it alone.
Answers to Correspondents p. 464
A Home-Maid (voice, health), Nell Adair (repertoire)

Number 30 (24 July 1880)
Three Years of a Girl's Life Ch. 8* pp. 465–8
Quite a Lady Ch. 2 pp. 469–71
How to Play the Harmonium (King Hall) pp. 472–3
The Dress of the Month pp. 477–8
Illustration shows woman at piano p. 477

Number 31 (31 July 1880)
Three Years of a Girl's Life Ch. 9 pp. 481–3
Girton College (J. A. Owen) pp. 492–3
Vocal music is a course of study, and an American student remembered choral music after dinner.
Answers to Correspondents pp. 495–6
Eulalie (violin), Racquet and Ball (piano), L. E. Alldridge (theory)

Number 32 (7 August 1880)
Three Years of a Girl's Life Ch. 10 p. 497
Our Own Colleges pp. 502–3
Includes music instruction offered at colleges in Britain that women may attend.
Quite a Lady Ch. 3 pp. 504–5
Illustration 'By degrees the trembling voice stopped' p. 505
Answers to Correspondents pp. 511–12
Reata (piano, practising, nuisance), Nannerel (piano)

Number 33 (14 August 1880)
Three Years of a Girl's Life Ch. 11 pp. 513–15
'Forget Me Not!' (music score) (Alma Sanders) pp. 524–6
Answers to Correspondents p. 527–8
Lorna Doone (terms), Kathleen (voice)

Number 34 (21 August 1880)
Three Years of a Girl's Life Ch. 12 pp. 529–31
Quite a Lady Ch. 4 pp. 534–5

Answers to Correspondents pp. 543–4
   A Magpie (repertoire), A Staunch Conservative (pronunciation), Hoodie (piano, practising, nuisance), Zacbra (music history and appreciation), Esther Dolaro (hymn repertoire), Madame Angot (repertoire)

Number 35 (28 August 1880)
Three Years of a Girl's Life Ch. 13 pp. 545–7
Once Again: A Ballad Story pp. 549–50
How to Accompany a Song (Lindsay Sloper) p. 552
Answers to Correspondents p. 560
   Olivia (voice)

Number 36 (4 September 1880)
Three Years of a Girl's Life Ch. 14* pp. 561–4
'Good-bye!' (music score) (J. W. Hinton, Words from *The Sunday at Home*) pp. 568–70

Number 37 (11 September 1880)
Three Years of a Girl's Life Ch. 15 pp. 577–9
Wrapped in the Robe of Mercy pp. 580–2
   Rhoda Burns is playing the piano at her twenty-first birthday party when her beau, Dr Falconer, arrives.
   Illustration 'He stood listening to the sweet, full notes' p. 581
Answers to Correspondents pp. 591–2
   Marian and Sweet Seventeen (organ), Madcap Jo (voice, health), Bessie Kilburn (terms)

Number 38 (18 September 1880)
Three Years of a Girl's Life Ch. 16 pp. 593–6
The New Violinist pp. 598–9
   Thirteen-year-old Mademoiselle Terresina Tua obtained the first prize for violin playing at the French Conservatoire.
Timothy's Welcome: A Ballad Story pp. 605–6

Number 39 (25 September 1880)
Three Years of a Girl's Life Ch. 17 pp. 609–11
How to Play the Harp (John Thomas) p. 616
Answers to Correspondents (Music heading) pp. 623–4
   First column to include Music as separate heading.
   Emmeline and Jessamine (terms), Genevra (voice), Ruvegmyrics (voice), Alta (voice, performance nerves, piano), Minnie Haha (repertoire), C.H.S (general), Reussuscite (piano, nuisance)

Volume 2 (October 1880–24 September 1881)

Number 40 (2 October 1880)
How to Improve Your Piano Playing (Lady Benedict) pp. 11–13
Answers to Correspondents p. 15
   Mabel (theory), Amy Thomas (music education), Flossie (general)
I Love Old Songs (poem) (Anne Beale) p. 16

Number 41 (9 October 1880)
The Queen o' the May (Anne Beale) Ch. 1 pp. 22–3
   At age six, motherless Madeline (May) Goldworthy is sent from London to live with her great-grandparents in the coal-mining district of Wales. Musical from an early age, May later takes organ lessons, sings in a choral competition at the Crystal Palace and uses her musical talent to help support her family.
A Lullaby (music score) (Joseph Barnby) pp. 24–5
A Song for Julia (poem) (Sarah Geraldina Stock) p. 28
   Illustration of woman playing harp p. 29
Answers to Correspondents p. 32
   Florence (repertoire)

Number 42 (16 October 1880)
The Queen o' the May Ch. 2 pp. 38–9
My Work Basket pp. 40–1
   Includes instructions for making a pianoforte front in four panels representing the seasons.
Illustration 'A Pianoforte Front' p. 41
Answers to Correspondents pp. 46–7
   E.A.L.C. (repertoire), Amy (general), Hilda (applied music)

Number 43 (23 October 1880)
The Queen o' the May Ch. 3 pp. 57–8
Answers to Correspondents pp. 63–4
   Amy Sims (voice, health)

Number 44 (30 October 1880)
Songs Without Music: 'Darby and Joan' p. 68
The Foundation of All Good Breeding (S.F.A. Caulfeild) pp. 73–5
   A well-bred person refrains from talking in a setting where someone is playing the pianoforte or singing by request.
The Queen o' the May Ch. 4 pp. 78–9
Answers to Correspondents p. 80
   Demoiselle Francaise (voice)

Number 45 (6 November 1880)
What Is 'a Correct Musical Taste'? (G. A. Macfarren) pp. 83–4
   Correct musical taste is good musical taste; that is, learning to appreciate the beautiful in music. Fitting music to the occasion and showing interest for simple melodies over 'manipulative ability' shows good taste; applying secular pieces to church use does not. (p. 84).
'Aspirations!' (poem) (M.M.P.) p. 88
The Queen o' the May Ch. 5 pp. 89–91

Answers to Correspondents p. 96
   Annie (voice), Ekdkiktkhk (general), M.L.M. (general), Organist's Sister (music education)

Number 46 (13 November 1880)
The Queen o' the May (Anne Beale) Ch. 6 pp. 102–3
Trust (music score) (Berthold Tours, Words C. A. Moberly) pp. 104–7
Answers to Correspondents p. 112
   Victoria (music education), A Bookworm (No. 2) (repertoire), Witch of Macbeth (violin, piano, performance etiquette, terms)

Number 47 (20 November 1880)
The Queen o' the May Ch. 7 pp. 116–18
How to Form a Small Library Part 2 pp. 122–3
   'You are musical, of course', the anonymous author states and recommends a hymnal and a book on music theory, as well as *The Girl's Own Annual*, as part of a girl's personal library (p. 123).
Varieties (Mendelssohn at the Piano) pp. 126–7
Answers to Correspondents pp. 127–8
   Iolette (voice, health), Floy (piano)

Number 48 (27 November 1880)
The Queen o' the May Ch. 8 pp. 135–6
Banbury Cross: A Ballad Story (Edward Oxenford) pp. 137–8
Answers to Correspondents p. 144
   Emmeline Marie Laurence (repertoire), Hazeldyne (piano)

Number 49 (4 December 1880)
The Queen o' the May Ch. 9 pp. 145–7
On Part-Singing (Henry Leslie) p. 151
   Discusses forming choral music classes or societies, in part to improve congregational singing, and reminds prospective members 'There is no royal road in art.'
Answers to Correspondents p. 160
   Iresene (organ, health), The Evergreen Sisters (performance etiquette), Esmeralda (piano), Gladys Clarke (voice, practising, health)

Number 50 (11 December 1880)
The Queen o' the May Ch. 10 pp. 166–7
'When the Tide Comes In': A Ballad Story p. 168
My Work Basket pp. 172–3
   Includes instructions for an embroidered wicker case for knitting or music.
Answers to Correspondents p. 176
   Pearl (general)

Number 51 (18 December 1880)
The Queen o' the May Ch. 11 pp. 177–9

Number 52 (25 December 1880)
The Queen o' the May Ch. 12 pp. 194–5
All From a Little Kindness: A Christmas Story (A. M.) pp. 196–8

Returning home from taking parish organist Mr Barton, her music master, some Christmas gifts, Gertrude (Gertie) Colborne comes upon a young boy and his mother, who has fainted. Both are brought to the Colborne house. When, as the Colborne's Christmas dinner guest, Mr Barton is persuaded to sing solos from his new oratorio, the young woman discovers her long-lost father from his voice.
The Singers (poem) (Longfellow) p. 201
Answers to Correspondents pp. 206–7
    Poppet Jane (repertoire)
An Old Christmas Carol (music score) p. 208

Number 53 (1 January 1881)
The Queen o' the May Ch. 13 pp. 209–11
In the Churchyard (music score) (Humphrey J. Stark, Words Knight Summers) pp. 216–18
Answers to Correspondents pp. 222–3
    Chrissie (voice, health)

Number 54 (8 January 1881)
The Queen o' the May Ch. 14 pp. 234–5
Varieties (Music in the Drawing-Room) pp. 238–9
Answers to Correspondents pp. 239–40
    Trixie (voice, health), T.E.S. (organ), Blue Bell (general), Trudie (voice, health)

Number 55 (15 January 1881)
The Queen o' the May Ch. 15 pp. 245–7
Answers to Correspondents pp. 255–6
    Toujours Gai (repertoire), Portia (performance etiquette), Little Mac and Georgina (repertoire), Semiramis (memory work)

Number 56 (22 January 1881)
The Queen o' the May Ch. 16 pp. 258–60
The Worker: A Ballad Story (F. E. Weatherly) p. 267
Answers to Correspondents pp. 270–1
    Little Chryssie (piano)

Number 57 (29 January 1881)
Music (poem) p. 273
The Queen o' the May Ch. 17 p. 277
New Music p. 287
    States intent to offer a monthly list of new music 'with short descriptions of their character, which will enable the girls to make a wise selection for themselves'.

Number 58 (5 February 1881)
The Queen o' the May Ch. 18 pp. 294–5
The Dead Heart (music score) (Gordon Saunders) pp. 300–2
Answers to Correspondents pp. 303–4
    Stephanotis (pronunciation)

Number 59 (12 February 1881)
The Queen o' the May Ch. 19 pp. 310–11
Answers to Correspondents pp. 318–19
    Little Imp (voice), Sunflower (voice)

Number 60 (19 February 1881)
The Queen o' the May Ch. 20 p. 325
The Stream of Life: A Ballad Story (Cotsford Dick) pp. 330–1

Number 61 (26 February 1881)
The Queen o' the May Ch. 21 pp. 347–8
New Music p. 349
How to Play the Guitar (Madame Sidney Pratten) pp. 350–1
Answers to Correspondents pp. 351–2
   A Young Cook (general)

Number 62 (5 March 1881)
The Queen o' the May Ch. 22 pp. 357–9
The Mountaineer's Bride: Tyrolienne for the Voice (music score) (Sir Julius Benedict) pp. 360–2
Varieties (A Division of Time for the Musical) p. 366

Number 63 (12 March 1881)
The Queen o' the May Ch. 23 pp. 374–5
Answers to Correspondents pp. 383–4
   Jennie (performance etiquette), Nellie Radford (general)

Number 64 (19 March 1881)
Twenty-One pp. 388–9
The Queen o' the May Ch. 24 pp. 390–1

Number 65 (26 March 1881)
Seasonable Dress and How to Make It pp. 401–2
   Illustration 'Practising' shows a pianist playing a grand piano while four young women gather around p. 401
The Queen o' the May Ch. 25 pp. 403–4
How to Sing in Public (Antoinette Sterling) p. 409
New Music p. 413
Answers to Correspondents (Music heading) pp. 415–16
   Barbiton (violin), Hauteur (performance etiquette), Edith A. W. (general), Terpsichore (harmonium), Flossy (voice), Irene, Helen M. and Ada (general), Marie (voice, performance etiquette)

Number 66 (2 April 1881)
Jocund Spring (illustration) plate facing p. 417
   Notated music staff with text 'Spring's delights are all reviving, Verdant leaflets clothe each spray, Hawthorn buds give joyful tiding, Welcome news! 'tis blythe May-day'.
From Strength to Strength: A Story of Two English Girls (Alice King) Ch. 1 pp. 417–19
   When 16-year-old heiress Ella Ringwood is sent to live with her elderly Uncle Matthew Lindhurst and his sister Nancy at Larcombe Priory, she insists on having a companion, so Ruby Stanton, a merchant's daughter, is brought into the home. Ruby has a 'clear silvery voice, and a correct musical ear', but when she sings and plays, Miss Nancy claims a headache, and Ella says she hates music (p. 470).
The Queen o' the May Ch. 26 pp. 430–1
Answers to Correspondents pp. 431–2
   Mignon (general), Katherine C. (applied music)

70 *Catalogue of musical content*

Number 67 (9 April 1881)
From Strength to Strength Ch. 2 pp. 434–5
The Queen o' the May Ch. 27 pp. 436–9
A Sister's Lullaby: For Violin and Pianoforte (music score) (Lady Lindsay of Balcarres) pp. 440–2
Answers to Correspondents pp. 447–8
  Red Riding Hood (practising, health), Mempsey (piano, terms)

Number 68 (16 April 1881)
From Strength to Strength Ch. 3 pp. 449–51
'The Children of the City' (Anne Beale) pp. 454–5
Answers to Correspondents pp. 462–3
  Sangerin (music education), Osprey of Enehar (general), Ruth (theory)

Number 69 (23 April 1881)
From Strength to Strength Ch. 4* pp. 469–71
'For a Song' (poem) (M. W.) p. 472
Answers to Correspondents pp. 479–80
  Terpischore (music education, performance etiquette), Patience (repertoire)

Number 70 (30 April 1881)
From Strength to Strength Ch. 5 pp. 481–3
How to Play the Concertina (Richard Blagrove) pp. 488–9
New Music p. 493
Useful Hints (Discoloured Pianoforte Keys) p. 494
Answers to Correspondents pp. 494–5
  Lady Beth (music education), Sister (memory work), I.O.G.T. (flute), Sylvanus (general), Katharine (copyright), Poppies in Corn (terms), A. A. (Chester) (guitar), A.H.B. (general)

Number 71 (7 May 1881)
Michaelmas Daisy (Sarah Doudney) Ch. 1 pp. 497–8
  A Cinderella story occurs when recently orphaned Daisy Garnett is sent at age 16 to live with her uncle's family and her cousins. Music making is used as a diversion to reveal more important plot developments in which Daisy becomes an heiress.
Margaret (music score) (Edwin M. Lott, Words Gertrude Moberly) pp. 500–1
Our Patty's Victory; or, A White Hand (Fairleigh Owen) Ch. 1 pp. 506–7
  Amy Blake's offer to teach Patty Holme piano goes awry, showing how the desire to play often is based on the wrong reasons. Patty wants to teach piano to augment her family's farm income, but lacks a musical background. Pianist Amy Blake has her mind set on the fame and fashion of the concert stage.
From Strength to Strength Ch. 6 pp. 510–11
Answers to Correspondents pp. 511–12
  Minnie Huff (violin, music potential), M. C. (practising), Crooked Pin (page turning)

Number 72 (14 May 1881)
Michaelmas Daisy Ch. 2 pp. 513–15
From Strength to Strength Ch. 7 pp. 519–20
Our Patty's Victory Ch. 2 pp. 525–7
Answers to Correspondents pp. 527–8
  Zerlina (voice, health), Kate (piano, instrument maintenance), Frances (general), Niobe (terms), Ada Thompson (piano drape)

Number 73 (21 May 1881)
Michaelmas Daisy Ch. 3 pp. 532–3
How to Play Mendelssohn's 'Songs Without Words' (Lady Benedict) Part 1 pp. 537–8
From Strength to Strength Ch. 8 pp. 538–9
Our Patty's Victory Ch. 3 pp. 540–2
Answers to Correspondents pp. 543–4
    Evangeline, S.A.B., Margaret, Devoir and Jessie (music education), Ada (piano front), Ami (general), Pet Lamb (voice, health), Scotch Tabby (performance etiquette)

Number 74 (28 May 1881)
Michaelmas Daisy Ch. 4 pp. 545–7
How to Play Mendelssohn's 'Songs Without Words' Part 2 pp. 548–9
'Years Ago': A Ballad Story (Helen Marion Burnside) pp. 550–1
From Strength to Strength Ch. 9 pp. 552–3
New Music pp. 555–6
Our Patty's Victory Ch. 4 pp. 556–8
Answers to Correspondents (Music heading) p. 559
    Tippe (music copying), Little Em (terms), Ju (performance etiquette), Elfin (voice), Young Pianist (music education), A.S.M. (music education)

Number 75 (4 June 1881)
From Strength to Strength Ch. 10 pp. 566–7
Michaelmas Daisy Ch. 5* pp. 569–71
Seven Days (poem) (Clara Thwaites) p. 573
Answers to Correspondents pp. 575–6
    Amphion (general), Sela (repertoire)

Number 76 (11 June 1881)
Michaelmas Daisy Ch. 6* pp. 577–9
Varieties (The Dawn of Genius) p. 579
From Strength to Strength Ch. 11 pp. 580–1
On Method in Teaching the Pianoforte (Edwin M. Lott) pp. 582–3
Answers to Correspondents pp. 590–1
    Spring Daisy (general), Wildgoose (piano), Miandia (voice, music potential)

Number 77 (18 June 1881)
Michaelmas Daisy Ch. 7 pp. 593–5
My Work Basket pp. 596–7
    Includes instructions for making an embroidered music case to keep songs clean and tidy.
Illustration 'Design for Embroidered Music Case' p. 597
From Strength to Strength Ch. 12 pp. 598–9
The Rose (music score) (The Rev. F. Peel, Words The Hon. C. F. Fox) pp. 601–2
Answers to Correspondents pp. 607–8
    Two Hazels (violin, nuisance)

Number 78 (25 June 1881)
Michaelmas Daisy Ch. 8 pp. 609–11
New Music pp. 622–3
Answers to Correspondents pp. 623–4
    Gypsy Queen (general), A Young Disciple (repertoire), M.D.C. (general), E. K. (national anthem)

72   *Catalogue of musical content*

Number 79 (2 July 1881)
Michaelmas Daisy Ch. 9 pp. 629–31
My Treasures: A Ballad Story (Nella Parker) pp. 634–5
From Strength to Strength Ch. 13 pp. 635–7
Answers to Correspondents (Music heading) pp. 639–40
   Edwyna (voice), A. R. (general), Wild Rose (piano), A Fanciful Fiddler (violin), Penelope (music education), Fatimore (organ, piano, voice), Nessie (voice), Beth (performance etiquette), Minnie (music history and appreciation, copyright), Ruspini (violin, health), M.A.W. (pronunciation)

Number 80 (9 July 1881)
Michaelmas Daisy Ch. 10* pp. 641–3
The Brook (music score) (Mrs Tom Taylor, Words Alfred Tennyson) pp. 648–9
From Strength to Strength Ch. 14 pp. 650–1

Number 81 (16 July 1881)
Michaelmas Daisy Ch. 11* pp. 657–9
From Strength to Strength Ch. 15 pp. 668–9
Answers to Correspondents (Music heading) pp. 670–2
   Irish Linnet (terms, voice), Susie Pitcher (general), Mina (piano)

Number 82 (23 July 1881)
Michaelmas Daisy Ch. 12 pp. 673–5
In the Garden (illustration) p. 681
   A woman is playing the violin in this scene of women and children.
From Strength to Strength Ch. 16 pp. 686–7
Answers to Correspondents pp. 687–8
   May (composition, music publishing)

Number 83 (30 July 1881)
Michaelmas Daisy Ch. 13 pp. 694–6
From Strength to Strength Ch. 17 pp. 701–2
New Music p. 703
Answers to Correspondents p. 704
   Annie (general)

Number 84 (6 August 1881)
Michaelmas Daisy Ch. 14 pp. 705–7
The Old Pot-pourri Jar (poem) (Helen Marion Burnside) p. 713
From Strength to Strength Ch. 18 pp. 714–15
Answers to Correspondents pp. 719–20
   Cecil Burn (organ)

Number 85 (13 August 1881)
Michaelmas Daisy Ch. 15 pp. 721–3
The Child's Mission: A Ballad Story (Mary Mark Lemon) p. 723
Anecdote of Haydn (C.H.P.) p. 731
From Strength to Strength Ch. 19 pp. 732–4
Answers to Correspondents pp. 734–6
   La Reine Rose (music education), Cecilia (piano, practising), Susannah (music teaching), Maid Margaret (voice), Marlborough and Copenhagen (repertoire), Fancy (Ontario) (repertoire), Etha Barrow (terms), Shirley (voice, music education)

Number 86 (20 August 1881)
'I Love Old Songs' (music score) (J. W. Hinton, Words Anne Beale) pp. 740–1
Varieties (Handel Made Simple) p. 744
From Strength to Strength Ch. 20 pp. 744–5
Michaelmas Daisy Ch. 16 pp. 745–7
Answers to Correspondents (Music heading) pp. 750–1
  Lady White (repertoire), Blanche (repertoire, piano, music education, terms), A New Subscriber (general)

Number 87 (27 August 1881)
From Strength to Strength Ch. 21 p. 753
Michaelmas Daisy Ch. 17 pp. 758–9
How to Purchase a Piano and Keep It in Good Order (A Professor of Music of sixty years' standing) pp. 761–2
New Music p. 762
Answers to Correspondents (Music heading) pp. 767–8
  Mildred Daisy (harmonium, organ), Nemophilia (music as profession, concertina), Mercy (music education), Wilfred Willie (general), May Gosling (instrument maintenance), Three Americans (terms), A Hopeful Amateur and Stephanie (repertoire, copyright), A Country Girl (voice, page turning)

Number 88 (3 September 1881)
Both in the Wrong Chs 1, 2* pp. 769–70
  When Mr Tremaine's new wife, Evelyn, sits at the piano and sings, her powerful, well-trained voice is 'full of subtle sweetness and tender, pathetic melody' (p. 771).
The Constancy of Love (music score) (Alma Sanders, Words Anne Beale) pp. 772–4
'Just Out' p. 775
  Encourages musical girls to practise piano diligently once they have left school, for some day they might 'be required to play the organ in church, the harmonium at meetings, to accompany friends in part or solo singing, and at all times you will be able to give a great deal of pleasure to those around you who are fond of music'.
Michaelmas Daisy Ch. 18 pp. 778–9
The Girl's Own: An Occasional Page of Amateur Contributions pp. 780–1
  Includes essay on 'Music' by 16-year-old Iris.
Answers to Correspondents pp. 782–4
  Tyro (practising), Poodle (voice, practising), Florence Fisher (voice, health), Minna (repertoire), Queen o' the May (voice), Rosalind (voice), Mabulette (piano, instrument maintenance), Iota (general), Lizzetta (concertina)

Number 89 (10 September 1881)
Michaelmas Daisy Ch. 19 pp. 785–7
New Music p. 787
How to Improve One's Education (J. P. Mears) Part 2 pp. 794–6
  Gives recommendations for practising on piano and on harmonium.
Both in the Wrong Ch. 3 pp. 796–8
Answers to Correspondents (Music heading) pp. 799–800
  Inesille (general), Janie (general), Edythe Lotus (general), M.A.W. (terms), H.M.DG. (repertoire)

Number 90 (17 September 1881)
Michaelmas Daisy Ch. 20 pp. 801–3

Both in the Wrong Ch. 4 pp. 804–5
Women and Music p. 814
  An extract from Frederick Crowest's *Phases of Musical England.*
Answers to Correspondents pp. 814–16
  Katy Croome and Punch (music education), E.F.L. (repertoire)

Number 91 (24 September 1881)
Michaelmas Daisy Ch. 21 pp. 817–19
Varieties (The Greatest Effect in Music; Ordinary Faults in Piano Playing – *Pauer*; For Those Who Sing Out of Tune – *Coleridge*) p. 823
Answers to Correspondents (Music heading) pp. 823–4
  Dorette (general), E.M.T. (Aintab, Syria) (general), Honor Bright (general), L. M. (terms), E.S.P. (general), Buttercup (general)

Volume 3 (1 October 1881–30 September 1882)

Number 92 (1 October 1881)
Answers to Correspondents pp. 14–15
    Fun (voice), Picklefork and Tongs (practising), Clara (piano)

Number 93 (8 October 1880)
How to Play Beethoven's Sonatas (Lady Benedict) Part 1 pp. 25–6
Answers to Correspondents (Music heading) p. 32
    Keziah (violin), Musk (music education), Evangeline (music history and appreciation), Olive (music history and appreciation), Alberta (terms), A.B.C. (general), Theresa W. (general), Mary S. B. (instrument maintenance, piano), Patiently Waiting (choral singing)

Number 94 (15 October 1881)
Answers to Correspondents (Music heading) pp. 47–8
    B.I.A. (piano), N. B. (general), F. and H. (terms), Aesthete (repertoire), Troublesome (terms), Smut (violoncello)

Number 95 (22 October 1881)
New Music p. 51
Answers to Correspondents (Music heading) pp. 62–3
    Poodle (practising), Kely (general), E.M.K. (terms, pronunciation), Puella (concertina), E. (general), T.E.S. (composition)

Number 96 (29 October 1881)
Le Dernier Papillon (music score) (Edwin M. Lott) pp. 72–3
Answers to Correspondents (Music heading) pp. 79–80
    Muriel, Mabel, Alice (general), Katie M. C. and Marie (music education)

Number 97 (5 November 1881)
In the Gloaming – (Ballad Picture No. 1) (illustration) (Charles Green) plate facing p. 81
How to Play Beethoven's Sonatas Part 2 pp. 81–4
    Illustration 'How to Play Beethoven Sonatas' shows a young woman at the piano p. 81
Answers to Correspondents (Music heading) pp. 95–6
    Clarissa (general), R.S.V.P. (harmonium, instrument maintenance), Sunflower (performance etiquette), A.G.B. (music education), Honeysuckle (general)

Number 98 (12 November 1881)
What Would You Like to Be? (M. R.) p. 103
    Three young girls ponder what they would like to be when they grow up; life intervenes to modify Nellie Graham's dream of a singing career.
Kind Words (music score) (Cotsford Dick, Words Helen Marion Burnside) pp. 104–6
Answers to Correspondents (Music heading) pp. 110–12
    Guest, W. K., and Kitty (music education), Nitsna (music education), A City Sparrow (general), Susie K. (performance etiquette), Marabella (voice), A West Indian (general), A.L.P. (general), Anxiety (music education), Saxon's Pet (general), Sunderland (repertoire), Pearl (pronunciation)

Number 99 (19 November 1881)
The Mind and the Health (Medicus) pp. 115–16
    Encourages readers to take up hobbies, of which music is most pleasant and healthful. A violinist as well as a physician, the author recommends that instrument as 'the only

Catalogue of musical content

perfect one in the world'. Readers wanting 'good sound lungs' should take up singing 'to defy colds and coughs with all their attendant ills' (p. 116).

The Four Periods: I. School-Life (Alice King) pp. 123–4
Repeats the admonition that unless a girl has real musical talent, she should not pursue it.

Answers to Correspondents (Music heading) p. 127
St. Cecilia (general), Inquisitive Viva (music education), Virgilia (musician work), M. S. Music (general)

Number 100 (26 November 1881)
New Music pp. 134–5

Number 101 (3 December 1881)
'Christmas Festivity': A Musical Acrostic for Juvenile Parties (Music, Words George Lomas) pp. 153–6
Includes music scores.

Answers to Correspondents (Music heading) pp. 159–60
Moss Rose (music education), Blue Rose (general), Etna (repertoire), Topsy (terms), An Invalid (general), Lizzie B. (general), Blanche Arundel (repertoire), Santa Lucia (general)

Number 102 (10 December 1881)
New Music p. 167
'Christmas Festivity' (cont.) pp. 171–4
Varieties (In Praise of Good Music) p. 174
Answers to Correspondents (Music heading) pp. 175–6
Chataigne (repertoire), Inquisitive (general), L'Allegro (practising, nuisance), Gratitude (general), Birdie (piano), Alice O'Brien (music history and appreciation), Jeune Pianiste (music history and appreciation), Cluny (zither, concertina, choosing instrument)

Number 103 (17 December 1881)
Forgive and Forget (music score) (Madame Sainton-Dolby, Words S.E.G.) pp. 180–2

Number 104 (24 December 1881)
How to Play Beethoven's Sonatas Part 3 pp. 194–5
Answers to Correspondents p. 207
Anxious Maggie (performance etiquette, practising), A Crooked Sixpence (general), Jessamine (general)

Number 105 (31 December 1881)
A Christmas Carol (music score) (Cotsford Dick) p. 216
New Music p. 219
Answers to Correspondents (Music heading) pp. 222–3
E.M.S. (general), Rochifan (practising, nuisance), Kate J. Silley (piano), Margaret Daw (terms), Isabel (general)
The Girl's Own: An Occasional Page of Amateur Contributions p. 224
Includes essay on 'Music' by Augusta Klein, age 15½.

Number 106 (7 January 1882)
How to Play Beethoven's Sonatas Part 4 pp. 233–4
Answers to Correspondents (Music heading) pp. 239–40
A Saxon Dane (sight-reading, memory work), Beethoven's Sonatas (piano), Anxious Queenie and Allegro (music education), An Orphan Girl (general)

Number 107 (14 January 1882)
The Mandolin (X. X.) pp. 244–5
  Illustration 'The Mandolin' shows a young woman playing the mandolin p. 245
Chimes of Evening (music score) (Franz Abt, Words Edward Oxenford) pp. 248–50
Answers to Correspondents pp. 254–5
  Pussy-Cat (general)

Number 108 (21 January 1882)
Old Court Dresses (poem) (Clara Thwaites) pp. 264–5
Varieties (How to Compose an Overture) p. 270
Answers to Correspondents pp. 270–1
Violet (general)

Number 109 (28 January 1882)
New Music pp. 284–5
Answers to Correspondents (Music heading) pp. 286–7
  Cynthia (general), Claitha (theory), Mops (theory), Jessie (voice), Bride of Triermain (harmonium), Kitten (piano, practising, nuisance, reading music)

Number 110 (4 February 1882)
A Cradle Song (Suggested by an air of Chopin's) (poem) (Maggie Macdonald) plate facing
  p. 289
Answers to Correspondents pp. 303–4
Joe the Violinist (general)

Number 111 (11 February 1882)
Sea Waves (music score) (Charles H. Bassett) pp. 308–9
Answers to Correspondents (Music heading) pp. 318–20
  Paddiana (general), Codfish (music history and appreciation), Birdie (general), Stella (piano), Rushlight and Kate Smith (music history and appreciation), Impromptu (applied music)

Number 112 (18 February 1882)
New Music p. 331
Answers to Correspondents (Music heading) pp. 334–6
  Anna (terms, applied music), Ignoramus (applied music), Flossy (terms), A.F.R. (music education), Melissa (general), E.Z.B. (theory, music history and appreciation), Marian (digitorium), Marie Henriquez Molores (organ, health)

Number 113 (25 February 1882)
New Music p. 339
Answers to Correspondents (Music heading) pp. 351–3
  Flying Dutchman (guitar), Sweet Birdie (piano), May (general), Anxious (music education), Maple Leaf (piano purchase), Ugly Duckling (music teaching), Hyacinth (general), Blanche (general)

Number 114 (4 March 1882)
L'Allegrezza (music score) (Annie E. Nash) pp. 364–5
Answers to Correspondents pp. 366–8
  Daisy (instrument maintenance, piano), Sea Anemone (repertoire)

Number 115 (11 March 1882)
Women of Intellect: Jane Austen pp. 378–9
  Although not an accomplished musician, Austen was fond of music and practised early in the morning to avoid annoying her family members.

78   *Catalogue of musical content*

Varieties (The Music of a Cheerful Heart) p. 382
Answers to Correspondents (Music heading) pp. 382–3
> Ella (general), Muriel (practising), Mary (general), Queenie King (general, voice, health), B.M.G. and Only an Ivy Leaf (repertoire), Lieder ohne Worte (violin), Juno (music education), Une Reveur Fille (terms, repertoire)

Number 116 (18 March 1882)
New Music pp. 394–5
Answers to Correspondents (Music heading) pp. 399–400
> Eva (piano, instrument maintenance), E.P.S. (mandolin), Clio (general), A Cornish Lassie (general), Lieder ohne Worte (music education), Lady Charles (zither), Glendarroch (general), Linnet (violin), Sentimentalist (terms), Margaret Constance (piano), Zerline (general), Dot (metronome)

Number 117 (25 March 1882)
A Bridal Song (poem) (Mrs G. Linnaeus Banks) p. 404
New Music p. 407
Answers to Correspondents (Music heading) pp. 415–16
> Violet (piano), Roucale (general), Dolly (theory), Gracie (guitar), Coral (terms), A Welshwoman and E.G.F. (music education), Claudine and Ambitious (mandolin), Olivette (performance etiquette)

Number 118 (1 April 1882)
An Unattractive Girl Ch. 1* pp. 417–19
> Mara Johnstone, a governess-pupil at a ladies' school, takes her music along with her to a concert given by the elder students but does not perform. On another occasion she finds it useless to practise in the family's shabby, cold drawing room.

Absent Friends (music score) (C. E. Rawstorne, Words Sarah Doudney from *Leisure Hour*) pp. 428–9
Answers to Correspondents (Music heading) pp. 431–2
> Heather Cup (terms), One Who Is Fond of Music (general), Mary L. A. (guitar), Irene and Organist (music education), Susie (general)

Number 119 (8 April 1882)
An Unattractive Girl Ch. 2* pp. 436–7
New Music p. 437
The Girl's Own: An Occasional Page of Amateur Contributions pp. 444–5
Includes poem 'Life's Music' by 15½-year-old Olive Hawthorne. (p. 444)
Answers to Correspondents (Music heading) pp. 446–8
> Sunflower (repertoire), A Teazer (organ, harmonium), Minch and Co. (voice), Rory (voice), Lena Wood (voice, health), Madcap Violet (performance etiquette), Trv. (repertoire), Edgitha (voice, repertoire), Heather (terms)

Number 120 (15 April 1882)
New Music p. 451
An Unattractive Girl Ch. 3 pp. 460–2
Answers to Correspondents pp. 463–4
> Geraldine B. (repertoire), Dot and Tap (repertoire)

Number 121 (22 April 1882)
New Music p. 471
Answers to Correspondents (Music heading) pp. 479–80

Catalogue of musical content 79

An Ambitious Strummer (music education), Shamrock (voice), An Admirer (general), Rosalind (repertoire), White Puss (general), A Female Clerk (general), J.B.C. (copyright)

Number 122 (29 April 1882)
The North London Collegiate School for Girls pp. 494–6
  Music is a heard when a student plays hymns on the organ for morning prayer; in hallways when she plays a march as students file out to their classes; in afternoon music lessons; in class singing; and even in the gymnasium, where students exercise to piano music.
  Illustration 'The Gymnasium of the North London Collegiate School for Girls' plate facing p. 494

Number 123 (6 May 1882)
Answers to Correspondents (Music heading) pp. 510–12
  Cherry Blossom (general), N.H.AT. and E.O.K. (music history and appreciation), Nokomis (repertoire), Pimpernel (harp), Nan (general), Home, Sweet Home (general)

Number 124 (13 May 1882)
Canzonette (music score) (Walter Wesché, Words from *Measure for Measure*) pp. 516–18
Answers to Correspondents pp. 527–8
  Swallow (violin), Judy (terms), Treble (general), Ortrud (music education)

Number 125 (20 May 1882)
New Music p. 539
Answers to Correspondents (Music heading) pp. 542–3
  Little Eleven Years Old (repertoire), Mollie Hawn (repertoire), Chertie (general), Trudie and Hermione (theory), M.W.P. (Yarmouth) (repertoire)

Number 126 (27 May 1882)
Answers to Correspondents pp. 558–60
  Lizzie (Surrey) (general)

Number 127 (3 June 1882)
New Music p. 567
Varieties (Bird-Like – *Victor Hugo*) p. 574
Answers to Correspondents pp. 575–6
  Daisy Heathcote (performance etiquette)

Number 128 (10 June 1882)
The Golden Thread (music score) (Mrs Tom Taylor) pp. 580–3
Honor Grant; or, Her Mother's Ring pp. 585–6
  Music and singing are among the lessons orphan Honor Grant shares with cousin Alice Hope when adopted by her wealthy aunt and uncle.
New Music p. 586
Answers to Correspondents (Music heading) pp. 591–2
  Jumbo (violin), Happy (general), Valentine (violin), Muriel Abney B. (general), Heather (repertoire), Violinist (instrument maintenance)

Number 130 (24 June 1882)
Thoughts on Practising (Lady Lindsay of Balcarres) pp. 617–19
New Music pp. 620–1
Answers to Correspondents pp. 622–4
  T. Johnstone (xylophone)

Number 131 (1 July 1882)
May Goldworthy (Anne Beale) Ch. 1 pp. 625–7
  In the sequel to 'Queen o' the May', May Goldworthy, who has become a professional concert singer in London, returns to her Welsh village as the new bride of cousin Meredith and resumes her role among family and friends, which includes singing and playing harmonium for the benefit of others.
Night Hymn at Sea (music score) (Natalie, Words Mrs Hemans) pp. 628–30
Answers to Correspondents (Music heading) pp. 638–9
  Annie Smith (general), Roma Crossby (general), Flora McDonald (general), Highland Lassie (music education), O. P. and F.C.G. (general), Letty (music education), K.A.N. and Little Dorrit (music education), Tottie (terms), Blue Bell (music history and appreciation), In Haste (terms), H.I.J.S.G.F. (general)
The Maiden and the Poppy (poem) p. 640

Number 132 (8 July 1882)
May Goldworthy Ch. 2 pp. 641–3
New Music pp. 652–3
  Illustration 'Trying Over New Music' p. 652
Answers to Correspondents (Music heading) pp. 654–6
  Musical Nell (theory, organ, piano, instrument maintenance)

Number 133 (15 July 1882)
May Goldworthy Ch. 3 pp. 661–3
New Music p. 663
The Song of Summer (poem) (Sydney Grey) p. 664
Varieties (How Two Friends Parted) p. 671
Answers to Correspondents (Music heading) pp. 671–2
  Winnie (organ, harmonium), Bo (repertoire), Dormouse (music teaching), A Lover of Music (general)

Number 134 (22 July 1882)
The Nightingale's Song (poem) (Harriet L. Childe-Pemberton) p. 676
New Music p. 683
Musical Graces Before and After Meat pp. 684–5
  The editor offers scores for three simple 'musical graces' for singing in schools, families, businesses and other institutions where girls and women assemble at meal times.

Number 135 (29 July 1882)
May Goldworthy Ch. 4 pp. 689–91
Illustration 'Mendelssohn's Wedding March' p. 689
Answers to Correspondents (Music heading) pp. 703–4
  Dinicus (violin), Vinaigrette (music teaching), Amie (piano, nuisance), Silver Sails (music teaching, piano), Josephine (violin, viola), Edelia (violin), Millie (voice), Eudochia (voice), Ildica (practising), Florence (violin)

Number 136 (5 August 1882)
New Music p. 708
'They Say There Is Anguish' (music score) (Ernst Helmer, Words Everard Clive) pp. 712–14

Number 137 (12 August 1882)
New Music p. 726
Answers to Correspondents (Music heading) pp. 734–5
  Fribbel (music education)

Number 138 (19 August 1882)
New Music p. 741
The Organist (poem) (M.W.) p. 745
    Illustration ''Twas somebody's soul that spoke' shows a male organist; a woman with sheet music in her lap sits beside the organ p. 744
Answers to Correspondents (Music heading) pp. 750–1
    F.Q.B. (voice), Learannie (terms), Clara Conningham (terms), A Subscriber (general), Ecila Yram (music education)

Number 139 (26 August 1882)
Answers to Correspondents (Music heading) pp. 767–8
    Inquisitive (music education), Signora Hiabella Frangerini (terms), Elsie (music education), E.S.B. (terms), Gabrielle (repertoire), Buttercup (voice), Watford Lassie (repertoire), Amateur Vocalist (music history and appreciation), A Lover of The Girl's Own Paper (repertoire)

Number 140 (2 September 1882)
The Tryst (music score) (Mary Carmichael, Words W. Davies) pp. 772–4

Number 141 (9 September 1882)
New Music p. 791
Answers to Correspondents (Music heading) pp. 798–800
    Farmer's Daughter (repertoire), Janie (repertoire)

Number 142 (16 September 1882)
Answers to Correspondents (Music heading) pp. 814–16
    Rosetta Bertini (voice), Lady Marion Seymour (music education), A Would-Be Player (terms), Confidence (repertoire), Condor (repertoire), Galatea (music history and appreciation), 'Secretary to Choral Society' (general), Rose and Maggie (music education), Iona and Catherine Seaton (music education)

Number 143 (23 September 1882)
New Music p. 827
Answers to Correspondents pp. 830–2
    A. Farley (music education), Wee Birdie (general)

Number 144 (30 September 1882)
The Gift of Song (poem) (Mrs G. Linnaeus Banks) p. 844
New Music p. 846
Answers to Correspondents pp. 846–8
    Topsey (piano, practising, nuisance)

Christmas Roses
Extra Christmas Part for Volume 3 (1881)
Christmas (music score) (Ciro Pinsuti, Words S.E.G.) pp. 9–11
Christmas Games for Young and Old (Ruth Lamb) pp. 12–15
    Gives directions for Magic Music, a hide-and-seek game using piano, and describes a 'charming rehearsal' of Haydn's Toy Symphony in the author's drawing room (p. 16).
Noël; or, Earned and Unearned (Grace Stebbing) pp. 17–23
    When a church offers Nessie Cartwright, who needs a paying job, an organist post, her rich friend cannot understand why Nessie would choose work over her friend's generosity. The story reinforces middle-class Victorian values: When in financial need, women should earn money by suitable work rather than accept charity, however well intended.

Miss Mignonette (E. M. Hordle) pp. 29–31
    Miss Mignonette, who is alone in the world, teaches music and plays organ at Wychley Church.

Silver Sails
Extra Summer Number for Volume 3 (1882)
Mildred Ashcroft (L. C. Silke) pp. 25–31
    Thoughts of piano practice, crewelwork and painting are equally dreary to 23-year-old Mildred Ashcroft as she gazes listlessly out the window on a wet August afternoon. 'I hate practising, unless I have anyone to play duets with me, or there is a new song to try over', she tells her aunt (p. 26).

The Mother and the Child (poem) (Cotsford Dick) p. 35

A Romance of a Summer Night (James Mason) pp. 54–5
    Alice Stewart is playing ''Twas in that garden beautiful' from *The Siege of Rochelle* on piano for her widowed mother when interrupted by a letter from friend Maggie Anson. Alice stops playing and goes to Maggie where, when asked to play piano, Alice finishes the piece.

The Reapers (music score) (Franz Abt, Words E. Oxenford) pp. 58–60

Volume 4 (7 October 1882–29 September 1883)

Number 145 (7 October 1882)
Bound to Earth Ch. 1 pp. 1–3
    When Mr Leslie demands some after-dinner music, daughter Fanny sings 'an Italian 'bravura song' (p. 58). Her friend Grace Hardinge follows with a Beethoven sonata. Grace's parents are poor but take her to London's classical concerts to learn how to interpret good music. 'It is as good for Grace as a lesson from one of the greatest masters', her mother says (p. 369).
Laura Leigh: A Tale of Highbridge Paper Mills (M. M. Pollard) Ch. 1 pp. 12–14
    As a governess, after dinner the eponymous heroine must play duets with her pupils Gerty and Ethel to exhibit their musical ability and occasionally 'join with them in singing their simple infantile songs' (p. 274).
Varieties (A Hint to Singers; Singers and 'Wrapping Up') p. 15
Answers to Correspondents p. 15
    Nessie in Australia (general), Lillie (general)

Number 146 (14 October 1882)
Bound to Earth Ch. 2 pp. 17–19
New Music p. 19
Love Having Once Flown (music score) (C. A. Macirone, Words Sir Philip Sydney) pp. 20–2
Laura Leigh Ch. 2 pp. 28–30
Varieties (Advice to Lady Vocalists; To Preserve the Throat in Singing) p. 31
Answers to Correspondents p. 32
    Lover of Music (violin, choosing instrument)

Number 147 (21 October 1882)
Bound to Earth Ch. 3* pp. 33–5
Margaret's Neighbours (Dora Hope) pp. 35–6
    Anxious for her children to sing well, Margaret Trent taught them little hymns and songs before they could speak. Daily governess, Miss Baines, approves, for singing is a delightful amusement best taught to youngsters first by ear rather than by notes. Margaret's neighbour Lulu Lancaster, a beginning violinist, learns from a master that she lacks finesse, the 'soul' that lets the violin speak to the heart, which comes with long life and knowledge of the world's 'sorrow and sadness' (p. 535).
Laura Leigh Ch. 3 pp. 42–3, 46
New Music p. 46
Answers to Correspondents (Music heading) pp. 46–7
    After Years of Waiting (general), Poma Parva Matura (general), Musical (sight-reading), Letitia (piano), Dormouse (general), Trotty Green (voice, health), Perseverance (general)

Number 148 (28 October 1882)
Bound to Earth Ch. 4* pp. 58–9
New Music pp. 62–3

Number 149 (4 November 1882)
Time at the Ferry (music score) (Lady Benedict, Words Jetty Vogel) pp. 68–70
Laura Leigh Ch. 4 pp. 71–2
Bound to Earth Ch. 5 pp. 76–8
Varieties (At an Evening Concert) pp. 78–9
Answers to Correspondents pp. 79–80
    Edith D. (music education), Wainright (music education)

84   *Catalogue of musical content*

Number 150 (11 November 1882)
Bound to Earth Ch. 6* pp. 88–90
   Illustration 'And began playing the duetto' shows Grace playing a Mendelssohn lieder for her friends Fanny and Helen p. 89
Laura Leigh Ch. 5 pp. 92–4
Answers to Correspondents (Music heading) p. 95
   Heather (repertoire), Lily of the Valley (general), J. Wood (general), A Plain-Looking Girl (metronome), Leslie (general), Marie Harwood (general)

Number 151 (18 November 1882)
Laura Leigh Ch. 5 (cont.) pp. 102–3
New Music p. 103
On Singing Sacred Music (Madame Edith Wynne) pp. 105–6
Bound to Earth Ch. 7 pp. 107–9
Varieties (The End of Music – *H. K. White*) p. 109
Answers to Correspondents pp. 111–12
   Mary Buchanan (general), Juanita (voice, health)

Number 152 (25 November 1882)
Margaret's Neighbours pp. 117–19
Charity: A Ballad Story p. 119
Correct Clothing, and How It Should Be Made (A Lady Dressmaker) pp. 120–2
   Illustration 'Winter Dress' shows a woman playing an upright piano as three young women listen p. 120.
Bound to Earth Ch. 8 pp. 125–7
Answers to Correspondents pp. 127–8
   Mignonette (general)

Number 153 (2 December 1882)
An Old Dutch House (M. M. Pollard) Ch. 1* pp. 129–30
   Maria De Velde invites her young cousin Anna to live with her and buys a piano so that Anna can keep up her practising. The evening before Anna's fiancé Oscar leaves to pursue a medical degree, he finds Anna playing a sonata on the parlour piano. 'It is my last night here', he says, 'and yet you pay more devotion to Beethoven than you do to poor me; shut up the piano for once, and come with me into the garden' (p. 146).
Laura Leigh Ch. 6 pp. 137–9
Bound to Earth Ch. 9 pp. 141–3
Answers to Correspondents (Music heading) pp. 143–4
   Evangeline Hatch (repertoire), J.P.A. (general), Mena (music education), True Blue (general), Lizzie and Nellie (voice, health), A Young Sufferer (violin), Creole (general), Corncrake (applied music), Murrie (repertoire), Gracy M. (repertoire), Cherith (theory)

Number 154 (9 December 1882)
An Old Dutch House Ch. 2* pp. 145–7
Lessons of the Gorses (music score) (Alice Mary Smith [Mrs Meadows White], Words Elizabeth Browning) pp. 152–3
Laura Leigh Ch. 7 pp. 154–5
Bound to Earth Ch. 10 pp. 157–9
Answers to Correspondents (Music heading) p. 159
   Cerita (general), Margaret (piano), A Musical Student (music education), Poppie (general)

Catalogue of musical content 85

Number 155 *(16 December 1882)*
An Old Dutch House Ch. 3 pp. 161–3
Laura Leigh Ch. 8 pp. 165–6
Varieties (For the Musical) p. 167
New Music p. 170
Margaret's Neighbours pp. 171–2*
Bound to Earth Ch. 11 pp. 173–4
Answers to Correspondents (Music heading) pp. 175–6
  Veritas Vincit (violin, repertoire), Miss Waldrom (general), Daisy Florence Cameron (general), Denverita (violin, choosing instrument), Keynote (general), Lady Psyche (mandolin), Faith, Hope, and Charity (piano), Moss Rose (mandolin), A Zigzag (repertoire)

Number 156 *(23 December 1882)*
Laura Leigh Ch. 9 p. 177
The Angels' Song (music score) (C. H. Purday, Words Frances Ridley Havergal) p. 181
Christmas Hymn (poem) (J. E.) p. 186
Bound to Earth Ch. 12 pp. 189–91
Answers to Correspondents (Music heading) p. 191
  Admirer of 'G.O.P.' (music teaching)

Number 157 *(30 December 1882)*
An Old Dutch House Ch. 4 pp. 193–5
His Heart's Desire p. 195
  After hearing a cathedral boy chorister sing 'O rest in the Lord, wait patiently for him', an elderly man recalls his own days as a boy chorister. As a man, he mistakenly made earthly wealth and then power his focus, and achieved his heart's desire for love and wisdom only when death came to him in his pew and his soul winged its flight to heaven.
New Music p. 204

Number 158 *(6 January 1883)*
Bound to Earth Ch. 13 pp. 213–15
Genius or Perseverance (Mary Selwood) p. 215
  Girls who hope a good fairy suddenly will endow them with the desired talent as a pianist must instead be their own fairies, for they can play well 'if they really *wish* it' and persevere (p. 215).
New Music p. 219
For a Little While (poem) (Louisa Grey) p. 220
Laura Leigh Ch. 10 pp. 220–3
Answers to Correspondents (Music heading) p. 223
  Jenny Bell (general), Aldyth (voice, health), Ruby Norman (music education), Cymraes (violin), Ocean (pronunciation), A Rover (music history and appreciation)

Number 159 *(13 January 1883)*
Laura Leigh Ch. 11 pp. 225–6
New Music p. 227
Bound to Earth Ch. 14 pp. 230–31
A Sweet Singer (poem) (Harriette Smith Bainbridge) p. 232
Answers to Correspondents (Music heading) pp. 238–40
  Papillotten-Fraulein (voice), M. H. (mandolin), Puck (general)

86 *Catalogue of musical content*

Number 160 (20 January 1883)
Laura Leigh (Ch. 12) pp. 241–3
Evenings with our Great Living Composers (James Mason) I. Richard Wagner pp. 245–7
   Twelve musical friends meet weekly for six weeks to discuss and perform the works of popular living composers.
The Slumber Song (music score) (G. Feldstein, Words Maggie Macdonald) pp. 248–9
Bound to Earth Ch. 15 pp. 250–1
Margaret's Neighbours pp. 253–5

Number 161 (27 January 1883)
Laura Leigh Ch. 13 pp. 257–9
My Mother (poem) (The Rev. William Cowan) p. 262
Bound to Earth Ch. 16 pp. 270–1
Answers to Correspondents (Music heading) pp. 271–2
   Lover of Music (voice), Violin (theory), Furneaux (general)

Number 162 (3 February 1883)
Laura Leigh Ch. 14* pp. 273–4
Varieties (An Alphabetical Note) p. 278
Bound to Earth Ch. 17 pp. 282–3
New Music p. 283
Afternoon in February (music score) (Mrs Tom Taylor, Words Longfellow) pp. 284–5

Number 163 (10 February 1883)
Laura Leigh Ch. 15 pp. 292–3
New Music pp. 293–4
Bound to Earth Ch. 18 pp. 297–8
Answers to Correspondents pp. 302–4
   Lily of Willow-Street (instrument maintenance, piano keys)

Number 164 (17 February 1883)
Bound to Earth Ch. 19 pp. 305–7
New Music p. 311
On a Blackbird Singing During Divine Service (poem) (Alice King) p. 313

Number 165 (24 February 1883)
Margaret's Neighbours pp. 322–3
Laura Leigh Ch. 16 pp. 334–5
Answers to Correspondents (Music heading) pp. 335–6
   L'May (composition), Evolym (repertoire), Daisy Dymond (music education, piano, instrument maintenance), Frederica (piano, memory work), Ludwig the Pious (music education), A. A. (piano), Laurie (general)

Number 166 (3 March 1883)
Bound to Earth Ch. 20 pp. 338–9
New Music p. 339
Winter Entertainment in Villages (Gentianella) pp. 348–9
   Village entertainments are within the scope and ability of young women willing to manage the event. Author offers step-by-step guidance.
Laura Leigh Ch. 17 pp. 349–51

Number 167 (10 March 1883)
Bound to Earth Ch. 21 pp. 353–5
Answers to Correspondents (Music heading) pp. 366–7
    Lucie Hart (piano, practising, nuisance), Zukeika (repertoire), A Blue-Ribbon Wearer (voice, music potential), Apollo (piano, instrument maintenance), Gladys Spenser (harmonium, piano)

Number 168 (17 March 1883)
Bound to Earth Ch. 22* pp. 369–71
Margaret's Neighbours pp. 374–5
New Music pp. 382–3
Answers to Correspondents (Music heading) pp. 383–4
    Hope (music education), E. C. (general), An Admiring Subscriber (piano), One Who Wishes to Improve (applied music), Kee Wee (terms), Cherrie (general, harmonium), Couradin (general), Captain Greek's Sister (voice), Pina (music education)

Number 169 (24 March 1883)
Bound to Earth Ch. 23 pp. 385–7
Evenings with Our Great Living Composers II. Charles Gounod pp. 387–9
Andante: For Violin and Pianoforte (music score) (Arthur Bunnett) pp. 392–5

Number 170 (31 March 1883)
New Music pp. 405–6
A Few Words on Musical Training (A Head Music Mistress) pp. 406–7
Answers to Correspondents p. 415
    Hiawatha (general)

Number 171 (7 April 1883)
A Long Lane with a Turning (Sarah Doudney) Ch. 1 pp. 417–20
    Cassie Decke with her 'flute-like' soprano, Mary Berrithorne, James Listowe with his 'trumpet-notes' and Arthur Beachley enjoy singing quartets together (p. 466). When Cassie, the Varner's adopted daughter, agrees to sit with the Scrooge-like elderly Jacob Varner, she often sings him to sleep with a plaintive little ballad.
Spring (music score) (Cotsford Dick, Words Sydney Grey) pp. 421–3
The Foster Sisters: A Story in Four Chapters (Louisa L.J. Menzies) Ch. 1 pp. 424–6
    Newborn infants Geraldine Anderson and Nora O'Hara, of different social classes, become foster sisters when Eileen O'Hara offers to take in Geraldine, who is not thriving under anxious mother Rachel Anderson's care. Both Geraldine and Nora are musical as young women and have sweet voices, though Geraldine's is cultivated, and Nora's is not.
Bound to Earth Ch. 24 pp. 430–1
Answers to Correspondents pp. 431–2
    A Young Violinist (music history and appreciation)

Number 172 (14 April 1883)
A Long Lane with a Turning Ch. 2 pp. 433–5
A Few Words on Musical Training (A Head Music Mistress) pp. 435–6
The Foster Sisters Ch. 2* pp. 436–8
    Illustration 'The rich young voice of the pleasant maid rose clear and sweet' p. 437
New Music p. 439

88 Catalogue of musical content

Number 173 (21 April 1883)
A Long Lane with a Turning Ch. 3 pp. 449–52
The Foster Sisters Ch. 3 pp. 452–4
Margaret's Neighbours pp. 454–5
Bound to Earth Ch. 25 pp. 462–3
Answers to Correspondents (Music heading) pp. 463–4
    Mima (applied music), Q. in the Corner (general), Forget-Me-Not (music education), Quartuor (music history and appreciation), Ethel (practising), Sunflower (theory), Manouri (general), Good Templar (voice, health)

Number 174 (28 April 1883)
A Long Lane with a Turning Ch. 4 pp. 465–7
The Foster Sisters Ch. 4 pp. 475–6
Answers to Correspondents (Music heading) pp. 479–80
    Ninon (general), Scotia (general), Crusoe (general), Snowdrop (voice, general)

Number 175 (5 May 1883)
A Long Lane with a Turning Ch. 5 pp. 481–3
New Music p. 483
The Ivy Green: A Sequel to ''Twas in a Crowd' (Mrs J. A. Owen) Ch. 1* pp. 488–90
    After her rich uncle brings orphaned Nora Grey from San Francisco to London and then suffers financial ruin, Norah seeks paid employment. With her piano background of Beethoven sonatas and Mendelssohn lieders, she gets a position as resident governess for the Speeding's daughter Lilly. When Norah plays several Chopin waltzes from memory 'with great brilliance and feeling', Mr Speeding offers her 'every opportunity' to keep up with her music (p. 500).
Answers to Correspondents (Music heading) pp. 494–6
    Dagmar B. (voice, copyright), Edward P. Sharp (applied music), D.E.F. (applied music), Emily Keen (applied music), Hope (music education), Alma (terms, metronome), Milly Macree (voice, practising), Alma (applied music), Dolce St. Cecilia (memory work, terms), Jolette Carhitton (general), Purple Pansy (general), Darkie (practising society)

Number 176 (12 May 1883)
A Long Lane with a Turning Ch. 6 pp. 497–500
The Ivy Green Ch. 2* pp. 500–2
The Spirit of Mine Eyes (music score) (John Gledhill) pp. 505–7
Answers to Correspondents pp. 510–11
    A Lady Violinist (general)

Number 177 (19 May 1883)
The Ivy Green Ch. 3 pp. 513–15
A Long Lane with a Turning Ch. 7 pp. 518–19
New Music p. 519
Answers to Correspondents pp. 527–8
    Ignoramus (general)

Number 178 (26 May 1883)
Margaret's Neighbors pp. 534–5, 537*
The Ivy Green Ch. 4 pp. 536–7
A Long Lane with a Turning Ch. 8* pp. 540–2

Answers to Correspondents (Music heading) p. 543
   Cook and Admirer of Music (repertoire), Brown Eyes (violin), Green Gosling and Timo (voice), Snowdrop (repertoire), Sophy Munro (violin), Polyphemus (voice, health)

Number 178 (2 June 1883)
How to Sing at Sight (Edwin M. Lott) pp. 547–8
A Long Lane with a Turning Ch. 9 pp. 548–50
Answers to Correspondents (Music heading) pp. 558–60
   A Student of Music (metronome), Little Tulip (voice, applied music), Bertha M. Stirling (music history and appreciation), Talkative Lucy (memory work), A Music Lover (piano), Lady Ditch (music history and appreciation), A Country Girl (violin), Roy (general), Lover of The Girl's Own Paper (music teaching)

Number 180 (9 June 1883)
New Music p. 564
A Long Lane with a Turning Ch. 10 pp. 565–7
My Work Basket pp. 568–9
   Includes instructions for making a music basket.
   Illustration 'Music Basket' p. 568
Margaret's Neighbours pp. 570–1
Answers to Correspondents p. 576
   Masculine Curiosity (repertoire)

Number 181 (16 June 1883)
A Long Lane with a Turning Ch. 11 pp. 577–80
Answers to Correspondents (Music heading) pp. 591–2
   Jessie R. (voice), Noel (violin), Mayflower (general), Katie (health, voice), Bryde (harp, guitar), A Troubled One (piano, practising), Edith Domberg (violin)

Number 182 (23 June 1883)
A Long Lane with a Turning Ch. 12 pp. 593–4
Village Bells (music score) (Charles Bassett) pp. 595–7
Evenings with our Great Living Composers III. Franz Liszt pp. 598–600
Answers to Correspondents (Music heading) p. 607
   Clarence W. (general), Clara C. (voice, health), Veilchen (violin)

Number 183 (30 June 1883)
A Long Lane with a Turning Ch. 13 pp. 609–11
Answers to Correspondents (Music heading) pp. 623–4
   Winniefred (repertoire), Lady Rickety (piano, instrument maintenance), Water Lily (composition), A Young Musician (general), Carrie (general)

Number 184 (7 July 1883)
A Long Lane with a Turning Ch. 14* pp. 625–7
Her Only Child (music score) (Louisa Gray, Words Fred E. Weatherly) pp. 632–3
Answers to Correspondents pp. 639–40
   D. Cox (voice)

Number 185 (14 July 1883)
A Long Lane with a Turning Ch. 15 pp. 641–3
New Music p. 643

90 *Catalogue of musical content*

Answers to Correspondents (Music heading) pp. 655–6
   Ida. M. Freeman (violin), Cobweb (repertoire), An Israelitish Woman (music history and appreciation), Brownie (repertoire), Psyche (repertoire), J.E.M. and Daffodil (general), Pansey (general), Hope (general)

Number 186 (21 July 1883)
A Long Lane with a Turning Ch. 16 pp. 657–9
Margaret's Neighbours pp. 666–7
New Music p. 667
Effie's Afternoon Tea (Dora Hope) Ch. 1* pp. 669–70
   Bimonthly meetings that Effie Wills and her friend Ruth Harley organize for their acquaintances to work on needlework and crafts to benefit charity include music and singing. Musical girls are asked in advance to perform, and they are considering combining a musical society with their work.

Number 187 (28 July 1883)
A Long Lane with a Turning Ch. 17 pp. 673–5
Effie's Afternoon Tea Ch. 2* 685–7
Answers to Correspondents (Music heading) p. 688
   Marie (piano, general), Lily of the Valley (general), Aunt Cockletop (mandolin), Otto's Girl (general), Church (general), Judy (general), H. A. (voice), One Who Is Anxious (music education), Little Dora (violin), W.H.E.L. (music education), Super-Tonic (copyright), Mervaide (piano), Primrose (voice, tonic sol-fa), Florence M. E. (repertoire), Napoli (practising), R.S.V.P. (sight-reading)

Number 188 (4 August 1883)
A Long Lane with a Turning Ch. 18 pp. 689–91
Evening Clouds (music score) (Edwin M. Lott) pp. 694–6
Evenings with Our Great Living Composers IV. Sir Julius Benedict pp. 698–9
Answers to Correspondents (Music heading) pp. 703–4
   Organist (organ), Yarkastad (piano, applied music), Myosotis (repertoire), Two Victorian Maidens (general), Alice S. (music education), Enid (terms), An Opening Bud (voice), Carmen and Doralice (violin), Vere Haldane (general), Dolly (general), Tarantelle and Arabesque (piano, practising), Andante (voice), A Late One (music teaching)

Number 189 (11 August 1883)
A Long Lane with a Turning Ch. 19* pp. 705–7
New Music p. 711
Answers to Correspondents pp. 719–20
   Lucini Marcello (general)

Number 190 (18 August 1883)
A Long Lane with a Turning Ch. 20 pp. 721–3
New Music p. 724
Answers to Correspondents pp. 735–6
   Oenone (music education)

Number 191 (25 August 1883)
A Long Lane with a Turning Ch. 21 pp. 737–9
Margaret's Neighbours pp. 739–40

Number 192 (1 Sept. 1883)
A Long Lane with a Turning Ch. 22 p. 759

All in Vain (Ballad) (music score) (Franz Abt, Words Edward Oxenford) pp. 760–2
Answers to Correspondents (Music heading) pp. 766–8
   E. R. and Elizabeth H. (music education), Corinne (terms), Lilac B. (repertoire), A Dublin Lassie (violin), Marsh Mallow (general), Grateful Rosebud (repertoire), Effie Moseley (general), Tebam (general), Snowdrop (metronome), Tonic Sol-Fa (musician pension), Lizzie M. S. (practising society), Great Reader of the 'G.O.P'. (organ, repertoire), Well-Wisher (voice), Portia (piano), Wilhelmina (general), A.A.G. (music teaching), Iolanthe, Aeneid, and Marcia (theory), Edmar (H. L.) (music teaching), Kemps (music education)

Number 193 (8 September 1883)
A Long Lane with a Turning Ch. 23 pp. 769–70
New Music p. 774
Evenings with Our Great Composers V. Rubenstein pp. 777–9

Number 194 (15 September 1883)
Answers to Correspondents pp. 799–800
   Hina (terms), Scribendibus (general), Motherless Ethel (guitar)

Number 195 (22 September 1883)
A Girl's Morning Hymn (poem) (C. A. Macirone) pp. 801–2
Clara Schumann (La Mara) pp. 808–11
Illustration 'Madame Schumann' p. 809
Answers to Correspondents (Music heading) pp. 814–15
   Musician (general), Rosamond (violin), Dora (music education), Edith M. Nordkyn (terms), Hans (voice, practising), Diffident (Darenth) (piano)
The Merry Harvest Time (music score) p. 816

Number 196 (29 September 1883)
Higher Thoughts on Girls' Occupations: Music (Alice King) pp. 822–3
   Girls with musical aspirations fall into two categories – the bullfinches and the parrots. The first group, who show evidence of talent at an early age, should be nourished in their musical studies. The second group should be encouraged to apply their time to nonmusical pursuits.
Evenings with Our Great Living Composers VI. Sir George Alexander Macfarren pp. 827–8
Margaret's Neighbours pp. 829–30
Answers to Correspondents (Music heading) pp. 831–2
   Minnie Wood (music history and appreciation), Female Cetewayo (music education), Gavotte (practising society), Ellen (music history and appreciation, theory)

Christmas Carillon
Extra Christmas Number for Volume 4 (1882)
Mildred Austin's Two Christmas Eves (M. M. Pollard) pp. 7–13
   In a good daughter/bad daughter dichotomy with a hint of deserved outcomes, the story pits selfless Mildred Austin, who fills in at the last moment for a soloist singing, 'I know that my Redeemer liveth', against her sister Floy, too engrossed in her novel-reading to look after their blind mother.
The Christmas Guest (poem) (Helen Marion Burnside) p. 33
Our Christmas Treat to the Poor (Dora Hope) pp. 34–7
   An account of several meetings at which music is a part. At a Mothers' Meeting in the Sunday-school room adjoining the church, a young woman plays 'sweet music' on the piano that replaces the usual harmonium. Hymns, carols, part songs and temperance songs are also sung (p. 34).

Illustration 'The next orator was more successful' shows a young woman at a piano on the platform p. 36

A Christmas Carol (music score) (Alfred Scott Gatty) pp. 40–1

Old Christmas Carols (The Rev. H. R. Bramley and John Stainer) pp. 49–51
Includes music scores.

The Whisperer: A Sketch (Sarah Doudney) pp. 52–6
School friend Bella Wylde sings a song to Charity Galton about the rose being the envy of other whispering flowers. Charity is the rose about whom other 'friends' whisper.

Summer Quiet
Extra Holiday Number for Volume 4 (1883)

The Lost Flora (Anne Beale) pp. 3–8
Orphans Lucy Stanmore and her brother Felix move from London to the Sussex hamlet of Millford where he sets up a medical practice. The piano came with them but does not respond to Lucy's touch as she practises – her mind is troubled by dwindling finances and lack of paying patients.

Illustration 'Gazing at the photograph of her dear father' shows Lucy in the parlour with a piano with its open sheet music in the background p. 5

Merrie England I. 'Oh, How Should I Your True Love Know!' (music score) (C. A. Macirone) pp. 20–3

A Dream of Heaven (poem) (G. Collingwood Banks) p. 56

Volume 5 (6 October 1883–27 September 1884)

Number 197 (6 October 1883)
Esther (Rosa Nouchette Carey) Ch. 1* pp. 5–7
>Carrie Steadman plays beautifully but seldom practises, thinking it a waste of time 'to devote so much time to a mere accomplishment' (p. 6). Her sister Esther is indignant: 'Waste of time to sing to mother!' (p. 199)

Answers to Correspondents (Music heading) pp. 15–16
>Shields (general), C.A.M. (general), Terpsichore (violin), Mountain Maiden (terms), An Eldest Daughter (organ), Topsey (music history and appreciation), Corncrake (applied music), Daisy W. (repertoire), Lily Pearl (general)

Number 198 (13 October 1883)
New Music p. 19
Esther Ch. 2 pp. 20–2
Singing (Lady Macfarren) Part 1 p. 23
Work for All: I. Introductory, II. Teaching pp. 25–7
>Because music is so laborious an occupation, the author does not recommend it as a means for young middle-class women who must leave home to earn a living.

Answers to Correspondents (Music heading) pp. 30–1
>Monica (music history and appreciation, organ), Violet (piano), Nina (general), Lily Williams (general), Mischievous Mollie (violin), A Lover of Singing (voice, tonic sol-fa)

Number 199 (20 October 1883)
Singing Part 2 pp. 33–4
Esther Ch. 3 pp. 36–8
Varieties (St. Cecilia) p. 42
Answers to Correspondents (Music heading) pp. 46–7
>Atlantis (general), E.R.A., Castellino, and Others (general), L. M. (organ, harmonium), Emmie (music teaching, music education), Nemo and A Danish Girl (music education), Bonnie Leslie (general), Veritas (piano, theory), Emma B. (bagpipe, music history and appreciation), Timidy (repertoire), Hawthorn Blossom (repertoire)

Number 200 (27 October 1883)
Esther Ch. 4 pp. 52–4

Number 201 (3 November 1883)
Singing Part 3 pp. 66–7
New Music p. 67
Esther Ch. 5 pp. 68–70
Old Times (music score) (Franz Abt, Words Edward Oxenford) pp. 72–4

Number 202 (10 November 1883)
Esther Ch. 6 pp. 81–3

Number 203 (17 November 1883)
Sunbeams (poem) (Annie Bentley) p. 97
>Illustration 'Ah! would there were no storm nor gloom' shows a woman musician p. 97

Esther Ch. 7 pp. 99–102
French Girls (Anne Beale) pp. 105–6

94   *Catalogue of musical content*

The Paris Conservatoire is among the institutions where French girls may obtain an education. If the student intends to make music a profession, she finds the work very laborious and intellectually demanding. But, Beale adds, 'this is the same everywhere' (p. 106).
[New] Music p. 107
Answers to Correspondents pp. 110–12
   Una Bona (instrument maintenance, piano keys), A Fiddlestick (practising, violin)

Number 204 (24 November 1883)
Esther Ch. 8 pp. 116–9

Number 205 (1 December 1883)
Esther Ch. 9* pp. 129–31
   Illustration 'Singing her the hymns she loves' p. 129
Answers to Correspondents pp. 142–4
   Grundy (pronunciation)

Number 206 (8 December 1883)
Esther Ch. 10 pp. 145–7
New Music p. 158
Answers to Correspondents pp. 159–60
   Aunt Sukey (terms)

Number 207 (15 December 1883)
The Power of Music (C. A. Macirone) First Letter pp. 163–5
   First in a series of articles written as letters titled 'A Plea for Music'.
Esther Ch. 11 pp. 165–7
Answers to Correspondents (Music heading) pp. 173–6
   Bella Rokesmith (piano), Leofwine (voice, piano, sight-reading), Tortoise (terms, music history and appreciation), Enquirer (piano), Viola (violin, music history and appreciation), Marguerite (voice)

Number 208 (22 December 1883)
Esther Ch. 12 pp. 181–3
The Girl's Own Carol (music score) (Joseph Barnby) pp. 184–5
The Girl's Own Carol (illustration) (M. Ellen Edwards) plate facing p. 186
Answers to Correspondents pp. 191–2
   Emily (voice), A Fair-Haired Girl, Par Nom. (page turning)

Number 209 (29 December 1883)
Esther Ch. 13* pp. 197–9
Answers to Correspondents pp. 206–8
   M. Willis (practising society)

Number 210 (5 January 1884)
Her Violin: A Sketch in Sepia Ch. 1 pp. 209–10
   On her first visit to London, 18-year-old German violinist Frida Bunn successfully debuts Hungarian Demetri von Szantó's sonata, bringing his love. When her mercenary father will not consent to the betrothal, Frida lives only to play and plays only for the income it brings. Confronting her father, who has withheld and lied about her earnings, leads to his death and Frida's own lengthy illness. With Demetri's help, Frida recovers with a new sense of happiness and contentment, though tinged with sadness and 'an almost exaggerated fear of hasty words and reckless speeches' (p. 262).

Esther Ch. 14 pp. 212–14
Common Errors in Daily Life (James Mason) III. Errors in Taste pp. 214–16
   Two common errors are made in music when girls with no natural liking for it are expected to play the piano as a stock accomplishment and when amateurs perform 'what is not far removed from trash'. Author advises musicians to play easy pieces well rather than difficult ones 'in second-rate style' (p. 216).

Number 211 (12 January 1884)
Esther Ch. 15 pp. 228–31
Her Violin Ch. 2 pp. 232–5
   Illustration 'The soft and gentle melancholy of the composition filled Frida's soul with longing and regret' p. 232
Higher Thoughts on Housekeeping (Alice King) pp. 235–6
   Some girls are born housekeepers; others are born musicians. Girls with real talent for music should let it come first in their education but still give some time to cookery and household matters.
New Music p. 239
Answers to Correspondents pp. 239–40
   Isa (organ)

Number 212 (19 January 1884)
Esther Ch. 16 pp. 241–3
New Music pp. 243–4
Her Violin Ch. 3 pp. 250–1
Answers to Correspondents (Music heading) pp. 255–6
   Staccato (harp), Ein Madchen (piano, instrument maintenance), B.B.J., (terms), Ambitious Welsh Lassie (music education), Iolanthe (performance nerves), Gwen Owen (voice), Ianthe (theory, music education), Violet (general), Seventeen (music education), Juliet (practising society), Cecilia (tonic sol-fa), Student (music history and appreciation), Clare Tonbridge (piano), Little Worrit (general), Oona (tonic sol-fa), A Very Anxious Inquirer (music education), Laura Halfpenny (piano), Goody Two-Shoes (piano), Edwintine Crossley (piano, music potential)

Number 213 (26 January 1884)
Esther Ch. 17 pp. 257–9
Her Violin Ch. 4 pp. 260–2
   Illustration 'In the old castle' p. 261
A Plea for Music (Clara A. Macirone) Second Letter pp. 268–70
   Following her introductory 'The Power of Music', Macirone devotes six additional letters urging a system of music education in girls' schools equivalent to that found in boys' schools, which she deems superior, though not entirely satisfactory.
Answers to Correspondents (Music heading) pp. 271–2
   Josephine (copyright), Jubal (music history and appreciation), L'Ainee (terms, music teaching), Ynnaej and Minnie-Ha-Ha (music copying, musician work)

Number 214 (2 February 1884)
Esther Ch. 18 pp. 277–9
New Music p. 287
Answers to Correspondents pp. 287–8
   One Who Would Work (music education)

Number 215 (9 February 1884)
Esther Ch. 19 pp. 289–91
New Music p. 295
My 'At Home', and How I Managed It pp. 298–9

Number 216 (16 February 1884)
Esther Ch. 20 pp. 305–7
Lucy (music score) (Myles B. Foster, Words Wordsworth) pp. 308–9
Answers to Correspondents pp. 318–20
   Rhoda (national anthem)

Number 217 (23 February 1884)
Esther Ch. 21 pp. 321–3
A Plea for Music Third Letter pp. 330–2
Answers to Correspondents (Music heading) pp. 335–6
   Vixen (voice), Music (general), Little One (voice, flute)

Number 218 (1 March 1884)
Esther Ch. 22 pp. 341–3
Work for All: Music pp. 347–8
   After stating that only those girls with a natural gift for music should make it their profession, the author, who favours teaching more science of music than mechanical proficiency, devotes most of the article to London's schools of music and the scholarships open to female candidates.
Answers to Correspondents (Music heading) pp. 351–2
   Marion W. (voice, applied music), Annie (voice), Annie C. (theory), Rose-Bush (music history and appreciation), Musical Cone (voice), Judie (organ, music education), Bella Donna (general), Sad Musician (music teaching)

Number 219 (8 March 1884)
Esther Ch. 23 pp. 356–8
New Music p. 359

Number 220 (15 March 1884)
Esther Ch. 24 pp. 373–5
[New] Music p. 383
Answers to Correspondents pp. 383–4
   Flossy (memory work)

Number 221 (22 March 1884)
True Love Never Dies (music score) (Annie Nash, Words William Gaspey) pp. 396–8

Number 222 (29 March 1884)
New Music p. 404
Varieties (The Association of Music) p. 407
A Plea for Music Fourth Letter pp. 410–12
Answers to Correspondents pp. 414–6
   Auntie (repertoire), Twenty-Three (practising, nuisance)

Number 223 (5 April 1884)
The Rose and the Dewdrop (music score) (C. A. Macirone, Words from 'Pearls of Faith' by Edwin Arnold) pp. 420–4

Answers to Correspondents (Music heading) pp. 431–2
    E. H. (page turning), Music (voice), Rose Ruddach (general), Isabella (piano, nuisance), A Lover of Music (general), Clara G. (general), E.M.W. (music education), Gabrielle (repertoire), A Blue-Eyed Welsh Lassie (voice), Elsie (general), Two Puzzled Lassies (general)

Number 224 (12 April 1884)
Varieties (Singers! Look to Your Feet) p. 435
Singing in Church (Myles B. Foster) p. 436
    Readers who pay for expensive singing lessons to master ballads during the week should give equal attention to singing church hymns in congregation and choir stalls on Sundays.
New Music p. 444
Signora Teresina Tua p. 445
    A 15-year-old violinist creating quite a sensation on the Continent.

Number 225 (19 April 1884)
A Plea for Music Fifth Letter pp. 457–9
Answers to Correspondents pp. 463–4
    Auf Wieder Sehen (repertoire)

Number 226 (26 April 1884)
Answers to Correspondents (Music heading) pp. 478–80
    Lady Lilian (applied music), Reader of the 'G.O.P.' (piano), Kate Frances B. (general), Chachamorena (publishing music), Lyra (music history and appreciation), Two Scamps (music history and appreciation)

Number 227 (3 May 1884)
Within Sight of the Snow: A Story of a Swiss Holiday (Lily Watson) Chs 1, 2 pp. 481–4
    Esther Fielding, a pianoforte teacher living in genteel poverty, travels to Switzerland. When she plays Mendelssohn and Beethoven for guests gathered around the piano in the hotel dining room one evening, Herr Lichtenstein, a professor at the Leipsic Conservatoire, critiques her performance as expressive but faulty in execution; she lets her feelings run away with her. From him Esther learns to view her music as a noble art and to live her life harmoniously and worthy of her lofty calling.
New Music pp. 484–5
Answers to Correspondents pp. 494–5
    Dunce (violoncello), Fairfax (repertoire)

Number 228 (10 May 1884)
Within Sight of the Snow Ch. 3 pp. 504–7
A June Song (poem) (Mary Rowles) p. 508
Answers to Correspondents pp. 511–12
    Barbara (music history and appreciation)

Number 229 (17 May 1884)
The Physical Education of Girls (Mrs Wallace Arnold) pp. 516–18
    During the years in which her figure is being formed, the young girl sitting at the piano has no support for her back, which becomes weary and sinks to one side. Supervised moderate bodily exercise in the form of calisthenics 'will do much to correct – nay, prevent – this mischief' (p. 516).

98 *Catalogue of musical content*

New Music p. 518
The Broken Chord (poem) (The Rev. Samuel K. Cowan) p. 520
Within Sight of the Snow Ch. 4 pp. 524–8
Answers to Correspondents p. 528
   Rose, Shamrock, and Thistle (practising)

Number 230 (24 May 1884)
A Sketch for the Pianoforte (music score) (Arthur Carnall) pp. 532–4
Within Sight of the Snow Ch. 5 pp. 536–40
Answers to Correspondents (Music heading) pp. 543–4
   A. M. and Never Despair (general, terms), The Sands (choosing instrument, harp, violin), Damaris Standfast (Bristol) (voice), Delta (music education), Agnes and Johanna C. (music education), A. Macdonald (instrument maintenance, piano)

Number 231 (31 May 1884)
Within Sight of the Snow Ch. 6 pp. 548–50
Answers to Correspondents (Music heading) p. 559
   Frida Bunel (violin), Mena (music history and appreciation)

Number 232 (7 June 1884)
Answers to Correspondents (Music heading) pp. 575–6
   Maria (piano, health), Vauline Girhardi (piano, health), Seventeen Minus the Sweetness (general)

Number 233 (14 June 1884)
A Plea for Music Sixth Letter pp. 580–1
New Music p. 589

Number 234 (21 June 1884)
The Lord Is My Shepherd: A Sacred Song (music score) (C. E. Rawstorne) pp. 596–8
New Music p. 600
Answers to Correspondents (Music heading) pp. 607–8
   Two Shoes (general), E.W.W. (general), Esposito (general), Linda (music education), Annoyed One (harmonium), Mignonette (voice), Ella (voice), Jennie B. (practising society, music education)

Number 235 (28 June 1884)
New Music p. 615
Answers to Correspondents p. 623
   Daisy (voice, repertoire)

Number 236 (5 July 1884)
New Music p. 627
Varieties (The Influence of Music) p. 631
Celia and Her Legacy (M. E. Hullah) Ch. 1 pp. 632–4
   Mr Hewing, a widowed neighbor hosting a musical party, tells daughter Maria that she can ask Janie Lake, who takes piano lessons with her at the Hewing's house, to play so that people will know of her 'if it should ever be necessary for her to make her own way in the world; it would be useful to her future career' (p. 729).

Number 237 (12 July 1884)
Celia and Her Legacy Ch. 2 pp. 641–3
New Music p. 647

Catalogue of musical content 99

Charity Begins at Home (Sarah Doudney) Chs 1, 2 pp. 649–51
    For health reasons, Florence Otway, a young wife with two young daughters, has returned to England from India, where her husband works. She teaches piano pupils, among them Rosalie Fenwood, a good student who learns from her teacher that 'charity begins at home'.

Number 238 (19 July 1884)
A Plea for Music Seventh Letter pp. 660–2
The Streamlet (music score) (The Rev. R. F. Dale, Words M. A. Smart) p. 664
Varieties (Mozart's Observations on a Lady's Pianoforte Playing, from *Life and Works of Mozart, by A. Whittingham*) p. 669
Celia and Her Legacy Ch. 2 (cont.) pp. 669–70
Answers to Correspondents (Music heading) pp. 670–1
    A Motherless Girl (reading music), Inquisitive Mouse (organ, music history and appreciation), Berengaria Perrot (performance etiquette), White Coral (violin), A. P. (music education), Nora Alvescott (voice), Kate Greenaway (general), Old Hag (voice), Ignoramus (applied music), Violetta (performance etiquette), Frances C. (general), Beth (voice), Patience (voice), Mendelssohn (music education)

Number 239 (26 July 1884)
New Music p. 675
Charity Begins at Home Chs 3, 4 pp. 683–4
Answers to Correspondents (Music heading) pp. 687–8
    Caracus Cocoa (practising), Inkbottle (music teaching)

Number 240 (2 August 1884)
What Girls Can Do to Hush 'the Bitter Cry' (Mrs S. A. Barnett, of Whitechapel) pp. 691–2
    After enumerating work that can be done at home, the author suggests that girls organize concerts to bring pleasure to the impoverished women and men of the working classes.
Celia and Her Legacy Ch. 3 pp. 697–8
Varieties (Not at All Musical) pp. 698–9
Answers to Correspondents (Music heading) pp. 703–4
    Major (practising), Mamie (music teaching), Roman (voice), A Foreign Bird (voice)

Number 241 (9 August 1884)
Our Holiday in Quimper (E. Macirone) pp. 708–11
    Includes music scores for two old Breton melodies overheard and arranged by C. A. Macirone.
Answers to Correspondents (Music heading) pp. 719–20
    Rhoda (practising society), Anxious Inquirer (tonic sol-fa)

Number 242 (16 August 1884)
Musical Notes p. 727
    Musical notation for A Musical Thunderstorm – Beethoven's Pastoral Symphony; Music in China – the air 'The Seven Brothers'; A Storm in Music – Wagner's *Die Walküre*.
On the Tuning of Stringed Instruments p. 727
Celia and Her Legacy Ch. 4* pp. 728–30
Answers to Correspondents (Music heading) pp. 735–6
    Rhoda M. (practising society), A. M. (publishing music), Old Crochetty (piano, health, repertoire), Moses (copyright)

Number 243 (23 August 1884)
New Music p. 744
The Blackbird and the Choir (music score) (Edwin M. Lott, Words Alice King) pp. 744–7
Answers to Correspondents (Music heading) pp. 751–2
   Dolly Penrith (music education), Distressed One (piano, performance nerves)

Number 244 (30 August 1884)
Our Holiday in Quimper (cont.) pp. 756–9
Celia and Her Legacy Ch. 5 pp. 763–4
Answers to Correspondents pp. 767–8
   Vera (repertoire)

Number 245 (6 September 1884)
Andante Scherzoso: For the Pianoforte (music score) (Myles B. Foster) pp. 780–1
Answers to Correspondents (Music heading) pp. 783–4
   Roy's Wife (music history and appreciation), May Davies (voice) A Lover of Music (piano), Excelsior (music education)

Number 246 (13 September 1884)
Celia and Her Legacy Ch. 6 pp. 792–4

Number 247 (20 September 1884)
Varieties (Music and Morals) p. 808

Number 248 (27 September 1884)
Celia and Her Legacy Ch. 7 pp. 830–1
Answers to Correspondents (Music heading) pp. 831–2
   St. Cecilia (music education), Marmion (voice, health), An Empty Vessel (general), Annette (general), Bella (piano), Veronica (applied music), C.A.J. (repertoire), Blanche (repertoire)

Winter Leaves
Extra Christmas Part for Volume 5 (1883)
The Christmas Angels (music score) (Elizabeth Philp, Words R. L. Gales) pp. 10–12

Sunlight
Extra Summer Number for Volume 5 (1884)
Tiny's Birthday Gift (Rosa Nouchette Carey) pp. 3–7
   As her birthday gift, Florence (Tiny) Redingcote invites cousins Cathy Williams, who gives music lessons, and Etta Williams, who is an invalid, for a month's stay at her home, Ellesere. The month turns into a permanent, happy home for them.
How We Sang Rounds and Catches (Nanette Mason) pp. 21–3
   Some of the friends who share 'Evenings with Our Great Living Composers' in Volume 4 gather to learn about and sing rounds and catches. Article includes music scores.
'Must We Part, and Part So Soon?' (music score) (Franz Abt, Words Edward Oxenford) pp. 42–6

Volume 6 (October 1884–27 September 1885)

Number 249 (4 October 1884)
The Mountain Path (Lily Watson) Ch. 1* pp. 1–4
  Possessing a good ear but no great talent, Lilian Brooke, deformed from a childhood injury, turns to music and, with lessons from a first-rate master and painstaking practice, becomes an excellent amateur pianist. Lilian's sister Helen is shocked that for Adela Gascoigne, a brilliant soprano who studied in Paris, music is all about society and invitations to people's houses, since Helen and her family consider music a noble art worthy of love and reverence.
How to Make a Metronome pp. 11–12
Answers to Correspondents (Music heading) pp. 14–15
  Picciola (piano), Ignorant (concertina), Flora Bradbroke (general), Harmonious Blacksmith (music history and appreciation), Bernard, B.C.T. M.L., Ethel, Mysotis, Marie, Christie (music education), Pianette, Dix-Sept, Country Girl, H.C.W. (general), White Cockade (composition), Cunobelin (piano), A Waif on Life's Ocean (general), Agnes (music potential), Union Jack (general), Lover of Music (voice)

Number 250 (11 October 1884)
For Listeners at Instrumental Concerts I. The 'Strings' of the Orchestra pp. 20–2
Varieties (Lovers of Music) p. 27
The Mountain Path Ch. 2 pp. 28–30
Answers to Correspondents (Music heading) pp. 31–2
  Effie Deans (terms, guitar), Helen Danvers (general), Ellen, Anxious One (piano), Maria Orford (banjo, mandolin, choosing instrument), E. B. Morris (national anthem)

Number 251 (18 October 1884)
The Mountain Path Ch. 3 pp. 33–5
The Fairies: Scherzo for the Pianoforte (music score) (Ernst Pauer) pp. 36–9

Number 252 (25 October 1884)
The Mountain Path Ch. 4 pp. 49–51
New Music p. 55
Answers to Correspondents pp. 62–3
  Urania (violin)

Number 253 (1 November 1884)
The Mountain Path (Lily Watson) Ch. 5 pp. 65–7
New Music p. 69

Number 254 (8 November 1884)
The Mountain Path Ch. 6* pp. 81–3
  Illustration 'And trilled away like a bird' shows Adela singing p. 81
Love Is Ours (music score) (Louisa Bodda-Pyne, Words H. Barrington) pp. 84–6
Village Bands (Alice King) pp. 91–2
  Focuses on management of village bands, which should be an amusement and relaxation for its members and help to teach sobriety and high morality.
Answers to Correspondents pp. 94–5
  Alice W. (general)

Number 255 (15 November 1884)
A Girl's Room (poem) (Clara Thwaites) p. 104
  Poem not musical in title or text but has musical illustration.

102 *Catalogue of musical content*

The Mountain Path Ch. 7 pp. 109–12
Answers to Correspondents p. 112
   Ossianna (general)

Number 256 (22 November 1884)
The Mountain Path Ch. 8 pp. 113–15
Varieties (Woman's Work) p. 115
Answers to Correspondents pp. 127–8
   A Future Musician (music student lodging)

Number 257 (29 November 1884)
Varieties (The Singing of Jenny Lind) p. 131
New Music p. 142

Number 258 (6 December 1884)
The Mountain Path Ch. 9 pp. 145–7
A Norwegian Melody (music score) (Edvard Grieg) pp. 148–9
Varieties (Music in Type; New Zealand Chants) p. 156
Answers to Correspondents pp. 159–60
   A.S.M. (general)

Number 259 (13 December 1884)
Varieties (Highland Music) p. 167
New Music p. 171
The Mountain Path Ch. 10 pp. 172–4
Answers to Correspondents (Music heading) pp. 174–5
   Clover (general), Tricksy (terms), Poppy (practising, nuisance), Jeanie Anderson (general), Busy Bee (repertoire), Gladys (voice), A Country Girl (guitar, violin, choosing instrument), Frank's Wife (guitar), Vixen (guitar), Hopeful Musician (piano), The Emmet (piano), Learner (violin), Modest Violet (general), A Young Musician (general), Sweet Seventeen Pansy (practising society), Elaine (violin), Uninteresting One (music education), Lily of the Valley (zither), Blue Hose (voice, piano), Lutonia Ragged Robin (terms), Pem Hope (violin, musician salary)

Number 260 (20 December 1884)
Varieties (Musical Decoration – *Grove Dictionary of Music*) p. 184
The Mountain Path Ch. 11 pp. 188–90

Number 261 (27 December 1884)
The Mountain Path Ch. 12* pp. 193–5
   Illustration 'The little deformed girl sat down without an instant's hesitation' shows Lilian at the piano p. 193

Number 262 (3 January 1885)
The Mountain Path Ch. 13 pp. 209–11
Come Home Again (music score) (C. A. Macirone, Words *old MS*) pp. 212–14
Correspondence Awaiting the Editor (Music heading) pp. 223–4
   Lover of Music (piano, music education, practising, nuisance), F.A.V.I. (voice, choral singing), Musicus (music education), Primrose (piano), Pygmalion (instrument maintenance, piano)

Number 263 (10 January 1885)
A Reverie in St. James's Hall (poem) (Clara Thwaites) p. 232
   Illustration 'Unfold, O sweet musicians, / Your secret art to me' p. 233
The Mountain Path Ch. 14 pp. 236–8
New Music pp. 238–9

Number 264 (17 January 1885)
Music and Method at a German Conservatoire (Eleanore d'Esterre-Keeling) p. 247
   Describes instruction at the conservatoire in Stuttgart, ending with the advice never to make musical perfection the end 'but rather as the means by which to attain a far nobler end'.
The Mountain Path Ch. 15 pp. 253–6

Number 266 (31 January 1885)
The Mountain Path Ch. 16 pp. 273–5
In Memoriam p. 276
   An appreciation of Mrs Meadows White (Alice Mary Smith before marriage).
   Illustration 'Mrs. Meadows White' p. 276
Varieties (Guitars in Fashion) pp. 286–7

Number 267 (7 February 1885)
'Tendresse' (Album Leaf) (music score) (Walter Macfarren) pp. 292–4
Taught His Way: The Story of a Life's Purpose Ch. 1 pp. 296–8
   Florence Hamilton wants to be a missionary. From friend Nellie Heywood, who sings and plays the piano to please her brother Ralph and keep him from bad influences outside the home, Florence learns of a different kind of 'mission' closer to home as aunt to her brother's two motherless daughters.
The Mountain Path Ch. 17 pp. 300–3
Answers to Correspondents (Music heading) pp. 303–4
   E. M. Harcourt (repertoire), A Cat (general), Teddy's Own (voice, health), Leeds, A. G. (piano), Ill Sunce Follo Mansy (organ), Nellie (music copying), A. S., A Beginner (composition), Tennis Ball (practising society), Ursie (general), A Lover of the 'G.O.P.' (melodeon), Lover of Music (music education), Lover of Music (Birmingham) (piano, nuisance), Sunflower (practising)

Number 268 (14 February 1885)
Taught His Way Ch. 2* pp. 309–11
   Illustration 'The Musical Evening' shows Nellie and her brother Ralph at Lady MacIvor's home p. 309
New Music p. 311
The Mountain Path Ch. 18 pp. 316–19

Number 269 (21 February 1885)
The Mountain Path Ch. 19 pp. 321–3
New Music p. 327
Taught His Way Ch. 3 pp. 330–2
Varieties (Voice Cultivation) pp. 334–5
Answers to Correspondents pp. 335–6
   Warwickshire Lass (choral singing)

Number 270 (28 February 1885)
Taught His Way Ch. 4 pp. 340–1
Women as Hymn Writers, and What They Have Done (The Rev. T. B. Willson) pp. 346–7
The Mountain Path Ch. 20 pp. 347–50
Answers to Correspondents pp. 351–2
   Nineteen (piano)

Number 271 (7 March 1885)
The Mountain Path Ch. 21 pp. 364–6

104   *Catalogue of musical content*

Answers to Correspondents (Music heading) pp. 367–8
   Sylvia (general), Helen (viola, zither, piano, mandolin, guitar, choosing instrument), Miss Grace Massy (secretary) (practising society), Jeanie (voice), S.A.S. (piano, practising, nuisance), Admirer of 'G.O.P.' (general), G.H.P. (general)

Number 272 (14 March 1885)
New Music p. 375
The Mountain Path Ch. 22 pp. 380–3
Aunt Diana (Rosa Nouchette Carey) Ch. 1 pp. 385–7
   After her mother dies, 16-year-old Alison Merle spends two years with her Aunt Diana Carrington. While away from home, violinist Greville Moore tutors her in music, Latin and British history. Aunt Diana's Wednesdays are an occasion for singing part songs and other music making. Back home again, Alison plays sister Mabel's accompaniments.

Number 273 (21 March 1885)
On Taste in the Choice of Songs (C. A. Macirone) First Letter pp. 390–2
The Mountain Path Ch. 23 pp. 396–9

Number 274 (28 March 1885)
Aunt Diana Ch. 2 pp. 401–3
A Wish (music score) (Mrs Tom Taylor) pp. 404–5
The Mountain Path Ch. 24 pp. 412–15
Answers to Correspondents pp. 415–16
   Ray C. (pronunciation), Biddy (pronunciation), Autumn Leaves (piano)

Number 275 (4 April 1885)
Varieties (Wagner Quizzed by Dumas – *Leisure Hour*; Of What Use is Music? – *Shakespeare*; Nonsense About Music – *Frederic L. Ritter*) p. 419
Aunt Diana Ch. 3* pp. 420–3
   Illustration 'Lost in enjoyment of the sweet sounds he had conjured up' shows Greville Moore playing violin p. 421
Answers to Correspondents (Music heading) pp. 430–2
   Jumbles (general), E.H.T. (music teaching), Moonlight Sonata (terms), Effie Deans (applied music, violin), Annie and Lucie (voice), A Black Sheep (organ, piano), Minna (theory, music history and appreciation), Flageolet (flute, flageolet, nuisance), Wild Flower (music education)

Number 276 (11 April 1885)
The Valley's Queen (music score) (Elizabeth Philp, Words F. B. Doveton) pp. 436–8
Aunt Diana Ch. 4* pp. 440–3
A Chorus for May (poem) (M. M. Pollard) p. 448

Number 277 (18 April 1885)
Aunt Diana Ch. 5 pp. 462–4
Answers to Correspondents (Music heading) p. 464
   A French Lover of G.O.P. (general), Muriel (voice, health), Aufwiedersehn (composition), Grateful Candienne (performance etiquette), Una (piano, music education)

Number 278 (25 April 1885)
New Music p. 467
Aunt Diana Ch. 6 pp. 476–9

Number 279 (2 May 1885)
For Old Sake's Sake (music score) (Lady William Lennox, Words Helen Marion Burnside) pp. 484–6
Aunt Diana Ch. 7* pp. 489–91
Answers to Correspondents (Music heading) pp. 494–6
   White Geranium (voice, health), A King's Daughter (violin, music and Christianity), B.B.P. (music education)

Number 280 (9 May 1885)
For Listeners at Instrumental Concerts II. Wind and Percussion Instruments pp. 499–502
Aunt Diana Ch. 8* pp. 509–11
Answers to Correspondents (Music heading) pp. 511–12
   Jeanie Mac L. (practising society), Anxious to Learn (general)

Number 281 (16 May 1885)
Aunt Diana Ch. 9 pp. 513–15
Women as Hymn Writers (The Rev. T. B. Willson) pp. 522–3

Number 282 (23 May 1885)
The Harp of Life (poem) (The Rev. Samuel K. Cowan) p. 531
Aunt Diana Ch. 10 pp. 536–9
Answers to Correspondents (Music heading) pp. 543–4
   Jemima (harp), Isodora (piano), Flossie (piano, music history and appreciation), W.F.C. (banjo), Maria B. (practising society)

Number 283 (30 May 1885)
Aunt Diana Ch. 11* pp. 545–7
On Taste in the Choice of Songs Second Letter pp. 548–50
Answers to Correspondents (Music heading) p. 559
   Emily Dodwell (violoncello), Interested Reader (France) (general), Julia (music education), Elsie (music teaching), Violin (violin), Lottie (music and Christianity)

Number 284 (6 June 1885)
Varieties (Playing the Piano by Machinery; Musical Talent – *Mozart*) pp. 562–3
Blanche Elmslie's Programme (Lady William Lennox) Chs 1, 2 pp. 564–5
   To support her mother and herself after her father's sudden death, Blanche Elmslie, a fair violinist, gives lessons and prepares for a recital. A French professor of music mentors Blanche gratuitously, and the debut is a tremendous success, assuring her future as a professional musician.
Merrie England: 'Here's to the Maiden of Bashful Fifteen' (music score) (C. A. Macirone) pp. 566–8
Aunt Diana Ch. 12 pp. 572–5
New Music pp. 575–6
Answers to Correspondents p. 576
   Pickle (piano), Elfie (voice, health)

Number 285 (13 June 1885)
Aunt Diana Ch. 13 pp. 584–7
Blanche Elmslie's Programme Ch. 2 pp. 591–2

Number 286 (20 June 1885)
Aunt Diana Ch. 14 pp. 593–5
Blanche Elmslie's Programme Ch. 3 pp. 596–7

106 *Catalogue of musical content*

Number 287 (27 June 1885)
Blanche Elmslie's Programme Ch. 4 pp. 611–13
  Illustration 'As a token of his good wishes for her success' shows Blanche admiring a gift from her mentor before her recital p. 613

Number 288 (4 July 1885)
Pianoforte Fronts: And How to Decorate Them (Fred Miller) pp. 628–9
Aunt Diana Ch. 15 pp. 629–31
On Taste in the Choice of Songs Third Letter pp. 634–5

Number 289 (11 July 1885)
Aunt Diana Ch. 16 pp. 641–3
My Love Is Dead (music score) (Mary Carmichael, Words P. B. Marston) pp. 644–7
Varieties (An Old Air; From the Temple at Jerusalem) p. 652
New Music pp. 654–5
Answers to Correspondents (Music heading) pp. 655–6
  Tib or Lib (piano), Adela (general), Gertrude C. (piano, pronunciation), Constance (voice), Fedora (general), Millicent (harp, instrument maintenance), Ivanhoe (terms), Eta (repertoire, theory), Marigold (organ), May Cavendish (music history and appreciation)

Number 290 (18 July 1885)
Aunt Diana Ch. 17 pp. 666–8
Varieties (A Hint for Singers – *Mrs Edmond Wodehouse*) p. 668

Number 291 (25 July 1885)
New Music p. 679
The Jubilee Singers at Grosvenor House (Anne Beale) pp. 686–7
  Review of the Fisk University Jubilee Singers' tour of Europe and the choir's concert in Grosvenor House and performance on behalf of the Princess Louise Home, a favourite *TGOP* charity.
Answers to Correspondents (Music heading) pp. 687–8
  Amateur (general), Musical Student (practising, nuisance, music education), S. C. (piano), Literary and Scientific (military bands), Would-Be-Musician (music copying)

Number 292 (1 August 1885)
Aunt Diana Ch. 18 pp. 694–6
On Taste in the Choice of Songs Fourth Letter pp. 696, 698–9
The Harvest Moon (illustration) p. 697
  A woman plays the piano as moonlight streams through the window into the room

Number 293 (8 August 1885)
Aunt Diana Ch. 19 pp. 705–7
Old Songs (music score) (Suchet Champion, Words Anne Beale) pp. 708–9

Number 294 (15 August 1885)
Varieties (The Music of Rossini – *Gustave Chouquet*; A Violin-Playing Monarch) p. 727
Aunt Diana Ch. 20 pp. 730–2
New Music pp. 732–3
Answers to Correspondents (Music heading) pp. 735–6
  Little Nell (applied music), Frank's Nellie (general), Pointz (music education), Forget-Me-Not (music education), Florida (general)

Number 295 (22 August 1885)
Aunt Diana Ch. 21 pp. 738–9
Answers to Correspondents pp. 751–2
    Nooch (organ, piano), Evelyn (terms, music history and appreciation), Theodora (music education), Lily Meville (applied music)

Number 296 (29 August 1885)
Answers to Correspondents pp. 767–8
    Lady Constance (violin, practising, nuisance)

Number 297 (5 September 1885)
The Belle of Birchwoods; or, The Uses of Adversity (Sarson C. J. Ingham) Ch. 1 pp. 769–71
    Ella Stennett's husband, John, thinks his new bride, who plays the piano, has a position to maintain as a married woman, so he is disappointed that she is not willing to outplay her guests. Ella, however, has a different view: 'The music itself ought to be first, and then all the professors of it will fall into their places naturally.' (p. 798)
Varieties (Black and White; A Musical Surname) p. 772
Aunt Diana Ch. 22* pp. 776–9
Answers to Correspondents pp. 783–4
    A Wild Daisy (practising society)

Number 298 (12 September 1885)
Aunt Diana Ch. 23 pp. 786–7
Minuet and Trio: From a Suite for Orchestra (music score) (Myles B. Foster) pp. 788–90
New Music pp. 796–7
    Illustration, 'A Duet' p. 796
The Belle of Birchwoods Ch. 2* pp. 798–9
Answers to Correspondents p. 800
    A Madressee (general), Fidelis (pronunciation)

Number 299 (19 September 1885)
Music and Scripture (E. B. Leach) pp. 808, 810–11
    Music as an accomplishment tends to overshadow 'its standing as a moral and spiritual power' (p. 808).
The Belle of Birchwoods Ch. 3 pp. 811–12
Answers to Correspondents (Music heading) pp. 815–16
    An Irish Girl (Irish harp), Amateur (general), Ruby (music education), Unknown to Fame Yet (voice, health), An Irish Girl (general), Brunette (piano), Eva Lenton (repertoire)

Number 300 (26 September 1885)
Aunt Diana Ch. 24* pp. 817–19
Dress: In Season and in Reason (A Lady Dressmaker) pp. 824–6
    Illustration 'Spotted velvet and satin bodice and zouave jacket bodice' shows young women waiting near double doors engraved 'Musik Zimmer' p. 825
The Belle of Birchwoods Ch. 4 pp. 828–30
Answers to Correspondents (Music heading) pp. 831–2
    Bessie (composition), Admirer of Beethoven (piano, practising, nuisance), Eva (performance nerves)

'Snowdrifts'
Extra Christmas Number for Volume 6 (1884)

The Organist's Niece (M. M. Pollard) pp. 3–12

> Frank Rendell, a bank clerk new to the city, meets Beatrice Vaughan through a mutual friend but lets his cousin guide him into a glamorous social life that threatens his relationship with her. Beatrice is a musician who takes over her uncle, Mr Halle's, organist duties when he falls ill.

Yuletide (poem) p. 16

Our Ain Fireside (Medicus) pp. 19–20

> Singing is excellent exercise for the voice and gives strength and vigour to the lungs. But fireside songs should be quiet in character – 'the parlour is not a concert-room. Give us melody, pathos, and feeling, but do not scream.' (p. 20)

Old Christmas Carols pp. 21–3

> Illustrations 'Carols in the olden time – in the "parlour" ' p. 21; 'Carols in the olden time – in the street' p. 23

The Angels of the Bells: A Cantatina for Two Sopranos and a Contralto (music score) (Myles B. Foster, Words Helen Marion Burnside) pp. 24–31

Our Chief Composers (illustration) plate facing p. 32

> Illustrations of Mrs Tom Taylor, John Thomas, Sir George Macfarren, Myles B. Foster, Clara Macirone, Sir Julius Benedict and Sir John Stainer

An Angel Unawares (Mrs G. Linnaeus Banks) pp. 32, 34–7

> Augusta Evering misses brother Ernest and Cousin Wilfred 'dolefully' when they are away at Cambridge 'to make men of them, and not milksops; they had been too long within sound of the harpsichord and spinning wheel' (p. 35). She plays over Wilfred's favourite airs and sings his favourite songs in his absence.

Twilight Visions (poem) (Sarah Doudney) p. 40

'Acquired Abroad': A Christmas Story (Louisa Emily Dobree) pp. 56–8

> To qualify for a morning governess position to support her blind mother and herself, Ellice Creswell is tempted to claim that her French has been acquired abroad, when in fact she has only visited Paris. After seeking her mother's counsel, Ellice declines the position and then takes solace on the organ bench of her village church. The rector, in need of an organist, hears Ellice playing and, after learning of her troubles, offers her the position.

> Illustration 'My child, what is the matter?' shows Ellice at the organ p. 57

'Sheets of Daisies'
Extra Summer Part for Volume 6 (1885)

On the Cromer Cliffs (Constance Evelyn) pp. 3–21

> Madge Bryant finds her work as chief lady music teacher drudgery and wants to return to the younger pupils. 'It's bad enough to teach the subjects that one hates, but it's worse to have to count an everlasting 1, 2, 3, 4, to some lovely little bit of Mozart or Haydn, and then in the end to hear it murdered all the way!' she complains to her sister Mimi (pp. 3–4).

> Illustrations, 'The music Louie was making' p. 10; 'I think he must have been listening to the music' p. 11

The Art of Packing (Dora Hope) pp. 22–3

> Advice to pack all music and books in the bottom of the trunk suggests that musical women travel with their music.

The Brook and the Wave (music score) (Cécile S. Hartog, Words Longfellow) pp. 27–9

Volume 7 (3 October 1885–25 September 1886)

Number 301 (3 October 1885)
Only a Girl-Wife (Ruth Lamb) Ch. 1 pp. 11–13
  After-dinner music at the Crawford's house contrasts two types of singers. Grace Steyne, the rector's daughter, is far behind the 'girl-wife' hostess Ida in brilliancy and style but has a fine voice that she uses 'with true musical taste', not attempting anything beyond her ability. Grace's music making is a labour of love – she plays the organ at church and trains the village choir, 'not a very easy task when scarcely any of the members knew their notes so as to read the music' (p. 366).
  Illustration 'I was almost as deep in my book as you were in your paper' shows Dr Fereday and wife Grace at the breakfast table with a piano in the background p. 12

Number 302 (10 October 1885)
Only a Girl-Wife Ch. 2 pp. 22–3
Varieties (The History of the Piano) p. 30
Answers to Correspondents pp. 30–1
  Nightingale (general)

Number 303 (17 October 1885)
Only a Girl-Wife Ch. 3 pp. 33–5
'Rise Up, My Love!' (music score) (The Countess of Munster, Words from 'The Song of Solomon') pp. 36–7
Answers to Correspondents (Music heading) pp. 47–8
  Lieder ohne Worte (music education), Bessie (composition), A Grateful Reader (music education), A Lover of the G.O.P. (lesson etiquette), Soldier's Daughter (general), Sirius (repertoire), An Anxious One (voice), Green Leaves (repertoire), Hyacinth (piano, instrument maintenance), Fugue (general), Eldonia (music history and appreciation)

Number 304 (24 October 1885)
Answers to Correspondents pp. 63–4
  Sally Brass (general)

Number 305 (31 October 1885)
Only a Girl-Wife Ch. 4 pp. 66–7
New Music p. 71
Answers to Correspondents (Music heading) pp. 79–80
  An Anxious Reader (applied music, pronunciation), A Middle-Aged One (general), H. G. (practising society), Vera Hugo (applied music), Rita (violin), Nil Desperandum (general), O.T.M.U.L. (general), Mountain Violet (applied music), Green Hat (Austria) (zither), Fanny E. (voice)

Number 306 (7 November 1885)
Only a Girl-Wife Ch. 5 pp. 81–3
Three Social Evenings (Anne Beale) pp. 86–7
  During one of three social gatherings of young women members of the Y.W.C.A., some 50 members formed a choir for a 'Service of Song' to sing hymns for the 200 girls in the audience.
Varieties (Perfect Singing) p. 87
Answers to Correspondents (Music heading) pp. 95–6
  F.E.R.F. (music education), Hermione (music education)

110   *Catalogue of musical content*

Number 307 (14 November 1885)
Only a Girl-Wife Ch. 6 pp. 102–4

Number 308 (21 November 1885)
Only a Girl-Wife Ch. 7 pp. 113–15
Varieties (Starting Too High) p. 115
Stay, Fleeting Hour (music score) (Franz Abt, Words Edward Oxenford) pp. 116–18

Number 309 (28 November 1885)
Only a Girl-Wife Ch. 8 pp. 142–3
Answers to Correspondents p. 144
    Pussy (voice, nuisance)

Number 310 (5 December 1885)
Varieties (A Daughter's Criticism) p. 147
Only a Girl-Wife Ch. 9 p. 153

Number 311 (12 December 1885)
Only a Girl-Wife Ch. 10 pp. 169–71
An Impromptu (illustration) (R. Catterson Smith) plate facing p. 171
    A young woman is playing the violin.
New Music p. 171
Answers to Correspondents (Music heading) pp. 174–5
    Jenny (practising society), Reta (violin, music as accomplishment)

Number 312 (19 December 1885)
See, the Dawn from Heaven Is Breaking! A Christmas Carol (music score) (W. C. Cusins, Words Thomas Moore) pp. 180–3
Only a Girl-Wife Ch. 11 pp. 188–90

Number 313 (26 December 1885)
Courtleroy (Anne Beale) Ch. 1 pp. 193–5
    After Mimica Marmont foils her languid uncle Reginald Le Roy's suicide attempt, she asks Barbra (Barbara), the curate's daughter, to sing sacred music to him. Barbara, a mezzo-soprano, chooses Handel, followed by Mozart's 'Voi che sapete', a favourite of Mr Leroy.

Number 314 (2 January 1886)
Courtleroy Ch. 2 pp. 210–11
Only a Girl-Wife Ch. 12 pp. 221–3
Answers to Correspondents (Music heading) pp. 223–4
    Gwenneth Leighton (terms), Bluebell (harmonium, instrument maintenance), Jeannie W. (voice), Piano Soloist (piano, instrument maintenance), Rita (voice), One Who Is Striving Hard to Learn (general), Norman-Neruda (music education), E.T.E. (general), Patience (voice), A Primrose (New Zealand) (voice)

Number 315 (9 January 1886)
Only a Girl-Wife Ch. 13 pp. 225–7
Courtleroy Ch. 3 pp. 230–1
New Music pp. 236–7
Answers to Correspondents (Music heading) pp. 239–40
    The Editor's Friend (terms, applied music), Sarah J. F. (theory), Purslow (music education)

Catalogue of musical content   111

Number 316 (16 January 1886)
A Doubting Heart (poem) (Clara Thwaites) p. 241–2
Only a Girl-Wife Ch. 14 pp. 242–3
Afternoon in February (music score) (E. Silas, Words Longfellow) pp. 244–6
Courtleroy Ch. 4 pp. 253–4
Answers to Correspondents (Music heading) pp. 255–6
    Ein Musikschulerine (music education), Edelgitha (terms), Pearla (repertoire), A.B.J. (theory), Jeanette Brown (piano), Olive Fifteen and Touchstone (music history and appreciation, piano)

Number 317 (23 January 1886)
Courtleroy Chs 5, 6 pp. 257–60
Varieties (Murdering Music) p. 263
Answers to Correspondents pp. 270–1
    Fire Gone Out (general)

Number 318 (30 January 1886)
Only a Girl-Wife Ch. 15 pp. 273–5

Number 319 (6 February 1886)
Courtleroy Chs 7, 8 p. 289–91
A Perilous Road Ch. 1 pp. 298–9
    For 17-year-old Marietta Stefani in a small Tuscan village, the opportunity to study singing in Florence offers a means to reverse her struggling family's financial setback. But despite warnings, Marietta lets her head be turned by her new life. Realizing her folly, Marietta stops singing in public but shares her gift of song with family, friends and charities and thanks God that she turned back from the perilous road on which she had started.
Only a Girl-Wife Ch. 16 pp. 301–3
Answers to Correspondents (Music heading) p. 303
    Nanny and Nancy (lesson etiquette), Annie Lee (practising society), Gwenllian (repertoire), Pansy, Leonie (music education), Well-Wisher (terms), Way (general), Brenda (musical pitch), Tommy D. (violin), Eta (repertoire), An Amateur Organist (general), Mina (general)

Number 320 (13 February 1886)
A Perilous Road Ch. 2 pp. 306–7
Only a Girl-Wife Ch. 17 pp. 308–10
Courtleroy Ch. 9 pp. 316–17
Answers to Correspondents (Music heading) pp. 318–20
    Dot (practising society), Edina (general), Bella (music history and appreciation), A Would-Be Composer (music history and appreciation), Denna (pronunciation, music history and appreciation), A Curious One (pronunciation), Joan (violin), Pink Rosebud (applied music), Pinkie (ocarina instrument), W.B.S. (general), Nella (terms), A Daughter of Israel (general), Expectation (music education), Phibby (terms), Mary Deane (dulcimer)

Number 321 (20 February 1886)
A Little Mazourka: In Memory of Chopin (Born March 1, 1809) (music score) (Myles B. Foster) pp. 324–5
A Perilous Road Ch. 3 pp. 326–7
Courtleroy Ch. 10 pp. 333–4
The Music for the Month pp. 334–5

112 Catalogue of musical content

Number 322 (27 February 1886)
A Perilous Road Ch. 4 pp. 339, 341
Dress: In Season and in Reason (A Lady Dressmaker) pp. 337–9, 340
  Illustration 'Indoor Costume' shows a young woman playing a grand piano while four other young women, two holding sheet music, gather nearby p. 340
Only a Girl-Wife Ch. 18 pp. 342–3
Courtleroy Ch. 11 pp. 350–1

Number 323 (6 March 1886)
Courtleroy Chs 12, 13 pp. 353–6
Varieties (Women in Music – *Haweis*; Diligent Practising) p. 356
A Widow Bird Sate Mourning (music score) (Maude Valérie White, Words Shelley) pp. 357–9
Only a Girl-Wife Ch. 19* pp. 366–8

Number 324 (13 March 1886)
Only a Girl-Wife Ch. 20* pp. 369–71
  Illustration 'There was more singing' p. 369
Courtleroy Ch. 14 pp. 377–9
Answers to Correspondents (Music heading) pp. 383–4
  Dupont, J.M.S. (general), Lothian Lass (composition), S.D.F. (general), Excelsior (voice, health), A Would-Be Singer (voice), E. W. (piano)

Number 325 (20 March 1886)
Only a Girl-Wife Ch. 21 pp. 385–7
Varieties (Musical Instruments) p. 391
Courtleroy Ch. 15 pp. 397–8

Number 326 (27 March 1886)
Courtleroy Chs 16, 17 pp. 401–4
The Music for the Month pp. 413–14
Answers to Correspondents (Music heading) pp. 415–16
  Crabstick (piano), Pris (music history and appreciation), Ivy Murray (practising society), Macduff (practising society), Martha (general), R.L.I.S. (music education), Jenny Lind (voice), Joan of Arc (organ), M. B. (copyright), A. D. (voice)

Number 327 (3 April 1886)
Only a Girl-Wife Ch. 22 pp. 418–19
Berceuse (music score) (Cécile S. Hartog) pp. 420–2
Courtleroy Chs 18, 19 pp. 426–8

Number 328 (10 April 1886)
Only a Girl-Wife Ch. 23 pp. 436–8
Stay-at-Home Girls: Our Y.W.C.A. Branch (Dora Hope) pp. 438–40
  Mrs Mayhew suggests that her two stay-at-home daughters start a singing class at a newly opened Y.W.C.A.
Courtleroy Ch. 20 pp. 446–7

Number 329 (17 April 1886)
Courtleroy Chs 21, 22 pp. 449–52

Number 330 (24 April 1886)
Courtleroy Ch. 23 pp. 466–7
Varieties (Music in Earnest) p. 467

The Music for the Month p. 471
Only a Girl-Wife Ch. 24 pp. 478–80
Answers to Correspondents p. 480
  Noira (general)

Number 331 (1 May 1886)
Courleroy Ch. 24 pp. 486–7
Only a Girl-Wife Ch. 25 pp. 488–91
Varieties (Mozart as a Musical Prodigy – *Hullah*) p. 494
Answers to Correspondents (Music heading) pp. 495–6
  A.L.A.M. (general), Ruby H., Apitum (general), Violet H. (general), Bad Linnet (metronome)

Number 332 (8 May 1886)
Courtleroy Ch. 25 pp. 502–3
O Yes! O Yes! O Yes! Part-Song for Mixed Voices (music score) (C. A. Macirone, Words from 'Roxburghe Ballads', 1500) pp. 504–8
Answers to Correspondents p. 512
  A Daughter of Israel (general)

Number 333 (15 May 1886)
Courtleroy Ch. 26 pp. 526–7
Varieties (A Proud Musician) p. 527

Number 334 (22 May 1886)
Courtleroy Chs 27, 28 pp. 530–33
The Music for the Month pp. 540–1

Number 335 (29 May 1886)
Wood Engraving as an Employment for Girls (Richard Taylor) Part 3 pp. 548–50
  Illustration 'An Example of Modern Engraving' shows a clarinetist and a flutist, both male p. 549
Dress: In Season and in Reason (A Lady Dressmaker) pp. 552–4
  Illustration 'Gown with flounces of woolen lace, and gown of plain beige' shows two women at a piano, one with sheet music in hand p. 552
Courtleroy Ch. 29 pp. 555–6

Number 336 (5 June 1886)
Amateur Choirs; Their Organisation and Training (An Organist) pp. 563–5
Courtleroy Chs 30, 31* pp. 572–4
Answers to Correspondents pp. 575–6
  A.K.L. (repertoire), Braneless (general)

Number 337 (12 June 1886)
Courtleroy (Ann Beale) Ch. 32 pp. 582–3
Answers to Correspondents pp. 591–2
  The Sparrows and Robin (music history and appreciation)

Number 338 (19 June 1886)
A Letter on Musical Rhythm (Oliveria Prescott) pp. 601–2
  Writing to My Dear Pupil, Prescott explains rhythm at its most basic as 'a balance of sounds', then moves in steps up 'the rhythmic ladder' (p. 601).
Courtleroy Chs 33, 34 pp. 603–6

114 *Catalogue of musical content*

Answers to Correspondents (Music heading) pp. 607–8
   Pianist (repertoire), Kathleen O'Moore (voice, practising), Excitable Jack (voice), Carnation (voice), Molly (terms), Havelock (voice), 'Guyella' (piano), Jeanie Scrubschall (general), Somerset (general), Violet (violin), Kathie L. C. (voice), A Doctor's Daughter (violin)

Number 339 (26 June 1886)
Notices of New Music pp. 612–13
'My Little Knight' (music score) (Elizabeth Philp, Words Astley Baldwin) pp. 614–15
Courtleroy Ch. 35 pp. 619–21

Number 340 (3 July 1886)
Courtleroy Ch. 36 pp. 630–2
Answers to Correspondents (Music heading) pp. 639–40
   Violet (general), Lady Floss (zither), Henrietta (music history and appreciation)

Number 341 (10 July 1886)
Courtleroy Chs 37, 38* pp. 641–4
Mona Spinning (music score) (Mary Carmichael, Words Alice Cary) pp. 645–7

Number 342 (17 July 1886)
Courtleroy Ch. 39 pp. 659–60
How to Choose a Pianoforte, and Keep It in Order First Letter pp. 664–7
   Illustration 'Sixty Years Ago' shows young woman sitting at a keyboard p. 665
Answers to Correspondents (Music heading) pp. 670–2
   Mary K. (piano, practising), Anxious One (voice), Punch and Judy (violin), Daisy (performance etiquette), Only Daughter (harp piano), L'Extra (voice, health), Clare (repertoire), A New Zealand Girl (general)

Number 343 (24 July 1886)
Notices of New Music pp. 677–8
Courtleroy Ch. 40 pp. 683–4
Answers to Correspondents (Music heading) pp. 687–8
   Katie Green (tonic sol-fa), An Ugly Duckling (terms, music history and appreciation), Il Penseroso (repertoire), Forget-Me-Not (general), Sweet (?) Seventeen (voice)

Number 344 (31 July 1886)
Courtleroy Ch. 41 pp. 694–5

Number 345 (7 August 1886)
Courtleroy Chs 42, 43 pp. 706–8
How to Choose a Pianoforte, and Keep It in Order Second Letter pp. 714–16
Answers to Correspondents (Music heading) pp. 719–20
   Singer (voice), Perplexity (general), Lily Wilson (harmonium), Mother Bunch (theory), Violet and Elflede (voice, health), A Constant Reader (general), Two Business Girls (general)

Number 346 (14 August 1886)
Courtleroy Ch. 44 pp. 721–3
Signs and Tokens (poem) (Frances Hurrell) p. 728
Evening (music score) (Gordon Saunders) pp. 732–5

Number 347 (21 August 1886)
Courtleroy Ch. 45 pp. 746–8
Answers to Correspondents (Music heading) pp. 751–2

Ecclesia (general), Autumnal Leaves (piano), White Violet (composition), Muriel Hen (piano, repertoire, practising), Queen Bess (voice)

Number 348 (28 August 1886)
Courtleroy Chs 46, 47 pp. 754–6
Dress: In Season and in Reason (A Lady Dressmaker) pp. 760–2
    Illustration 'In a garden under the pines' shows a woman playing a piano located under a large parasol p. 761

Number 349 (4 September 1886)
Between School and Marriage pp. 769–70
    Rather than dawdling time away irresponsibly, girls should use it constructively. The valuable hours between ten and one o'clock 'should be occupied with study, music (if you really have a taste for it), or the learning of some useful art by which you could earn your living if required to do so' (p. 770).
Courtleroy Ch. 48 pp. 771–2
How to Choose a Pianoforte and Keep It in Order Third Letter pp. 772–5
    Illustration 'A Gossip' shows two young women at a piano p. 773

Number 350 (11 September 1886)
Courtleroy Chs 49, 50 pp. 785–8
The Band of Hope (Stay-at-Home Girls) (Dora Hope) pp. 789–90
    A weekly meeting for children to teach them abstinence from alcohol always includes a good deal of singing and recitations and the giving of prizes.

Number 351 (18 September 1886)
Courtleroy Chs 51, 52 pp. 801–3
How to Choose a Pianoforte, and Keep It in Order Fourth Letter pp. 811–13

Snow-Drops
Extra Christmas Part for Volume 7 (1885)
A Christmas Rose: Cantatina for Girls' Voices (music score) (Myles B. Foster, Words Clara Thwaites) pp. 17–22
A Musical Romance (Beatrice Harraden) p. 23
    As Edward, a dying elderly cellist, reminisces about love lost, that love, Marie, comes to visit. Each takes the blame for letting the other go: he for focusing too much on fame and music, she for cruel selfishness. A final kiss, and Edward dies in Marie's arms.
The Zither Player (poem) (Sydney Grey) p. 24
Illustration 'The Zither Player' (Charlotte Hamfel) p. 25
The 'Toy Symphony': A Recollected Tale (Jetty Vogel) pp. 38–9
    Fräulein Schmidt, a German music teacher, invites neighbors to her home on Christmas Eve and, to break the ice, has each play an instrument as she performs Haydn's 'Toy Symphony' on the piano.
Christmas Thoughts (poem) (Sarah Doudney) p. 40
Martin Spencer's Luck: A Story of Mendelssohn's Christmas Music pp. 42–3
    When physician Martin Spencer suffers a serious spinal injury after being thrown from his horse, his resolute and cheerful fortitude effects a complete cure. A cure he devises for his invalid wife brings him recognition and a valuable appointment at a London hospital. Such is the 'luck' of the tale that began with the unnamed aunt narrator playing Mendelssohn's 'Christmas Music' on the piano.
Music at Home (Alexandra Thompson) pp. 50–1

116 Catalogue of musical content

After discussing music's role in domestic harmony, the author focuses on the rudiments of a solid music education, with suggestions on how to practice, what to play, performance etiquette and performance nerves.

The 'Girl's Own' Musical Calendar for 1886 pp. 62–4
Month-by-month list of composers' birthdates.

Lily Leaves
Extra Summer Number for Volume 7 (1886)

'Consider the Lilies' (poem) (Julia) p. 45

Margaret Dane; or, An English Girl in a German Home (Florence Wilson) pp. 49–55
As companion to two German girls, Margaret Dane and her charges, whose voices blend harmoniously in duets, attend twice-weekly concerts, which are 'quite equal to good music lessons' (p. 51).

Gathering Cowslips: Retrospect (music score) (Mrs Tom Taylor) pp. 57–9

Harvest Hymn (poem) (The Rev. Canon Fleming) p. 60

Varieties (A Note for Vocalists) p. 64

Volume 8 (2 October 1886–24 September 1887)

Number 353 (2 October 1886)
The Amateur Church Organist (The Hon. Victoria Grosvenor) pp. 4–5
   Urges readers with musical talent and leisure to qualify themselves as amateur organists for churches in agricultural and suburban parishes unable to pay a professional organist.
Varieties (The Moonlight Sonata) p. 7
Romance: For Violin and Pianoforte (music score) (Professor Sir G. A. Macfarren) pp. 12–14

Number 354 (9 October 1886)
Girls' Friendships Ch. 1 pp. 24–6
   Music offers an example of true friendship when Alice, who does not like music, enjoys a concert because of the keen interest with which friend Maud listens to every note. Study of a common interest such as music, not for the sake merely of doing something but rather for the earnest use to which it will be put, characterizes a high level of friendship.

Number 355 (16 October 1886)
Notices of New Music p. 42
Varieties (Twenty-Four Notes in One Bow) p. 47

Number 356 (23 October 1886)
Varieties (Beethoven in Germany) p. 61

Number 357 (30 October 1886)
Historical Sketches of Musical Forms (Myles B. Foster) Sketch 1 The Oratorio and Passion Music (Sacred Drama) pp. 70–1
Answers to Correspondents pp. 79–80
   A.G.O.E. (memory work)

Number 358 (6 November 1886)
Girls' Friendships Ch. 2 pp. 83–4
Answers to Correspondents pp. 95–6
   Naughty One (practising etiquette), Florence (music as accomplishment)

Number 359 (13 November 1886)
Answers to Correspondents (Music heading) pp. 111–12
   Annie James (voice, performance etiquette), Gertrude May (general), A. Andrews (practising society), Fiddlestring (composition), Sister Elizabeth (theory), Narcissus (music education), Snowdrop, No. 100 (voice), Tyza Worrall (performance etiquette)

Number 360 (20 November 1886)
Notices of New Music pp. 116–17
Varieties (The Composer and the Sea-Captain) pp. 119–20
The Birds: Duet (music score) (C. A. Macirone, Words J. T. Coleridge) pp. 122–5
Answers to Correspondents (Music heading) p. 128
   M.L.P. (practising society), Old Man's Darling (general), Courtleroy (tonic sol-fa), Romola (music history and appreciation), A Greek Girl (repertoire)

Number 361 (27 November 1886)
Historical Sketches of Musical Forms Sketch 2 Opera (Secular Musical Drama) pp. 141–3
Answers to Correspondents p. 143
   Alberta Roxley (general), Jack (applied music)

118   *Catalogue of musical content*

Number 362 (4 December 1886)
The Amateur Choir Teacher (The Hon. Victoria Grosvenor) pp. 149–50
   Building on a thorough knowledge of music, the choir teacher must show 'untiring patience, which will bear with stupidity, carelessness, want of zeal, deficient ear, bad pronunciation, and all the thousand and one difficulties which beset choirs' (p. 149).
Answers to Correspondents pp. 159–60
   Curious (music history and appreciation, repertoire)

Number 363 (11 December 1886)
Answers to Correspondents (Music heading) pp. 175–6
   Dinah (banjo, choosing instrument), Rob Roy (organ, music history and appreciation), Mary Bird (flute, clarionette, music history and appreciation)

Number 364 (18 December 1886)
A Song for the Old Year (poem) (M. M. Pollard) p. 184

Number 365 (25 December 1886)
Notices of New Music p. 203
Answers to Correspondents pp. 207–8
   Hope (pronunciation), Inquisitive Girl (music history and appreciation)

Number 366 (1 January 1887)
Girls' Friendships Ch. 3 pp. 222–3
The Inheritance of a Good Name (Louisa Menzies) Ch. 1 pp. 236–8
   Mark Fenner, son of a deceased military officer, accepts a job at his mother's cousin Miles Ecclin's London publishing firm. Ecclin, who had lost both his wife and child years ago, invites Mark's mother and sister Eveline to move into his house, where Mark already is his guest. Eveline is a musician and fills Ecclin's house with laughter and song once again.

Number 367 (8 January 1887)
Answers to Correspondents pp. 239–40
   Young Inquirer (general), Three Ignorant Schoolgirls (general)

Number 368 (15 January 1887)
Berceuse (music score) (J. W. Hinton) pp. 244–5
The Inheritance of a Good Name Ch. 2 pp. 249–50
Answers to Correspondents p. 256
   Dotty (pronunciation), Snowdrop and Ivyleaf (general)

Number 369 (22 January 1887)
Hints on Practising Singing and Preserving the Voice (An Experienced Teacher) pp. 261–2
The Inheritance of a Good Name Ch. 3 pp. 266–8

Number 370 (29 January 1887)
The Inheritance of a Good Name Ch. 4* pp. 275–7
   Illustration 'He started back, dazzled' shows Mark Fenner's surprise and joy when he recognizes his mother and his sister Eveline, who is playing *Lieder ohne Worte* on the piano in Ecclin's home. p. 277
Historical Sketches of Musical Forms Sketch 3 Cantatas and Church Music pp. 278–9

Number 371 (5 February 1887)
The Blossom (music score) (Mary Carmichael, Words William Blake) pp. 292–4
Girls' Friendships Ch. 4 pp. 302–3

Answers to Correspondents (Music heading) p. 304
  G. C. (general), A Berkshire Lass (zither), Marion (music education), Maggie (mandolin), I.F.D. (music copying)

Number 372 (12 February 1887)
Dreaming of Spring (poem) (Jessie M. E. Saxby) p. 312
Varieties (Musical Performers) pp. 318–19
Answers to Correspondents (Music heading) pp. 319–20
  Allegro (music history and appreciation), Claire Elliot (general), An Old Maid of 24 (song repertoire), Brownie M.C.B. (voice)

Number 373 (19 February 1887)
Varieties (How to Play at Sight – *Ernst Pauer*) p. 324
How to Take Care of a Violin (C.H.P.) pp. 332–3
Answers to Correspondents pp. 335–6
  Birne (voice, practising), A Lady Student of Music (music education, lesson etiquette)

Number 374 (26 February 1887)
Historical Sketches of Musical Forms Sketch 4 Madrigals and Secular Part Music pp. 342–3
Varieties (Music Run Mad) p. 343
New Music pp. 349–50
Answers to Correspondents pp. 351–2
  Heliotrope (New Zealand) (voice)

Number 375 (5 March 1887)
Answers to Correspondents (Music heading) pp. 367–8
  Five Years Subscriber (health, piano), Gingerbottle (music history and appreciation)

Number 376 (12 March 1887)
Varieties (A Lesson in Music) p. 375
Touching the Pianoforte (Oliveria L. Prescott) pp. 377–8
  Told from the pianoforte's point of view, 'for truly it does repeat what all we say to it' through how we touch its keys (p. 378).
Love's Summer Dream (music score) (Lady William Lennox, Words G. W. Gilbart Smith) pp. 380–2

Number 377 (19 March 1887)
Varieties (Good Reasons for Learning Singing) p. 398
Answers to Correspondents pp. 399–400
  K.M.W. (voice, health), Mona (song repertoire), Sarnia (music teaching, choral singing)

Number 379 (2 April 1887)
Rondino in G: For Pianoforte (music score) (C. A. Macirone) pp. 428–30

Number 381 (16 April 1887)
In the Days of Mozart: The Story of a Young Musician (Lily Watson) Ch. 1 pp. 449–52
  In 1761, 10-year-old Rudolph and his 11-year-old sister, Elsa, children of a widowed officer, are left with their grandfather in Salzburg. Their music master, Leopold Mozart, encourages Rudolph's playing, but not Elsa's. Like Mozart's children, who are characters in the story, the young girls play a supportive role to their more talented brothers.
Varieties (Haydn in London) p. 454
A Chorus for May (poem) (M. M. Pollard) p. 457
Notices of New Music pp. 460–1
  Illustration of female guitarist p. 460

120 *Catalogue of musical content*

Answers to Correspondents (Music heading) pp. 463–4
    Old Reader (music education), Lassie (voice), Maude (music history and appreciation), One of Your Girls (voice, health), White Heather (voice, health), T.O.A.O. (harmonium), Scotia (harmonium)

Number 382 (23 April 1887)
Girls as Pianoforte Tuners: A New Remunerative Employment pp. 465–6
    Illustration 'Beginning work in earnest' p. 465
Historical Sketches of Musical Forms Sketch 5 Folk Songs pp. 466–8
In the Days of Mozart Ch. 2 pp. 476–7

Number 383 (30 April 1887)
In the Days of Mozart Ch. 3 pp. 482–3

Number 384 (7 May 1887)
In the Days of Mozart Ch. 4 pp. 498–9
Answers to Correspondents (Music heading) pp. 511–12
    Minerva (voice, performance nerves, health), Muriel (voice), Mabel, Florence (music history and appreciation), Euterpe, Pollie Juggar (memory work), Melusina (zither), Viola (voice), Laura (theory), 'Modest Violet' (repertoire)

Number 385 (14 May 1887)
On Learning to Sing (Madame Lemmens-Sherrington) pp. 514–15
In the Days of Mozart Ch. 5 pp. 516–17

Number 386 (21 May 1887)
In the Days of Mozart Ch. 6 pp. 534–5
Song: 'While Cuckoos Are Calling' (poem) (Clara Thwaites) p. 536
The Day of Rest (music score) (Cotsford Dick) pp. 540–1
Answers to Correspondents (Music heading) p. 544
    Debutante (music pension), Acorn (violin), M. M. and Baby (general), Chorister (music history and appreciation)

Number 387 (28 May 1887)
In the Days of Mozart Ch. 7 pp. 548–50
Notices of New Music p. 551
An Analysis of Beethoven's Sonata in G Minor, Op. 49, No. 1 (Oliveria Prescott) pp. 555–6

Number 388 (4 June 1887)
The Thistle: A Flower Ballad (music score) (C. A. Macirone, Words The Earl Lytton) pp. 565–7
In the Days of Mozart Ch. 8 pp. 574–5

Number 389 (11 June 1887)
In the Days of Mozart Ch. 9 pp. 581–3
    Illustration 'Whenever Leopold Mozart was at home he would encourage and stimulate his protégé' p. 581
Varieties (Faults in Pianoforte Playing – *Ernst Pauer*) p. 591

Number 391 (25 June 1887)
'La Génte Anglaise': A Sketch of Bohemian Life (H. E. Gray) Chs 1, 2* pp. 609–12
    Mariana Ross, a minister's daughter, was given the sobriquet 'la génte Anglaise' while an art student in France. Mariana's Bohemian lifestyle and choice of music – she seats

Catalogue of musical content 121

herself at the piano in her studio and sings a contralto aria from Berlioz's *Faust* – contrasts with her father's Wesleyan ways. As he crosses the hall to invite her to accompany him to church, 'The wild music of his daughter's song strikes on his ear as a profanation of the holy day.' (p. 611)
Illustration 'Will you come with me, my dear?' shows the minister talking with Mariana, who is seated at the piano p. 609
Notices of New Music p. 615
In the Days of Mozart Ch. 10 pp. 618–19
Answers to Correspondents p. 623
 A Pretty Girl (?) (general)

Number 392 (2 July 1887)
'La Génte Anglaise' Chs 3, 4 pp. 625–6
A Summer Song (poem) (J. Huie) p. 632
In the Days of Mozart Ch. 11 pp. 632, 634–5
Varieties (Advice to Musical Students; Haydn's Wife) p. 635
Under the Waves: A Pianoforte Piece (music score) (H.A.J. Campbell) pp. 636–7

Number 393 (9 July 1887)
In the Days of Mozart Ch. 12 pp. 642–4
'La Génte Anglaise' Ch. 5 pp. 648, 650

Number 394 (16 July 1887)
'La Génte Anglaise' Chs 6, 7 pp. 657–9
Notices of New Music p. 666
Varieties (A Singer's Terms) p. 669
In the Days of Mozart Ch. 13 pp. 670–1

Number 395 (23 July 1887)
In the Days of Mozart Ch. 14 pp. 673–6
 Illustration 'How Elsa thrilled with joy and pride' p. 673
Transformed: A New Serial Story Ch. 1 pp. 682–3
 When someone proposes a little music one evening, Frank Warren sings Schubert's 'Erl König', followed by 'Muth' from *Die Winterreise*. 'Courage', Miss Leslie muses. 'Yes – that was what so many of us wanted. And had not he wanted it when he composed that song? Did he not compose it to give himself courage? Else how could it so exactly express itself?' (p. 715)

Number 396 (30 July 1887)
Transformed Ch. 2 pp. 696–700
Varieties (In Praise of Music – *Chappell*) p. 702
Evensong (poem) (J. Huie) p. 702
Answers to Correspondents (Music heading) p. 703
 Madeline (violin, music history and appreciation), Bertha (violin), Elphanta (Cape Colony) (voice, health, practising)

Number 397 (6 August 1887)
Transformed Ch. 3* pp. 714–15
In the Days of Mozart Ch. 15 pp. 717–19
Answers to Correspondents p. 719
 Milkmaid (instrument maintenance, piano keys)
Hail to the Chief! Boat Song (music score) (Mrs Tom Taylor, Words Sir Walter Scott) p. 720

122 *Catalogue of musical content*

Number 398 (13 August 1887)
In the Days of Mozart Ch. 16 pp. 721–4
  Illustration 'Bravo, my young first violin' p. 721
My Work Basket pp. 732–3
  Includes instructions for making a music case and a piano cover.
  Illustrations 'A Music Case' p. 732; 'Piano Cover' p. 733
Varieties (Saving a Violin) p. 735

Number 399 (20 August 1887)
Transformed Ch. 4 pp. 737–8
On Singing (Madame Lemmens-Sherrington) pp. 741–2
In the Days of Mozart Ch. 17 pp. 743–4
Varieties (The Dolls of a Musician; Pianoforte Practising) p. 751

Number 400 (27 August 1887)
Transformed Ch. 5 pp. 767–8
Answers to Correspondents p. 768
  Lady Ethel (repertoire)

Number 401 (3 September 1887)
Transformed Ch. 6 pp. 769–70
Lo! the Herald (music score) (Franz Abt, Words Edward Oxenford) pp. 772–4
In the Days of Mozart Ch. 18 pp. 781–3
Varieties (Notes on the Bagpipes – *Dr Ogilvie*) p. 783
Answers to Correspondents p. 784
  M. H. (violoncello), Veronica (voice)

Number 402 (10 September 1887)
In the Days of Mozart Ch. 19 pp. 795–7

Number 403 (17 September 1887)
Transformed Chs 7, 8, 9 pp. 804–5
On Learning to Sing (Madame Lemmens-Sherrington) p. 811

Number 404 (24 September 1887)
In the Days of Mozart Ch. 20 pp. 824–6

Feathery Flakes
Extra Christmas Part for Volume 8 (1886)
Five Letters (Jetty Vogel) pp. 14–15
  Katherine Wilson sings for her invalid friend Sybil Maurice. Her voice is like herself – 'it had capabilities but stood in great need of training' (p. 14).
Vera; or, A Good Match (R. Mitchell) pp. 17–25
  Vera Couldrey wants to earn her living as a musician, but her practicing is mechanical, undisciplined and unfocused, not boding well for plans to teach youngsters the piano and the violin.
Gold, Frankincense, and Myrrh: Cantatina for Girls' Voices, in Three Parts (music score) (Myles B. Foster, Words Clara Thwaites) pp. 38–45
An Hour a Day for a Year (James Mason) pp. 57–8
  A daily hour of practice will carry the musician far in a year. One attentive hour is better than three careless hours.

Novelties for the Christmas Tree (S. R. Canton) pp. 59–61
   Novelties include a music holder and a monkey orchestra.

Victoria's Laurel
Extra Summer Part for Volume 8 (1887)
A Story of an Angle Window (Ruth Lamb) pp. 50–60
   Norah Pease is a 'born musician' with a well-cultivated voice whose delightful singing owes more to her 'natural gifts' than to her teaching (p. 58). For Richard Maynard Whitmore, the favoured seat in the angle window in his Mere Side home now will ring with Norah's voice rather than an echo of his deceased mother.

Volume 9 (1 October 1887–29 September 1888)

Number 405 (1 October 1887)
My Musical Training; or, What I Did with a Hundred Pounds (Anna Williams) Part 1 pp. 5–7
    First-hand account of a voice student in Naples offers a reality check for readers contemplating music study abroad.
Answers to Correspondents (Music heading) p. 15
    Maria L. (piano, practising, terms), Mary (music history and appreciation), Nil Desperandum (terms, guitar), Viola (terms), Nora (music history and appreciation)

Number 406 (8 October 1887)
One Little Vein of Dross (Ruth Lamb) Ch. 1 pp. 17–19
    Musical Mrs Beauchamp asks her prospective daughter-in-law, Olive Stafford, if she, too, is musical. Olive describes herself as loving and appreciating good music but lacking talent for it. 'I am not even an average player', she says. 'I suppose, then, you play a little. Most young ladies say that, in these music-murdering days', responds Mrs. Beauchamp, in a tone that Olive thinks unnecessarily sarcastic. 'I do not even profess so much', Olive replies. 'I thought it would be waste of time to attempt what I was never likely to do well' (p. 43). Her frankness pleases Mrs Beauchamp.
My Musical Training Part 2 pp. 22–3
'The Lady I Love' (music score) (The Countess of Munster, Words Frederick Locker) pp. 29–31
Answers to Correspondents (Music heading) p. 32
    Amy Wood (music education), Her Own Choice (voice, health), Judy (piano, instrument maintenance), Ivanhoe (music history and appreciation), Dolly (music history and appreciation)

Number 407 (15 October 1887)
A Competition in Musical Composition (Examiner John Stainer) p. 40
One Little Vein of Dross Ch. 2* pp. 41–3
Answers to Correspondents (Music heading) p. 48
    Kate B. (terms, violin), Ruth (music history and appreciation), Forget-Me-Not (harp)

Number 408 (22 October 1887)
One Little Vein of Dross Ch. 3 pp. 49–51
New Music p. 61
Answers to Correspondents p. 64
    Ivy (general)

Number 409 (29 October 1887)
The Girls' Year; or, January to December Spent with Pleasure and Profit (James Mason) pp. 75–7
    Three young women friends, who finished their schooling 15 months ago, begin a monthly programme of 'self-culture and mutual improvement' that includes studying and performing a piece of music (p. 75).
One Little Vein of Dross Ch. 4 pp. 78–9

Number 410 (5 November 1887)
The Stories of Famous Songs (Isabella Fyvie Mayo) pp. 86–7
    'Auld Robin Gray'
One Little Vein of Dross Ch. 5 pp. 92–4

[Answers to] Correspondents pp. 95–6
    Writing 'To the Editor of "The Girl's Own Paper"', the president of the 'Girls' Practising Club' in Holcombe, New Zealand, describes the start-up of her organization that includes musical evenings.

Number 411 (12 November 1887)
Romance, for Violin and Pianoforte (music score) (G. A. Macfarren) pp. 100–3
Answers to Correspondents (Music heading) pp. 111–12
    Polyhymnia (theory), Short (music history and appreciation), Ruthie (repertoire), Anxiety (voice, health), Young Lady of Twelve (pronunciation, general)

Number 412 (19 November 1887)
One Little Vein of Dross Ch. 6 pp. 126–8

Number 413 (26 November 1887)
One Little Vein of Dross Ch. 7 pp. 129–31
The Girls' Year pp. 138–41
New Music p. 141
Answers to Correspondents (Music heading) p. 144
    Cordella (general), A Subscriber (music education)

Number 414 (3 December 1887)
Victory Is in Truth Ch. 1* pp. 145–7
    When Mary Wonham's father (a carpenter) and mother (a cook) purchase a lodging house on Portman Square in London and prosper, they send their daughter to a fashionable French boarding school but expect her help when she returns home. 'There'll still be time to play the pianer to us of evenings and read over some of your lessons', her father says. 'It won't never do for you to forget all we've paid such a pile o' money for you to learn.' (p. 146)
    Illustration 'She turned round towards him' shows Mary at the piano p. 145
One Little Vein of Dross Ch. 8 pp. 154–6
A Christmas-tide Remembrance (music score) (C. A. Macirone, Words Mrs Norton) pp. 157–9

Number 415 (10 December 1887)
Victory Is in Truth Ch. 2 pp. 166–7
One Little Vein of Dross Ch. 9 pp. 168–71

Number 416 (17 December 1887)
Notices of New Music pp. 177–8
    Illustration 'At the Organ' shows a female organist p. 177
One Little Vein of Dross Ch. 10 pp. 178–80
Victory Is in Truth Ch. 3* pp. 184–7

Number 417 (24 December 1887)
One Little Vein of Dross Ch. 11 pp. 193–5
Historical Sketches of Musical Forms (Myles B. Foster) Instrumental pp. 196–7
    Five other Sketches found in Volume 8.
Victory Is in Truth Ch. 4 pp. 198–9
Homeward Bound: A Sailor's Song to His Wife (poem) (Alex. Hayes) p. 200
The Stories of Famous Songs (Isabella Fyvie Mayo) pp. 200, 202–4
    About song writer Carolina, Baroness Nairne

126 *Catalogue of musical content*

Number 418 (31 December 1887)
The Girls' Year pp. 221–3
Notices of New Music p. 224
Answers to Correspondents p. 224
   Marjery (music as accomplishment)

Number 419 (7 January 1888)
On the Choice of Pianoforte Pieces (Ernst Pauer) Part 1 pp. 228–9
One Little Vein of Dross Ch. 12 pp. 232, 234–5
To Chloris (music score) (George J. Bennett, Words Robert Burns) pp. 238–9

Number 420 (14 January 1888)
One Little Vein of Dross Ch. 13 pp. 241–3
The Story of Famous Songs (Isabella Fyvie Mayo) pp. 244–5
   'The Marseillaise'
The Bailiff's Daughter p. 252
   Illustrated song text with music score.
The Bailiff's Daughter of Islington pp. 253–6
   Illustrated song text.

Number 421 (21 January 1888)
The Bailiff's Daughter of Islington (cont.) pp. 257–9
One Little Vein of Dross Ch. 14 pp. 270–2

Number 422 (28 January 1888)
The Story of a Sorrow pp. 273–4
   When vocalist Madeline Taunton's fiancé dies in a hansom on his way to hear her sing an oratorio, she is devastated and stops singing after the concert. On a visit to her friend's country home, a young child's fall from a tree and his request that Madeline sing away his pain breaks the spell at last, and Madeline's 'rich, soft, melancholy tones, full of tenderness and pathos' are heard again (p. 274).
Notices of New Music p. 275
The Girls' Year pp. 284–6
Answers to Correspondents p. 288
   Medical Aid (disability, music potential)

Number 423 (4 February 1888)
One Little Vein of Dross Ch. 15 pp. 289–91
Rêverie (music score) (J. W. Hinton) p. 295

Number 424 (11 February 1888)
The Stories of Famous Songs (Isabella Fyvie Mayo) pp. 315–16
   'There's Nae Luck About the House'
One Little Vein of Dross Ch. 16 pp. 316–18

Number 425 (18 February 1888)
One Little Vein of Dross Ch. 17 pp. 320–3
Correspondence (Music heading) p. 336
   Idalia, Demerara (general), Queenie and Heliotrope (voice, practising), Ethel Winifred (music education), Madrigal (music history and appreciation)

Number 426 (25 February 1888)
Notices of New Music p. 349
The Girls' Year pp. 350–2

Number 427 (3 March 1888)
On the Choice of Pianoforte Pieces Part 2 pp. 356–7
One Little Vein of Dross Ch. 18 pp. 358–60
Answers to Correspondents p. 367
    Ottilie von Radzitz (music history and appreciation)

Number 428 (10 March 1888)
One Little Vein of Dross Ch. 19 pp. 369–72
Gavotte (music score) (H.A.J. Campbell) pp. 372–4
Answers to Correspondents p. 384
    N.M.S. (piano, instrument maintenance)

Number 429 (17 March 1888)
One Little Vein of Dross Ch. 20 pp. 396–8
Answers to Correspondents (Music heading) pp. 399–400
    Marion Clark and Ethel Winifred (voice, music education), Lobster and Crab (terms), Pretty Floss (music history and appreciation), Ermine (piano, music potential), Our Piano (piano, instrument maintenance)

Number 430 (24 March 1888)
Notices of New Music p. 404
The Result of the Competition in Musical Composition: The Best Settings of Longfellow's Poem, 'The Rainy Day' p. 405
Our Next Musical Composition p. 405
Beethoven's Sonata in E Flat, Op. 7: Analysis of Its Design and Harmony (Oliveria Prescott) pp. 408, 410–12

Number 431 (31 March 1888)
One Little Vein of Dross Ch. 21 pp. 417–20
The Girls' Year pp. 428–30
Answers to Correspondents (Music heading) p. 432
    Olive (terms), Patience Moberley (music education), S.E.B. (music education), A Would-Be Singer (voice, performance)

Number 432 (7 April 1888)
The Rainy Day (music score) (Ethel Harraden, Words Longfellow) pp. 436–40
    Winner of ten-guinea first prize in first musical composition competition.
A May Song (poem) (Mary Rowles) p. 444
One Little Vein of Dross Ch. 22 pp. 446–8

Number 433 (14 April 1888)
On the Choice of Pianoforte Pieces Part 3 pp. 454–5
The Telegraph's Song (poem) (Helen Marion Burnside) p. 456
One Little Vein of Dross (Ruth Lamb) Ch. 23 pp. 456–9

Number 434 (21 April 1888)
Miss Pringle's Pearls (Mrs G. Linnaeus Banks) Ch. 1 pp. 465–7
    When Aunt Phillis Penelope Pringle visits niece Barbara, married to Stephen Heathfield of Upland Farm, their daughter Mabel plays her new piano pieces. Then Aunt Pringle calls the family together to sing 'The Evening Hymn' to her accompaniment. 'Her voice had been well-trained, and her touch of the keys was that of a mistress.' (p. 539) Mabel continues her music when away at boarding school, and on her return pronounces the old pianoforte 'execrable, no better than a jingling tin-kettle' and talks her father into a new

one (p. 637). Mr Heathfield asks Miss Pringle, who substitutes as organist at Shepperley Church, for advise on the purchase.
One Little Vein of Dross Ch. 24 pp. 472, 474

Number 435 (28 April 1888)
The Girls' Year pp. 485–7
Miss Pringle's Pearls Ch. 2 pp. 491–2

Number 436 (5 May 1888)
The Gladness of Nature (music score) (C. A. Macirone, Words Cullen Bryant) pp. 501–3
Miss Pringle's Pearls Ch. 3 pp. 507–9

Number 437 (12 May 1888)
The Stories of Famous Songs (Isabella Fyvie Mayo) pp. 517–19
  The American Marching Song 'John Brown'
Miss Pringle's Pearls Ch. 4 pp. 520–3
Notices of New Music p. 523

Number 438 (19 May 1888)
On the Choice of Pianoforte Pieces Part 4 pp. 534–5
Miss Pringle's Pearls Ch. 5* pp. 537–9

Number 439 (26 May 1888)
Miss Pringle's Pearls Ch. 6 pp. 545–7
The Girls' Year pp. 549–51

Number 440 (2 June 1888)
The Bachelors in Central Italy (John Francis Brewer) pp. 568–72
  Illustration 'St. Cecilia' (Raphael) p. 569
Miss Pringle's Pearls Ch. 7 pp. 572–4

Number 441 (9 June 1888)
Miss Pringle's Pearls Ch. 8 pp. 589–91
Educational Classes Y.W.C.A. (Anne Beale) p. 591
  For young women engaged in business, the Y.W.C.A. offers advanced piano among its more practical classes.

Number 442 (16 June 1888)
The Wondrous Cross (music score) (Myles B. Foster, Words Dr Watts) pp. 596–9
Miss Pringle's Pearls Ch. 9 pp. 606–7
Answers to Correspondents p. 608
  Stella (general)

Number 443 (23 June 1888)
Miss Pringle's Pearls Ch. 10 pp. 609–11
The Girls' Year pp. 612–15
Notices of New Music p. 615
Handel's Mother pp. 622–3
Answers to Correspondents pp. 623–4
  One of the Girls (instrument purchase, piano)

Number 444 (30 June 1888)
Deborah: Poet and Musical Composer pp. 635–7
  Through biblical judge and prophet, Deborah and her appointed army commander Barak, the Lord gave the Israelites victory over the Canaanite army. 'Deborah's song has

preached a sermon to us', the unnamed *TGOP* author writes, 'and from her song we may be taught the sin of sitting at ease in our homes, and not identifying ourselves with such Christian enterprise as may be within our reach' (p. 657).
Miss Pringle's Pearls Ch. 11* pp. 637–9

Number 445 (7 July 1888)
Frances Ridley Havergal (Alice King) pp. 643–5
   As a poet with a good singing voice, Havergal not only wrote books of sacred song and music but also led the hymns in religious meetings.
   Illustration 'Frances Ridley Havergal' p. 644
Miss Pringle's Pearls Ch. 12 pp. 645–7
Varieties (Wonders of Pianoforte Playing) p. 647
'Leal' (music score) (Suchet Champion, Words Chas. J. Rowe) pp. 652–3

Number 446 (14 July 1888)
Miss Pringle's Pearls Ch. 13 pp. 657–60
Answers to Correspondents p. 672
   May (music teaching)

Number 447 (21 July 1888)
A Village Concert (poem) (Helen Marion Burnside) p. 680
Miss Pringle's Pearls Ch. 14 pp. 683–5

Number 448 (28 July 1888)
   The Girls' Year pp. 701–3

Number 449 (4 August 1888)
Miss Pringle's Pearls Ch. 15 pp. 709–11
Answers to Correspondents p. 720
   Annie Laurie (general)

Number 450 (11 August 1888)
Miss Pringle's Pearls Ch. 16 pp. 721–4
Evensong: Duet for Girls' Voices (music score) (C. A. Macirone, Words from an old Proverb) pp. 728–31

Number 451 (18 August 1888)
Miss Pringle's Pearls Ch. 17 pp. 741–3

Number 452 (25 August 1888)
The Girls' Year pp. 753–6
Miss Pringle's Pearls Ch. 18 pp. 758–9

Number 453 (1 September 1888)
Miss Pringle's Pearls Ch. 19 pp. 769–71
Nocturne (music score) (H.A.J. Campbell) p. 781
Answers to Correspondents pp. 783–4
   M.A.R. (instrument maintenance, piano keys)

Number 454 (8 September 1888)
Miss Pringle's Pearls Ch. 20 pp. 790–2
The Stories of Famous Songs (Isabella Fyvie Mayo) pp. 796–7
   'Home, Sweet Home', 'Sally in Our Alley'

130 *Catalogue of musical content*

Number 455 (15 September 1888)
Notices of New Music pp. 801–2
　Illustration 'A New Song' p. 801
Miss Pringle's Pearls Ch. 21 pp. 805–8

Number 456 (22 September 1888)
Saturday Afternoon (poem) (E. O.) p. 817
The Girls' Year pp. 818–20
Miss Pringle's Pearls Ch. 22 pp. 824–6
Answers to Correspondents (Music heading) p. 832
　Oboe (music history and appreciation, piano, practising, nuisance, music as accomplishment), Molly Maloney (general)

Number 457 (29 September 1888)
Miss Pringle's Pearls Ch. 23 pp. 836–8
Answers to Correspondents p. 843
　Dubious (composition)

Evergreen
Extra Christmas Part for Volume 9 (1887)
'Give!' A Canon, with Intermezzo (music score) (Myles B. Foster, Words Adelaide Ann Procter) pp. 11–15
Lady Ella (poem) (Jessie M. E. Saxby) p. 56
　Nonmusical poem with musical illustration.
A Winter Evening of Old English Music (James Mason) pp. 62–4
　The friends featured in 'Evenings with our Great Living Composers' in Volume 4 devote an evening to songs and ballads of Old England.

'Rosebud Garden'
Extra Summer Part for Volume 9 (1888)
Dear Miss Meg (Ruth Lamb) pp. 3–15
　Lady Longridge thinks granddaughter Margaretta's singing voice is like a railway whistle. But Mrs Moffit takes an interest in Meg (Margaretta) and teaches her music. Within two years, Meg's 'wonderful voice' is the talk of the neighbourhood (p. 11).
'Only a Professional' (Lily Watson) pp. 28–33
　Among passengers crossing the English Channel to the Continent is violinist Herr von Erckmann, who has played at St James's Hall. Story touches on a rank-conscious society that does not treat musicians with respect. A tenor serenading the passengers during dinner turns out to be Violetta Fortescue's brother. As the sister of a strolling musician, surely she can marry an eminent violinist 'and nobody will venture to say that I have stooped in choosing – only a professional!' (p. 33)
A Wedding Song (poem) (Sydney Grey) p. 36
The Rainy Day (music score) (Amelia Corper, Words Longfellow) pp. 44–7
　Winner of five-guinea second prize in the first musical composition competition.
The Royal Conservatorium of Music at Leipzig pp. 50–1

Volume 10 (6 October 1888–28 September 1889)

Number 458 (6 October 1888)
Our Bessie (Rosa Nouchette Carey) Ch. 1 pp. 1–4
 Edna Sefton, whom Bessie Lambert visits in London, sings charmingly. When Edna refuses to sing for her brother Richard, Bessie offers to sing him a pretty ballad or two. Richard, who has a fine musical ear, is much pleased.
The Art of Translating Verse for Music (Lady Macfarren) p. 4
Answers to Correspondents p. 15
 Miss Annie Graham (practising society)

Number 459 (13 October 1888)
Violins and Mittenwald (Emma Brewer) Ch. 1 pp. 20–2
 In a series of articles, author describes her visit to the Bavarian town of Mittenwald to learn how its violins are made and then turns to women who play it (see Ch. 9). Continued under 'Mittenwald and Its Violins'.
Pianoforte Duet Playing (Walter van Noordin) p. 24
 First in five-part series; other parts under 'Pianoforte Duets and Pianoforte Duet Playing'.
Our Bessie Ch. 2 pp. 29–31

Number 460 (20 October 1888)
Our Bessie Ch. 3 pp. 36–8
Oh, Why Not Be Happy? 'A Quoi bon Entendre les Oiseaux' (music score) (A. C. Mackenzie, Words Victor Hugo, trans. Leopold Wray) pp. 44–7
Answers to Correspondents p. 48
 Aurepine and Bookworm (general, nuisance)

Number 461 (27 October 1888)
Our Bessie Ch. 4 pp. 49–51
Notices of New Music pp. 62–3
Answers to Correspondents (Music heading) p. 63
 A Lover of Music (general), Essy W. (violin), Anxious Inquirer (general), D. Denham (violin), Coppers (music history and appreciation), Mary B. (buglette)

Number 462 (3 November 1888)
The Stories of Famous Songs (Isabella Fyvie Mayo) pp. 74–5
 'The Village Blacksmith', 'Excelsior', 'The Old Clock on the Stairs'
Our Bessie Ch. 5 pp. 78–80
Answers to Correspondents (Music heading) p. 80
 One Trying to be Patient (general), Rose Lanach (voice, music potential), An Organist and Wild Rose (organ, music history and appreciation), Lottie Mosley (repertoire)

Number 463 (10 November 1888)
Our Bessie Ch. 6 pp. 82–3
Withered Flowers (music score) (H.A.J. Campbell, Words from German of W. Müller) pp. 92–4
Pianoforte Duets and Pianoforte Duet Playing p. 95

Number 464 (17 November 1888)
Our Bessie Ch. 7 pp. 108–9
Answers to Correspondents p. 111
 Dollypig (accordion, voice), May Bird (instrument maintenance, piano keys)
Evensong (poem) (J. Huie) p. 112

132   *Catalogue of musical content*

Number 465 (24 November 1888)
Our Bessie Ch. 8 pp. 114–15
Mittenwald and Its Violins Ch. 2 pp. 122–4
Notices of New Music p. 127

Number 466 (1 December 1888)
How to Play the Banjo (Frank Mott Harrison) pp. 132–4
   Illustration 'The Banjo' p. 133
Our Bessie Ch. 9* pp. 136–8
Answers to Correspondents p. 144
   A Subscriber (harp, health)

Number 467 (8 December 1888)
'Those Silv'ry Sounds' (music score) (Ethel Harraden, Words Gertrude Harraden) pp. 149–51
Our Bessie Ch. 10* pp. 157–9
Answers to Correspondents p. 160
   A Little Mother (music history and appreciation), W.F.M. (general), Laura Alex Smith (repertoire)

Number 468 (15 December 1888)
Report on the Musical Competition (Adjudicator Sir John Stainer) p. 173
   For pianoforte piece in two movements describing Sorrow and Joy.
Our Bessie Ch. 11 pp. 174–5
Answers to Correspondents (Music heading) p. 176
   Martha (voice, music history and appreciation), Lover of Music (music history and appreciation)

Number 469 (22 December 1888)
Our Bessie Ch. 12* pp. 178–9
Pianoforte Duets and Pianoforte Duet Playing p. 187
Answers to Correspondents p. 192
   Fanny Hensel (voice, health), A Mother (music as accomplishment), M. R. (piano)

Number 470 (29 December 1888)
Notices of New Music pp. 193–4
   Illustration 'Song Pictures I' p. 193
Mittenwald and Its Violins Ch. 3 pp. 194–5

Number 471 (5 January 1889)
Our Bessie Ch. 13* pp. 209–11
Answers to Correspondents p. 223
   Doll-Fig (concertina)
A Song of the Moments (poem) (Mary Rowles Jarvis) p. 224

Number 472 (12 January 1889)
Our Bessie Ch. 14 pp. 230–1
Answers to Correspondents (Music heading) p. 239
   Maid of Cym (violin, choosing instrument), C. Skinner (violin), Student of Music (viola)

Number 473 (19 January 1889)
Mittenwald and Its Violins Ch. 4 pp. 243–4
Pianoforte Duets and Pianoforte Duet Playing p. 245
Our Bessie Ch. 15 pp. 246–7

Number 474 (26 January 1889)
Our Bessie Ch. 16 pp. 262–3

Number 475 (2 February 1889)
Our Bessie Ch. 17 pp. 281–3
The Burden of the Wind (music score) (Ernst Helmer, Words Lady Elliot) pp. 284–7
Answers to Correspondents (Music heading) p. 288
   Storm (piano, instrument maintenance), Frankie (whistling), Chryse (music history and appreciation), D. P. (repertoire)

Number 476 (9 February 1889)
Pianoforte Duets and Pianoforte Duet Playing p. 293
The Stories of Famous Songs (Isabella Fyvie Mayo) pp. 294–5
   'The Watch on the Rhine', 'What Is the German's Fatherland?', 'The Sword Song'
Notices of New Music p. 295
Our Bessie Ch. 18 pp. 302–3
Answers to Correspondents p. 304
   Scamp (music education)

Number 477 (16 February 1889)
Our Bessie Ch. 19 pp. 310–11

Number 478 (23 February 1889)
Our Bessie Ch. 20 pp. 321–3
Mittenwald and Its Violins Ch. 5 pp. 326–7

Number 479 (2 March 1889)
The Better Light (music score) (The Rev. W. J. Foxell, Words Mrs Payne-Smith) pp. 342–3
The Twin-Houses (Anne Beale) Part 1 Ambition pp. 344–6
   Fred Oliver, a clerk with a self-described 'magnificent voice', is determined to leave Merriton to make his fortune as a musician in London (p. 344). But once there, Fred learns that to make it as a public singer requires more time, teaching and practice than he is willing to give, so he drifts onto music-hall stages instead. A serious illness ends his music career but teaches him a lesson about self-glorification.
Our Bessie Ch. 21 pp. 347–8
Answers to Correspondents (Music heading) p. 352
   Mibbie (practising society), Constance (voice, music education), Roy Raymond (general)

Number 480 (9 March 1889)
Our Bessie Ch. 22 pp. 355–7
'Come Unto Me' (poem) (Mrs G. Linnaeus Banks) p. 360
   Illustration 'Waft the young echoes over land and sea, / "Come, oh, ye weary, come for rest to Me"' shows woman at organ accompanying a female vocalist p. 361
   The Twin-Houses Part 2 A Start for London pp. 360, 362
Answers to Correspondents p. 367
   Fiddler (instrument maintenance, harp)

Number 481 (16 March 1889)
The Twin-Houses Part 3 Fruit of Discontent pp. 369–71
Our Bessie Ch. 23 pp. 381–3
Answers to Correspondents p. 384
   Lover of Music (instrument maintenance, piano), A Devonshire Dumpling (music history and appreciation)

134 *Catalogue of musical content*

Number 482 (23 March 1889)
Mittenwald and Its Violins Ch. 6 pp. 390–1
The Twin-Houses Part 4 Home, Sweet Home pp. 393–4
Our Bessie Ch. 24 pp. 396–8
Varieties (The Music of the Future) p. 399
Answers to Correspondents (Music heading) p. 400
   Banjo (banjo), Lucie (voice, health), Joseph Spink (music history and appreciation), Samivel Weller (music history and appreciation)

Number 483 (30 March 1889)
New Music and Musical Events p. 407
Answers to Correspondents p. 416
   An Inquirer E. (piano, health)

Number 484 (6 April 1889)
Mittenwald and Its Violins pp. 430–1
Correspondence (Music heading) p. 432
   N. C. (music education), A Bideford Lassie (lyre), Brock Dish (general)

Number 485 (13 April 1889)
Song of the Spring (poem) p. 433
Old Memories (music score) (Charles Vincent, Words Arthur Burchett) pp. 437–9

Number 488 (4 May 1889)
Memories (illustration) (from Frank Dicksee painting) plate facing p. 481
   A young woman pianist.
The Hill of Angels (Lily Watson) Ch. 1* pp. 487–90
   Author includes a lesson about musical etiquette when hotel guests encourage Herr Lichtenstein to continue an impromptu recital in the music room. 'I shall play with pleasure', he responds, 'so long as people do not laugh and talk and walk about the room. If they are not still', he says, shrugging his shoulders, 'then, you see, the instrument cannot speak to them, and the labour is thrown away to make them understand.' (p. 638)
   Illustration 'I have made up my mind to publish' shows Evelyn Hope telling cousin Dottie Lancaster of her plan in front of a piano with open sheet music p. 489
Mrs. Hemans (Alice King) pp. 490–1
   Poet Felicia Hemans possessed considerable musical talent. When middle aged, she studied music at Liverpool and began setting her verses to music.
Answers to Correspondents (Music heading) pp. 495–6
   Hopeful (music teaching), A Constant Reader (terms), Iddie Stanley (terms)

Number 489 (11 May 1889)
Mittenwald and Its Violins Ch. 8 pp. 498–9
Mazurka in C Minor (music score) (Ethel M. Boyce) pp. 500–3
The Hill of Angels Ch. 2 pp. 504–7

Number 490 (18 May 1889)
Haymaking Song (poem) (Sydney Grey) p. 520
The Hill of Angels Ch. 3 pp. 521–3

Answers to Correspondents p. 528
   Nine Years' Subscriber (general)

Number 491 (25 May 1889)
The Hill of Angels Ch. 4 pp. 532–5
New Music p. 541

Number 492 (1 June 1889)
How to Play the Zither pp. 552–4
   Illustration 'The Zither' p. 553
The Hill of Angels Ch. 5 pp. 556–8

Number 493 (8 June 1889)
The Hill of Angels Ch. 6 pp. 561–3
Mittenwald and Its Violins Ch. 9 pp. 563–5
   Illustration 'The Sisters Milanello' p. 564
Love versus Money (L. Sharp) Ch. 1* pp. 566–7
   Rich young heiress Leslie Barton is sick of her empty social butterfly life and wants more to life than admiration. Wandering to the piano to get away from after-dinner gossip, Leslie begins to play 'some soft, sweet Nocturne'; more music and singing follow (p. 567).

Number 494 (15 June 1889)
Love Versus Money Ch. 2 pp. 582–3, 585
The Hill of Angels Ch. 7 pp. 585–7

Number 495 (22 June 1889)
Song-Summer Days (poem) (John Huie) p. 593
The Hill of Angels Ch. 8 pp. 594–5
Love Versus Money Ch. 3* pp. 596–8
A Blossom That Never Dies (music score) (Cécile S. Hartog, Words Caroline Radford) pp. 603–5

Number 497 (6 July 1889)
Varieties (Musical Families) p. 631
Art Needlework (Helen Marion Burnside) pp. 636–7
   Includes instructions for making a piano back.
   Illustration 'Piano Back' p. 637
The Hill of Angels Ch. 9* pp. 637–9

Number 498 (13 July 1889)
Sunday Song: 'O Saviour, I Have Nought to Plead' (music score) (C. A. Macirone) pp. 645–7
The Hill of Angels Ch. 10 pp. 654–5

Number 499 (20 July 1889)
The Hill of Angels Ch. 11 pp. 657–9
Musical Design for Musical Babes: Analysis of the Slow Movement of Beethoven's Sonata in D, Op. 28 (Oliveria Prescott) pp. 662–3, 665–6
The Dream of Home (illustration) p. 664
   A young woman plays an ancient stringed instrument.
Answers to Correspondents p. 672
   Dagmar Valerian (voice, music education)

136 *Catalogue of musical content*

Number 500 (27 July 1889)
Nocturne (poem) (William Cartwright Newsam) p. 673
The Hill of Angels Ch. 12 pp. 686–7

Number 501 (3 August 1889)
The Hill of Angels Ch. 13 pp. 689–91

Number 502 (10 August 1889)
The Hill of Angels Ch. 14 pp. 706–7
Good-Night! A Serenade (music score) (Myles B. Foster, Words Sarah Doudney) pp. 708–11

Number 503 (17 August 1889)
How to Teach the Elements of Music (Helen Kenway) p. 728
Mademoiselle Merle: A Sketch (P. W. Roose) pp. 728–31
    Details the piano lessons that Mademoiselle Merle, a daily French governess for young English ladies living in Geneva, gives to her pupils.
    Illustration 'A Lesson' p. 729
The Hill of Angels Ch. 15 pp. 731–3
Answers to Correspondents p. 736
    Constant Reader (music education)

Number 504 (24 August 1889)
The Hill of Angels Ch. 16 pp. 750–1

Number 505 (31 August 1889)
The Hill of Angels Ch. 17 pp. 755–6

Number 506 (7 September 1889)
The Hill of Angels Ch. 18 pp. 774–6
Answers to Correspondents (Music heading) p. 783
    N. C. (music education), Snowdrop (mandolin), Laburnum (music education)

Number 507 (14 September 1889)
Prelude (music score) (H.A.J. Campbell) p. 790
The Hill of Angels Ch. 19 pp. 791–2

Number 508 (21 September 1889)
The Hill of Angels Ch. 20 pp. 814–15
Answers to Correspondents pp. 815–16
    Queen Dido (piano, performance etiquette)

Number 509 (28 September 1889)
Correspondence p. 827
    A Music Teacher (general)

Household Harmony
Extra Christmas Number for Volume 10 (1888)
Household Harmony (James and Nanette Mason) pp. 3–4
    Uses musical terms to describe household harmony: 'Some tempers are like violin strings out of tune; with them, who can expect either melody or harmony from the family orchestra?' (p. 3)
The Wrong Colour: A Christmas Story (Luke Lovart) pp. 22–5
    In an otherwise unmusical story, an old woman train traveler's discrete imbibing to warm her cold feet on a train is described in musical terms of fugue and variations.

Clara's Christkind (J. A. Owen) pp. 32, 34–5
> Clara Steinmetz, a 15-year-old invalid with a weak spine, is a wood carver; in another room of the house, Helen Graham is a musician of great promise who works as a governess by day and at her piano in the evening.

Miss Angel's Last Christmas pp. 37–43
> Governess Magdalene Angel's very chequered life has left her poor and friendless after rejecting Ewan McReady's love over 30 years ago. Christmas afternoon finds them both at the same church service, where Ewan's singing brings the two back together.

'In Vesture White': A Song and Chorale for Christmas-tide (music score) (Myles B. Foster, Words The Rev. Richard Wilton) pp. 54–9

Rosemary
Extra Summer Number for Volume 10 (1889)
A Polish Melody (music score) (Gordon Saunders) pp. 28–31

Nobody's Holiday; or, An August and September Spent in Good Company pp. 42–4
> Hester Grey, who spends August and September at home in London instead of away, is saturated by lodgers' musical making – perhaps rather 'a pandemonium of discords': No. 1, practising a classical piece for piano and violins; No. 3 cultivating the banjo; No. 4, picking out hymn tunes with two fingers. A large, loud street-organ performs nearby (p. 42).

Varieties (Robert Schumann on Chopin's Playing His Own Etudes) p. 64

Volume 11 (5 October 1889–27 September 1890)

Number 510 (5 October 1889)
Kathleen's 'Handful' Ch. 1 pp. 1–3
 Kathleen O'Kelly is a natural singer with two young stepsisters in her charge. Lady Dacre, who resides in the same lodging house, asks Kathleen, whose voice thrills her, to sing to her and plays her accompaniment. Lady Dacre, who once had a fine voice, offers to 'make a musician' of Kathleen, who refuses – her stepsisters come first in her life (p. 259).
On Careful Treatment of the Voice (A Few Hints to Beginners) (Lisa Lehmann) pp. 4–5
Answers to Correspondents (Music heading) pp. 15–16
 Olive Wood, Daisy, Nona (music education), Tootsie (terms), Sonus (terms), M.S.C. (general), Maria von C. (general), Win (general), Welsh Maid (crwth instrument), Zillah (harmonium)

Number 511 (12 October 1889)
Work, Wait, Win (Ruth Lamb) Ch. 1 pp. 16–18
 John (Jack) Simpson loses the family estate when his father dies after disastrous financial speculations. While lodging temporarily with the former caretakers of the estate, Jack receives an anonymous gift – a pianette, which he plays to the delight of his landlords, who sing along to his hymns with cracked, tremulous, bagpipe-like voices.
Impressions of Celebrated Pianoforte Pieces (Ernst Pauer) pp. 20–1
Kathleen's 'Handful' Ch. 2 pp. 22–3
Answers to Correspondents p. 32
 An Irish Girl (musical confusion)

Number 512 (19 October 1889)
My Love Is Near! (music score) (Rosalind Frances Ellicott, Words Mabel Parsons) pp. 36–9
Work, Wait, Win Ch. 2 pp. 44–5
Kathleen's 'Handful' Ch. 3 pp. 46–8
Answers to Correspondents p. 48
 Viola (violin)

Number 513 (26 October 1889)
Kathleen's 'Handful' Ch. 4 pp. 50–1
Dress: In Season and in Reason (A Lady Dressmaker) pp. 56–8
 Illustration 'Back of Cashmere Gown' shows a woman at the piano p. 57
Work, Wait, Win Ch. 3 pp. 62–4

Number 514 (2 November 1889)
Kathleen's 'Handful' Ch. 5 pp. 65–7
Impressions of Celebrated Pianoforte Pieces (Ernst Pauer) p. 69
Work, Wait, Win Ch. 4 pp. 70–1
Answers to Correspondents (Music heading) p. 79
 K. Pilkington (composition), Mona and M. D. (voice, health, piano, instrument maintenance), Mary (violin, instrument maintenance), Musicus (general)

Number 515 (9 November 1889)
Work, Wait, Win Ch. 5* pp. 81–3
 Illustration 'That their cottage roof should shelter a piano was a something too good to be true' p. 81

Varieties (A Whimsical Singer) p. 83
See! the Swallows Circle O'er Us (music score) (Franz Abt, Words Edward Oxenford) pp. 84–5
Kathleen's 'Handful' Ch. 6 pp. 92–4

Number 516 (16 November 1889)
Kathleen's 'Handful' Ch. 7 pp. 98–9
Work, Wait, Win Ch. 6 pp. 108–10

Number 517 (23 November 1889)
Kathleen's 'Handful' Ch. 8 pp. 114–15
Work, Wait, Win Ch. 7 pp. 118–20
'Attraction!' A Melody in Two Keys (C Minor) (Mary L. Pendered) pp. 123–4
    Author uses a creative approach to contrast good and bad character traits in vocalist Cicely Percival and her social beau Larry, whose jealousy and social lifestyle, respectively, place them in the key of C Minor in the story's first part. When both learn the 'consciousness of usefulness' in the second part, the mode modulates to C Major, and their mutual attraction leads to marriage (p. 140).
Answers to Correspondents (Music heading) pp. 127–8
    Musical Box (music history and appreciation), Young Music Teacher (music teaching), Stella (voice, health), R. A. Davies (composition)

Number 518 (30 November 1889)
Work, Wait, Win Ch. 8 pp. 133–5
'Attraction!' A Melody in Two Keys (C Major) pp. 140–1
Kathleen's 'Handful' Ch. 9 pp. 142–3

Number 519 (7 December 1889)
Kathleen's 'Handful' Ch. 10 pp. 145–7
Three 'Album Leaves': Solitude, Despair, Peace (music score) (Myles B. Foster) pp. 148–51
Work, Wait, Win Ch. 9 pp. 157–9

Number 520 (14 December 1889)
Work, Wait, Win Ch. 10 pp. 161–3
The Study of Harmony (A. D. Swift) pp. 164–5
Kathleen's 'Handful' Ch. 11 pp. 166–7
Answers to Correspondents (Music heading) p. 175
    Liza L. (repertoire), A Student R.A.M. (piano, practising, health), Miss Jones (repertoire), Alice Marina (music education), Tenby Girl (general), Madcap (banjo), Perseverance (musician work)
New Music p. 176

Number 521 (21 December 1889)
The Girls of Today (A Templar) pp. 179–80
    Reaction to Catherine Milnes Gaskell's 'The Women of To-day' recently printed in *Nineteenth Century*. Lady Gaskell noted a high standard of perfection expected in women of to-day; A Templar extends Gaskell's argument to the large middle-class readership of *TGOP*. Both authors use musical accomplishments as an example to make their points.
Work, Wait, Win Ch. 11 pp. 186–7
Kathleen's 'Handful' Ch. 12 pp. 189–91
The Grandest Love-Song (poem) (H. M. Burnside) p. 192

140 *Catalogue of musical content*

Number 522 (28 December 1889)
Kathleen's 'Handful' Ch. 13* pp. 193–5
   Illustration 'With her hands full of flowers, singing some Irish ballad' p. 193
Work, Wait, Win Ch. 12 pp. 197–9
The London Y.W.C.A. (The Hon. Emily Kinnaird) p. 199
   The Young Women's Christian Association has opened two gymnasiums, and musical drill is offered at the Cloudesley Institute on Barnsbury Street. Music classes are taught as well.

Number 523 (4 January 1890)
Work, Wait, Win Ch. 13 pp. 209–12
Visions of the Departed (poem) (Anne Beale) p. 216
   Illustration 'The orphaned maiden tunes her harp and weeps' p. 217
Kathleen's 'Handful' Ch. 14 pp. 222–4
Answers to Correspondents (Music heading) p. 224
   Salammbo (piano, health), An Old Subscriber (general), Ariel (general), Faded Autumn Leaf (guitar), M. N. (Brighton) (voice, health), Musica (music teaching), E.A.C. (general), Australian Lassie (theory), F.E.R. (general)

Number 524 (11 January 1890)
Varieties (A Lover of Music; A Philosophic Musician; Who Invented the Tuning Fork) p. 227
Cradle Song (music score) (Mrs Tom Taylor, Words from Blake's 'Song of Innocence') pp. 228–30
Kathleen's 'Handful' Ch. 15 pp. 233–5
Work, Wait, Win Ch. 14 pp. 238–9

Number 525 (18 January 1890)
Work, Wait, Win Ch. 15 pp. 248, 250–1
Kathleen's 'Handful' Ch. 16 pp. 254–5

Number 526 (25 January 1890)
Kathleen's 'Handful' Ch. 17* pp. 257–9
The Popular Concerts (R.W.R.) pp. 262–3
   A fond account of the Popular Concerts in St James's Hall on Saturday afternoons and Monday evenings throughout London's winter season.
Notices of New Music p. 272
Answers to Correspondents (Music heading) p. 272
   Verena (applied music, practising society), Our Bessie (violin), Lover of Music (music education), Bashful Fifteen (voice), Nineteen (general)

Number 527 (1 February 1890)
Faithful (music score) (C. A. Macirone, Words Mary Cowden Clarke) pp. 276–9
A Hymn of the Night (poem) (J. Huie) p. 280
Work, Wait, Win Ch. 16 pp. 281–2
Kathleen's 'Handful' Ch. 18 pp. 286–8

Number 528 (8 February 1890)
Work, Wait, Win Ch. 17 pp. 289–91
Kathleen's 'Handful' Ch. 19 pp. 302–3

Number 529 (15 February 1890)
Kathleen's 'Handful' Ch. 20 pp. 310–11
Work, Wait, Win Ch. 18 pp. 315–17

Catalogue of musical content 141

Answers to Correspondents (Music heading) p. 320
  E. Wolf (general), A Reader of 'G.O.P'. (performance nerves), Mary B. (music history and appreciation), W.M.M. (music education)

Number 530 (22 February 1890)
Kathleen's 'Handful' Ch. 21 pp. 321–3
Work, Wait, Win Ch. 19 pp. 334–5

Number 531 (1 March 1890)
Kathleen's 'Handful' Ch. 22 pp. 339–40
Allegro (music score) (H.A.J. Campbell) pp. 348–9
Work, Wait, Win Ch. 20 pp. 350–1

Number 532 (8 March 1890)
Aldyth's Inheritance (Eglanton Thorne) Ch. 1 pp. 353–6
  At least four characters in this tale are musical. Aldyth Lorraine and her aunt play the piano; Captain Walker plays violin; and sister Gladys Stanton sings. A visit from Captain Walker contrasts two styles of musical accomplishment. Aldyth, who is playing his accompaniments, had studied music thoroughly, 'attained a brilliant touch, and played with a rare power and expression'. Gladys, whose voice lacks 'accuracy and finish', had studied 'in a superficial, half-hearted fashion'; her singing was 'very faulty, and her choice of songs poor' (p. 646).
Kathleen's 'Handful' Ch. 23 pp. 363–4
Work, Wait, Win Ch. 21 pp. 365–7

Number 533 (15 March 1890)
Work, Wait, Win Ch. 22 pp. 369–72
Aldyth's Inheritance Ch. 2 pp. 374–5

Number 534 (22 March 1890)
Aldyth's Inheritance Ch. 3 pp. 386–8, 390
Schoolgirl Troubles, and How to Cope with Them (Nanette Mason) p. 391
  Discussing 'One's Own Self for an Enemy', author uses music as an example of girls who want to be great pianists, for instance, but only if it requires no more than about three lessons.
Work, Wait, Win Ch. 23* pp. 396–8
Song (poem) (Jno. Finnemore) p. 400

Number 535 (29 March 1890)
Aldyth's Inheritance Ch. 4 pp. 406–7
Notices of New Music p. 411
Work, Wait, Win Ch. 24 pp. 414–16
The Orphan's Easter Hymn (poem) (Anne Beale) p. 416
  Illustration 'The Orphans' Easter Hymn' plate facing p. 416

Number 536 (5 April 1890)
Aldyth's Inheritance Ch. 5 pp. 417–20
Work, Wait, Win Ch. 25 pp. 421–3
Notices of New Music p. 427
Shine Out, Stars! (music score) (R. Thorley Brown, Words T. Moore) pp. 428–30
Answers to Correspondents (Music heading) pp. 431–2
  Tressida (music education), Excelsior S. V. (theory, correspondence course), C.A.R. (piano, music education), Vivo (lesson etiquette), Judy (guitar), St. Cecilia (music education), Sissy (voice, repertoire), Nemo (composition), Miss Jefferis (practising society)

142 *Catalogue of musical content*

Number 537 (12 April 1890)
'Charlie Is My Darling' (Anne Beale) Ch. 1* pp. 433–6
  Belle Dauncey has 'a clear, pleasant voice' and often breaks out in song, singing old Jacobite ditties by ear; 'Charlie is my darling', which reminds her of her brother, is a favourite (p. 436). Her niece Marjory, Charlie's child, complains as she practises at her grandfather's house, saying she cannot get any tone out of the old piano. She tells Belle that she has joined a practicing union 'and is bound to practice an hour a day' (p. 534).
Aldyth's Inheritance Ch. 6 pp. 443–4
Work, Wait, Win Ch. 26 pp. 445–7
Answers to Correspondents (Music heading) p. 448
  Verna (piano, applied music), One Very Anxious (music teaching, music potential)

Number 538 (19 April 1890)
Work, Wait, Win Ch. 27 pp. 450–1
Aldyth's Inheritance Ch. 7 pp. 458–61
'Charlie Is My Darling' Ch. 2 pp. 461–3
Answers to Correspondents (Music heading) p. 464
  Rehoboth (zither), White Wings (music teaching)

Number 539 (26 April 1890)
From the Artistic World: The Diary of the Early Artistic Days of Natalie Janotha (Her Mother) pp. 465–7
'Charlie Is My Darling' Ch. 3 pp. 478–80
Answers to Correspondents (Music heading) p. 480
  A Lover of Music (applied music), Arbutus (theory, applied music), Ezra (composition), Wallflower (general), Intended Learner of Singing (tonic sol-fa)

Number 540 (3 May 1890)
'Charlie Is My Darling' Ch.4 pp. 481–3
Ella's Experiences (Mary E. Hullah) Ch. 1* pp. 484–6
  After Ella Farrington's mother dies, the orphaned young woman is placed as a pupil-teacher at Oak House. On a holiday visit to Tor Cottage with one of her young pupils, Ella sings and plays piano accompaniments during an informal musical evening.
Aldyth's Inheritance Ch. 8 pp. 486–8
A Retrospect (music score) (Myles B. Foster) pp. 490–4
Answers to Correspondents (Music heading) p. 496
  Eirdach (applied music), Rehoboth (zither), Yum Yum (violoncello), Portia (general), Freda D. (general), North Wales (harmonium), K. Williams (theory)

Number 541 (10 May 1890)
Varieties (In Dread of a Trumpet; The Power of Music) p. 499
Aldyth's Inheritance Ch. 9 pp. 500–1
Ella's Experiences Ch. 2* pp. 504–8
'Charlie Is My Darling' Ch. 5 pp. 510–12
Answers to Correspondents (Music heading) p. 512
  A Toiler in Art (applied music), Kathleen (theory), M. A. (practising society)

Number 542 (17 May 1890)
Aldyth's Inheritance Ch. 10* pp. 514–15
Ella's Experiences Ch. 3 pp. 519–20, 522
'Charlie Is My Darling' Ch. 6* pp. 522–6
Answers to Correspondents p. 528
  M.I.C. (repertoire)

Number 543 (24 May 1890)
'Charlie Is My Darling' Ch. 7* pp. 534–6
Ella's Experiences Ch. 4 pp. 536–40
Aldyth's Inheritance Ch. 11* pp. 542–4
Answers to Correspondents p. 544
    Portia (voice)

Number 544 (31 May 1890)
From the Artistic World pp. 546–7
'Charlie Is My Darling' Ch. 8 pp. 558–60

Number 545 (7 June 1890)
'Charlie Is My Darling' Ch. 9 pp. 561–4
From the Artistic World pp. 566–7
Aldyth's Inheritance Ch. 12 pp. 573–5
Varieties (Advice to Young Pianists; The New Church Organ) p. 575
Answers to Correspondents p. 576
    Ivy Lee (digitorium), Anxious Girl (violin, health)

Number 546 (14 June 1890)
Aldyth's Inheritance Ch. 13 pp. 577–9
Varieties (What Music Can Do – *Richter*) p. 579
'Charlie Is My Darling' Ch. 10 pp. 588–90
Answers to Correspondents (Music heading) pp. 591–2
    Hetty (voice), Misterioso (piano, practising), Amy Firth (practising society, memory work)

Number 547 (21 June 1890)
Aldyth's Inheritance Ch. 14 pp. 594–7
'Charlie Is My Darling' Ch. 11 pp. 601–3
The Exiles (music score) (Suchet Champion, Words Dora Gillespie) pp. 604–6

Number 548 (28 June 1890)
'Charlie Is My Darling' Ch.12* pp. 610–12
Aldyth's Inheritance Ch. 15 pp. 621–3
Answers to Correspondents p. 624
    Golden Gertie (voice)

Number 549 (5 July 1890)
'Charlie Is My Darling' Ch. 13 pp. 625–8
The Story of a Summer (E. C. Vansittart) Ch. 1* pp. 632, 634
    Winifred Tafford, who has an artist's eye and a musician's ear, is unable to draw on either for consolation, for both are uncultivated. Keenly alive to the influence of music, she might have found relief in 'the magic power of song' when confronted with her current separation from her family (p. 632).
Aldyth's Inheritance Ch. 16* pp. 637–9

Number 550 (12 July 1890)
Aldyth's Inheritance Ch. 17* pp. 643, 645–6
A Summer Song (poem) (Helen Marion Burnside) p. 649
The Story of a Summer Ch. 2 pp. 649–50
Mary Morison (music score) (George J. Bennett, Words Robert Burns) pp. 651–3
'Charlie Is My Darling' Ch. 14 pp. 654–6

144 *Catalogue of musical content*

Answers to Correspondents (Music heading) p. 656
    Alpha Beta (sight-reading, piano), White Rose (music education), F. W. Ellis (violoncello, instrument maintenance), A Yawner (voice, health), Elizabeth S. M. (health), M.M.E.L.B., Este es Nuestro Secreto Sabe (general)

Number 551 (19 July 1890)
Aldyth's Inheritance Ch. 18* pp. 662–4
'Charlie Is My Darling' Ch. 15 pp. 666–8
The Story of a Summer Ch. 3 pp. 670–1
Answers to Correspondents (Music heading) pp. 671–2
    Gertrude (general), I.L.M. (voice)

Number 552 (26 July 1890)
Aldyth's Inheritance Chs 19, 20 pp. 673–8
Women's Clubs in London (Sophia F. A. Caulfeild) Part 2 pp. 678–9
    Author mentions music practising societies among the numerous clubs and societies devoted to the general and more specialized education of girls of all classes.
'Charlie Is My Darling' Ch. 16 pp. 683–5
The Story of a Summer Ch. 4 pp. 686–7

Number 553 (2 August 1890)
'Charlie Is My Darling' Ch. 17 pp. 689–92
A Guitar Melody (poem) (Mary Rowles Jarvis) p. 696
    Illustration 'A Guitar Melody' p. 697
Aldyth's Inheritance Ch. 21 pp. 701–3

Number 554 (9 August 1890)
Aldyth's Inheritance Ch. 22 pp. 705–7
Music Among the Working Girls of London (A. M. Wakefield) pp. 715–16
    Brief account of the annual music festival held by the Working Girls' Club Union in which choirs from its 27 branches compete for prizes.
'Charlie Is My Darling' Ch. 18 pp. 718–20

Number 555 (16 August 1890)
Aldyth's Inheritance Chs 23, 24 pp. 722–5
'Charlie Is My Darling' Ch. 19 pp. 734–6

Number 556 (23 August 1890)
Aldyth's Inheritance Ch. 25 pp. 737–40
'Charlie Is My Darling' Ch. 20 pp. 741–3

Number 557 (30 August 1890)
Aldyth's Inheritance Chs 26, 27 pp. 755–7
Varieties (A Tragic Chorus; Killed by Music) p. 759
'Sorrow' – 'Joy' (music score) (Fanny Scholfield Petrie) pp. 763–5
    Winner of ten-guinea first prize in *TGOP*'s second musical composition competition.
'Charlie Is My Darling' Ch. 21 pp. 766–8

Number 558 (6 September 1890)
'Charlie Is My Darling' Ch. 22 pp. 769–72
On the Practice of Duet-Singing (Florence Campbell Perugini) pp. 774–5
Aldyth's Inheritance Chs 28, 29 pp. 780–3

Number 559 (13 September 1890)
Notices of New Music pp. 785–6
 Illustration 'Trying It Over' p. 785
Varieties (Music as Medicine; A Cure for Deafness) p. 787
'Charlie Is My Darling' Ch. 23 pp. 795–7
Aldyth's Inheritance Ch. 30 pp. 798–800
Answers to Correspondents (Music heading) p. 800
 Harmony (theory), Salmon and Physic (terms), Lily (voice, health), Scotch Thistle (music education), Golden Hair (music education), Annie F. (voice)

Number 560 (20 September 1890)
'Charlie Is My Darling' Ch. 24 pp. 802–4
Aldyth's Inheritance Ch. 31 pp. 806–7

Number 561 (27 September 1890)
Aldyth's Inheritance Ch. 32 pp. 817–20
'Charlie Is My Darling' Ch. 25 pp. 820–4

'Christmas Cherries'
Extra Christmas Number for Volume 11 (1889)
Milly's Christmas Guest (Rosa Nouchette Carey) pp. 3–11
 Because of a ticketing error, Madame Virginie Dormay, a music teacher from Islington, has been let off the train at Castleton instead of Carlisle. Milly Copeland takes Virginie and dog Rough home with her to wait out a storm and take the next train to Carlisle.
Our Connie (C. N. Carvalho) pp. 12–16
 Connie Beauchamp is attentive to her father in the evenings, seeing that his books and chessmen are ready on hand and his favourite songs on the piano. She loves music, and 'her clear tones raised in song' are a signal for her father to come to her (p. 14).
Crumpled Rose Leaves (Sarson C. J. Ingham) pp. 31–6
 A poem set to music sings itself over in Paulina Elmore's mind on a lonely walk outside on a November day: 'Withering, withering, all are withering'. She invites her niece Carlina to come for Christmas and bring 'a pile of music' and a companion, but no mention is made of Carlina opening that music while visiting her aunt (p. 33).
Christmas Day in a London Hospital pp. 38–9
 A harmonium is wheeled into each ward successively for nurses and patients to sing hymns.
Christmas Bells (poem) p. 39
The Queen of Arcadee: Pastoral Operetta (Herbert Harraden) pp. 40–5
 Includes music scores.
Silence and Song (Lily Watson) pp. 52–7
 That contralto Pauline Lucas must rest from singing for an indefinite period to restore her health is devastating to her. If lacking the 'exceptional brilliancy' marking the queens of song, Pauline's oratorio career nonetheless had been 'creditable and successful' (p. 54). At St Hilda's seaside resort, Pauline overhears a lodger singing 'O Rest in the Lord' – it is a former pupil who, now motherless, asks her former teacher to become her traveling companion. Pauline's favourite aria brings hope and the realization that no work 'truly and conscientiously done, is ever altogether lost' (p. 57).

Gillyflowers
Extra Summer Number for Volume 11 (1890)
The Songs of Tyrol (The Rev. John Kelly) pp. 6–8
Includes music scores.
'Wandering Wings' (Sarson C. J. Ingham) pp. 19–22
    In a rare creative moment, Grace Vilmar sits down at her piano and picks out notes to accompany 'The Dying Cottage Girl'. She is pleased with her efforts that 'admirably blended the verses with a strain which had a "dying fall"' (p. 19).
    Illustration 'Still holding the book' shows Grace Vilmar at the piano p. 21
Romance for Violin: With Pianoforte Accompaniment (music score) (Myles B. Foster) pp. 28–32

Volume 12 (4 October 1890–26 September 1891)

Number 562 (4 October 1890)
Averil (Rosa Nouchette Carey) Ch. 1 pp. 1–3
    Pianist Lottie Jones takes lessons and practices scales before breakfast; Annette Ramsey never learned music but enjoys hearing others play. Herr Faber, a pianist engaged to play at a lawn party they attend, offers a lesson in musical etiquette: 'It is all in the day's work,' he mutters afterward. 'To make music for those who do not listen! Bah! It is thankless work!' (p. 147)
Some Types of Girlhood; or, Our Juvenile Spinsters (S.F.A. Caulfeild) Part 1 pp. 4–5
    Author warns musicians, who 'as a rule, are very genial, good-natured, light-hearted folk' against being a nuisance when practising: 'Those only who have resided, as a sandwich, between the crossfire of two pianos, or two sopranos of the singing sisterhood, can at all appreciate the pandemonium to which they are condemned!' (p. 197)
    Illustration 'Musical' depicts a musical girl p. 4
Varieties (On a Bad Singer) p. 15

Number 563 (11 October 1890)
Greyfriars: A Story for Girls (Evelyn Everett-Green) Ch. 1 pp. 17–19
    While at Greyfriars, Aunt Esther, who is a good pianist with 'brilliant accuracy of touch' and whose music is much in demand in the evenings, helps her niece Jessie improve her playing 'wonderfully'. Jessie's Aunt Gostling finds it 'galling' that in contrast her own daughter Bertha 'could hardly struggle through a schoolgirl piece without breaking down or slurring over every little difficulty' (p. 322).
Averil Ch. 2 pp. 28–9
Answers to Correspondents (Music heading) pp. 31–2
    Scriptor (organ), Kilarney (general), M.F.E. Ormsby (repertoire, charity entertainments)

Number 564 (18 October 1890)
Greyfriars Ch. 2 pp. 37–9
Averil Ch. 3 pp. 42–3
Mille Amitiés (music score) (G. J. Bennett) pp. 44–5

Number 565 (25 October 1890)
Greyfriars Ch. 3 pp. 49–51
On the Technique of the Pianoforte: A Practical Talk to Earnest Students (Fanny Davies) pp. 52–3
Notices of New Music p. 55
Averil Ch. 4 pp. 62–3
Answers to Correspondents (Music heading) p. 64
    Brittania (viol, music history and appreciation), Gwendoline (instrument maintenance, piano keys), Miss S. H. Allen (practising society), An Only Girl (general)

Number 566 (1 November 1890)
Averil Ch. 5 pp. 65–8
Greyfriars Ch. 4 pp. 73, 75–6

Number 567 (8 November 1890)
Averil Ch. 6* pp. 82–3
Greyfriars Ch. 5 pp. 86–7, 89
Varieties (A Musical Degree for Handel) p. 94

148 *Catalogue of musical content*

Number 568 (15 November 1890)
Averil Ch. 7* pp. 102–4
Greyfriars Ch. 6 pp. 104–7
Varieties (Musical Progress) p. 107
'Think upon Me' (Sacred Air) (music score) (C. A. Macirone, Words Neh. v. 19) pp. 108–10
Answers to Correspondents (Music heading) p. 112
    Tam O'Shanter (piano, violin, choosing instrument), A Stitch in Time (violin, health), Amy Hill (general)

Number 569 (22 November 1890)
Greyfriars Ch. 7 pp. 113–15
High Failure: A Story in Three Scraps (Vera) pp. 118–19
    Margaret Tremayne plays carols on the piano while guests gather around during a Christmas party.
Averil Ch. 8 pp. 120, 122–3
Answers to Correspondents (Music heading) p. 127
    Undine (guitar, violin, choosing instrument)

Number 570 (29 November 1890)
Averil Ch. 9 pp. 132–4
Greyfriars Ch. 8 pp. 139–41

Number 571 (6 December 1890)
Averil Ch. 10* pp. 145–7
Music Hath Charms (A. Mabel Culverwell) Chs 1, 2 pp. 156–7
    Madeline Stuart has been taking lessons from the parish organist since age 13. She has to think about her livelihood, for the four Stuart siblings are orphans and must make their own ways in life. Providentially, the parish organist's untimely arm injury puts Madeline on the organ bench as his substitute for the Christmas season, leading to a position as music governess.
Greyfriars Ch. 9 pp. 157–9

Number 572 (13 December 1890)
Averil Ch. 11 pp. 162–3
Varieties (Music – *Pope*) p. 167
Music Hath Charms Ch. 3 pp. 168, 170
Greyfriars Ch. 10 pp. 170–2
Black and White Heroism: Stories from the Abolition Crusade (Ascott R. Hope) Part 3 pp. 172–5
    Illustration 'A slave no longer' shows a man playing a banjo p. 173
Answers to Correspondents (Music heading) p. 175
    Bab (psaltery, music history and appreciation), Alpha Beta (practising society), May Blossom (music potential), Salammbo (general)
The Snowflake's Song (poem) (Samuel K. Cowan) p. 176

Number 573 (20 December 1890)
Greyfriars Ch. 11 pp. 177–9
Averil Ch. 12 pp. 182–3
Music Hath Charms Ch. 4 pp. 187–8

Number 574 (27 December 1890)
Greyfriars Ch. 12 pp. 193–5
Some Types of Girlhood Part 2 pp. 196–7
Averil Ch. 13 pp. 204–6

Number 575 (3 January 1891)
Greyfriars Ch. 13 pp. 210–12
Averil Ch. 14 pp. 222–3
Answers to Correspondents p. 224
   Miss Florence Griffith (practising society), Marguerite (practising society)

Number 576 (10 January 1891)
Averil Ch. 15 pp. 225–7
Greyfriars Ch. 14 pp. 231–4
Answers to Correspondents p. 239
   Primrose (Yokohama) (repertoire), T. H. (music education)

Number 577 (17 January 1891)
Greyfriars Ch. 15 pp. 242–4
Some Types of Girlhood Part 3 pp. 244–6
Averil Ch. 16 pp. 254–5
Answers to Correspondents (Music heading) p. 256
   Piano, Organ, Violin (composition), A Mother (wasted time, nuisance), Zenobia (voice, nuisance)

Number 578 (24 January 1891)
Greyfriars Ch. 16 pp. 257–9
Averil Ch. 17 pp. 270–2

Number 579 (31 January 1891)
Greyfriars Ch. 17 pp. 273–5
Andante Pastorale: For the Pianoforte or American Organ (music score) (Myles B. Foster) pp. 278–9
Averil Ch. 18 pp. 285–7
Answers to Correspondents p. 288
   D.W.M. Anderson (repertoire)

Number 580 (7 February 1891)
Averil Ch. 19 pp. 290–1
The Violin – Its Pains and Pleasures (W. Lawrence Liston) I. Gradus ad Parnassum pp. 292–3
   Addresses how readers with younger sisters just beginning 'to flounder about in the first slough of difficulties' in violin playing can supervise their practice (p. 292).
Greyfriars Ch. 18 pp. 301–3

Number 581 (14 February 1891)
Averil Ch. 20 pp. 305–7
There Are Ripples on the Ocean: Song (poem) (Clara Thwaites) p. 312
Greyfriars Ch. 19 pp. 317–19
Answers to Correspondents (Music heading) p. 319
   A. (violin), Almida (general), Cousin Fanny (repertoire), Violin (general), Sparrow (reading music, voice, health), Hayburn Crescent (music education)

Number 582 (21 February 1891)
Greyfriars Ch. 20* pp. 321–3
Averil Ch. 21 pp. 334–6
Answers to Correspondents p. 336
   Molly (practising society)

150   Catalogue of musical content

Number 583 (28 February 1891)
Greyfriars Ch. 21 pp. 337–9
Averil Ch. 22 pp. 350–1
Answers to Correspondents p. 352
   Kate Wren (piano, practising)

Number 584 (7 March 1891)
Averil Ch. 23 pp. 354–5
Edelweiss (music score) (Natalie Janotha) pp. 356–8
Edelweiss: Note on Mademoiselle Janotha's Pianoforte Piece (Marion Chappell) p. 359
Greyfriars Ch. 22 pp. 366–8
Answers to Correspondents p. 368
   Muriel (voice, musician work)

Number 585 (14 March 1891)
Averil Ch. 24 pp. 369–71
My Song (poem) (M. Hedderwick Browne) p. 376
Greyfriars Ch. 23 pp. 380–2
The Violin – Its Pains and Pleasures II. Parnassus pp. 382–3
   Addressing the young violinist who has reached Parnassus and has emerged from solitary scales and studies, author focuses on chamber music as the '"happy hunting ground" of every true amateur' (p. 382).
Answers to Correspondents p. 384
   Cathie (zither)

Number 586 (21 March 1891)
Greyfriars Ch. 24 pp. 385–7
Answers to Correspondents pp. 398–9
   Farmaringo (music teaching), Peggoty (practising)

Number 587 (28 March 1891)
Notices of New Music p. 411
Answers to Correspondents (Music heading) p. 416
   M. A. (voice), Hopeful M.T.B. (mandolin, violin, choosing instrument), Sonata (piano, practising), Olive (general), Eva (voice, health), Cecile Dene (composition), T. H. (general), Nellie America (general)

Number 588 (4 April 1891)
Answers to Correspondents p. 432
   Bashful Seventeen (terms)

Number 589 (11 April 1891)
Thou Sing'st to Her: Old Song 1606 John Danyel (poem) p. 433
Mendelssohn's 'Song without Words', in G, Op. 62, No. 4 (Oliveria Prescott) p. 443
Answers to Correspondents p. 447
   Flora (mandolin, banjo, choosing instrument)

Number 590 (18 April 1891)
An Idyl (music score) (The Countess of Munster) pp. 452–4

Number 591 (25 April 1891)
The Beauty of Evenness (Bee Orchis) p. 471
   Practising societies are an example of organizations that suffer when leaders have fitful moods and initial enthusiasm for the project wanes.

Answers to Correspondents pp. 479–80
    M. H. (violoncello)

Number 592 (2 May 1891)
Blest as the Immortal Gods: Duet for Mezzo-Soprano and Alto (music score) (C. A. Macirone, Words Sappho) pp. 492–5
Answers to Correspondents p. 496
    F. von H. and S.R.N. (practising society), Amy Firth (practising society)

Number 593 (9 May 1891)
Varieties (The Rival Singers) p. 503

Number 594 (16 May 1891)
Notices of New Music pp. 513–14
    Illustration 'The Gentle Music of a Bygone Day' (from J. M. Strudwick painting) p. 513
Sloane Garden House (Anne Beale) pp. 526–7
    A residential club for ladies of slender incomes. The facility's public portion includes music rooms for general use. Musical instruments are prohibited outside of these rooms, and no playing is allowed overnight.
Answers to Correspondents (Music heading) pp. 527–8
    Jenny (music history and appreciation), Mousey (violin, piano), Scotchie (general), Ignoramus (guitar, piano, choosing instrument), Marie Agnes (applied music)

Number 595 (23 May 1891)
Answers to Correspondents (Music heading) p. 544
    June Rose (general), Brown Betty (piano, instrument maintenance), An Orphan (harmonium, music teaching), Pansy (piano), F.G.X.Z. (piano, repertoire), Dottie W. (music education)

Number 596 (30 May 1891)
Varieties (Useful Music) p. 551

Number 598 (13 June 1891)
Some Remarks on Modern Professional Pianoforte Playing (William Porteous) pp. 589–90
    Describes the two recognized schools of pianoforte playing – the Classical style of Sir Charles Hallé, and the Emotional or Romantic style exemplified in Anton Rubinstein.
Answers to Correspondents (Music heading) p. 591
    Violin (violin), Bella (music history and appreciation, theory), Alex (music history and appreciation), Miss Florence Griffith (practising society)

Number 599 (20 June 1891)
Minuet and Musette (music score) (H.A.J. Campbell) pp. 596–8
Malvolia (Alice Macdonald) pp. 600–2
    Janet Neal, a poor music teacher, receives a letter from 'Malvolia', who describes herself as a 'rich, beautiful, beloved, talented' – yet also restless and unhappy – 20-year-old who considers giving up everything for music, to become a world-famous singer (p. 601). Janet replies, and a correspondence ensues before she learns that it is all a hoax.
Song of the Workers (poem) (Mary Rowles Jarvis) p. 603

152 Catalogue of musical content

Number 600 (27 June 1891)
Malvolia pp. 614–15
Answers to Correspondents (Music heading) pp. 623–4
> Miss A. Graham (practising society), Ada (music history and appreciation), Evelyn (general), Mary Elizabeth (music of the spheres), Damaris (music history and appreciation, national anthem)

Number 601 (4 July 1891)
A Fortunate Exile: A Story of Swiss School Life (Lily Watson) Ch. 1 pp. 625–7
> Fortunately for 17-year-old Honor Drayton, an English student at a Swiss boarding school, an inept piano performance of one of Mendelssohn's *Songs Without Words* leads to an opportunity to learn singing, her heart's desire, and to cultivate her pure contralto voice.

Summer Song (music score) (Cécile Hartog) pp. 628–30
Youth (poem) (Ida J. Lemon) p. 633
Varieties (The Music of a Cheerful Heart) p. 634

Number 602 (11 July 1891)
A Fortunate Exile Ch. 2 pp. 641–4
Notices of New Music p. 653
Answers to Correspondents p. 656
> D.W.F. (hymn composition)

Number 603 (18 July 1891)
A Fortunate Exile Ch. 3 pp. 657–9
Answers to Correspondents p. 672
> I.M.F. (repertoire)

Number 604 (25 July 1891)
A Fortunate Exile Ch. 4 pp. 673–5

Number 605 (1 August 1891)
School-Day Remembrances pp. 692–3
> Author describes the 'Close' – the breaking up function before the summer holidays. As entertainment, each girl performed upon the piano, but only advanced pupils played solos. 'Quartettes were the order of the day', and if not brilliant, at least they were a pretty sight as the younger girls played their simple pieces (p. 692).

Hints on Pianoforte Teaching (A. D. Swift) pp. 693–4
Midst Granite Hills: The Story of a Dartmoor Holiday (Eglanton Thorne) Ch. 1 pp. 694–6
> Grace Erith, a music governess, has given up her position to nurse her brother back to health following his time at university. An admirer offers a cottage in Dartmoor for his convalescence; in return, Grace serves as organist at the village church.

A Fortunate Exile Ch. 5 pp. 696–9
> Illustration 'Isabel slipped the paper among the bushes' shows a young woman musician in a garden p. 697

Number 606 (8 August 1891)
A Fortunate Exile Ch. 6 pp. 705–7
Midst Granite Hills Ch. 2 pp. 708–9
A Rhyme of Songs (poem) (Augusta Hancock) p. 712
Thoughts on the Higher Education of Women (A Man) pp. 713–14
> The average, well-educated woman should be educated through the ordinary degree course and then study those special subjects 'which will cultivate the taste and increase the imagination', such as harmony and counterpoint for those who are musical.

Catalogue of musical content 153

The Out-bound Bark (music score) (Gordon Saunders, Words Albert E. Drinkwater) pp. 715–19
Answers to Correspondents (Music heading) p. 720
 G. S. Knights (violin), Trumpeter (voice), General 'Jack' (music education)

Number 607 (15 August 1891)
Song of the Fisherman's Wife (poem) (W. D.) p. 721
A Fortunate Exile Ch. 7 pp. 728–30
Midst Granite Hills Ch. 3 pp. 732–4
Answers to Correspondents p. 736
 A. M. (music history and appreciation)

Number 608 (22 August 1891)
A Fortunate Exile Ch. 8 pp. 737–9
Midst Granite Hills Ch. 4 pp. 746–7
Answers to Correspondents (Music heading) p. 751
 Anxious to Know (music education)
Solo (poem) (C. P.) p. 752

Number 609 (29 August 1891)
A Fortunate Exile Ch. 9 pp. 758–9
Midst Granite Hills Ch. 5 p. 763
Answers to Correspondents (Music heading) p. 768
 Fond of Music (general), Rosalinde (general), Twinkling Star (practising society)

Number 610 (5 September 1891)
Tessa and Tonine: A Story for Younger Girls (An Italian Countess) Chs 1, 2, 3, 4 pp. 769–72
 Tessa Dolfini, a very young orphan, plays violin on the streets of London for money or food for her sick twin brother Tonine. When the twins are kidnapped to line the pockets of an unscrupulous man, his scheme to profit financially from the 'entertaining' labour of children is exposed when a clergyman and his wife discover and rescue the children, convert them to Christianity and find them loving homes.
A Fortunate Exile Ch. 10 pp. 780, 782–3
Answers to Correspondents (Music heading) p. 784
 Marian (music history and appreciation), Jessica (repertoire), Jack (voice), Iris (terms), Juanita (general, nuisance)

Number 611 (12 September 1891)
A Fortunate Exile Ch. 11 pp. 785–7
Tessa and Tonine Chs 5, 6 pp. 795–7
Allegreto Giojoso: For the Pianoforte or American Organ (music score) (Myles B. Foster) pp. 798–9
Answers to Correspondents (Music heading) p. 800
 Fairy Lilian (applied music), A Reader of the 'G.O.P.' (applied music, piano, terms), Cedar Tree (music history and appreciation), Beginner (terms)

Number 612 (19 September 1891)
An Evening Recital (poem) (Constance Morgan) 'Prelude' and 'Symphony' p. 802
 Illustration (untitled) shows women and a piano p. 801
A Fortunate Exile Ch. 12 pp. 810–12
Tessa and Tonine Chs 7, 8, 9, 10 pp. 812–15
Answers to Correspondents (Music heading) p. 816
 Letty S. Smith (music education), Gipsy Juggins (practising society), Lightfoot (general)

Number 613 (26 September 1891)
A Fortunate Exile Ch. 13 pp. 820–3

Virgin Snow
Extra Christmas Number for Volume 12 (1890)
The Pedlar: A Pastoral (Herbert Harraden) pp. 54–61
  Includes music scores.

Meadow-Sweet
Extra Summer Number for Volume 12 (1891)
Little Kindnesses (Evelyn Upton) pp. 26–7
  Author cautions readers to 'beware of vexing your nervous neighbours by practising on the piano with open windows' (p. 27). Kindness also should extend to family members who might not find one's singing or playing charming to the ears.
Cousin Madeline pp. 34–51, 53
  When Madeline St Just moves into her Uncle Ethelred's house, one of Cousin Agatha's first questions is whether she plays and sings. 'Yes', says Madeline, who does both and has had good masters. 'I am very fond indeed of music.' (p. 38)
With the Tide: Holiday Duet for Pianoforte (Myles B. Foster) pp. 54–9
A Singing Lesson (poem) (C. P.) p. 61
  Illustration 'A Singing Lesson' p. 60

Volume 13 (3 October 1891–24 September 1892)

Number 614 (3 October 1891)
The Studio Mariano (Eglanton Thorne) Ch. 1* pp. 1–4
> All Maud Marian cares about is her art, and she has her heart set on another winter in Rome where she can resume her lessons and trips to art galleries. Her careless playing after dinner of an air from a new opera she heard in Rome suggests that Maud's fascination is with the city's art, not its music.

The Old Songs and the New (poem) (Helen Marion Burnside) p. 9
> Illustration 'Those quaint old ballads that linger / So long in the heart and ear' p. 8

Answers to Correspondents (Music heading) p. 16
> Annie Finburgh (organist salary), Elizabeth (repertoire), Barnby (repertoire), Emma (voice, musician work, performance etiquette), Heather (repertoire)

Number 615 (10 October 1891)
A Lonely Lassie (Sarah Tytler) Ch. 1 pp. 17–20
> The condition of an open grand piano in the Hayter's drawing room represents the house's lack of a home-like atmosphere when Flora Macdermot arrives. 'It was as if a spell of reckless neglect and indifference was on everything' with the instrument's discoloured keys, unpolished, stained case and carelessly strewn sheets of soiled, torn music (p. 276).

New Employments for Girls (S.F.A. Caulfeild) Part 1 pp. 20–1
> Focuses on suitable means by which upper-class young women can supplement their small, private fortunes. Suggests that musical girls whose families object to public performance sing and play instead for remuneration at private receptions.

The Studio Mariano Ch. 2 pp. 28–30
Answers to Correspondents (Music heading) p. 31
> Nellie (music history and appreciation), Soprano (music history and appreciation)

Number 616 (17 October 1891)
A Lonely Lassie Ch. 2 pp. 36–8
The Studio Mariano Ch. 3 pp. 41–3
Romance (music score) (Clara Schumann) pp. 44–7

Number 617 (24 October 1891)
A Lonely Lassie Ch. 3 pp. 50–2
Out-Door Games From Over the Sea Part 1 pp. 56–8
The Studio Mariano Ch. 4 pp. 58–9
Answers to Correspondents (Music heading) p. 64
> Willing One (organ-accordion), A Princess of Thule (zither), Olive Wyaille (theory), Yellow Topaz (organ), Fudge (dance music, general), Musical (music education), Lady Maud (violin), Monica (applied music), Letty Smyth (music education), Louise (music education)

Number 618 (31 October 1891)
A Use for Old Pianos p. 71
> How to turn an unused upright piano into a combination bookcase, writing desk and cabinet.

A Lonely Lassie Ch. 4 pp. 75–6
Answers to Correspondents (Music heading) p. 80
> Edythe (guitar, banjo, choosing instrument), A.L.M. (music education), Old Gold, etc. (violin, music history and appreciation), Marianne (music history and appreciation)

156 *Catalogue of musical content*

Number 619 (7 November 1891)
My Home in the Close Ch. 1* pp. 81–3
 Orphaned 18-year-old Gertrude Barlett finds life with her aunt Frances in the Close of Dulminster Cathedral 'deadly dull', with evenings only of piano playing or cribbage (p. 82). But after a narrow escape from Russian rebels when on a trip to the Continent, Gertrude gladly returns to the calm of the Close, where the routine becomes more interesting with singing lessons added to her daily piano practice.
 Illustration 'With bent head and clasped hands' shows Gertrude at the piano p. 81
The Studio Mariano Ch. 5 pp. 85–6
Plain Words to Schoolgirls (The Ven. Archdeacon Wilson) pp. 89–90
 Cautions girls not to overdo the intellectual side of education. Social duties, which include music making, are 'one of the developments of the soul' and should not make one selfish or unsociable (p. 89).
A Lonely Lassie Ch. 5 pp. 90–1
How French Girls Are Employed (Helen Zimmern) pp. 93–5
 From 'The Young Girl's Practical Guide in the Choice of a Profession' compiled by Madame Pacquet-Mille and recently published in Paris. Zimmern excerpts the list of studies and admission requirements for musical artists at the Conservatoire, which she considers 'the best preparatory institution of the kind on the whole continent' (p. 93).

Number 620 (14 November 1891)
The Studio Mariano Ch. 6 pp. 97–9
Bessie Gilbert (Alice King) pp. 100–1
 Scarlet fever at age three left Bessie Gilbert blind, but she was taught music and had a correct musical ear. As a young woman, she was equally talented on harp, piano and guitar. Her flexible voice mastered operatic arias and old ballads alike.
A Lonely Lassie Ch. 6 pp. 101–3
My Home in the Close Ch. 2 pp. 108–11
Answers to Correspondents p. 112
 A Wandering Dove (repertoire), Logwood Blossom (Jamaica) (repertoire)

Number 621 (21 November 1891)
A Lonely Lassie Ch. 7 pp. 113–16
 Illustration 'Flora was, as a matter of course, a good deal teased by Dick, who would tell all sorts of good and bad stories of Scotchmen' shows Flora at the piano p. 113
My Home in the Close Ch. 3* pp. 116–18
Out-Door Games From Over the Sea Part 2 pp. 120–2
The Studio Mariano Ch. 7 pp. 122–4
Answers to Correspondents p. 128
 Soubrette (general)

Number 622 (28 November 1891)
My Home in the Close Ch. 4 pp. 129–31
Notices of New Music pp. 131–2
A Lonely Lassie Ch. 8 pp. 133–5
The Studio Mariano Ch. 8 pp. 139–41

Number 623 (5 December 1891)
A Lonely Lassie Ch. 9 pp. 146–9
Out-Door Games From Over the Sea Part 3 pp. 152–5
The Studio Mariano Ch. 9 pp. 156–9

Number 624 (12 December 1891)
The Studio Mariano Ch. 10 pp. 161–4
A Lonely Lassie Ch. 10 pp. 174–5
Answers to Correspondents (Music heading) p. 176
   Ambitious One (piano, health), Sonata (music history and appreciation), E. M. (digitorium)

Number 625 (19 December 1891)
A Christmas Carol (poem) (S.F.A. Caulfeild) p. 177
The Studio Mariano Ch. 11 pp. 178–80
Love and Laughter (music score) (C.H.H. Parry, Words Arthur Butler) pp. 180–2
Song of the Early Christians, Meeting in the Catacombs, in Secret by Night (from 'Vivia perpetua', a dramatic poem by S. F. Adams) p. 183
A Lonely Lassie Ch. 11 pp. 190–1
Answers to Correspondents (Music heading) p. 191
   Pink Jacket (music history and appreciation), Lover of Music (general)

Number 626 (26 December 1891)
A Lonely Lassie Ch. 12 pp. 193–6

Number 627 (2 January 1892)
A Lonely Lassie Ch. 13 pp. 210–11
Music (illustration) p. 216
   A young woman plays an ancient stringed lyre.
A Chameleon (Alice Macdonald) Chs 1, 2 pp. 217–18
   Camilla Blake, who finds the piano 'awfully slow', drops it and takes up the banjo instead (p. 247).
The Studio Mariano Ch. 12 pp. 220–2

Number 628 (9 January 1892)
The Studio Mariano Ch. 13 pp. 226–9
A Chameleon Chs 3, 4 pp. 235–6
A Lonely Lassie Ch. 14 pp. 237–8
Answers to Correspondents p. 239
   Gretchen (national anthem, music history and appreciation)

Number 629 (16 January 1892)
The Studio Mariano Ch. 14 pp. 241–4
A Chameleon Chs 5, 6* pp. 247, 249
Some Celebrated Female Musicians: St. Cecilia (J. F. Rowbotham) pp. 251–2
A Lonely Lassie Ch. 15 pp. 253–5
Answers to Correspondents (Music heading) p. 256
   Semi-Quaver (music education), Muriel, E. D. (copyright), Dodo (music history and appreciation), A.A.C. (banjo, choosing instrument), Charity (music teaching), L'Eglantine (violin), Sans Sentiment (general), Mozart-Bach (piano, health)

Number 630 (23 January 1892)
Pincushions (B.C.) pp. 257–9
   Includes pincushions shaped like a violin and a banjo.
The Studio Mariano Ch. 15 pp. 261–3
Out-Door Games From Over the Sea Part 4 pp. 264–6
A Chameleon Ch. 7 p. 267
Answers to Correspondents pp. 271–2
   Pansy R. (harmonium)

Number 631 (30 January 1892)
A Lonely Lassie Ch. 16* pp. 276–8
Sola (poem) p. 288
    Anonymous response to poem 'Solo' in *TGOP* Volume 12.
Duetto (poem) (C. P.) p. 288

Number 632 (6 February 1892)
A Lonely Lassie Ch. 17 pp. 289–92
Out-Door Games From Over the Sea Part 5 pp. 300–1
The Studio Mariano Ch. 16 pp. 302–3

Number 633 (13 February 1892)
The Studio Mariano Ch. 17 pp. 305–8
A Lonely Lassie Ch. 18 pp. 317–18
Answers to Correspondents pp. 319–20
    Carrie (copyright)

Number 634 (20 February 1892)
A Lonely Lassie Ch. 19 pp. 323–4
Antiphon: Daylight Fades Away (music score) (C. A. Macirone, Words George MacDonald) pp. 324–6
The Studio Mariano Ch. 18 pp. 328–31
Answers to Correspondents (Music heading) p. 336
    An Innocent (zither), Judy (music education)
    Illustration 'A Banjo Enthusiast'

Number 635 (27 February 1892)
A Lonely Lassie Ch. 20 pp. 338–40
The Studio Mariano Ch. 19 pp. 342–3
Frau Dr. Clara Schumann: A Short Sketch of Her Life (The Countess A. Von Bothmer) pp. 348–9
Varieties (Printed Music in England) p. 350

Number 636 (5 March 1892)
A Lonely Lassie Ch. 21 pp. 353–6
New Employments for Girls Part 2 pp. 362–3
    Piano tuning offers remunerative employment for girls.
The Studio Mariano Ch. 20 pp. 364–6
Answers to Correspondents (Music heading) p. 368
    Dolce Carmen (guitar, mandolin, choosing instrument), Dorothy F. (sight-reading), Birdie (general), M. Garry (general)

Number 637 (12 March 1892)
A Lonely Lassie Ch. 22 pp. 369–71
Out-door Games From Over the Sea Part 6 pp. 372–4
Notes on Songs of Tennyson: With Reference to Their Musical Settings (William Porteous) pp. 374–5
Varieties (Sweet Music) p. 377
The Studio Mariano Ch. 21 pp. 378–80

Number 638 (19 March 1892)
The Studio Mariano Ch. 22 pp. 385–7
A Battle with Destiny (John Saunders) Chs 1, 2 pp. 392–4
    In a series of calamities, Owen Stanard dies suddenly before he can pay his £47,000 debt, marry and fulfil the provisions of his father Benjamin's will and inherit his estate.

Owen's son Colonel Paul, recently returned from military service in India, thus inherits Castle Stanard and his father's enormous debt. During this time of adversity, daughter Jeanie's playing and singing of sacred music such as 'O Rest in the Lord' brings comfort to her father and herself.
Under the Greenwood Tree (music score) (Myles B. Foster, Words William Shakespeare) pp. 396–8

Number 639 (26 March 1892)
The Studio Mariano Ch. 23 pp. 401–4
A Battle with Destiny Ch. 3 pp. 406–7
Answers to Correspondents (Music heading) p. 416
    Miss Rees (practising society), Mabel (music history and appreciation), Ana Mana (sight-reading, practising society), Kathleen (choral singing), Queenie (practising)

Number 640 (2 April 1892)
The Studio Mariano Ch. 24 pp. 417–19
A Battle with Destiny Ch. 4 pp. 430–2
Answers to Correspondents (Music heading) p. 432
    Rosebud (music lessons), May (composition), Wilhelmina (applied music), Sweet Seventeen (mandolin), Heather (music teaching), Jess of the D'Urbervilles (general), Nina (violin, music history and appreciation), Music Mad (general)

Number 641 (9 April 1892)
Sackcloth and Ashes (Ruth Lamb) Ch. 1 pp. 433–5
    Landlord Mr Richard Cutclose considers a tenant's sewing machine a good security. A piano, however, is better. The former he associates with 'hard toil, scanty pay, and the lower classes'; the latter, with gentility and leisure. 'In his better-class houses a piano is part of the necessary furniture, even when little used; and as a rule its presence is a test of respectability, of rents duly paid, and tenants who only move at long intervals, mostly to better themselves.' (p. 502)
Elegy: For the Harmonium or American Organ (music score) (Myles B. Foster) pp. 436–8
A Battle with Destiny Ch. 5 pp. 445–6
Answers to Correspondents (Music heading) p. 447
    Ada C. Gibbons (music education), Anxious Pattie (castanets), Mezzo (voice, nuisance)

Number 642 (16 April 1892)
Sackcloth and Ashes Ch. 2 pp. 449–52
A Battle with Destiny Ch. 6 pp. 458–9

Number 643 (23 April 1892)
A Battle with Destiny Ch. 7 pp. 465–7
Sackcloth and Ashes Ch. 3 pp. 474–5
Some Celebrated Female Musicians: Sappho (J. F. Rowbotham) pp. 478–9
Answers to Correspondents (Music heading) pp. 479–80
    Grateful Reader (banjo, guitar, concertina, organ-accordion), Nancy (piano, music teaching), Theodora (pronunciation)

Number 644 (30 April 1892)
Sackcloth and Ashes Ch. 4 pp. 482–4
A Battle with Destiny Chs 8, 9 pp. 494–5
Answers to Correspondents p. 496
    F.E.W. (terms)

Number 645 (7 May 1892)
Sackcloth and Ashes Ch. 5* pp. 501–3
The Tuner and the Tuning (poem) William Luff) p. 505
A Battle with Destiny Ch. 10 pp. 506–7
Romance: For Violin and Pianoforte (music score) (J. T. Field) pp. 508–9

Number 646 (14 May 1892)
Sackcloth and Ashes Ch. 6 pp. 514–15
A Battle with Destiny Ch. 11 pp. 524–6

Number 647 (21 May 1892)
Sackcloth and Ashes Ch. 7 pp. 529–31
A Battle with Destiny Ch. 12 pp. 536, 538

Number 648 (28 May 1892)
A Battle with Destiny Ch. 13 pp. 545–7
Sackcloth and Ashes Ch. 8 pp. 556–9
Answers to Correspondents p. 560
    Would-Be Vocalist (general), All Sorts (zither)

Number 649 (4 June 1892)
Sackcloth and Ashes Ch. 9 pp. 561–4
A Battle with Destiny Chs 14, 15 pp. 566–7
Some Celebrated Female Musicians: Jenny Lind (J. F. Rowbotham) pp. 570–1
Up the Steep Hillside Ch. 1 pp. 572–3
    Playing second violin in a string quartet at the Davey's Norwood home is a heady experience for Mary Pollard. She has to do some soul searching regarding her musical ambitions. Deciding, like many real-life contemporaries, that 'it would be the most delightful thing in the world' to study at Guildhall School of Music, Mary has to consider 'How much had vanity and ambition to do with that conclusion, and how much a genuine love of music?' (p. 598)

Number 650 (11 June 1892)
Sackcloth and Ashes Ch. 10 pp. 578, 580–2
Up the Steep Hillside Ch. 2* pp. 586–7
A Battle with Destiny Ch. 16 pp. 590–1

Number 651 (18 June 1892)
A Battle with Destiny Ch. 17 pp. 595–6
Up the Steep Hillside Ch. 3* pp. 597–8
Summer Days (poem) (Ellen Thorneycroft Fowler) p. 601
Sackcloth and Ashes Ch. 11 pp. 603–5
Notices of New Music p. 605
Answers to Correspondents (Music heading) p. 607
    Little May (voice, applied music, health), Beatrice (choral singing), Muriel E. D. (copyright)

Number 652 (25 June 1892)
A Battle with Destiny Chs 18, 19 pp. 609–11
Up the Steep Hillside Ch. 4 pp. 611–12
Sackcloth and Ashes Ch. 12 pp. 619–20
Answers to Correspondents (Music heading) p. 623
    A Lover of Music (violin, music history and appreciation, organ), An Orphan (general), Viola (music history and appreciation)

Catalogue of musical content 161

Number 653 (2 July 1892)
A Lesson from Nature (poem) (The Rev. William Cowan) p. 625–6
Sackcloth and Ashes Ch. 13 pp. 626–8
A Battle with Destiny Ch. 20 pp. 634–5
Answers to Correspondents pp. 639–40
   Fairy (lyre, music history and appreciation), Dorothy (practising, nuisance)

Number 654 (9 July 1892)
A Battle with Destiny Ch. 21 pp. 646–7
Aubade (music score) (H.A.J. Campbell) pp. 652–3
Sackcloth and Ashes Ch. 14 pp. 654–6

Number 655 (16 July 1892)
Sackcloth and Ashes Ch. 15 pp. 657–9
The Glee Maidens (J. F. Rowbotham) pp. 663, 665
   To gain proficiency in music, ambitious village girls in the Middle Ages often became itinerant musicians while traveling to one of the great cities in Europe for music study. Recognized by their colourful mode of dress, these 'glee maidens' remained safe and were respected for their performances on a number of instruments including violin, flute, lute and guitar.
A Battle with Destiny Ch. 22 pp. 667–9
Varieties (Poverty at the Piano) p. 670

Number 656 (23 July 1892)
A Battle with Destiny Ch. 23 pp. 679–80
Sackcloth and Ashes Ch. 16 pp. 685–7

Number 657 (30 July 1892)
A Battle with Destiny Ch. 24 pp. 690–1
Sackcloth and Ashes Ch. 17 pp. 701–3
Answers to Correspondents (Music heading) p. 704
   Marvel (music education), Daisy (repertoire), Lover of music (guitar, banjo), Edith H. Muir (piano)

Number 658 (6 August 1892)
A Battle with Destiny Ch. 25 pp. 705–7
Sackcloth and Ashes Ch. 18 pp. 718–20

Number 659 (13 August 1892)
A Battle with Destiny Chs 26, 27 pp. 725–7
Varieties (Without Ears for Music) p. 727
Sackcloth and Ashes Ch. 19 pp. 731–3

Number 660 (20 August 1892)
Sackcloth and Ashes Ch. 20 pp. 737–40
Christine Nisson (J. F. Rowbotham) pp. 740–1
Varieties (The Power of Music) p. 743
A Battle with Destiny Chs 28, 29 pp. 748–9
Answers to Correspondents p. 751
   Florence (music education)

Number 661 (27 August 1892)
Sackcloth and Ashes Ch. 21 pp. 754–5
Crusaders' March: For the Harmonium or American Organ (music score) (Myles B. Foster) pp. 756–8

162 Catalogue of musical content

A Battle with Destiny Ch. 30 pp. 766–7
Answers to Correspondents (Music heading) p. 768
   A. Brooks (practising societies), Secretary (music education), Wayland Smith (general), Twelve Years' Contributor (general), R.P.W.S. (mandolin), Emily Hartland (practising society), Edith Q. (repertoire), Madge (general)

Number 662 (3 September 1892)
Sackcloth and Ashes Ch. 22 pp. 773–5
A Battle with Destiny Ch. 31* pp. 779–80

Number 663 (10 September 1892)
Sackcloth and Ashes Ch. 23 pp. 787–9
A Battle with Destiny Chs 32, 33 pp. 797–8
Answers to Correspondents p. 799
   Madame St. Pierre (piano, repertoire)

Number 664 (17 September 1892)
Sackcloth and Ashes Chs 24, 25 pp. 802–6
A Battle with Destiny Ch. 34 pp. 810–11
Answers to Correspondents p. 816
   Marie Stuversant (music potential)

Number 665 (24 September 1892)
Sackcloth and Ashes Ch. 26 pp. 819–21
Meditation: For the Harmonium or American Organ (music score) (Myles B. Foster) p. 822
A Battle with Destiny Ch. 35 pp. 826–7

Love-Light
Extra Christmas Number for Volume 13 (1891)
A Modern Martyr pp. 3–12, 14–19
   When Marjorie Hunter visits the Winthrops, the guests engage in music making after dinner. Marjorie, who plays the piano 'with taste', has an excellent ear and has been well taught, joins the curate Mr Hewson as cellist and Dora Winthrop as violinist in a Beethoven trio (p. 10).
'Nearer, My God, to Thee' (poem) (The Rev. William Cowan) p. 33
Old Daddy Christmas: A Musical Allegory (Herbert Harraden) pp. 34–41
   Includes music scores.
A Daily Governess pp. 42–3, 45
   Miss Shenstone not only is diligent with the needle, but has the knack of getting the best work out of others for the benefit of those in need. When guests assemble and fingers are flying, Miss Shenstone occasionally plays for the women or treats them with a ballad sung in her rich contralto voice. 'Decidedly, Miss Shenstone aimed at things higher than mere needlework.' (p. 45)

Maidenhair
Extra Summer Number for Volume 13 (1892)
A Mountain Idyl: An Episode from the Life of Ludwig II, King of Bavaria (Elizabeth Highfield) p. 4–11
   Letters exchanged between Bavarian King Ludwig II and Fräulein Elisabeth von Rebach recount his immoderate interest in the works of and friendship with Richard Wagner.
The Zither Player (illustration) p. 12
   A young woman is playing the zither.

Jennie's Wooing (music score) (Cécile Hartog, Words Emma C. Dowd) pp. 13–15
A Summer Hymn (poem) (Catherine P. Craig) p. 17
A Song of Briar Roses (poem) (Mary Rowles Jarvis) p. 24
A Girl's Patience (C. J. Blake) pp. 43–8
    When 15-yer-old Edith Harley comes to live with her Aunt Rachel at Silchester, the elderly woman enquires about the girl's capabilities and accomplishments. Although fairly good at French, Edith claims no natural talent for music, having been taught but not practised piano regularly. 'As for the music', her aunt says, 'I don't believe in making girls who can't tell the National Anthem from the Old Hundredth, strum on the piano whether they like it or not. You may learn drawing instead.' (p. 46)
A Disguised Blessing (La Petite) pp. 56, 58–63
    Damaris Calendar, Hazelcopse's new schoolmistress, undertakes some much-needed reform in the village. After starting a night school for working lads and a girls' club, she takes on the organist duties on Sundays and forms a choir from her musical scholars and older parishioners.

Volume 14 (1 October 1892–30 September 1893)

Number 666 (1 October 1892)
Little Miss Muffet (Rosa Nouchette Carey) Ch. 1* pp. 1–3
> Effie Beresford's mother wants her daughter, like other young ladies, to 'be able to play nicely on the piano', which she thinks is a reasonable demand (p. 2). But when Effie, who practised a 'stupid' accompaniment 'for at least two hours' nonetheless plays it badly, her aunt Isobel advises, 'Half an hour's daily practice is better than two hours every week or so.' (p. 150)

Answers to Correspondents (Music heading) p. 15
> Would-Be Songstress and Edith Daisy (voice), D. B. (practising society)

All Thy works shall praise Thy Name (illustration) p. 16
> An angel is playing a stringed instrument.

Number 667 (8 October 1892)
The Little Girl in Grey: A Story of Two Continents (Horace Townsend) Prologue, Ch. 1 pp. 17–20
> Dorothy Datchett, raised in England, is on a steamer bound for the United States. The purser who has heard her beautiful voice wants Dorothy to sing for an after-dinner concert, but the two elderly matrons of the planning committee overrule him. When a performer cancels at a moment's notice, however, Dorothy is persuaded to sing. Knowing nothing of modern music, she sings old-fashioned English ditties and ballads and turns a failing programme into a success.

Little Miss Muffet Ch. 2 pp. 30–1
Answers to Correspondents p. 32
> Little Ivy (general)

Number 668 (15 October 1892)
Little Miss Muffet Ch. 3 pp. 34–5
The Artistic Life of Louisa Pyne (Ruth Lamb) Ch. 1 pp. 36–7
> Illustration 'Miss L. Pyne' p. 37

The Little Girl in Grey Ch. 2* pp. 44–5

Number 669 (22 October 1892)
The Little Girl in Grey Ch. 3 pp. 50–1
Hidden Love (music score) (Edvard Grieg, Words Björnson, English trans. F. Corder) pp. 52–3
Little Miss Muffet Ch. 4 pp. 62–3

Number 670 (29 October 1892)
The Little Girl in Grey Ch. 4 pp. 70–1
Notices of New Music p. 71
Marquetry Wood-Staining pp. 75–7
> Illustrations Fig. 2 Marquetry by Riesner and Fig. 3 Floral Marquetry show musical designs pp. 75, 76

Miss Brewson and Miss Smith (Ida Lemon) pp. 78–80
> Housemates Caroline Brewson and Martha Smith, more like sisters than friends, were apprentice dressmakers together before starting a joint establishment. Both had been sopranos in an amateur choral society so feel assured in their musical powers. When Mr Burton, a middle-aged bachelor seeking a steady, smart wife, visits, Miss Smith sings

Catalogue of musical content 165

in her thin voice; Miss Brewson, whose voice is superior to her friend's, has 'no desire to show-off' (p. 78).
Answers to Correspondents p. 80
    Martha Byam (violin)

Number 671 (5 November 1892)
The Little Girl in Grey Ch. 5 pp. 81–3
My Father's Ward (La Petite) Ch. 1 pp. 89–90
    Two brief mentions of music making suggest that this accomplishment is still important in the daily lives of young women in the old rambling house at Blackheath. In the first, Lilian Chardwell's father asks her to give him a song; in the second, Candace (Candy) Gordon is playing piano.
The Artistic Life of Louisa Pyne Ch. 2 pp. 91–2
Little Miss Muffet Ch. 5 pp. 94–5

Number 672 (12 November 1892)
Little Miss Muffet Ch. 6 pp. 97–9
To Dolly (music score) (C. Hubert Parry) pp. 100–1
My Father's Ward Ch. 2* pp. 104–6
The Little Girl in Grey Ch. 6* pp. 108–9

Number 673 (19 November 1892)
My Father's Ward Ch. 3 pp. 113–14
Little Miss Muffet Ch. 7 pp. 118–19
The Little Girl in Grey Ch. 7 pp. 126–7
Answers to Correspondents (Music heading) pp. 127–8
    Cauliflower (general), Harmony (terms, applied music), A.N.H. (dulcimer, cithara, music history and appreciation), Marion (theory)

Number 674 (26 November 1892)
My Father's Ward Ch. 4* pp. 129–30
    Illustration 'She was playing' shows Candy at the piano p. 129
Little Miss Muffet Ch. 8 pp. 134–5
The Little Girl in Grey Ch. 8 pp. 139–40

Number 675 (3 December 1892)
The Little Girl in Grey Ch. 9 pp. 145–7
Little Miss Muffet Ch. 9* pp. 150–1
The Artistic Life of Louisa Pyne Ch. 3 pp. 154–5
Answers to Correspondents (Music heading) p. 160
    A Fiddler (violin), A Working Girl (violin), Ethel and Inez (piano), X.Y.Z. (general), Doubtful Harmony (composition)

Number 676 (10 December 1892)
Little Miss Muffet Ch. 10* pp. 161–3
Aunt Lu's Legacy Ch. 1 pp. 172–3
    When Irene Northam sees Lucindy West – Aunt Lu – on the kerb after a fall, she takes the elderly woman to her own lodgings before taking her home. The two become friends, and both are musical. During a visit, Aunt Lu, who once 'must have possessed rare skill', plays 'I know that my Redeemer liveth' on a sweet-toned piano (p. 182). Other melodies

follow, sung in a high quavering voice to which Irene adds her soft contralto. Irene's offering is 'O Rest in the Lord'.
The Little Girl in Grey Ch. 10 pp. 174–5

Number 677 (17 December 1892)
The Piano and the Player (poem) (William Luff) p. 177
Little Miss Muffet Ch. 11* pp. 178–9
Minuet (music score) (Myles B. Foster) pp. 180–1
Aunt Lu's Legacy Ch. 2* pp. 182–3
The Little Girl in Grey Ch. 11 pp. 188–90
Answers to Correspondents (Music heading) p. 191
    Sam Bo (practising society), N.I.E.P. (music potential), F. M. (composition), Sandilli (Cape Colony) (music history and appreciation)

Number 678 (24 December 1892)
Christmas Mummers in Sweden (illustration) p. 193
    Musicians are among the merrymakers.
Little Miss Muffet Ch. 12 pp. 194–5
Aunt Lu's Legacy Ch. 3 pp. 199–200
The Little Girl in Grey Ch. 12 pp. 206–7

Number 679 (31 December 1892)
Little Miss Muffet Ch. 13 pp. 210–11
Aunt Lu's Legacy Ch. 4 pp. 219–20

Number 680 (7 January 1893)
Little Miss Muffet Ch. 14 pp. 230–1
The Little Girl in Grey Ch. 13 pp. 237–9

Number 681 (14 January 1893)
Little Miss Muffet Ch. 15 pp. 241–3
'On Richmond Hill' (music score) (arr. C. A. Macirone) pp. 244–6
The Artistic Life of Louisa Pyne Ch. 4 pp. 247–8
The Little Girl in Grey Ch. 14 pp. 252–4

Number 682 (21 January 1893)
Little Miss Muffet Ch. 16 pp. 258–9
The Little Girl in Grey Ch. 15 pp. 268, 270–1
The Roman Singer (illustration) p. 269
    A young woman not actively singing.

Number 683 (28 January 1893)
Little Miss Muffet Ch. 17 pp. 285–6
Notices of New Music p. 287

Number 684 (4 February 1893)
Little Miss Muffet Ch. 18 pp. 294–5
'A Fateful Number': A Tale of Amalfi (Mrs Frank W. W. Topham) Ch. 1* pp. 296–8
    In Italy's Amalfi Hills, Tessa, a young peasant with a lovely singing voice, is considered 'a wicked little witch, who bewitches everyone who comes near her' (p. 297). When ill, Tessa seeks solace in her mandolin.

Catalogue of musical content 167

Answers to Correspondents (Music heading) p. 304
   Miss A. E. Blunt (practising society), Clematis (applied music), A Would-Be Musician (guitar, zither, banjo-zither, choosing instrument), Woodstock and A Would-Be Songster (music education), Miss L. Feary (theory, correspondence course), Violinist (general)

Number 685 (11 February 1893)
Little Miss Muffet Ch. 19 pp. 305–7
'My Love' (music score) (Charles P. Banks) pp. 308–11
A Fateful Number Ch. 2 pp. 312–14
A Fit of the Blues (Medicus) pp. 315–16
   Lassitude and weariness are best treated by taking an antibilious pill or two rather than by reading a romance or playing sad music on the piano or violin.
Answers to Correspondents pp. 319–20
   Joan (performance etiquette, piano, general)

Number 686 (18 February 1893)
A Fateful Number Ch. 3* pp. 321–3
   Illustration 'She even went so far as to play on her little mandolin' p. 323
Little Miss Muffet Ch. 20 pp. 326–7
Answers to Correspondents (Music heading) p. 336
   Amelia (voice), Topsy-Turvy (music history and appreciation), A.L.R. (music history and appreciation), Lina (repertoire)

Number 687 (25 February 1893)
The Artistic Life of Louisa Pyne Ch. 5 pp. 340–1
Little Miss Muffet Ch. 21 pp. 342–3
Varieties (The Singer's Work – *Charles Santley*) p. 346
A Fateful Number Ch. 4 pp. 347–8
An Old Song Ended (illustration) (from Frank Cox painting) plate facing p. 352
   A young woman looking out the window has a guitar at her side.

Number 688 (4 March 1893)
The Organist's Daughter Ch. 1 pp. 356–8
   Ivy Gardiner takes over her father's organist duties when his health fails. Confident in the role, she also meets with the parents of his piano pupils to encourage continued lessons under her tutelage.
Little Miss Muffet Ch. 22 pp. 364–5

Number 689 (11 March 1893)
'Heard melodies are sweet, but those unheard are sweeter' (illustration) (from Edith Martineau picture) p. 376
   A young woman with a violin in hand.
My Music (poem) (Constance Morgan) p. 377
The Organist's Daughter Ch. 2 pp. 377–9
Varieties (Envying the Cats) p. 381
Little Miss Muffet Ch. 23 pp. 382–3
Answers to Correspondents (Music heading) p. 384
   Ama (harp, health), G.C.P. (music student lodging), Carrie (voice, health), Farmer's Daughter (general), Nora (composition), Nell (practising society)

168 *Catalogue of musical content*

Number 690 (18 March 1893)
Little Miss Muffet Ch. 24 pp. 385–7
The Organist's Daughter Ch. 3 pp. 392, 394
Supplication: For Harmonium or Pianoforte (music score) (Myles B. Foster) p. 395

Number 691 (25 March 1893)
Varieties (High and Low Notes – *Santley*) p. 403
The Artistic Life of Louisa Pyne Ch. 6 pp. 406–7
Notices of New Music p. 407
Answers to Correspondents p. 416
    Carrie (music history and appreciation)

Number 692 (1 April 1893)
Our Poets' Corner: William Cowper (1731) p. 423
    Cowper was a hymn writer who, with John Newton, compiled the *Olney Hymns*.
Next-Door Neighbours: A Story for Girls (Evelyn Everett-Green) Ch. 1 pp. 424–7
    Max Tresham, a college student with a fine baritone voice, meets contralto Regina Stanley-Devenish at a musical evening and hears her sing. Max could tell that 'she was a true artist and a true musician' who had had excellent training (p. 495). Regina plays Max's accompaniment. Regina's comment to her hostess about Max offers an authorial opinion about a current musical practice: 'Yes, and he sang very well, too. I am so glad you do not yield to the growing fashion of having all the music done by second-rate professionals that interest nobody. I would much rather hear amateur performances – one likes to hear one's friends.' (p. 444)

Number 693 (8 April 1893)
How to Drape (T. J.) Part 2 pp. 435–7
    Illustration of draped piano p. 436
Next-Door Neighbours Ch. 2* pp. 440–3
    Illustration 'In the Walnut Tree' shows Susie Tresham sitting on a tree branch playing guitar p. 441
Answers to Correspondents (Music heading) pp. 447–8
    A.L.P. (music education), Marie (composition), Miss L. Feary (theory, correspondence course), Mezzo-Soprano (voice)

Number 694 (15 April 1893)
Next-Door Neighbours Ch. 3 pp. 450–1
'I Publish the Bans of Marriage'; or, My Sister's Wedding, and How We Organized It' Part 1 pp. 452–3
    Details the organ music chosen for the occasion.
Spring Song (poem) p. 464

Number 695 (22 April 1893)
Next-Door Neighbours Ch. 4 pp. 476–9

Number 696 (29 April 1893)
A New Hymn Tune (music score) (C. A. Macirone) p. 493
Next-Door Neighbours Ch. 5* pp. 494–5

Number 697 (6 May 1893)
My First Appearance (E. Meredith Cartwright) pp. 501–2
   After her father dies, the singer has to give up her studies at the German Conservatoire and teach music rather than perform. Her first professional engagement as a singer is on a barge, arranged by an agent who works on commission.
Next-Door Neighbours Ch. 6 pp. 510–11

Number 698 (13 May 1893)
Varieties (Girls and Singing – *Reminiscences of Charles Santley*) p. 517
Next-Door Neighbours Ch. 7 pp. 524–5
Answers to Correspondents (Music heading) p. 527
   E. H. Hobart (practising society), Banjo (dulcimer), Pussie (practising society), Vox Humana and Would-Be Musician (organ), 'Kathleen Mavourneen' (repertoire), Lulu (piano, repertoire), Lucy E. (general)

Number 699 (20 May 1893)
The Music of the Emerald Isle (Annie W. Patterson) pp. 537–8
   Patterson, a Dublin organist, composer, author and first woman to earn a doctorate in music by examination in 1889, from the Royal University of Ireland two years after earning her Bachelor of Music and Bachelor of Arts from the same institution, writes about her native Celtic music.
Sing, Sweet Warblers (music score) (Franz Abt, Words Edward Oxenford) pp. 540–1
Next-Door Neighbours Ch. 8 pp. 542–3

Number 700 (27 May 1893)
Next-Door Neighbours Ch. 9 pp. 548–50

Number 701 (3 June 1893)
Next-Door Neighbours Ch. 10 pp. 572–4
Answers to Correspondents (Music heading) p. 575
   Macniven (music education), Rosaline and Musical Belle (music teaching), Eunice (harmonium, health), Sanandshire (general), H.B. (music history and appreciation), Miss Muffet (piano, nuisance), Bessie (Washington) (repertoire, music history and appreciation)
'Pansies for Thoughts' (illustration) p. 576
   A women from olden times holds a stringed instrument.

Number 702 (10 June 1893)
Song: – 'Come to Me, O Ye Children' (music score) (C. A. Macirone, Words W. H. [sic] Longfellow) pp. 580–3
Next-Door Neighbours Ch. 11 pp. 584–7

Number 703 (17 June 1893)
Varieties (The Divine Art of Music – *Carlyle*) p. 595
Next-Door Neighbours Ch. 12 pp. 604–6
[Notices of New] Music pp. 606–7

Number 704 (24 June 1893)
Varieties (An Extraordinary Musical Feat) p. 615
Next-Door Neighbours Ch. 13 pp. 621–3

170 Catalogue of musical content

Number 705 (1 July 1893)
Next-Door Neighbours Ch. 14 pp. 632–5
Varieties (The Piano – *J. S. Van Cleve*; Profitable Music Lessons) p. 635
How to Improve on the Violin (Gabrielle Vaillant) pp. 636–7
Answers to Correspondents p. 639
  Pippa Passes (practising society)

Number 706 (8 July 1893)
A Sudden Shadow (Laura G. Ackroyd) pp. 641–3
  When Helen is losing her eyesight, she asks her sister Faith to play for her, 'for in the twilight a little soft music is so comforting'. As Faith's 'fingers stirred lightly over the keys in one of Schubert's Impromptus, Helen sat thinking deeply, and knitting assiduously, "troubled," like Martha of old, "about many things"'. (p. 642)
The Birds Sing All the Year (poem) (Helen Marion Burnside) p. 648
Next-Door Neighbours Ch. 15 pp. 650–1
Answers to Correspondents (Music heading) p. 655
  Jessamine (applied music), Mab (piano, repertoire), D. L. (piano), Mary (theory, music education), Cramp's Housekeeper (violin), Beginner (terms)

Number 707 (15 July 1893)
Next-Door Neighbours Ch. 16 pp. 667–9

Number 798 (22 July 1893)
Next-Door Neighbours Ch. 17 pp. 686–8

Number 709 (29 July 1893)
The Three Little Clouds (music score) (C. E. Rawstorne, Words Kate Kellog) pp. 693–5
Next-Door Neighbours Ch. 18 pp. 696–8

Number 710 (5 August 1893)
Next-Door Neighbours Ch. 19 pp. 705–7

Number 711 (12 August 1893)
Next-Door Neighbours Ch. 20 pp. 722–3
Our Poets' Corner: Reginald Heber (1783) pp. 734–5
  Heber's poem 'From Greenland's icy mountains', set to music by Lowell Mason, is known as the missionary hymn.
Answers to Correspondents p. 735
  Prascovie (music as accomplishment)
A Wandering Minstrel (illustration) p. 736
  A young girl plays the harp.

Number 712 (19 August 1893)
Next-Door Neighbours Ch. 21 pp. 738–9
Gavotte (music score) (Myles B. Foster) pp. 740–1

Number 713 (26 August 1893)
Next-Door Neighbours Ch. 22 pp. 754–5

Number 714 (2 September 1893)
Next-Door Neighbours Ch. 23 pp. 770–2
My Godfather's Present (C.N. Carvalho) Ch. 1* pp. 776, 778
  When her father objects to her plan to use her godfather's £20 gift to go abroad, Catherine does what she usually does when in a temper – goes into the drawing room and plays the piano. Before finishing a Chopin nocturne, she had a less gloomy view of the situation.

Number 715 (9 September 1893)
Next-Door Neighbours Ch. 24 pp. 786–7
My Godfather's Present Ch. 2 pp. 790–1
A Cinderella (poem) (E. Nesbit) p. 792
    Illustration 'Cinderella' shows a young female musician of olden times p. 793
Answers to Correspondents p. 800
    Toodles (harmonium)

Number 716 (16 September 1893)
Our Life in a Country Village: An Actual Experience (A Country Girl) pp. 801–3
    Julia set up a 'charming room' in her village and wooed the sailors from the pubs when she sang 'Nancy Lee' and songs dear to their hearts (p. 803).
My Godfather's Present Ch. 3 pp. 809–10
Next-Door Neighbours (Evelyn Everett-Green) Ch. 25 pp. 812–14

Number 717 (23 September 1893)
Eventide (music score) (J. W. Hinton, Words Augusta Hancock) pp. 820–2
Next-Door Neighbours Ch. 26 pp. 826–7

Number 718 (30 September 1893)
Answers to Correspondents p. 843
    Miss Hettie Garrett (practising society)

Starshine
Extra Christmas Number for Volume 14 (1892)
St. Cecilia's Day at Rome (Eglanton Thorne) pp. 21–3
    Illustrations 'St. Ceciila' p. 21; 'Deathbed of St. Cecilia' p. 22
A Little Country Maid pp. 23–4
    Gertrude Crawford's singing, which 'had been the chief attraction in many a London drawing-room', brings the sweet voice of angels to the bedsides of workhouse inmates (p. 24).
An Old-Fashioned Christmastide: A Reverie (music score) (Ruth S. Cove) pp. 44–6
From a Good Old Stock (Ruth Lamb) pp. 47–55, 58–63
    Illustration 'A Rehearsal' shows a group of children singing p. 49
A Christmas Melody (poem) p. 64

Lily-White
Extra Summer Number for Volume 14 (1893)
Melany's Keepsake: A Story in Ten Chapters (Sarah Doudney) pp. 3–19
    Hearing 'The Lost Chord' sung, Melany Davie understands that in life's quest, some 'are weary and ill at ease' and feels drawn to help its singer Clara find that chord again (p. 15).
Intermezzo: Duet for Piano (music score) (George J. Bennett) pp. 34–7
In a Breton Castle (Buzzie) 43–9
    When the countess asks her new governess to play for her on the piano, she enters the castle drawing room and plays one of Mendelssohn 'Songs Without Words' from memory.

Volume 15 (7 October 1893–26 September 1894)

Number 719 (7 October 1893)
How to Sing in Oratorio (Esther Palliser) pp. 5–6
Answers to Correspondents (Music heading) p. 15
  E. Hartland (practising society), Student of Trin. Coll. (music history and appreciation), Curiosity (music education), A Working Girl (voice), Peterina (music education)

Number 720 (14 October 1893)
Changes: Song (music score) (Hamish MacCunn, Words Lady Lindsay of Balcarres) pp. 20–2
Answers to Correspondents (Music heading) p. 32
  Miss Meech and Anxious to Improve (practising society), Violet (applied music), Y.A.M. (piano, applied music), R. A. (sight-reading), Rustic (theory)

Number 721 (21 October 1893)
Notices of New Music p. 39

Number 722 (28 October 1893)
Varieties (Paying Music) p. 58

Number 723 (4 November 1893)
Beethoven (J. F. Rowbotham) Part 1 pp. 69–71
Answers to Correspondents (Music heading) p. 80
  W. H. Springfellow (music education), Meg (voice), Player (Camarthen) (violin, instrument maintenance), Impromptu (music education, nuisance), Kerry (banjo), I. M. Alix (theory, correspondence course), M. B. (Brisbane) (music teaching, correspondence classes), Lady Organist (organ, health, practising society), Nobody's Darling (Aleppo) (Irish harp), Dum Spiro Spero (piano, practising, nuisance)

Number 724 (11 November 1893)
Answers to Correspondents (Music heading) p. 95
  M. or N. (organ, music history and appreciation), A Native of the Golden Horn (Constantinople) (voice), Agnita (repertoire)

Number 725 (18 November 1893)
Answers to Correspondents (Music heading) p. 112
  Madge (piano, nuisance), Hilda (violin), A Constant Subscriber (general), B.E.S. (terms), Red Tail (general)

Number 726 (25 November 1893)
Answers to Correspondents (Music heading) p. 128
  Snowdrop (violin), A. C. Veneris (violin, instrument maintenance), Madge (theory, correspondence course), No Name (violin), A Would-Be Musician (banjo, Irish harp, choosing instrument), S. Williams (violin, health), Georgie (zither), F. R. Fisher (repertoire)

Number 727 (2 December 1893)
Come, Let Me Sing, Sweet Muse Sublime (poem) (C. P.) p. 136
  Illustration 'Come, let me sing, sweet muse sublime' p. 137
Answers to Correspondents (Music heading) p. 144
  L. E. (music education), Gertrude Dear (organ, repertoire), Enquiring Mind (terms), M. M. (piano)

Number 728 (9 December 1893)
Beethoven Part 2 pp. 148–50

Number 729 (16 December 1893)
Answers to Correspondents pp. 175–6
   Barbara (music history and appreciation)

Number 730 (23 December 1893)
Carol for Female Voices (music score) (William H. Hunt, Refrain from Longfellow's 'Norman Baron') pp. 179–81
Answers to Correspondents (Music heading) p. 192
   Elsie Dinsmore (voice, health), La Brum (general), C. Sharp (general), Allen (music education), Corona and Mazeppa (practising society), G. S. (voice), Wynifred (music history and appreciation)

Number 731 (30 December 1893)
The Coming of the King (poem) (Helen Marion Burnside) p. 205

Number 732 (6 January 1894)
Lassie (poem) (William T. Saward) p. 216
Answers to Correspondents (Music heading) p. 224
   L.E.E.L. (applied music), Doddie (practising, nuisance), Doubtful (applied music), Bee (theory), Ruby H. A. (general), E. G. (music education), Maggie (music student lodging), Louise (music history and appreciation), Monica (music education)

Number 733 (13 January 1894)
The Progress of Women's Work (S.F.A. Cauldfeild) Part 2 pp. 228–9
   Caulfeild expresses surprise that women 'have produced no works of importance, very beautiful song-composers as they have, in many instances, shown themselves', which she attributes to lack of training and opportunities to develop their inherent talent (p. 228).
Mendelssohn (J. F. Rowbotham) Part 1 pp. 237–8
   Illustration 'Mendelssohn' p. 237
Answers to Correspondents (Music heading) p. 239
   Ada (general, choosing instrument), Lizzie E. (composition), A Professional (general), Organist (organ, music history and appreciation), Dorothy (repertoire, barrel organ), Would-Be Mus. Doc. (music education)

Number 734 (20 January 1894)
Answers to Correspondents (Music heading) pp. 255–6
   Pitty Sing (voice), Miss E. Mackenzie (practising society), Lover of Music (violin), Rosalinda Queechy (voice, health), Maria (violin), Lenore (theory)

Number 736 (3 February 1894)
When Wilt Thou Come?' Song (poem) (Clara Thwaites) p. 281
   Illustration 'When wilt thou come, / And change my sigh to song?' p. 280
Notices of New Music p. 287
Answers to Correspondents p. 288
   Lancashire Lass (general)

Number 737 (10 February 1894)
Mendelssohn Part 2 pp. 292–3

174 *Catalogue of musical content*

Number 738 (17 February 1894)
Vocal Studies for Girls: For Solo, Duet, and Class Practice (Jacob Bradford) pp. 308–10

Number 739 (24 February 1894)
The Wards of St. Margaret's (Sister Joan) Ch. 1 pp. 321–3
 Constance Wilson is a musically accomplished young gentlewoman, nurse and sister in charge of a ward. One afternoon when off duty, she plays the piano in the nurses' lodgings and sings, unintentionally breaking a rule forbidding piano playing while the night-sisters are sleeping. The Matron, who overhears, is angry, not only because Constance may have disturbed sleeping nurses but also because drawing attention to oneself is unbecoming to a lady.
Answers to Correspondents pp. 332–5
 Kathleen Mavourneen (repertoire), A Young Man (general)

Number 740 (3 March 1894)
The Wards of St. Margaret's Ch. 2 pp. 348–50
The Piano-Player: A Life Picture (poem) (C. P.) p. 350
Answers to Correspondents p. 351
 Muriel (practising, voice, nuisance)

Number 741 (10 March 1894)
The Wards of St. Margaret's Ch. 3 pp. 366–7

Number 742 (17 March 1894)
A Little While Ago (music score) (Charles P. Banks, Words Sarah Doudney) pp. 372–4
The Wards of St. Margaret's Ch. 4 pp. 382–3

Number 743 (24 March 1894)
The Wards of St. Margaret's Ch. 5 pp. 385–7
'Like a Worm i' the Bud' (Anne Beale) Ch. 1 pp. 392–4
 Ivor Herbert, 'abandoned' son from a secret marriage, lives in the Arymor Union Workhouse. He is a gifted and versatile musician who wins first prizes for singing at the Eisteddfod in Arymor and later amazes listeners with his violin playing. After running away, he returns to Arymor years later to give a concert as Signor Rovi Singleton, 'the most celebrated composer and violinist of the age' (p. 810).
Varieties (He Was Not Musical) p. 397
Answers to Correspondents p. 400
 Dot and Matilda R. (copyright)

Number 744 (31 March 1894)
'Like a Worm i' the Bud' Ch. 2 pp. 410–12
The Wards of St. Margaret's Ch. 6 pp. 412–13

Number 745 (7 April 1894)
Parting Song (poem) (E. Nesbit) p. 417
'Like a Worm i' the Bud' Ch. 3 pp. 418–19
The Wards of St. Margaret's Ch. 7 pp. 428–9
Answers to Correspondents (Music heading) p. 432
 Mizpah (general), Spray of Pink Ti-Tree (New Zealand) (guitar, instrument maintenance)

Number 746 (14 April 1894)
'Like a Worm i' the Bud' Ch. 4 pp. 435–7
The Wards of St. Margaret's Ch. 8 pp. 444–5

Answers to Correspondents (Music heading) p. 448
   Buffalo (applied music), Pat (practising, nuisance), Tommy (repertoire), Rienzi (music history and appreciation), I.O.G.T. (repertoire)

Number 747 (21 April 1894)
The Wards of St. Margaret's Ch. 9 pp. 449–51
'Like a Worm i' the Bud' Ch. 5 pp. 454–5
Answers to Correspondents p. 464
   Robin (general)

Number 748 (28 April 1894)
The Wards of St. Margaret's Ch. 10 pp. 472–4
'Like a Worm i' the Bud' Ch. 6 pp. 474–6
Answers to Correspondents (Music heading) p. 480
   Fantasia (piano), Yankee Jack and L.F.C. (music education), J. St. John B. (repertoire), Molly (pronunciation), Mina (piano), Mrs. H. Rowson (circulating music), Wee One (British Guiana) (banjo)

Number 749 (5 May 1894)
The Wards of St. Margaret's Ch. 11 pp. 481–2
'Like a Worm i' the Bud' Ch. 7 pp. 485–7
'Our Little Genius' (Mary E. Hullah) Ch. 1* pp. 489–90
   When playing for an 'At Home' concert, Nora Croften, who has given up violin and always has an excuse for neglected piano lessons, breaks down, feeling 'utterly miserable and ashamed' during her performance from memory of Mendelssohn's 'Variations Sérieuses'. Too late, she wishes that she had practised the piece more diligently (p. 498). Illustration 'Leo took up his place on the other side of the music and howled' shows Nora's dog's response to her violin playing p. 488
Answers to Correspondents p. 495
   S.F.C. (voice, music teaching)

Number 750 (12 May 1894)
'Our Little Genius' Ch. 2* pp. 497–8
'Like a Worm i' the Bud' Ch. 8 pp. 506–7
French and Swiss Rounds pp. 508–9
   Includes music scores.
The Wards of St. Margaret's Ch. 12 pp. 510–11

Number 751 (19 May 1894)
The Wards of St. Margaret's Ch. 13 pp. 513–15
'Our Little Genius' Ch. 3 pp. 516–17
Sea of Life (poem) (Ethel Morgan) p. 521
   Illustration 'I gazed across the sea of life with youthful eyes' shows a young woman playing guitar p. 520
'Like a Worm i' the Bud' Ch. 9 pp. 525–7
Answers to Correspondents (Music heading) p. 528
   Frances (theory, correspondence class), B. A. (repertoire, music education), Elsa (flute), Penelope (general)

Number 752 (26 May 1894)
'Like a Worm i' the Bud' Ch. 10 pp. 530–2
The Wards of St. Margaret's Ch. 14* pp. 538–9

176 Catalogue of musical content

Varieties ('Her voice was sweet' – *Barry Cornwall*; 'Sweet the music of the step' – *J. R. Drake*) p. 539
'Our Little Genius' Ch. 4 p. 540–1
Answers to Correspondents p. 544
    Sal (music history and appreciation)

Number 753 (2 June 1894)
'Like a Worm i' the Bud' Ch. 11 pp. 547–9
Inspirations (poem) (Ethel Morgan) p. 552
    Illustration 'Oh, that my life might be / A beautiful melody' p. 553
The Wards of St. Margaret's Ch. 15 pp. 558–9
Answers to Correspondents p. 560
    Olivene (piano)

Number 754 (9 June 1894)
A Song of Love (poem) (Ethel Morgan) pp. 561–2
The Wards of St. Margaret's Ch. 16 pp. 562–3
'Like a Worm i' the Bud' Ch. 12 pp. 572–5
Answers to Correspondents (Music heading) pp. 575–6
    Bunnie (general, voice), Snowdrop (harp, violin, banjo, choosing instrument), Nom de Guerre (harp), L.C.V. (guitar), Edith (terms), Blenheim House School (repertoire), Annette (general), Stella (composition)

Number 755 (16 June 1894)
The Wards of St. Margaret's Ch. 17 pp. 577–9
Be Strong! (music score) (Myles B. Foster, Words Adelaide Proctor) pp. 580–2
'Like a Worm i' the Bud' Ch. 13 pp. 588–90
Answers to Correspondents (Music heading) p. 591
    E.I.L.L. (practising society), Daphne (theory), Daisy Grey (applied music), Meta (composition), Ethiopian (repertoire), Norah (organ, music education), Rowena (music education), Louie (voice), Matinka (violin), Connie Muir (performance nerves), 'Quartorze Ans' (pronunciation)

Number 756 (23 June 1894)
'Like a Worm i' the Bud' Ch. 14 pp. 598–600
The Wards of St. Margaret's Ch. 18* pp. 605–7
Answers to Correspondents p. 608
    E. Eckersley (repertoire), G. H. Elliott (repertoire)

Number 757 (30 June 1894)
'Like a Worm i' the Bud' Ch. 15 pp. 610–11
The Wards of St. Margaret's Ch. 19 pp. 620–2

Number 758 (7 July 1894)
'Like a Worm i' the Bud' Chs 16, 17 pp. 626–9
The Wards of St. Margaret's Ch. 20 pp. 634–6
Answers to Correspondents (Music heading) p. 640
    Minnie (applied music), Leonora Lear (general), T. D. Derrick, Strood and Lill (circulating music)

Number 759 (14 July 1894)
The Wards of St. Margaret's Ch. 21 pp. 646–7
'Like a Worm i' the Bud' Chs 18, 19 pp. 651–5

Catalogue of musical content 177

Number 760 (21 July 1894)
'Like a Worm i' the Bud' Ch. 20 pp. 658–9
Mazourka in E Minor, Op. 6 No. 1 (music score) (Natalie Janotha) pp. 660–3
The Wards of St. Margaret's Ch. 22 pp. 668–9

Number 761 (28 July 1894)
'Like a Worm i' the Bud' Ch. 21 pp. 676–8
The Wards of St. Margaret's Ch. 23 pp. 686–7
Answers to Correspondents (Music heading) p. 688
   Henrietta Richards (applied music), Madge (music education), Stella (practising, nuisance), Nellie Ball (guitar), Wakeful and E.T.L.L. (theory, correspondence course)

Number 762 (4 August 1894)
'Like a Worm i' the Bud' Chs 22, 23 pp. 692–5
The Wards of St. Margaret's Ch. 24 pp. 700–1

Number 763 (11 August 1894)
The Wards of St. Margaret's Ch. 25 pp. 709–10
Pianoforte Fingering p. 71
'Like a Worm i' the Bud' Ch. 24 pp. 715–18

Number 764 (18 August 1894)
The Wards of St. Margaret's Ch. 26 pp. 721–3
'Like a Worm i' the Bud' Chs 25, 26 pp. 731–4
Answers to Correspondents p. 736
   Ignoramus Katie (pronunciation)

Number 765 (25 August 1894)
'Like a Worm i' the Bud' Ch. 27 pp. 747–50

Number 766 (1 September 1894)
'Like a Worm i' the Bud' Chs 28, 29 pp. 754–7
Only (poem) (William T. Saward) pp. 760
Answers to Correspondents (Music heading) p. 768
   'Peter Augustine' (guitar), The Parish Fashion-Plate (general), Florence Edinger (circulating music), St. Ives (terms), A Cornish Lassie (page turning), Mandoline (music teaching), Rosie (general), A Constant Clapham Reader (piano), G. G. (repertoire), Awaiting a Reply (metronome)

Number 767 (8 September 1894)
'Like a Worm i' the Bud' Chs 29 (cont.), 30 pp. 770–3
Varieties (An Eccentric Organist) p. 773
'The setting sun, and music at the close, / As the last taste of sweets is sweetest last / Writ in remembrance more than things long past' – *Shakespeare* (illustration) p. 776
   Music making in the home with mother at piano, husband turning pages, son playing violin and daughter looking on at side of piano; three others listen nearby.

Number 768 (15 September 1894)
'Like a Worm i' the Bud' Chs 32, 33, 34 pp. 786–9
Varieties (The Pianoforte) p. 791
A Dream Within a Dream (Parable from the Divina Comedia) (poem) (Sarson C. J. Ingham) pp. 792, 794
Notes on Songs of Longfellow, and Some Musical Settings (William Porteous) pp. 798–9

178 Catalogue of musical content

Number 769 (22 September 1894)
'In Autumn Days' (music score) (Charles P. Banks, Words E. Matheson) pp. 804–6
'Like a Worm i' the Bud' Chs 35, 36, 37 pp. 809–12

Number 770 (29 September 1894)
'Like a Worm i' the Bud' Chs 38, 39, Conclusion pp. 818–21

The Morning of the Year[1]
Extra Christmas and New Year's Number for Volume 15 (1893)
Frontispiece: Souvenir du Premier Empire (from the painting by A. H. Bramtott, in the Salon Paris)
Christmas Morning (Sonnet) (The Editor)
The Black Tarn (Lady Margaret Majendie)
Pretty Dishes Made of Dried Fruits
Old Haidenbach's New Pupil (La Petite)
Accomplished Girls (G. Holden Pike)
The Faithful Sentinel (From a painting)
Where the Baboushka Dwells: A Christmas Legend
Concerning Muffs
The Love Between a Mother and Daughter: A Short Story
Victoria and Alberta. A Short Story
A Model Christmas Dinner, with Recipes
Fairy Kind-Heart: A Musical Story (Written, Composed Herbert Harraden)
Jul-tide in Sweden
A Song of Christmastide (Harriet Kendall)
On the Ice: A Sketch for Girls (A Middle-aged Woman)
Refining Fires
The Bride (poem) (Clara Thwaites)
Cakes for Christmas
Our Puzzle Poem
Varieties

Mignonette ('Little Darling')
Extra Summer Number for Volume 15 (1894)
Sweet-Gale (The Ven. Archdeacon Wynne) pp. 3–6
  Helen Preston, known as Sweet-gale, plays the 'not very tuneful' piano in a Scottish inn parlour for her father and guests (p. 5).
Two Sea Songs 'Sixteen' and 'Sixty' (poem) (Sarah Doudney) p. 12
Flower Song (poem) (E. Nesbit) p. 20
Varieties (The Grave of Mozart) p. 35
A Summer Morning (music score) (L. Meadows White, Words Edward Medland White) pp. 43–7
Only a Commercial Traveller (Margaret Littleton) pp. 59–60
  Miss Enid's singing of 'O Rest in the Lord' at the Lake of Geneva brings an elderly commercial traveler, whom she had befriended when others ridiculed him, back to God.

Note

1 I could not locate 'The Morning of the Year' Extra Christmas and New Year's Number but found its table of contents in the 25 November 1893 issue of *TGOP* in a 'Now Ready' notice, p. 128. I have listed those contents without speculating which might contain musical references.

Volume 16 (6 October 1894–28 September 1895)

Number 771 (6 October 1894)
Marsh Marigolds (Ada M. Trotter) Prologue, Ch. 1 pp. 1–3
 Ritchie Marphell takes over her father's church organist duties when his vision fails. Only 16 years old, she has trouble maintaining order during rehearsals when cantankerous male choir members challenge her ability to direct them. Ritchie's older sister Ruth, also a musician, chooses not to cultivate her contralto voice, because a singing career would be selfish when she is needed to run the farm during her father's progressive blindness.
The Blue-Eyed Maiden's Song (music score) (H.R.H. Princess Beatrice / Princess Henry of Battenberg, Words The Earl of Beaconsfield) pp. 4–6
Music in Social Life (Lady Macfarren) p. 11
 Advice for readers who host, attend and perhaps perform in musical 'At Homes'.
Answers to Correspondents p. 16
 Hilda (piano, instrument maintenance, piano keys), E.E.T. (general)

Number 772 (13 October 1894)
Her Own Way (Eglanton Thorne) Ch. 1 pp. 17–20
 Juliet Tracy wants to be a public singer, for its splendid life standing before an audience with every eye on her, 'listening spell-bound to her voice' (p.146). When permitted to take singing lessons from an Italian master, Juliet reads into his words only what she wants to hear rather than the truth, letting vanity fuel a dream that her vocal progress does not support.
 Illustration 'A visit was paid to Signor Lombardi' p. 145
Marsh Marigolds Ch. 2 pp. 30–1
Answers to Correspondents (Music heading) p. 32
 Violetta (music education), Darby and Joan (music history and appreciation), A Boy Reader (composition), Isleworth (piano), Violin (violin), Thirty-Two (musician work, choral singing), Emme (terms), Orange and Purple (piano, music history and appreciation), Der Erlkönig (music history and appreciation), Piccolina (mandolin)

Number 773 (20 October 1894)
Her Own Way Ch. 2 pp. 38–9
Marsh Marigolds Ch. 3 pp. 47–8

Number 774 (27 October 1894)
Marsh Marigolds Ch. 4 pp. 50–1
Her Own Way Ch. 3 pp. 59–61
Answers to Correspondents (Music heading) p. 64
 Eseh (voice, health), Sister to a B. A. (terms), B.S.M. (general), M.P.S. (organ), Queen Gwen (general)

Number 775 (3 November 1894)
Marsh Marigolds Ch. 5 pp. 65–7
 Illustration 'Oh, how good you are!' shows Ritchie on the organ bench speaking with her minister p. 65
Notices of New Music pp. 75–6
Her Own Way Ch. 4 pp. 76–8

Number 776 (10 November 1894)
Her Own Way Ch. 5 pp. 81–3
Marsh Marigolds Ch. 6 pp. 90–1

180 *Catalogue of musical content*

Answers to Correspondents (Music heading) p. 95
    Margaret Wilson (music education), Fairy (general), Viola (violin, piano, music education), L. Danby (piano, instrument maintenance, music education), Hiddigeigel (composition)

Number 777 (17 November 1894)
Marsh Marigolds Ch. 7 pp. 99–100
Her Own Way Ch. 6 pp. 102–3
Answers to Correspondents (Music heading) p. 111
    Rosie (piano, instrument maintenance), Carmita (West Indies) (music education), Eveline (theory), Constant Reader (voice), B. J. (violin, music history and appreciation)

Number 778 (24 November 1894)
Marsh Marigolds Ch. 8 pp. 114–15
The Girl's Outlook; or, What Is There to Talk About? (James and Nanette Mason) Part 1 pp. 115–17
    To avoid taking part in the petty gossip of rural life, three friends in a remote village, all in their early twenties, meet at least monthly to discuss what they have read, confining their conversation to current topics and events, including musical ones.
Her Own Way Ch. 7 pp. 118–19

Number 779 (1 December 1894)
Marsh Marigolds Ch. 9 pp. 129–30
Her Own Way Ch. 8 pp. 141–3

Number 780 (8 December 1894)
Her Own Way Ch. 9 pp. 145–7
Music (Osgood Hartier) p. 154
    The spirit of a homeless man wanders through the night into frugal and rich homes and, moved by Music, wanders to its source – a beautiful woman playing 'that saddest song that e'er was sung – 'Home, home, sweet, sweet home'" – then goes back out into the night.
Marsh Marigolds Ch. 10 pp. 157–9

Number 781 (15 December 1894)
'Tuning Up' (music score) (Natalie Janotha, Words Charles Peters from '*The Quiver*') pp. 164–6
Marsh Marigolds Ch. 11 pp. 167–8
A Worker's Song (poem) (Mary Rowles Jarvis) p. 168
Varieties (Good Musicians) p. 171
Her Own Way Ch. 10 pp. 174–5
Answers to Correspondents (Music heading) p. 176
    Desirée and Mermaid (violin, guitar, choosing instrument), A. Company (voice), Dodo (copyright), Winnifred (music education), Piping Bullfinch (music history and appreciation), Ruby (repertoire)

Number 782 (22 December 1894)
Marsh Marigolds Ch. 12 pp. 180–1
Her Own Way Ch. 11 pp. 188–90
Answers to Correspondents (Music heading) p. 191
    A Hampstead Reader (violin), Birdie (organ, music education), An Old Musician (musician pension), Innocence (voice)

Number 783 (29 December 1894)
The Girl's Outlook Part 2 pp. 204–5
Her Own Way Ch. 12 p. 206

Answers to Correspondents p. 208
   Mary (repertoire)

Number 784 (5 January 1895)
Marsh Marigolds Ch. 13 pp. 209–11
The Art of Accompanying: A Vocalist's Complaint (K. G.) p. 213
   K. G.'s question, why a good amateur accompanist is so hard to find at ordinary provincial concerts, prompts reactions printed in follow-on issues by C.A.M. ('On the Art of Accompanying' p. 415) and Lady William Lennox ('More About Accompaniments' p. 438).
Her Own Way Ch. 13 pp. 215, 217

Number 785 (12 January 1895)
Her Own Way Ch. 14 pp. 226–8
Marsh Marigolds Ch. 14 pp. 235–6
Answers to Correspondents p. 239
   Frances S. (music history and appreciation), Noiram Sivad (voice)

Number 786 (19 January 1895)
Her Own Way Ch. 15 pp. 242–4
Marsh Marigolds Ch. 15 pp. 254–5

Number 787 (26 January 1895)
Marsh Marigolds Ch. 16 pp. 258–9
The Girl's Outlook Part 3 pp. 267–8
Her Own Way Ch. 16 pp. 270–1

Number 788 (2 February 1895)
Marsh Marigolds Ch. 17 pp. 273–4
'Since I Was Young' (music score) (Theo. Marzials, Words May Probyn) pp. 276–8
Her Own Way Ch. 17 p. 279

Number 789 (9 February 1895)
Her Own Way Ch. 18 pp. 290–1
Marsh Marigolds Ch. 18 pp. 294–5
A Crescendo (poem) (Gertrude Harraden) p. 304

Number 790 (16 February 1895)
Her Own Way Ch. 19 pp. 306–7
Marsh Marigolds Ch. 19 pp. 309–10
Answers to Correspondents (Music heading) p. 319
   M.E.I. (wasted time, nuisance), Ruth (repertoire), Bonnie and Semie (practising society), Bo-Peep (mandolin, guitar, choosing instrument), A. M. (bagpipe, harp, music history and appreciation)

Number 791 (23 February 1895)
Her Own Way Ch. 20 pp. 320–4
The Girl's Outlook Part 4 pp. 324–6
Marsh Marigolds Ch. 20 pp. 326–7

Number 792 (2 March 1895)
Marsh Marigolds Ch. 21 pp. 347–8
Her Own Way Ch. 21 pp. 350–1

182   *Catalogue of musical content*

Number 793 (9 March 1895)
'Sweet and Low' (music score) (Emily, Lady Tennyson, arr. Natalie Janotha, Words Alfred Lord Tennyson) pp. 356–8
Marsh Marigolds Ch. 22 p. 359
Varieties (Music in China) p. 364
Her Own Way Ch. 22 pp. 365–6

Number 794 (16 March 1895)
Marsh Marigolds Ch. 23 p. 372
Her Own Way Ch. 23 p. 379

Number 795 (23 March 1895)
Marsh Marigolds Chs 24, 25 pp. 385–8
Her Own Way Ch. 24 pp. 390–1
The Girl's Outlook Part 5 pp. 396–7
Answers to Correspondents (Music heading) p. 399
  Beginner (metronome), Gipsy (zither, violoncello, harp, choosing instrument), Dingo (general), Rosemary (applied music, terms), Amateur (theory), Adam (general), Sally in Our Alley (voice)

Number 796 (30 March 1895)
Cousin Mona (Rosa Nouchette Carey) Ch. 1 pp. 401–3
  When their parents die, sisters Rufa and Joyce Gordon must live with different relatives. The Gordon household where Rufa lives is a quiet one, but Rufa gets permission to move a rented pianette into a room upstairs so she can practise her singing. When Cousin Mona asks Rufa to sing for her, Rufa chooses songs she thinks her cousin would like best. Cousin Mona is passionate about music and had a pretty voice that left her suddenly. She still sings in church, however: 'I do not think the angels mind how we sing, if we sing with our whole heart.' (p. 566)
Her Own Way Ch. 25 pp. 412–13
On the Art of Accompanying: Suggested by an Article in the 'G.O.P.' (C.A.M.) p. 415
  To C.A.M. – likely Clara Angela Macirone – responding to vocalist K. G.'s complaint ('The Art of Accompanying', p. 213), a good accompanist practises 'the art of effacing oneself to gain good for others'.

Number 797 (6 April 1895)
A Song of Spring (from Charles Jones painting) plate facing p. 417
  While not obviously musical, sheep in a meadow might be hearing their own song of spring.
Her Own Way Ch. 26 pp. 419–21
Women Workers' Songs (Lara Alex. Smith) pp. 422–3
  An overview of texts to songs that women spinning cloth, milking cows, herding sheep, threading beads and selling lavender sing as they work.
Cousin Mona Ch. 2 pp. 430–1

Number 798 (13 April 1895)
Handel (J. F. Rowbotham) Part 1 pp. 433–5
  Illustration 'Portrait of Handel' p. 433
Her Own Way Ch. 27 pp. 435–7
More About Accompaniments (Lady William Lennox) p. 438
  Echoing C.A.M.'s remarks on accompanying ('On the Art of Accompanying', p. 415), Lennox, a violinist, notes that the intuitive and prompt intervention of a good accompanist has saved a soloist in time of emergency.
Cousin Mona Ch. 3 pp. 438–40

Number 799 (20 April 1895)
Her Own Way Ch. 28 pp. 449–451
Cousin Mona Ch. 4* pp. 461–3

Number 800 (27 April 1895)
A Wilful Ward (Ruth Lamb) Ch. 1 pp. 465–7
    Cousins Kathleen Mountford and Geraldine Ellicott are both naturally gifted musicians, but whereas Kathleen is content with the facility gained from moderate effort, Geraldine works to turn her talent to best account. Kathleen wins praise for her charming voice and lovely touch, but she envies Geraldine's power that elicits the greater compliments of silence and awe.
The Girl's Outlook Part 6 pp. 469–70
Cousin Mona Ch. 5 p. 476

Number 801 (4 May 1895)
Cousin Mona Ch. 5 (cont.)* pp. 481–3
A Wilful Ward Ch. 2 pp. 490–2

Number 802 (11 May 1895)
Handel Part 2 pp. 499–500
    Illustration 'George Frederick Handel' (painted by Hudson) p. 501
A Wilful Ward Ch. 3 pp. 500, 502–3
Cousin Mona Ch. 6 pp. 507–9
Answers to Correspondents p. 512
    Dollie (practising)

Number 803 (18 May 1895)
Andante: For the Pianoforte (music score) (H.R.H. Hereditary Grand Duke of Hesse) pp. 516–17
Cousin Mona Ch. 7 pp. 518–19
A Wilful Ward Ch. 4 pp. 524–6
Answers to Correspondents (Music heading) p. 527
    B.Z.O. (violin), Anxious One (music teaching), Nan (zither), Gracie (piano, practising, nuisance), Zoé (practising society), Seize (piano)
Odds and Ends [Ugliness of the Piano] p. 528

Number 804 (25 May 1895)
A Wilful Ward Ch. 5* pp. 529–31
The Girl's Outlook Part 7 pp. 540–1
Cousin Mona Ch. 8 pp. 542–3

Number 805 (1 June 1895)
Cousin Mona Ch. 9 pp. 545–7
A Wilful Ward Ch. 6 pp. 549–51
A Story of 1857 (Ada M. Trotter) Ch. 1* pp. 553–5
    Isabel Alwyn and her friend Elise brought their English ways of life, including their musical accomplishments, with them to India where their military fathers are assigned. Isabel has a 'clear sweet soprano' voice, and Elsie, 'a rich contralto' (p. 554).

Number 806 (8 June 1895)
'Blind' (poem) (C.Y.F.) p. 565
Cousin Mona Ch. 10* pp. 566–7

Beatrice: A Study for Girls (Sarson C. J. Ingham) Part 1 pp. 568–71
   Illustration 'Music' (Konrad Kiesel) shows a young woman holding a medieval illuminated manuscript p. 569
A Wilful Ward Ch. 7 pp. 571–3
A Story of 1857 Ch. 2 pp. 573–4
Answers to Correspondents (Music heading) p. 575
   Alabama Coon (general), Madge (piano, instrument maintenance), Zenobia (music education), Lover of the Violin (general)

Number 807 (15 June 1895)
A Wilful Ward Ch. 8 pp. 581–3
Cousin Mona Ch. 11 pp. 590–1

Number 808 (22 June 1895)
A Wilful Ward Ch. 9 pp. 593–5
How I Painted a Tambourine (An Old Girl) p. 603
Cousin Mona Ch. 12 pp. 606–7

Number 809 (29 June 1895)
The Girl's Outlook Part 8 pp. 610–11
Eventide (music score) (Charles P. Banks, Words Adelina Fermi) pp. 612–14
A Wilful Ward (Ruth Lamb) Ch. 10 pp. 619–21

Number 810 (6 July 1895)
Cousin Mona Ch. 13 pp. 625–7
The Daughter of the House (S.F.A. Caulfeild) pp. 628–9
   New study and practical work such as cookery, flower arranging, home nursing and regular reading should follow a young woman's school days. Musical girls should keep up their practice, but only at times that will not inconvenience the household.
A Wilful Ward Ch. 11 pp. 637–9

Number 811 (13 July 1895)
A Wilful Ward Ch. 12 pp. 651–3
Cousin Mona Ch. 14 pp. 654–5
Answers to Correspondents p. 656
   Bo-Peep (repertoire)

Number 812 (20 July 1895)
A Wilful Ward Ch. 13 pp. 657–9
Cousin Mona Ch. 15 pp. 669–70

Number 813 (27 July 1895)
Cousin Mona Ch. 16 pp. 674–5
Living in Lodgings (Josepha Crane) pp. 677–8
   The woman choosing lodgings is told to inquire whether other lodgers' musical instruments might disturb her.
A Wilful Ward Ch. 14 pp. 686–7

Number 814 (3 August 1895)
Cousin Mona Ch. 17 pp. 689–91
A Wilful Ward Ch. 15 pp. 702–4

Catalogue of musical content   185

Number 815 (10 August 1895)
Varieties (How a Chinaman Described a Piano) p. 707
Cousin Mona Ch. 18 pp. 710–11
Mozart: His Life and Influence on the Development of Pianoforte Literature (Edgar Mills)
   Part 1 pp. 715–18
   Illustration 'Mozart at the Organ' (Photo Union, Munich) p. 716
A Wilful Ward Ch. 16 pp. 718–19

Number 816 (17 August 1895)
A Wilful Ward Ch. 17 pp. 721–3
Song (music score) (Frank Barât, Words Barham) pp. 724–7
Mozart Part 2 pp. 732–3
   Illustration 'Mozart's Tomb' p. 733
Cousin Mona Ch. 19 pp. 734–5

Number 817 (24 August 1895)
A Wilful Ward Ch. 18 pp. 738–40
Cousin Mona Ch. 20 pp. 747–8

Number 818 (31 August 1895)
A Wilful Ward Ch. 19 pp. 755–7
Cousin Mona Ch. 21 pp. 758–9
The Girl's Outlook Part 9 pp. 764–5
Answers to Correspondents p. 768
   Bo-Peep (repertoire)

Number 819 (7 September 1895)
Cousin Mona Ch. 22 pp. 769–71
A Wilful Ward Ch. 20 pp. 781–3
Answers to Correspondents (Music heading) p. 784
   Pattie (music history and appreciation), E. Litchy (piano, practising, nuisance), Happy Medium (circulating music), G.O.P. (music education)

Number 820 (14 September 1895)
A Wilful Ward Ch. 21 pp. 784–8
Cousin Mona Ch. 23 pp. 790–1
Answers to Correspondents (Music heading) p. 799
   T. A. Wilson (music education), Amy (copyright), Jessie (terms), Heather Bell (organ, piano)

Number 821 (21 September 1895)
Cousin Mona Ch. 24 803–5
The Girl's Outlook Part 10 pp. 808, 810
A Wilful Ward Ch. 22 pp. 811–13
Odds and Ends [The Harp] p. 816

Number 822 (28 September 1895)
A Wilful Ward Ch. 23 pp. 819–22

Robin Redbreast
Extra Christmas Number for Volume 16 (1894)
The Coming of the King: A Cantatina for Two Sopranos and a Contralto (music score) (Myles B. Foster, Words Helen Marion Burnside) pp. 22–9

London Pride
Extra Summer Number for Volume 16 (1895)
Adelaide's Reward (Percy Tarrant) pp. 1–7, 9–15, 17–23
   When Adelaide (Lally) Maxwell's uncle asks if she is musical, Lally replies that she loves music, can sing by note and also accompany at the piano. She had 'excellent teaching' and has a talent for music (p. 5).
My Little Boy Blue (Rosa Nouchette Carey) pp. 25–8, 30–1, 33
   Maud Oliver, a pianist and her father, a cellist, both love music and, with violinist Claude Russell, had 'quite a nice concert' (p. 26). 'Little Boy Blue' – Gaston Myers – is a 'droll little beggar' musician who plays violin and sings and, with the help of a benefactor, studies music in London and makes a splendid debut (p. 25).
   Illustration 'Maude' shows Maud at an upright piano p. 26
Sweet Lavender (music score) (Mary Carmichael, Words Helen M Burnside) pp. 52–5

Volume 17 (5 October 1895–26 September 1896)

Number 823 (5 October 1895)
The Green Cavalier's Song (music score) (H.R.H. Princess Henry of Battenberg, Words The Earl of Beaconsfield) pp. 4–6
Varieties (Out of Tune) p. 7
The Three Old Maids of Leigh (Lady Dunboyne) Ch. 1 pp. 8, 10
  When an entertainment is planned to benefit a hospital for the village, sisters Charlotte, Clara and Dorothy Leigh agree to perform. Dorothy's spirited Turkish march played on the 'well-known, much thumped on, Rectory semi-grand' serves as the overture; Clara sings Kingsley's ballad of the 'Three Fishers' and 'The Auld House' as an encore (p. 36).
Hymn Pictures – I (illustration) p. 9
  "And His that gentle voice we hear, / Soft as the breath of even, / That checks each fault, that calms each fear, / And speaks of Heaven – "

Number 824 (12 October 1895)
Half-a-Dozen Sisters (Evelyn Everett-Green) Ch. 1* pp. 17–19
  Guinivere, Beatrice and Misie, Norah, Gipsy (Marjorie) and Freda are the half-dozen Wilberforce sisters at the Larches. Pianist Guinivere is the musician among them. During a musical entertainment at their home, Lord Woodmayne disregards the musical code of etiquette and talks to Guinivere with the air of someone who has no intention of listening to 'second-rate music in a suburban drawing room' (p. 174).
Hints on Practising the Voice (Marguerite Macintyre) p. 20
The Three Old Maids of Leigh (Lady Dunboyne) Ch. 2* p. 21
Varieties (When Oratorios Began; Cottage Pianos) p. 30

Number 825 (19 October 1895)
The Three Old Maids of Leigh Chs 3, 4 pp. 36–7
Half-a-Dozen Sister Ch. 2 pp. 43–5
Answers to Correspondents p. 47
  Nan (viola de gamba)

Number 826 (26 October 1895)
Half-a-Dozen Sisters Ch. 3 pp. 53–5

Number 827 (2 November 1895)
Modern Women Song-Writers (Esther Esther Palliser) p. 68
Half-a-Dozen Sisters Ch. 4 pp. 69–71
Varieties (Music of the Olden Time) p. 78
Answers to Correspondents (Music heading) p. 79
  Clematis (music teaching), D.E.L.C. (applied music), Mary Anne (harp), Ethel (music education), Mabel France (general), Madge (psaltery), Dorothea (music student lodging), Iva (music education), Helen of Troy (banjo), A.L.D. (repertoire)

Number 828 (9 November 1895)
Half-a-Dozen Sisters Ch. 5 pp. 81–3
Answers to Correspondents (Music heading) p. 95
  Pansy Blossom (violin, health), May Blossom (terms), A Lover of Good Music (terms), Violet (terms), La Russie (music history and appreciation), Doreen (music education), Bien Aimé (repertoire), Amy (copyright)
Odds and Ends [Organ-Grinders]; [Jenny Lind] p. 96

188 *Catalogue of musical content*

Number 829 (16 November 1895)
Half-a-Dozen Sisters Ch. 6 pp. 98–9
Answers to Correspondents p. 111
   Judy (violin, instrument maintenance)

Number 830 (23 November 1895)
Half-a-Dozen Sisters Ch. 7 pp. 114–15
Answers to Correspondents (Music heading) p. 128
   Dwarf (piano, wasted time), Little John (music education), A.B.C. (music education)

Number 831 (30 November 1895)
Half-a-Dozen Sisters Ch. 8 pp. 142–3

Number 832 (7 December 1895)
Half-a-Dozen Sisters Ch. 9 pp. 150–1
A Christmas Carol (poem) (Rita F. Moss-Cockle) p. 152
Answers to Correspondents p. 159
   X.Y.Z. (music history and appreciation)

Number 833 (14 December 1895)
Half-a-Dozen Sisters Ch. 10* pp. 173–5
   Illustration 'He took not the slightest notice of looks thrown in his direction' shows a young woman playing the piano in a suburban drawing room p. 173

Number 834 (21 December 1895)
At a Concert (illustration) p. 184
   Two women and a man sit attentively at the Evening Concert identified on the programme.
Music's Empire (poem) (Andrew Marvell) p. 185
Half-a-Dozen Sisters Ch. 11 pp. 186–8
Answers to Correspondents p. 191
   Muriel (general)

Number 835 (28 December 1895)
Half-a-Dozen Sisters Ch. 12 pp. 198–9

Number 836 (4 January 1896)
'Not in Vain' (Marian Findlay) Ch. 1 pp. 209–10
   Helen Carlyle's 'foolish dreams' to marry a clergyman, visit the poor, teach Sunday school and play the organ at church and, failing that, to compose music change when she marries Edward (p. 235). When the neighborhood gossip, Miss Smith, expresses surprise that Helen's husband would let her sing 'O Rest in the Lord', Helen learns that her husband is an atheist. Her fervent prayers and untimely death rather than her music are instrumental in converting Edward to Christianity.
Half-a-Dozen Sisters Ch. 13 pp. 221–3

Number 837 (11 January 1896)
Half-a-Dozen Sisters Ch. 14 pp. 225–7
'There is sweet music here that softer falls / than petals from blown roses on the grass. *Tennyson*' (illustration) p. 233
   A young woman pianist accompanies a male violinist.
'Not in Vain' Ch. 2* pp. 235–6

Catalogue of musical content 189

Answers to Correspondents (Music heading) pp. 239–40
    Claribel (voice, health), Beta (circulating music), Mezzo-Soprano (voice, health), Music (instrument tuner), Miss I. E. Kent (practising society)

Number 838 (18 January 1896)
Half-a-Dozen Sisters Ch. 15 pp. 246–7
Cecil Frances Alexander (William Cowan) pp. 251–2
    Recalls the life and work of the recently deceased author of the hymn 'There Is a Green Hill Far Away'.
    Illustration 'Mrs. Alexander' p 251
'Not in Vain' Ch. 3 pp. 253–4
Varieties (Fifteen Minutes a Day) p. 255

Number 839 (25 January 1896)
'Not in Vain' Ch. 4 pp. 257–9
Half-a-Dozen Sisters Ch. 16 pp. 261–3

Number 840 (1 February 1896)
A Love Out of Tune (J. F. Rowbotham) Ch. 1 pp. 273–5
    Reginald Horton, a farmer's son, leaves home to pursue a career as a pianist. After a rocky start, his eventual success is a hollow victory when his father dies suddenly, greatly in debt. After promising to marry Reginald once he made his name in music, Mildred Vane, the rector's daughter and an organist, marries someone else.
Albumblatt (music score) (E. Humperdinck) pp. 276–7
Half-a-Dozen Sisters Ch. 17 pp. 278–9
Answers to Correspondents (Music heading) p. 288
    Mignon (music education), Margot (music history and appreciation), Lover of Music (music history and appreciation), Mona (general), Nita (theory), Amy (music history and appreciation), Rosalind (circulating music)

Number 841 (8 February 1896)
Half-a-Dozen Sisters Ch. 18 pp. 289–91
The Palace Wall (poem) (D.J.S.) p. 297
A Love Out of Tune Ch. 2 pp. 299–300

Number 842 (15 February 1896)
A Love Out of Tune Ch. 3 pp. 305–7
Half-a-Dozen Sisters Ch. 19 pp. 314–16
Answers to Correspondents (Music heading) p. 320
    D. M. (correspondence clubs), Florence (voice), Lall (general), Sunrise (repertoire), Trilby (pronunciation, music history and appreciation)

Number 843 (22 February 1896)
Half-a-Dozen Sisters Ch. 20 pp. 322–3
A Love Out of Tune Ch. 4 pp. 326–7
A Word About Her Rosenthal the Pianist p. 336

Number 844 (29 February 1896)
Half-a-Dozen Sisters Ch. 21 pp. 338–40

Number 845 (7 March 1896)
Half-a-Dozen Sisters Ch. 22 pp. 354–5
Answers to Correspondents (Music heading) p. 367
    Ada (general), Dover Cliffs (terms), A Contralto (voice), Ethel Milne (piano), A. L. (music education), J. Lewis (music education), Perplexed (composition)

Number 846 (14 March 1896)
Half-a-Dozen Sisters Ch. 23 pp. 370–2
Answers to Correspondents p. 384
    Nina Yeomans (music education), Cornish Maiden (voice)

Number 847 (21 March 1896)
Half-a-Dozen Sisters Ch. 24 pp. 397–9
Answers to Correspondents p. 399
    Pétite (terms)
'Golden Bright on Hill and Valley': An Easter Carol (music score) (Myles B. Foster, Words Florence Hoare) p. 400

Number 848 (28 March 1896)
New Serial Story: Other People's Stairs (Isabella Fyvie Mayo) Ch. 1 pp. 401–3
    Mrs Henderson is the driving force behind her daughter Gladys's singing lessons. Energized by the 'dreadful' discovery that other girls in the family circle are receiving praise for their singing, Mrs Henderson engages the finest foreign singing master she can find to teach her daughter, a rather indifferent pianist, to sing. Much to her mother's dismay, Gladys returns from her first lesson in tears, because the teacher has said she lacks a musical ear. The pronouncement devastates Mrs Henderson, who, unable to accept the truth, hushes it up instead with excuses.
Half-a-Dozen Sisters Ch. 25 pp. 414–15

Number 849 (4 April 1896)
Half-a-Dozen Sisters Ch. 26 pp. 417–19
Varieties (She Inherited It) p. 429
Other People's Stairs Ch. 2 pp. 430–1

Number 850 (11 April 1896)
Other People's Stairs Ch. 3* pp. 441–3
Marching Tune: 'One Foot Up, and One Foot Down': Old Nursery Rhyme for Girls' Voices (music score) (C. A. Macirone) pp. 444–7

Number 851 (18 April 1896)
A Child of Genius (Lily Watson) Ch. 1 pp. 449–51
    When Katharine Lovell's mother remarries, her disappointed daughter has to leave the German conservatoire where she is studying composition and piano and return home to Switzerland. When invited to live with her uncle's family in London, Katharine continues her education, but also learns long overdue lessons in selflessness and compassion, manifested when, poised on a professional career as a pianist, she puts that next step on hold in order to nurse her sick mother back to health.
    Illustration 'A girl sat by the window' shows Katharine surrounded by manuscript paper p. 449
Winifred's Home (Josepha Crane) Ch. 1 pp. 452–3

To May Dallingham visiting Winifred Despard, music piled untidily on the piano indicates poor housekeeping. Winifred is musical but refuses to play accompaniments for her husband to try out his voice after dinner, because it might wake the children.
Other People's Stairs Ch. 4 pp. 454–5

Number 852 (25 April 1896)
Other People's Stairs Ch. 5 pp. 466–7
A Child of Genius Ch. 2 pp. 475–6

Number 853 (2 May 1896)
Other People's Stairs Ch. 6 pp. 481–3
A Child of Genius Ch. 3 pp. 494–5
'Felix Mendelssohn': A Musically Illustrated Recitation (Annie W. Patterson) p. 496
    During this poetic tribute to Mendelssohn, a pianist can play appropriate selections from the composer's music softly in the background.

Number 854 (9 May 1896)
Other People's Stairs Ch. 7 pp. 499–501
A Child of Genius Ch. 4 pp. 501–2
Answers to Correspondents (Music heading) p. 511
    Engo di Santafior (music education), Viola (violin, music history and appreciation), Tootsie (violin, performance nerves), Nesta (voice)
Replies to Often-Asked Questions: '*Is Organ-playing bad for Girls?*' p. 512

Number 855 (16 May 1896)
Other People's Stairs Ch. 8 pp. 515–17
A Child of Genius Ch. 5 pp. 520–2
    Illustration 'Katharine's playing was distinguished by a wonderful verve and fire' p. 521
''Twas Johnnie's Favourite Song' (Gordon Stables) pp. 534–5
    Stables, a physician who also wrote under penname Medicus, was a violinist. In this excerpt from his medical practice, he tells how he used the power of music, played on a borrowed fiddle, to help a patient begin to mend her sorrow.

Number 856 (23 May 1896)
Other People's Stairs Ch. 9 pp. 530–1
Varieties (Foolish People) p. 531
Mazurka (music score) (Lady Thompson) pp. 532–4
A Child of Genius Ch. 6 pp. 542–3

Number 857 (30 May 1896)
Other People's Stairs Ch. 10 pp. 545–7
Winifred's Home Ch. 2* pp. 550–1
A Child of Genius Ch. 7 pp. 557–8
Varieties (Music Has Charms) p. 559

Number 858 (6 June 1896)
A Child of Genius Ch. 8 pp. 566–7
Other People's Stairs Ch. 11 pp. 573–4
Varieties (Is It So?) p. 574
Answers to Correspondents (Music heading) p. 576
    Student (music student lodging), Contralto (voice), Idaho (music education), A.E.J. (music education), C.E.C. and Popsie (zither), The Lady of Shalott (mandolin)

Number 859 (13 June 1896)
A Child of Genius Ch. 9 pp. 577–9
Other People's Stairs Ch. 12 pp. 589–90
Varieties (B. A. kindly sends us the following information) p. 591
    About St Paul's Cathedral choir.

Number 860 (20 June 1896)
Other People's Stairs Ch. 13 pp. 593–5
A Child of Genius Ch. 10 pp. 598–9

Number 861 (27 June 1896)
Other People's Stairs Ch. 14 pp. 612–13
A Child of Genius Ch. 11 pp. 619–20
Madame Schumann (J. F. Rowbotham) pp. 620–2
    Illustration 'Clara Schumann' (from F. Ganz photograph, Brussels) p. 621
Winifred's Home Ch. 3 pp. 622–3

Number 862 (4 July 1896)
A Child of Genius Ch. 12 pp. 630–1
Other People's Stairs Ch. 15 pp. 637–8
Answers to Correspondents p. 639
    Memory (general)

Number 863 (11 July 1896)
A Child of Genius Ch. 13 pp. 646–7
Other People's Stairs Ch. 16 pp. 654–5

Number 864 (18 July 1896)
Other People's Stairs Ch. 17 pp. 657–9
Winifred's Home Ch. 4 pp. 662–3
Sunset: A Lullaby (music score) (Ruth S. Cove) pp. 667–9
A Child of Genius Ch. 14 pp. 670–1

Number 865 (25 July 1896)
A Child of Genius Ch. 15 pp. 674–5
Other People's Stairs Ch. 18 pp. 685–6

Number 866 (1 August 1896)
Other People's Stairs Ch. 19 pp. 698–700
A Child of Genius Ch. 16 pp. 702–4
Answers to Correspondents (Music heading) p. 704
    A# (theory), Mother (practising, nuisance, wasted time), M.E.P. (general), Pretty Girl (?) (music education), Sorrowing Viola (general), Pansy (guitar), Rosemary (general), Chrysanthemum (voice), E. M. (repertoire)

Number 867 (8 August 1896)
A Child of Genius Ch. 17 pp. 705–6
A Trio (illustration) (from A. B. Donaldson painting) p. 712
    Two young women and a girl perform a string trio. The youngest, a violinist, sits in a chair too high for her feet to touch the floor.

England's Musical Past pp. 713–15
   Review of Frederick J. Crowest's *The Story of British Music*; the first volume had been published recently.
Other People's Stairs Ch. 20 pp. 715–16

Number 868 (15 August 1896)
Other People's Stairs Ch. 21 pp. 724–5
Varieties (Music in Japan) p. 727
A Child of Genius Ch. 18 pp. 733–4

Number 869 (22 August 1896)
A Child of Genius Ch. 19 pp. 742–3
Winifred's Home Ch. 5 pp. 746–7
Other People's Stairs Ch. 22 pp. 750–1
Answers to Correspondents (Music heading) p. 751
   Lover of Music (general), Organist (organ), Leila (music history and appreciation), Mona (national anthem), A. L. (piano), Rebecca and Others (general)

Number 870 (29 August 1896)
Other People's Stairs Ch. 23 pp. 753–5
Varieties (Musicians, Take Note) p. 759
A Child of Genius Ch. 20 pp. 766–7

Number 871 (5 September 1896)
A Child of Genius Ch. 21 pp. 774–5
Varieties (Three Things Needed) p. 775
Winifred's Home Ch. 6 pp. 778–9
Other People's Stairs Ch. 24 pp. 782–3

Number 872 (12 September 1896)
Other People's Stairs Ch. 25 pp. 786–7
A Child of Genius Ch. 22 pp. 790–1
A Song of Olden Days (illustration) p. 792
   A young woman has sheet music in hand.
The Music of the Past (poem) (Helen Marion Burnside) p. 793
Postlude: For Pianoforte or American Organ (music score) (Myles B. Foster) pp. 796–7

Number 873 (19 September 1896)
Song (poem) (L. G. Moberly) p. 809
A Child of Genius Ch. 23 pp. 811–12
Other People's Stairs Ch. 26 pp. 814–15

Number 874 (26 September 1896)
A Child of Genius Ch. 24 pp. 817–19
Other People's Stairs Ch. 27 pp. 820–1

Herald Angels
Extra Christmas Number for Volume 17 (1895)
Uncle Caleb's Choice pp. 2–10
   When Caleb Ayre's speculation in a mine finally pays off, he invites to his country home six nieces, nephews and second cousins from whom he plans to choose his heir.

Charlotte Ayres is loath to go without her friend Frances, who plays all her accompaniments, so Frances is invited too.

'Joy Cometh in the Morning': A Short Cantata for Girls' Voices (music score) (Mary Augusta Salmond, Words Helen Marion Burnside) pp. 18–25

Mother's Deputy (poem) p. 49

A Lullaby (poem) (William T. Saward) p. 53

Illustration 'Sing to me, Darling, sing something to-night' p. 52

The Carved Umbrella pp. 60–4

During her interview for a position in Russia supposedly to teach a little girl music, English and drawing, Rachel Grey, a daily governess in London, is mortified when her playing of a *Lieder ohne Worte* is met with an impatient, bored air.

Summer Spices
Extra Summer Number for Volume 17 (1896)

Summer Spices (Flower Songs) (poem) (Helen Marion Burnside) pp. 32–3

'A Good-Night Song in the Orphan School' (illustration) p. 40

Beethoven and the Blind Girl – A Surprise Visit (illustration) p. 44

A young woman is at the piano.

Barcarolle (from the 'Mountain Scenes') (music score) (Natalie Janotha, Op. 3) pp. 59–62

Varieties (She Refused to Sing) p. 63

Volume 18 (3 October 1896–25 September 1897)

Number 875 (3 October 1896)
Retrospection (music score) (H.R.H. the Princess Beatrice / Princess Henry of Battenberg, Words Charlotte Elliott) pp. 4–6

Number 876 (10 October 1896)
The White Rose of the Mountain (Anne Beale) Ch. 1 pp. 17–19
    Gwenllean Llewellen, who as a young girl sings and plays the harp, is pronounced 'not only the finest musician, but the first songstress of the Eisteddfod' (p. 190). Gwenllean uses her musical talent to support her family.

Number 877 (17 October 1896)
The White Rose of the Mountain Ch. 2 pp. 38–9
'Andante' (illustration) (from Etienne Azambie painting) p. 40
    A male pianist accompanies a young woman playing the violin while two other women listen.
Music-Copying as a Fine Art pp. 41–2
Answers to Correspondents (Music heading) p. 47
    Last column to include Music as a separate heading.
    Viola (voice), Nervous One (performance nerves)

Number 878 (24 October 1896)
A Competition for Professional Girls p. 57
    Musicians are among those eligible to compete in this announcement of a competition for girls who earn their livelihood in professional work not connected with the 'industrial class'.
The White Rose of the Mountain Ch. 3 pp. 57–9
Singers and Singing (The Countess Valda Gleichen) Part 1 pp. 60–1

Number 879 (31 October 1896)
The White Rose of the Mountain Ch. 4 pp. 69–71
Answers to Correspondents (Study and Studio) pp. 79–80
    First column to include Music replies under Study and Studio heading.
    Minnie M. Parish (composition), W. W. (applied music, pronunciation), E.N.G. (composition)

Number 880 (7 November 1896)
The White Rose of the Mountain Ch. 5 pp. 94–5
Answers to Correspondents p. 96
    Tone (music copying)

Number 881 (14 November 1896)
The White Rose of the Mountain Ch. 6 pp. 97–8
    Illustration 'David and Gwenllean' shows Gwenllean playing David's harp p. 97
Weep No More (music score) (William Hayman Cummings, Words John Fletcher (A.D. 1647) pp. 100–1
The Rehearsal (illustration) (from G. Moreau-de-Tours painting) plate facing p. 107
    Adults and children – one girl with violin in hand – stand behind a piano singing, as a woman accompanies them on piano.
Singers and Singing Part 2 p. 107
Answers to Correspondents p. 111
    Teddy's Molly Bawn (general)

196 *Catalogue of musical content*

Number 882 (21 November 1896)
The White Rose of the Mountain Ch. 7 pp. 114–15

Number 883 (28 November 1896)
The White Rose of the Mountain Ch. 8 pp. 132–4
Answers to Correspondents pp. 143–4
   Catherine S. (piano, typewriter)

Number 884 (5 December 1896)
A Shepherd with a Pipe (illustration) (from Giorgione painting) plate facing p. 145
The White Rose of the Mountain Ch. 9 pp. 155–7
Answers to Correspondents (Study and Studio heading) p. 160
   Elspeth (repertoire), Maida Vale (practising society)

Number 885 (12 December 1896)
The White Rose of the Mountain Ch. 10 pp. 173–4
Answers to Correspondents (Study and Studio heading) p. 175
   Syncopation (applied music), A Lover of Music (music education), Chaconne (sight-reading)

Number 886 (19 December 1896)
That Dear Old Song (poem) (Edward Oxenford) p. 177
   Illustration 'That dear old song' shows a woman violinist p. 177
A Song in a Dream (music score) (C. Villiers Stanford, Poem N. Breton) pp. 180–1
The Nightingale and the Robin: The Plea of a Minor Poet (poem) (Helen Marion Burnside)
   p. 184
The White Rose of the Mountain Ch. 11 pp. 190–1
Answers to Correspondents p. 191
   Lady Organist (organ)

Number 887 (26 December 1896)
The White Rose of the Mountain Ch. 12 pp. 193–6
Varieties (Music, Heavenly Maid) p. 205
Answers to Correspondents (Study and Studio heading) p. 208
   M. I. Rutter (music education)

Number 888 (2 January 1897)
The White Rose of the Mountain Ch. 13 pp. 221–2
Answers to Correspondents (Study and Studio heading) p. 223
   Lily of the Valley (voice), Dania (applied music), E. Marchbank (music education), Reader of Dear Old 'G.O.P.'

Number 889 (9 January 1897)
The White Rose of the Mountain Ch. 14 pp. 230–1

Number 890 (16 January 1897)
Longing (music score) (Ethel L. Watson, Words Matthew Arnold) pp. 244–7
The White Rose of the Mountain Ch. 15 pp. 249–51

Number 891 (23 January 1897)
The White Rose of the Mountain Ch. 16 pp. 257–9

Number 892 (30 January 1897)
The White Rose of the Mountain Ch. 17 pp. 282–3
Answers to Correspondents p. 288
   A Daughter of Jubal (organ)

Number 893 (6 February 1897)
A Song of Hope (poem) (I.K.N.) p. 297
The White Rose of the Mountain Ch. 18 pp. 301–2
Answers to Correspondents p. 304
   B.L.W. (voice, health)

Number 894 (13 February 1897)
'The Xylophone' (Priscilla Harrison) pp. 305–6
The White Rose of the Mountain Ch. 19 pp. 318–19
Answers to Correspondents (Study and Studio heading) p. 320
   Sophia (applied music)

Number 895 (20 February 1897)
The White Rose of the Mountain Ch. 20 pp. 333–4

Number 896 (27 February 1897)
Varieties (What Her Voice Was Good For) p. 339
Our Competition for Professional Girls p. 347
   Third-Prize winner is 'Pimpernel', an organist from Plumstead.
The White Rose of the Mountain Ch. 21 pp. 349–51

Number 897 (6 March 1897)
That Horrid Boy Next Door (May Gladwin) pp. 353–5
   Sisters Jo, Jeffie, Doll and Becky Doran find Cyril Montagu, the boy visiting next door, annoying until one day, when Jo begins to sing and play 'Old Folks at Home' on the schoolroom piano, he appears and confesses that he is homesick. Jo befriends the lonely, unhappy boy and, when he is dying of consumption not long afterward, she sings the song at his bedside.
The White Rose of the Mountain Ch. 22 pp. 365–7
Answers to Correspondents (Study and Studio heading) p. 368
   One of Our Girls (piano), S. (A reader of the dear old GIRL'S OWN PAPER) (terms), Jane Grey (voice), Strangers Yet (repertoire)

Number 898 (13 March 1897)
The White Rose of the Mountain Ch. 23 pp. 370–2
'The Old Refrain': Lines on the Death of a Chorister (music score) (The Rev. L. Meadows White, Words Edward Medland White) pp. 378–81

Number 899 (20 March 1897)
The White Rose of the Mountain Ch. 24 pp. 393–4
   Illustration 'A solo on the harp' shows a woman seemingly more concerned with her appearance than her playing p. 392
Odds and Ends [Spiders and Music] p. 400

Number 900 (27 March 1897)
The White Rose of the Mountain Ch. 25 pp. 410–11
Competition for Professional Girls: The Five Prize Essays pp. 412–15
   Includes third-prize essay by 'Pimpernel', organist from Plumstead pp. 413–14. A graduate of the Royal Academy of Music, 'Pimpernel' trained as a singer but could not get enough engagements, so she teaches music and plays the organ instead.

Number 901 (3 April 1897)
Music (poem) (G.K.M.) p. 417
   Illustration 'The Witching Cadence' shows a young woman pianist accompanying a male violinist p. 417

198   *Catalogue of musical content*

Girls and Their Pocket-Money pp. 418–19
   Author argues for giving girls regular pocket money to spend on hobbies and other worthwhile activities. Gives example of a father whose housekeeper daughter was not compensated but could spend the household budget surplus. A musical girl, she purchased a piano from these funds, much to her father's anger.
The White Rose of the Mountain Ch. 26 pp. 430–1
Answers to Correspondents (Study and Studio heading) pp. 431–2
   Marie (copyright), Catherine S. (typewriting, piano)

Number 902 (10 April 1897)
The White Rose of the Mountain Ch. 27 pp. 433–5
Pianoforte Practising (A. D. Swift) pp. 446–7
Answers to Correspondents (Study and Studio heading) p. 447
   Grace Eulalie (composition)
Summer is y-comen in (poem) p. 448
   The maidens in this illustrated poem play musical instruments.

Number 903 (17 April 1897)
The White Rose of the Mountain Ch. 28 pp. 454–5
An Easter Hymn (poem) (Somerville Gibney) p. 456
Answers to Correspondents (Study and Studio heading) p. 463
   Quester (violin)

Number 904 (24 April 1897)
Student-Life in Florence (Ellen) Letter 1 p. 477
   Ellen Aubert traveled to Florence to study singing. Letter 7 gives practical hints to her friend and correspondent who herself is following in Aubert's footsteps. For Letter 2, see 'Musical Art in Florence'.
The White Rose of the Mountain Ch. 29 pp. 478–9
Answers to Correspondents (Study and Studio heading) pp. 479–80
   Leo (composition), Violet (general, music education), White Violet (repertoire)

Number 905 (1 May 1897)
The White Rose of the Mountain Ch. 30 pp. 494–5

Number 906 (8 May 1897)
Time and the Maidens (poem) (Mildred Emra) p. 504
   One of the maidens in this illustrated poem is musical.
The White Rose of the Mountain Ch. 31 p. 507
Answers to Correspondents (Study and Studio heading) pp. 511–12
   Isabel E. Kent (practising society)

Number 907 (15 May 1897)
Varieties (Music – *Shakespeare*) p. 519
The White Rose of the Mountain Ch. 32 pp. 526–7
Answers to Correspondents (Study and Studio heading) pp. 527–8
   Annette (music education), Loveday (music education)

Number 908 (22 May 1897)
The White Rose of the Mountain Ch. 33 p. 535
Answers to Correspondents p. 544
   Maud (music history and appreciation)

Catalogue of musical content 199

Number 909 (29 May 1897)
The White Rose of the Mountain Ch. 34 pp. 546–7

Number 910 (5 June 1897)
The White Rose of the Mountain Ch. 35 pp. 566–7
Musical Art in Florence (A Student) p. 574
    Second of seven letters Ellen Aubert wrote under a different title. See 'Student-Life in Florence'.

Number 911 (12 June 1897)
Father of Love: Hymn for a Wedding (music score) (Myles B. Foster, Words Henry Hamilton) pp. 580–2
'Et in Arcadia, Ego' (poem) (Mildred Emra) p. 584
The White Rose of the Mountain Ch. 36 pp. 589–91

Number 912 (19 June 1897)
Answers to Correspondents (Study and Studio heading) p. 608
    Harmony (theory)

Number 914 (3 July 1897)
Answers to Correspondents (Study and Studio heading) p. 639
    Amateur Societies (practising society), Arbor Vitae (music copying), Perseverance (piano, repertoire), Stella Callingham and A. Minor (practising, music education)

Number 915 (10 July 1897)
A River Song (poem) (Clara Thwaites) p. 641
Answers to Correspondents (Study and Studio heading) p. 655
    A Lover of the Dear Old 'G.O.P.' (general), Feather Pen (reading music), Twiser (Brisbane, Queensland) (violin, music education)

Number 916 (17 July 1897)
Student-Life in Florence (A Student) Letter 3 p. 667

Number 917 (24 July 1897)
Varieties (A Left-Handed Compliment) p. 684
Answers to Correspondents (Study and Studio heading) pp. 687–8
    Mandilina (guitar)

Number 918 (31 July 1897)
Answers to Correspondents pp. 703–4
    Madge (music history and appreciation)

Number 919 (7 August 1897)
A Pretty Pianoforte Back pp. 708–9
    Illustration 'Painted Canvas or Painted Sacking Hanging for Back of Piano' p. 708
Varieties (How She Sang) p. 710
Answers to Correspondents (Study and Studio heading) pp. 719–20
    Bob's Sweetheart (song repertoire), A Lover of Music (music history and appreciation), R.A.K. (piano repertoire), Honey (performance nerves), 'Music Mad' (harpsichord, piano), Old English Songs (repertoire)

Number 920 (14 August 1897)
Student-Life in Florence (Ellen Aubert) Letter 4 p. 727

Answers to Correspondents pp. 735–6
   Tom Thumb (instrument maintenance, piano keys)

Number 921 (21 August 1897)
An Exiled Rose (poem) (Sarah Doudney) p. 737
   Illustration 'The land of the gourd and vine' shows a musical young woman p. 737

Number 922 (28 August 1897)
Student-Life in Florence (A Student / Ellen Aubert) Letter 5 p. 756

Number 923 (4 September 1897)
Answers to Correspondents (Study and Studio heading) p. 784
   E.N.G. (composition)

Number 924 (11 September 1897)
Mental Melodies (poem) (C.P.) p. 793
Student-Life in Florence (A Student / Ellen) Letter 6 p. 793
'Agatha's Choice' (A. Fraser Robertson) Ch. 1 pp. 797–8
   Agatha Ashley and Edward Templeton enjoy music. After dinner in the drawing room, he sings 'The Three Singers' in a voice that brings tears to her eyes. Both attend orchestra concerts.

Number 925 (18 September 1897)
Student-Life in Florence (A Student / Ellen Aubert) Letter 7 p. 803
'Agatha's Choice' Ch. 2 pp. 809–10
Answers to Correspondents (Study and Studio heading) p. 816
   Student (voice, piano, music education)

Number 926 (25 September 1897)
'Agatha's Choice' Ch. 3 pp. 822–3
Answers to Correspondents (Study and Studio heading) p. 827
   A. M. (composition)

Our Christmas Wreath
Extra Christmas Number for Volume 18 (1896)
The Result of a Song (Ellen A. Bennett) pp. 1–4
   When Evelyn Stuart, the celebrated singer Leonora Dolci, encounters a poor, elderly woman singing on the street to earn money to buy food for her sick husband, she takes her place and sings her 'Bird Song' to the delight of the gathering crowd. The result of the song benefits both the old couple's finances and Evelyn's love life.
Christmas Music (poem) (Sarah Doudney) p. 6
'So Pleasant' p. 33
   Agreeable women learned the art of pleasing when girls. Applied to music, one should oblige if possible when asked to sing or play, for music as an accomplishment is learned to please others.
Endymion: A New Song (music score) (Myles B. Foster, Words Longfellow) pp. 38–41
Clarice pp. 42–7
   Chris Vaughan thinks his sister Clare 'awfully lazy over her music', but when she plays a Schubert Impromptu 'with more feeling than power of execution', Mr Martindale, a potential suitor, thinks she need not envy any one's musical talent, for 'you have by instinct the power that many of us vainly spend years to acquire' (p. 42).

'Queen of Queens'
Diamond Jubilee Number for Volume 18 (1897)
'My Long Life. By Mary Cowden Clarke' p. 29–32
    'Notice' of autobiography of Mary Cowden Clarke, the Novello's eldest daughter and author of *The Shakespeare Concordance*, includes mention of the musical careers of the Novello family and description of a musical evening in their home at which Malibran, De Beroit and Mendelssohn performed.

Wild Orchises (Darley Dale) p. 37–9, 41–2
    While the six Manifold sisters all have nonmusical interests that take them away from home, their stepsister Cissy pursues twice-weekly music lessons, practices two hours daily and has a weekly lesson in harmony.

Volume 19 (2 October 1897–24 September 1898)

'A Reverie' (illustration) frontispiece
   Young woman plays a piano, on which rest a violin and a cello.
Chloe (illustration) (from Sir John Poynter painting) title page
   A young woman holds a lyre.

Number 927 (2 October 1897)
Sisters Three (Mrs Henry Mansergh) Ch. 1 pp. 1–3
   Norah is the musically gifted one of the seven Betrand siblings. She had taken violin lessons in London and by her own admission, plays 'beautifully', but had to give up lessons when her family moved. She is delighted when a neighbor arranges for her to take lessons with his violinist sister. Within three years she becomes 'a performer of no mean attainments' whose goal is to attend the Royal College of Music for further study (p. 354).
'If Loving Hearts Were Never Lonely – '; or, Madge Harcourt's Desolation (Gertrude Page) Ch. 1 pp. 8, 10–11
   The Cumberland home's silent, unvarying routine gives way to snatches of operatic arias and gay whistling when 18-year-old Madge Harcourt's brother Jack visits from London. Madge plays the piano but lets it slip when Jack is around – until her stepmother insists that she practise after a day of pleasure.
'Love Divine – All Love Excelling' (illustration) p. 9
   Young women as pianist and as vocalist.
A Painted Silk or Satin Pianoforte Front p. 12

Number 928 (9 October 1897)
'If Loving Hearts Were Never Lonely – ' Ch. 2* pp. 22–3, 25
Sisters Three Ch. 2* pp. 29–30

Number 929 (16 October 1897)
Sisters Three Ch. 3* pp. 34–6
'If Loving Hearts Were Never Lonely – ' Ch. 3 pp. 40–2

Number 930 (23 October 1897)
Sisters Three Ch. 4 pp. 51–2
'If Loving Hearts Were Never Lonely – ' Ch. 4* pp. 54–5
Answers to Correspondents (Study and Studio heading) pp. 63–4
   Evangeline (music history and appreciation), Courage (repertoire), Largo (theory), Evangeline (piano, guitar, mandolin, choosing instrument)

Number 931 (30 October 1897)
Sisters Three Ch. 5* pp. 66–7
'If Loving Hearts Were Never Lonely – ' Ch. 5 pp. 78–9

Number 932 (6 November 1897)
Sisters Three Ch. 6 pp. 81–3
Varieties (No Pieces Sold Here) p. 85
'If Loving Hearts Were Never Lonely – ' Ch. 6 pp. 94–5

Number 933 (13 November 1897)
'If Loving Hearts Were Never Lonely – ' Ch. 7 pp. 98–9
Sisters Three Ch. 7 pp. 106–7
Answers to Correspondents pp. 111–12
   Musician (music copying)

Catalogue of musical content 203

Number 934 (20 November 1897)
Notes on Two Choral Works by Johannes Brahms (William Porteous) I. German Requiem; II. A Song of Destiny pp. 114–15
Sisters Three Ch. 8 pp. 118–19
'If Loving Hearts Were Never Lonely – ' Ch. 8 pp. 122–3
Answers to Correspondents (Study and Studio heading) p. 127
    Norah Grayson (general)

Number 935 (27 November 1897)
'If Loving Hearts Were Never Lonely – ' Ch. 9 pp. 129–31
'Little Miss Penny' (Eleanor C. Saltmer) pp. 134–5
    Margaret Penny is a music teacher of limited means whose 'shabby-genteel' fashion style Lottie and her friend ridicule (p. 134). Unknown to them, Miss Penny has scrimped on clothes in order to give money to help Lottie's young cousin who is dying. When Lottie learns this, she vows never again to judge a person by her appearance.
Some Soprano Songs for Girls (Mary Augusta Salmond) p. 135

Number 936 (4 December 1897)
'If Loving Hearts Were Never Lonely – ' Ch. 10 pp. 152–5
Sisters Three Ch. 9 pp. 158–60
Answers to Correspondents (Study and Studio heading) p. 160
    May Blossom (piano, health), R.E.C. (Bath) (theory, music education), 'Advance' (music education), Would-Be Musician (theory)

Number 937 (11 December 1897)
Sisters Three Ch. 10 pp. 164–5
'If Loving Hearts Were Never Lonely – ' Ch. 11 pp. 170–1
Chorale: For Pianoforte or American Organ (music score) (Myles B. Foster) pp. 172–3
Questions and Answers p. 175
    'Our Open Letter-Box' heading includes music replies.
    A Lover of Poetry (repertoire), Miss Hill for E.A.T. (repertoire), Vera Vernon (repertoire)
Answers to Correspondents (Study and Studio heading) p. 176
    Vera Vernon (repertoire)

Number 938 (18 December 1897)
Sisters Three Ch. 11 pp. 176–9
'If Loving Hearts Were Never Lonely – ' Ch. 12 pp. 182–3
Some New Mezzo-Soprano Songs for Girls (Mary Augusta Salmond) p. 183

Number 939 (25 December 1897)
'If Loving Hearts Were Never Lonely – ' Ch. 13 pp. 194–5
Sisters Three Ch. 12 pp. 205–6

Number 940 (1 January 1898)
'If Loving Hearts Were Never Lonely – ' Ch. 14 pp. 210–11
Sisters Three Ch. 13 pp. 214–15
An Evening Hymn (poem) p. 217
Answers to Correspondents (Study and Studio heading) pp. 223–4
    Perseverance (repertoire), C.M.T.M. (music education)

Number 941 (8 January 1898)
'If Loving Hearts Were Never Lonely – ' Ch. 15 pp. 226–7
Sisters Three Ch. 14 pp. 236–7

204 *Catalogue of musical content*

Answers to Correspondents (Study and Studio heading) pp. 238–9
    T.I.G. (violin)

Number 942 (15 January 1898)
Sisters Three Ch. 15 pp. 241–3
'If Loving Hearts Were Never Lonely – ' Ch. 16 pp. 245–6
Johann Sebastian Bach (Eleonore D'Esterre-Keeling) pp. 248–51
    Illustrations 'J. S. Bach' p. 248; 'A Few Bars of Bach's MS. Music' p. 249; 'Bach's Introduction to Frederick the Great at Potsdam' p. 249; 'Bach's Birthplace' p. 250
Answers to Correspondents (Study and Studio heading) p. 255
    Contralto (general)

Number 943 (22 January 1898)
'If Loving Hearts Were Never Lonely – ' Ch. 17 pp. 258–60
Sisters Three Ch. 16 pp. 266–7
Allegro con Moto Agitato: For Pianoforte or American Organ (music score) (Myles B. Foster) pp. 268–9
Answers to Correspondents p. 272
    Carlotta (piano, musician work), Norma (piano), Miss Isabel Kent (practising society), E.A.B. (mandolin)

Number 944 (29 January 1898)
'If Loving Hearts Were Never Lonely – ' Ch. 18 pp. 274–6
Sisters Three Ch. 17 pp. 278–9

Number 945 (5 February 1898)
'If Loving Hearts Were Never Lonely – ' Ch. 19 pp. 289–91
Varieties (A Musical Sister) p. 295
Sisters Three Ch. 18 p. 302

Number 946 (12 February 1898)
Sisters Three Ch. 19 pp. 305–7
'If Loving Hearts Were Never Lonely – ' Ch. 20* pp. 317–19

Number 947 (19 February 1898)
'If Loving Hearts Were Never Lonely – ' Ch. 21* pp. 322–4
Musical Degrees for Our Girls (Annie W. Patterson) pp. 331–2
Sisters Three Ch. 20 p. 334

Number 948 (26 February 1898)
Sisters Three Ch. 21 pp. 338–9
'If Loving Hearts Were Never Lonely – ' Ch. 22 pp. 350–1
Answers to Correspondents pp. 351–2
    Miss S. Hill (repertoire), Mr William Wardrop (repertoire), Scotia (repertoire)

Number 949 (5 March 1898)
Sisters Three Ch. 22* pp. 353–4
    Illustration 'It was always a treat to hear her play' shows Norah playing the violin p. 353
'If Loving Hearts Were Never Lonely – ' Ch. 23 p. 358
Dick Hartwell's Fortune (Sarah Doudney) Ch. 1* p. 361
    In a gesture of compassion, Dick Hartwell gives £5 to a woman who has lost her meagre savings. 'The five-pound note belonged, strictly speaking, to the piano fund'. After Minnie Brace accepted his proposal, Dick started the fund to buy her a first-rate instrument.

'He was ready to gratify any wish of hers, and he would have done his best to get her a church organ if she had asked for it.' (p. 361) Dick spends the next month replenishing the fund.
Answers to Correspondents (Study and Studio heading) pp. 367–8
   Gurth (piano), Ivy Leaf (voice)

Number 950 (12 March 1898)
'If Loving Hearts Were Never Lonely – ' Ch. 24 pp. 372–4
A Song (poem) (William T. Saward) p. 377
   Illustration 'A Song' p. 376
Dick Harwell's Fortune Ch. 2* pp. 378–9
Sisters Three Ch. 23 pp. 382–3
Answers to Correspondents (Study and Studio heading) p. 384
   Jim and 'Lawson' (general)

Number 951 (19 March 1898)
Paderewski as a Composer (A. E. Keeton) p. 389
   Illustration 'M. Paderewski' p. 388
Dick Harwell's Fortune Ch. 3* pp. 390–1
'If Loving Hearts Were Never Lonely – ' Ch. 25 p. 391
Sisters Three Ch. 24 pp. 396–7
Answers to Correspondents (Study and Studio heading) p. 399
   High Sea (music education), Gentleman Reader (theory), R. H. Fletcher (violin)

Number 952 (26 March 1898)
The Bells of Spring (poem) (William T. Saward) p. 401
'If Loving Hearts Were Never Lonely – ' Chs 26, 27 pp. 402–3
Dick Hartwell's Fortune Ch. 4 pp. 405–6
Sisters Three Ch. 25 pp. 406–7

Number 953 (2 April 1898)
Sisters Three Ch. 26 pp. 422–3
The Sorrows of Girlhood (Lily Watson) Part 4 pp. 428–9
   Gives example of a girl training for a musical career with high hopes, when a violinist's cramp ends that beloved work. She bravely begins a new chapter of her life and becomes more successful with her pen than she would have with her violin.
Answers to Correspondents (Study and Studio heading) p. 432
   Porc-Épic (music education), Opera (Vienna) (opera)

Number 954 (9 April 1898)
Fairies (poem) (Constance Morgan) p. 441
Some Useful New Music (Mary Augusta Salmond) p. 441
Sisters Three Ch. 27 pp. 442–3
Answers to Correspondents (Study and Studio heading) pp. 447–8
   T. C. (composition)

Number 955 (16 April 1898)
In Spite of All (Ida Lemon) Ch. 1 pp. 449–2
   Norah Gilman and Beattie Margetson both sing as evening entertainment. Norah's voice, though uncultivated, is 'fresh and pure like a bird's' (p. 607). Beattie is just learning to sing. Her aunt Ella does not think much of Beattie's power of voice but knows that singing shows her off to advantage.

Answers to Correspondents (Study and Studio heading) p. 464
    E.N.G. (theory, correspondence course), May Blossom for A Lover of Poetry (repertoire)

Number 956 (23 April 1898)
In Spite of All Ch. 2 pp. 466–8
The Sea-Boy's Song (music score) (Sir George C. Martin, Words The Rev. H. C. Shuttleworth) pp. 476–8

Number 957 (30 April 1898)
In Spite of All Ch. 3* pp. 491–2

Number 958 (7 May 1898)
In Spite of All Ch. 4 pp. 497–500
'That Peculiar Miss Artleton' (Frances Lockwood Green) Ch. 1 p. 503
    Wealthy Miss Joan Artleton wears shabby clothing to see how her appearance affects how people treat her. When shop girl Clarice Day treats her with kindness, the wealthy woman takes her into her confidence and befriends her. Clarice, who has a sweet but uncultivated voice, takes her music along to lunch with Miss Artleton and sings 'Darby and Joan' to her own accompaniment.
Answers to Correspondents (Study and Studio heading) p. 512
    Natalie (health)

Number 959 (14 May 1898)
A New Idea for Treating a Piano Back (Fred Miller) pp. 516–17
    Illustration 'Embroidered Pockets to Hold Music' p. 516
'That Peculiar Miss Artleton' Ch. 2 p. 519
In Spite of All Ch. 5 pp. 524–6

Number 960 (21 May 1898)
In Spite of All Ch. 6 pp. 530–2
The Little Organ-Grinder (poem) (E. Nesbit) p. 536
Varieties (A Hundred Guineas a Lesson) p. 539
'That Peculiar Miss Artleton' Ch. 3 pp. 542–3
Answers to Correspondents (Study and Studio heading) p. 544
    Mabel (organ)

Number 961 (28 May 1898)
'That Peculiar Miss Artleton' Ch. 4 pp. 549–50
In Spite of All Ch. 7 pp. 550–1, 555

Number 962 (4 June 1898)
In Spite of All Ch. 8 pp. 561–3
'Glorified' Workmen's Dwellings Part 2 p. 567
    Aunt Mary offers advice to nieces Elsie and Annie who want to set up housekeeping in London. Knowing the girls are practical and ready to take useful hints, she asks whether they have kept up their music and will have a piano for which they will need a music stool. Aunt Mary then tells them how to convert an old croquet case into a music seat and box.
Answers to Correspondents (Study and Studio heading) pp. 575–6
    B. J. (piano, applied music), Pansy (song repertoire), A Devonian (music education), Dominant (music teaching)

Number 963 (11 June 1898)
In Spite of All Ch. 9 pp. 588–9
Answers to Correspondents (Study and Studio heading) pp. 591–2
    A Lover of Good Music (music teaching, practising society)

Number 964 (18 June 1898)
'The Father of the Symphony': Joseph Haydn (Eleonore D'Esterre-Keeling) pp. 596–8
    Illustration 'Joseph Haydn' p. 597
In Spite of All Ch. 10* pp. 605–7

Number 965 (25 June 1898)
In Spite of All Ch. 11 pp. 612–14
Answers to Correspondents (Study and Studio heading) pp. 623–4
    Violet (song repertoire), M.E.H. (composition), Pink Heather (repertoire), Doris (piano)

Number 966 (2 July 1898)
In Spite of All Ch. 12 pp. 625–8
Answers to Correspondents (Study and Studio heading) pp. 639–40
    Musical Jessie (music education)

Number 967 (9 July 1898)
In Spite of All Ch. 13 pp. 642–4
Answers to Correspondents p. 656
    Twins (general, nuisance)

Number 968 (16 July 1898)
My Land of Memories (poem) (Eric Broad) p. 657
    Illustration 'How sweet the secret bower' shows a musical young woman p. 657
In Spite of All Ch. 14 pp. 660–2

Number 969 (23 July 1898)
In Spite of All Ch. 15 pp. 674–6
New Music: Some Pretty Vocal Duets and New Two-Part Songs for Girls (Mary Augusta Salmond) p. 684
Answers to Correspondents (Study and Studio heading) pp. 687–8
    A Lover of Music (piano)

Number 970 (30 July 1898)
In Spite of All Ch. 16 pp. 693–5
Answers to Correspondents (Study and Studio heading) pp. 702–4
    An Independent One (music education)

Number 971 (6 August 1898)
In Spite of All Ch. 17 pp. 705–8
Answers to Correspondents (Study and Studio heading) pp. 719–20
    May (mandolin), Lover of Music (Irish harp, Welsh harp), Ethel Rimmer (repertoire)

Number 972 (13 August 1898)
In Spite of All Ch. 18 pp. 722–4
Some New Contralto Songs for Girls (Mary Augusta Salmond) p. 727

208 *Catalogue of musical content*

Number 973 (20 August 1898)
The Sea's Song (poem) (Nora Hopper) p. 737
In Spite of All Ch. 19 pp. 738–40
Varieties (Musical Enthusiasm) p. 740
Sunday Evening (illustration) p. 744
 A young woman is at a keyboard.
Some New Sacred Songs (Mary Augusta Salmond) p. 745
Answers to Correspondents (Study and Studio heading) pp. 751–2
 Castelfranc (general)

Number 974 (27 August 1898)
In Spite of All Ch. 20 pp. 754–6
Varieties (Which Horn?) p. 757

Number 975 (3 September 1898)
In Spite of All Ch. 21 pp. 770–2
Voices on the River (poem) (Edward Oxenford) p. 776
Her Last Oratorio (Greta Gilmour) Ch. 1 pp. 776, 778–9
 Jenny, a soprano suffering from an undisclosed terminal illness, dies during her performance of 'I Know That My Redeemer Liveth' after singing the words 'yet in my flesh shall I see God'.
Answers to Correspondents (Study and Studio heading) pp. 783–4
 Marjory (composition)

Number 976 (10 September 1898)
In Spite of All Ch. 22 pp. 786–8
Adagio ma non Troppo: For the Pianoforte or American Organ (music score) (Myles B. Foster) p. 789
New Helps to Music Study: For Younger Musicians (Mary Augusta Salmond) p. 791
Her Last Oratorio Ch. 2 pp. 793–4
Answers to Correspondents (Study and Studio heading) p. 799
 Bellum (repertoire)

Number 977 (17 September 1898)
Franz Schubert (Eleonore D'Esterre-Keeling) pp. 801–2
 Illustration 'Schubert' p. 801
In Spite of All Ch. 23 pp. 803–5
Answers to Correspondents (Study and Studio heading) pp. 815–16
 Soloist (musician work, choral singing)

Number 978 (24 September 1898)
In Spite of All Ch. 24 pp. 817–20
Varieties (A Well-Founded Belief) p. 823

Christmas Chimes
Extra Christmas Part for Volume 19 (1897)
'Cis': A Short Story pp. 18–21
 A music professor befriends the invalid child Dickey, who hears the noisy pupils in the rooms above, and his 22-year-old sister 'Cis', all residents of the same lodging house.
Chopin (illustration) p. 36
 A girl is playing the piano.

Birdie; or, A Houseful of Girls (C. N. Carvalho) pp. 57–9
   On a visit to Woodleigh, Lancaster meets friend Philip Rutherford's five sisters. The eldest, Victoria, and youngest, Birdie, are musical; Victoria is a cellist, and Birdie plays her accompaniments and also has a sweet voice but dislikes singing before strangers.

'Honied Hours'
Extra Summer Number for Volume 19 (1898)
One Summer-Time (Helen Boulnois) pp. 1–12
   When Betty Braintree plays the violin, schoolmistress Laura Landon, who has an ear for music and considers the violin the worst instrument of 'torture' when in unskilled hands, hears a quaint old melody in which 'Every note fell truly and sweetly, and with the wailing sadness that is characteristic of the violin.' (p. 6)

Volume 20 (1 October 1898–30 September 1899)

Number 979 (1 October 1898)
Autumn (poem) (V. R.) p. 8
A New Prize Competition: The Girl's Own Questions and Answers pp. 14–15
   Competition to ask 36 questions over three months for readers to answer. Question 8 of the first 12 is 'What are the characteristics of the music of Chopin?' Answer p. 366.
Varieties (Delight in Praising – *Walter S. Landor*) p. 15

Number 980 (8 October 1898)
About Peggy Saville (Jessie Mansergh / Mrs G. de Horne Vaizey) Ch. 1 pp. 17–18
   Fourteen-year-old Peggy boards with the Reverend Asplin and his family in England for schooling while her parents are in India. The vicar believes music is useful for girls but tailors its practice to their talent. Peggy does not pursue music; his daughter Esther, a scholar with minimal musical ability, spends minimal time on the piano, while Mellicent, who is not a scholar, focuses on the violin.
Twilight Music (illustration) p. 24
   Two women sit outdoors near an instrumental duo of men playing violin and cello.
Answers to Correspondents (Study and Studio heading) pp. 30–1
   'Génie' (repertoire)

Number 981 (15 October 1898)
About Peggy Saville Ch. 2 pp. 38–9
The Girl's Own Questions and Answers Competition p. 47
   Question 13. 'When did the pianoforte first come into use?' Answer p. 367.

Number 982 (22 October 1898)
About Peggy Saville Ch. 3* p. 54–5
Answers to Correspondents (Study and Studio heading) pp. 63–4
   Song Bird (metronome)

Number 983 (29 October 1898)
Girls As I Have Known Them (Elsa D'Esterre-Keeling) Part 1 The Sentimental Girl pp. 68–9
   In her irreverent look at Victorian girlhood, the author does not single out the Musical Girl, but makes musical references to the Vulgar Girl (Part 3) and the average Athletic Girl (Part 6).
About Peggy Saville Ch. 4 pp. 70–1
Answers to Correspondents (Study and Studio heading) p. 79
   Hetty Spier (general, choral singing), Bangalore (composition)

Number 984 (5 November 1898)
About Peggy Saville Ch. 5* pp. 90–1
Answers to Correspondents (Study and Studio heading) p. 95
   Ajax (composition)

Number 985 (12 November 1898)
Henry Purcell: The Pioneer of English Opera (Eleonore D'Esterre-Keeling) pp. 100–2
   Illustration 'Henry Purcell' p. 100
The New Soprano (illustration) p. 104
   A young woman entering the churchyard carries what is likely a prayer book and hymnal or book of music in her hand.

Orpheus (poem) (A. N.) p. 105
About Peggy Saville Ch. 6 pp. 109–10
Answers to Correspondents (Study and Studio heading) p. 112
    Betsy Trotwood (organ, applied music)
The Girl's Own Questions and Answers Competition p. 112
    Question 37. "What famous musical composition came to a violinist in a dream?" Answer p. 479.
    Question 42. "What saint was so able a musician that according to tradition an angel descended to earth enraptured with her melodious strains?" Answer p. 479.

Number 986 (19 November 1898)
About Peggy Saville Ch. 7 pp. 113–15
Girls As I Have Known Them (Elsa D'Esterre-Keeling) Part 2 The Witty Girl pp. 116–17
Answers to Correspondents (Study and Studio heading) pp. 127–8
    Smilloc (general), Clara J. Nicholson and Wyndhamite for Ethel Rimmer (repertoire), Irish Shamrock (repertoire)

Number 987 (26 November 1898)
About Peggy Saville Ch. 8 pp. 132–3
The Girl's Own Questions and Answers Competition p. 135
    Question 49. "What epidemic in Italy in the sixteenth century was cured by means of music?" Answer p. 525.

Number 988 (3 December 1898)
Varieties (A Lesson for a Choir-Singer) p. 147
About Peggy Saville Ch. 9 pp. 150–1
'Sister Warwick': A Story of Influence (H. Mary Wilson) Ch. 1* pp. 153–5
    In this sequel to 'In Warwick Ward' and 'In Monmouth Ward', it is not the nurse but rather her considerate friend who is the musician. Having invited Sister Warwick to her home, she 'played softly and quietly . . . bits of Beethoven, Handel, Mendelssohn' on a small chamber organ to refresh her friend's body and soul (p. 155).
Rules of Society (Lady William Lennox) Part 2 pp. 156–7
    When invited to a country house, if on a wet day the guest would rather work on her drawing or run through songs, and others want to play billiards or battledore, she should sacrifice her private inclinations and join the others.

Number 989 (10 December 1898)
About Peggy Saville Ch. 10* pp. 165–6
The Girl's Own Questions and Answers Competition p. 167
    Question 69. "Who was the father of English Cathedral music?" Answer p. 527.
The Fairy Governess: A Musical Story (Herbert Harraden) pp. 169–76
    Includes music scores.

Number 990 (17 December 1898)
About Peggy Saville Ch. 11 pp. 182–3, 185
'Sister Warwick' Ch. 2 pp. 185–6

Number 991 (24 December 1898)
About Peggy Saville Ch. 12 pp. 193–6
A Carol of Footprints (poem) (Nora Hopper) p. 201
'Sister Warwick' Ch. 3 p. 207

212 *Catalogue of musical content*

Number 992 (31 December 1898)
About Peggy Saville Ch. 13 pp. 211–12
Girls As I Have Known Them Part 3 The Vulgar Girl* pp. 212–13
'Sister Warwick' Ch. 4 pp. 220–1
Answers to Correspondents pp. 222–3
  Miss Florence E. Smith (practising society), Peterkin, and others for Ethel Rimmer (repertoire), 'A Lover of the G.O.P.' (repertoire)

Number 993 (7 January 1899)
Song (poem) (L.G. Moberly) p. 233
The Ruling Passion Ch. 1 pp. 233–5
  Elderly Professor Crowitzski, who attends the Monday Popular Concerts at Saint James's Hall, befriends Herbert Maxwell, a young aspiring singer.
About Peggy Saville Ch. 14 pp. 235–7
Answers to Correspondents (Study and Studio heading) pp. 239–40
  H.M.I. (composition), Wild Rose (composition), Soldier's Daughter and others for Ethel Rimmer (repertoire)

Number 994 (14 January 1899)
About Peggy Saville Ch. 15 pp. 250–2
The Ruling Passion Ch. 2 pp. 254–5
Answers to Correspondents (Study and Studio heading) pp. 255–6
  E.W.H. (voice)

Number 995 (21 January 1899)
About Peggy Saville Ch. 16 pp. 257–9
Two of the Greatest Afflictions of Girlhood: Blushing and Nervousness (The New Doctor) pp. 259–61
  The unpleasant sensations of blushing and nervousness often appear when one sings or plays before an audience for the first time, but usually vanish once the performer is comfortable in the role.
Answers to Correspondents (Study and Studio heading) pp. 271–2
  Marguerite (repertoire), Clarice (nuisance)

Number 996 (28 January 1899)
About Peggy Saville Ch. 17 pp. 278–9
Girls As I Have Known Them Part 4 The Moody Girl pp. 282–3

Number 997 (4 February 1899)
A Bridal Song (poem) p. 289
About Peggy Saville Ch. 18 pp. 294–5

Number 998 (11 February 1899)
About Peggy Saville Ch. 19 pp. 310–11
Answers to Correspondents (Study and Studio heading) pp. 319–20
  Carrie (clarionet, flute, music history and appreciation)

Number 999 (18 February 1899)
About Peggy Seville Ch. 20 pp. 330–2
Answers to Correspondents (Study and Studio heading) p. 335
  Nemo (composition), Laura (guitar), Piano (piano, instrument maintenance, piano keys)

Catalogue of musical content 213

Number 1000 (25 February 1899)
About Peggy Saville Ch. 21 pp. 337–40
Varieties (The Piano Has Been Sold) p. 341
Portrait Gallery of Contributors to 'The Girl's Own Paper' (illustrations) multi-page fold-out plate facing p. 344
   Includes photographs of composers for *TGOP*.
Girls As I Have Known Them Part 5 The Girl Who Goes in for Art pp. 348–9

Number 1001 (4 March 1899)
His Great Reward (R.S.C.) Ch. 1 p. 359
   Professional vocalist Marielle Heritage agrees to sing at St Jude's church. She and her widowed mother recently moved to York Road on limited means, and Marielle has taken voice pupils to supplement their tiny income. She chooses Gounod's 'There is a green hill far away' as her solo, 'and the singer sang as though her whole soul was wrapped up in the words and music' (p. 379).
About Peggy Saville Ch. 22 p. 365
The Girl's Own Questions and Answers: The Examiners Report on the First Twenty-Four Questions pp. 366–7
Answers to Correspondents pp. 367–8
   Marie (*The Stage*) (general)

Number 1002 (11 March 1899)
A Youthful Pianist (illustration) p. 369
   A young girl is playing a grand piano for half-a-dozen people clustered around it.
About Peggy Saville Ch. 23 pp. 374–5
His Great Reward Ch. 2 p. 379
Answers to Correspondents (Study and Studio heading) pp. 382–4
   Sefton Park (musical stammering), Fiddler (composition)
An Embroidered Pianoforte Back p. 384
   Illustration 'A Pianoforte Back' p. 384

Number 1003 (18 March 1899)
Some New Guitar Music p. 393
   Illustration 'The Guitarist' p. 392
About Peggy Saville Ch. 24 pp. 394–5
His Great Reward Ch. 3 pp. 397–8

Number 1004 (25 March 1899)
About Peggy Saville Ch. 25 pp. 410–12
His Great Reward Ch. 4 pp. 413–14

Number 1005 (1 April 1899)
Varieties (Classical Music) p. 420
About Peggy Saville Ch. 26 pp. 422–3

Number 1006 (8 April 1899)
About Peggy Saville Ch. 27 pp. 433–7
Sheila: A Story for Girls (Evelyn Everett-Green) Ch. 1 pp. 440–2
   Teens Sheila and Oscar Cholmondeley must split up to live with different relatives when their father dies. Sheila joins an uncle's family and becomes companion to Cousin Effie,

214   *Catalogue of musical content*

a sickly 23-year-old. Both Effie and Sheila are musical, but in different ways. When Isingford plans a bazaar with entertainments, Effie's singing is credible but elicits little praise. Sheila is in great demand as an accompanist. Story continues in Ch. 9 as 'Sheila's Cousin Effie: A Story for Girls'.

Answers to Correspondents (Study and Studio heading) p. 448
    Cecilia (practising, memory work), Mrs Walker (practising society), Sympathetic (music history and appreciation)

Number 1007 (15 April 1899)
'The Song the Raindrops Sing' (poem) (Augusta Bryers) p. 457
Sheila Ch. 2 pp. 461–2
Answers to Correspondents (Study and Studio heading) pp. 463–4
    E.M.M. (music education), Queenie Desmond (mandolin, music history and appreciation)

Number 1008 (22 April 1899)
Spring Song (poem) (E.M.W.) p. 472
Sheila Ch. 3* pp. 476–7
The Girl's Own Questions and Answers: The Examiners Report on the Second Twenty-Four Questions pp. 478–80
Answers to Correspondents (Study and Studio heading) p. 480
    In April (violin, memory work), A.V.D.G. (piano, terms), Eglaia (applied music), Earnest Student (music education)

Number 1009 (29 April 1899)
Success and Long Life to the 'G.O.P.' (music score) (M.B.F., Words Helen Marion Burnside) pp. 484–5
Sheila Ch. 4 pp. 486–7
Answers to Correspondents p. 496
    A Lonely Lover (concertina, accordion, choosing instrument)

Number 1010 (6 May 1899)
Sheila Ch. 5 pp. 497–9
Varieties (Words for Music) p. 499
Answers to Correspondents (Study and Studio heading) pp. 511–12
    Kyle and others for Gold Dust (song repertoire), S.W.H. (hymn repertoire), Bessie (song repertoire)

Number 1011 (13 May 1899)
Sheila Ch. 6 pp. 518–19
Varieties (No Time to Play on It) p. 519
Early Summer (illustration) p. 520
    Girl in a field plays a stringed instrument as some curious deer pause to listen.
The Girl's Own Questions and Answers: The Examiners Report on the Third and Last Twenty-Four Questions pp. 525–7
Answers to Correspondents p. 528
    Lucy Hood (music teaching)

Number 1012 (20 May 1899)
Sheila Ch. 7* pp. 530–1
Girls As I Have Known Them Part 6 The Athletic Girl* pp. 534–5

Number 1013 (27 May 1899)
Sheila Ch. 8* pp. 556–8
Answers to Correspondents pp. 559–60
  Mabel (terms), A.H.P. (pronunciation)

Number 1014 (3 June 1899)
Thomas Arne (The English Amphion) (Eleonore D' Esterre-Keeling) pp. 565–7
  Illustration 'Dr. T. Arne' p. 565
Sheila's Cousin Effie: A Story for Girls (Evelyn Everett-Green) Ch. 9 pp. 574–5
  Chapters 1–8 titled 'Sheila: A Story for Girls'.
Answers to Correspondents (Study and Studio heading) pp. 575–6
  Soda (piano), Four Years' Reader (general)
  Editor announces that he cannot return musical manuscripts sent for criticism.

Number 1015 (10 June 1899)
Sheila's Cousin Effie Ch. 10 pp. 577–9
Varieties (The Power of Music) p. 579
A Quiver of Quotations p. 581
  Includes 'Harmony, not melody, is the object of education. If we strive for melody we shall but end in producing discord.' – *Sewell*
On Some Points of Deportment in Singing (Florence Campbell Perugini) p. 583
On a Very Old Piano: Lately Seen in a London Shop Window, and Labelled, 'Cash Price, Two Guineas' (poem) p. 590
Some Holiday Music (Mary Augusta Salmond) p. 591
Answers to Correspondents (Study and Studio heading) pp. 591–2
  Rebecca (music history and appreciation)

Number 1016 (17 June 1899)
Sheila's Cousin Effie Ch. 11 pp. 602–4
Answers to Correspondents (Study and Studio heading) pp. 607–8
  Miss McC. (Germany) (composition), A Devonian (composition), Héré (composition), Tatiana (hymn repertoire), Bright Star (song repertoire), Sailor (song repertoire), Seaton Devon (song repertoire), K. A. (music teaching), St. Elmo (repertoire), L. W. (music history and appreciation)

Number 1017 (24 June 1899)
Sheila's Cousin Effie Ch. 12 pp. 614–15
Answers to Correspondents (Study and Studio heading) pp. 623–4
  Hildegarde Winter (practising, organ, repertoire)

Number 1018 (1 July 1899)
Last Year's Roses (poem) (Helen Marion Burnside) p. 633
Nocturne: For Pianoforte (music score) (Matthew Hale) pp. 634–6
Sheila's Cousin Effie Ch. 13 pp. 637–8

Number 1019 (8 July 1899)
Sheila's Cousin Effie Ch. 14 pp. 641–3
Varieties (Meaning in Music) p. 643
Answers to Correspondents (Study and Studio heading) pp. 655–6
  M. D. Jordan for Winton (repertoire)

216   *Catalogue of musical content*

Number 1020 (15 July 1899)
Sheila's Cousin Effie Ch. 15 pp. 667–8
Answers to Correspondents (Study and Studio heading) pp. 671–2
   An Ignorant Musician (reading music), G. R. and Mary Priscilla Cunningham (practising society), A Lover of Music (music education)

Number 1021 (22 July 1899)
Sheila's Cousin Effie Ch. 16 pp. 681–2

Number 1022 (29 July 1899)
Sheila's Cousin Effie Ch. 17 pp. 700–2
Answers to Correspondents (Study and Studio heading) p. 704
   Nil Desperandum (music teaching), Old Bournemouthian and others for Winton (repertoire), Rosemary (repertoire)

Number 1023 (5 August 1899)
Sheila's Cousin Effie Ch. 18 pp. 717–19
Answers to Correspondents (Study and Studio heading) pp. 719–20
   A Lover of the 'G.O.P.' (music history and appreciation)

Number 1024 (12 August 1899)
Sheila's Cousin Effie Ch. 19 pp. 721–3
'I Need Some Music' (Song, introducing theme of Chopin's Nocturne in G Major) (music score) (Thomas Ely, Words Norman R. Gale) pp. 730–2
Answers to Correspondents (Study and Studio heading) pp. 735–6
   French Canadian (music education), Daisy (piano), Sappho (music teaching), Bessie (repertoire)

Number 1025 (19 August 1899)
Sheila's Cousin Effie Ch. 20 pp. 748–9
Answers to Correspondents (Study and Studio heading) pp. 750–1
   Nydia (composition)

Number 1026 (26 August 1899)
Girls As I Have Known Them Part 7 The Old-Fashioned Girl pp. 757–8
Sheila's Cousin Effie Ch. 21 pp. 764–5
Answers to Correspondents (Study and Studio heading) pp. 767–8
   Royal Academy of Music (RAM) scholarship notice

Number 1027 (2 September 1899)
Girls as I Have Known Them (Elsa D'Esterre-Keeling) Part 8 The Beautiful Girl pp. 773–4
Sheila's Cousin Effie Ch. 22 pp. 774–5
Useful Cantatas and Operettas for Girls (Mary Augusta Salmond) p. 781

Number 1028 (9 September 1899)
Varieties (Musical Performers) p. 786
The Romanticism of Beethoven (Eleonore D'Esterre-Keeling) pp. 792–7
   Illustrations 'The House Where Beethoven Was Born' p. 792; 'Beethoven' p. 793; 'Countess Therese' p. 794; 'Room in Beethoven's House' p. 794; 'Beethoven, 1786–1827' p. 795; 'Relics of Beethoven' p. 796
Sheila's Cousin Effie Ch. 23 pp. 797–8
Answers to Correspondents (Study and Studio heading) p. 800
   Primrose (repertoire), Hopeful (music education)

Number 1029 (16 September 1899)
Sheila's Cousin Effie Ch. 24 pp. 813–14
Answers to Correspondents (Study and Studio heading) pp. 815–16
  Peggy (repertoire), Winton (applied music), An Old Subscriber for Winton (repertoire)

Number 1030 (23 September 1899)
Sheila's Cousin Effie Ch. 25 pp. 825–7
Girls As I Have Known Them Part 9 The Tall Girl and the Small Girl pp. 828–9
Answers to Correspondents (Study and Studio heading) p. 832
  Mrs C. L. Jackson for Ailsa (general), Disappointed (general), A Pilgrim in a Sunny Land (Beyrout, Syria) (general)

Number 1031 (30 September 1899)
Sheila's Cousin Effie Ch. 26 pp. 833–5
The Way to Arcady (poem) (Nora Hopper) p. 837
Answers to Correspondents (Study and Studio heading) pp. 842–3
  Zara (composition)

Winter Sweet
Extra Christmas Part for Volume 20 (1898)
The Old Maids' Christmas (Darly Dale) pp. 1–10
  Mabel, her mother and brothers visit the three 'old maid' aunts at Cornfield Hall for Christmas. Mabel and her brothers take part in a Boxing Day concert that features a violinist, the village choir and popular airs played by a bigotphone band in which all instruments are made from cardboard.
A Christmas Carol (poem) (Nora Hopper) p. 10
'The Frog Who Would A-Wooing Go' (G. D. Lynch) pp. 26–9
  A play for young people. Includes music scores.
Two Christmas Days in a Girl's Life (Eglanton Thorne) pp. 34–6, 38
  Geoffrey Ward is musical and persuades Gladys Wakefield to sing to his violin accompaniment. When in her sweet soprano she sings 'Should one of us remember, / One of us forget', rival Arthur Lawrie thinks she is singing to him.
Adelé (poem) (W. T. Saward) p. 41
'The Gladness of Winter' (music score) (Mary Augusta Salmond, Words Helen Marion Burnside) pp. 46–53

Sundrops
Extra Summer Part for Volume 20 (1899)
'The sweetest songs are those which tell of saddest thoughts' (illustration) p. 11
  A young woman is playing piano while another listens.
Gipsies: Song and Chorus for Girls' Voices (music score) (Ethel Harraden, Words Gertrude Harraden) pp. 27–30
The Forest Princess (Mary E. Hullah) pp. 36–8
  Fellow lodgers Paul Lissa, a poor German musician, and Maud Kincote, a music student from England, meet after an accident requiring Maud to stop playing violin for six months. Paul knows her story well – a student with high ambitions and slender means. But has she any talent?
Varieties (Advice to Pianoforte Students) p. 64

Volume 21 (7 October 1899–29 September 1900)

Number 1032 (7 October 1899)
Life's Trivial Round (Rosa Nouchette Carey) Ch. 1 pp. 1–3
> Miss Ashton, a fine, expressive pianist, would have liked to be a professional musician, but family responsibilities prevented it. Her performance one evening of a loud battle piece with 'pealing chords, like the sound of clarions and silver trumpets, as though a troop were marching to victory' is followed by a solemn, devotional Te Deum laudamus to the God of all battles (p. 68).

The Odd Girl Out (Ruth Lamb) Ch. 1 pp. 9–10
> Contrasts selfish heiress Miss Elce, who possesses a powerful and well-trained singing voice, with selfless Nellie Hope, who has a lovely voice but earns her living teaching piano.

Answers to Correspondents (Study and Studio heading) p. 16
> E. E. Phillips and others for Seaton Devon (repertoire), M. L. Stephen and W. W. for Sailor (repertoire)

Number 1033 (14 October 1899)
More About Peggy (Mrs George de Horne Vaizey) Ch. 1 pp. 17–19
> Peggy Saville is not inherently musical. When singing a ditty about her future husband, her attempt at the correct tune is so disastrous that her mother shakes with laughter. People think the tune is wrong, Peggy exclaimed. 'They don't understand that I'm improving on the original.' (p. 78)

My Heart Is Like a Summer Sea (poem) (Lady Lindsay) p. 24
The Odd Girl Out Ch. 2 pp. 24–6
Life's Trivial Round Ch. 2 pp. 28–9
Answers to Correspondents (Study and Studio heading) p. 31
> Réviellée (piano, applied music)

Number 1034 (21 October 1899)
More About Peggy Ch. 2 pp. 35–6
The Odd Girl Out Ch. 3 p. 37
Varieties (How to Practise Music) p. 39
Life's Trivial Round Ch. 3 pp. 44–6
Answers to Correspondents (Study and Studio) p. 48
> Lover of Hymns (repertoire)

Number 1035 (28 October 1899)
The Odd Girl Out Ch. 4 pp. 49–50
More About Peggy Ch. 3 pp. 52–3
Life's Trivial Round Ch. 4 pp. 54–5

Number 1036 (4 November 1899)
Royal Musicians (Eleonore D'Esterre-Keeling) Part 1 pp. 65–8
Life's Trivial Round Ch. 5* pp. 68–9
More About Peggy Ch. 4* pp. 77–9

Number 1037 (11 November 1899)
Life's Trivial Round Ch. 6 pp. 81–3
Varieties (First-Rate Voices Are Rare) p. 83
More About Peggy Ch. 5 pp. 93–5

Answers to Correspondents (Study and Studio heading) p. 96
   Maidie (repertoire), Laetus (?) Sorte Mea (repertoire), Wandering Minstrel (violin, instrument maintenance)

Number 1038 (18 November 1899)
Life's Trivial Round Ch. 7 pp. 98–9
More About Peggy Ch. 6* pp. 102–3
Varieties (Musical Advice) p. 107
Answers to Correspondents (Study and Studio heading) p. 111
   RAM scholarship notice, Sweet Seventeen (composition)

Number 1039 (25 November 1899)
More About Peggy Ch. 7* pp. 122–3
Life's Trivial Round Ch. 8 pp. 125–6
Some New Light Pianoforte Pieces for Girls (Mary Augusta Salmond) p. 126
Answers to Correspondents (Study and Studio heading) p. 127
   Ronia (choral singing)

Number 1040 (2 December 1899)
More About Peggy Ch. 8 pp. 133–5
How Music Speaks to Those Who Hear (Annie W. Patterson) pp. 137–8
Life's Trivial Round Ch. 9 pp. 141–3

Number 1041 (9 December 1899)
More About Peggy Ch. 9 pp. 145–8
Life's Trivial Round Ch. 10 pp. 158–9

Number 1042 (16 December 1899)
Life's Trivial Round Ch. 11 pp. 161–3
Varieties (An Early Start) p. 165
More About Peggy Ch. 10 pp. 168, 170–1

Number 1043 (23 December 1899)
More About Peggy Ch. 11 pp. 182–4
Life's Trivial Round Ch. 12 pp. 187–8

Number 1044 (30 December 1899)
More About Peggy Ch. 12 pp. 196–8
Life's Trivial Round Ch. 13 pp. 198–9
My Clothes Month by Month (The Lady Dressmaker) pp. 200–2
   Illustration 'Green cashmere gown tucked' shows a young woman with a guitar at a piano p. 201

Number 1045 (6 January 1900)
More About Peggy Ch. 13 pp. 209–11
Royal Musicians Part 2 pp. 212–15
A Lady to Her Musician (poem) (Lady Lindsay) p. 216
Life's Trivial Round Ch. 14 pp. 220–1
Answers to Correspondents (Study and Studio heading) p. 223
   M.D.G. (music education), Dora Bolton (St. Petersburg) (repertoire), Giusto for Wild Rosebud (repertoire), 'An Old Subscriber' for Faithful Heart (repertoire), Mrs Pewtress and others for Nell Gwynne (hymn text), Snowdrop (repertoire), Thomas Webster (general)

Number 1046 (13 January 1900)
Life's Trivial Round Ch. 15 pp. 225–7
More About Peggy Ch. 14 pp. 236–9
Answers to Correspondents (Study and Studio heading) pp. 239–40
    Réveillée (pronunciation), Irish Girl (composition), Inca (piano, voice), Irish Girl (composition), Violet for Nell Gwynne (hymn text)

Number 1047 (20 January 1900)
More About Peggy Ch. 15 pp. 246–7
Life's Trivial Round Ch. 16 pp. 253–5
Some Recent Violin and Violoncello Music (Mary Augusta Salmond) p. 255

Number 1048 (27 January 1900)
Life's Trivial Round Ch. 17 pp. 257–9
Varieties (Twelve Buried Musicians) p. 266
More About Peggy Ch. 16 pp. 268–70

Number 1049 (3 February 1900)
Life's Trivial Round Ch. 18 pp. 276–7
More About Peggy Ch. 17 pp. 284–7
Answers to Correspondents (Study and Studio heading) p. 288
    Zara (composition)

Number 1050 (10 February 1900)
Life's Trivial Round Ch. 19 pp. 293–4
More About Peggy Ch. 18 pp. 301–3

Number 1051 (17 February 1900)
Life's Trivial Round Ch. 20 pp. 310–11
More About Peggy Ch. 19 pp. 316, 318–19
Answers to Correspondents (Study and Studio) pp. 319–20
    V. V. (mandolin, piano)

Number 1052 (24 February 1900)
More About Peggy Ch. 20 pp. 325–7
Life's Trivial Round Ch. 21 pp. 331–3

Number 1053 (3 March 1900)
More About Peggy Ch. 21 pp. 337–40
Life's Trivial Round Ch. 22 pp. 342–3

Number 1054 (10 March 1900)
Life's Trivial Round Ch. 23 pp. 354–5
More About Peggy Ch. 22 pp. 362–3

Number 1055 (17 March 1900)
Life's Trivial Round Ch. 24 pp. 369–71
More About Peggy Ch. 23 pp. 374–6
Impromptu: For Pianoforte (music score) (Albert W. Ketèlbey) pp. 379–81
Answers to Correspondents (Study and Studio heading) pp. 383–4
    E.M.G. (Brisbane) (repertoire)

Number 1056 (24 March 1900)
Varieties (Answer to Twelve Buried Musicians) p. 387
More About Peggy Ch. 24 pp. 394–5
Answers to Correspondents (Study and Studio heading) pp. 399–400
   Guitar (repertoire, guitar)

Number 1057 (31 March 1900)
More About Peggy Ch. 25 pp. 411–13

Number 1058 (7 April 1900)
More About Peggy Ch. 26 pp. 429–31
Answers to Correspondents (Study and Studio heading) p. 432
   H.E.M. (theory, composition)

Number 1059 (14 April 1900)
More About Peggy Ch. 27 pp. 433–5
Answers to Correspondents (Study and Studio heading) pp. 447–8
   Pen-Ray (pronunciation, repertoire)

Number 1060 (21 April 1900)
Some Words in Season (Gordon Stables / Medicus) pp. 459–60
   Advises 'A Real Girl' to rise at a reasonable hour, take a bracing bath, dress sensibly and 'Paint, or play your fiddle or piano. It will amuse you and while away many a weary hour, though only one girl in a thousand can play well.' (p. 460)
Answers to Correspondents (Study and Studio heading) pp. 463–4
   F.E.G., Miss Isabel E. Kent, Miss Walker, Miss F. E. Smith, and Miss Cunningham (practising societies), Barum (composition)
New Songs for Sopranos (Mary Augusta Salmond) p. 464

Number 1061 (28 April 1900)
Royal Musicians Part 3 pp. 468–70

Number 1062 (5 May 1900)
Some New Contralto Songs for Girls (Mary Augusta Salmond) p. 487

Number 1063 (12 May 1900)
On Making the Best of It (A Middle-Aged Woman) pp. 502–3
   Uses a musical young woman to make her point: She thinks her home uncongenial. But the father who grumbles at the noise of practising sacrificed other plans to buy the grand piano for his daughter. The sisters who think her practising is a waste of time made a convenient music stand; and the brothers who laugh when she plays her mother's requests in the evening brag about her musical talent when at school. 'Your gift is not understood or appreciated, but you are loved, and is not that far better?' (p. 502)
The Song of the City (poem) (H.C.A.) p. 505
Answers to Correspondents (Study and Studio heading) p. 512
   Miss E. Gardiner (repertoire)

Number 1064 (19 May 1900)
Away to the Woodland Green: Two-Part Song (music score) (H.A.J. Campbell, Words H.G.F. Taylor) pp. 516–17
Song (poem) (L. G. Moberly) p. 521

222   *Catalogue of musical content*

Illustration 'Song' shows a woman and a girl in a garden where the younger is playing a stringed instrument p. 520

Number 1066 (2 June 1900)
Answers to Correspondents (Study and Studio heading) pp. 559–60
  Ruth (voice, music education), Wood Violet (song repertoire), A. M. (repertoire), Milly (repertoire)

Number 1067 (9 June 1900)
Answers to Correspondents (Study and Studio heading) p. 575
  M.D.G. (piano, applied music)

Number 1069 (23 June 1900)
Royal Musicians Part 4 pp. 593–6
Answers to Correspondents (Study and Studio heading) pp. 607–8
  Miss Bealey (practising society), Restless (music education)

Number 1070 (30 June 1900)
Girls as Students (Lily Watson) pp. 619–20
  Exhorts musical girls, 'in the interest of health, beauty and of Art itself' to avoid pressure of excessive practice that leads to nervous exhaustion (p. 620).

Number 1071 (7 July 1900)
Answers to Correspondents (Study and Studio heading) pp. 639–40
  Nerina (hymn repertoire), Irene (repertoire), E.K.W. (repertoire), Toby (repertoire), Spero Meliora (repertoire), Amabel McDonald for C. Winifred James (repertoire), Jane Stirling for Dora Bolton (repertoire), Winnifred Arathoor (ladies orchestra)

Number 1072 (14 July 1900)
The Master of Sedgewick Hall (C. N. Carvalho) Ch. 1 pp. 651–2
  After dinner at the rectory, the rectors' daughters perform – Maisie's 'very indifferent rendering of Chopin' followed by Laura's performance of 'Robin Adair' in her clear, sweet voice, which faltered at the end, causing her to stop abruptly (p. 663). The song reminds her of Robin Sedgewick, the falsely accused son whom his father banished and whom she still loves.

Number 1073 (21 July 1900)
Because You Love Me (music score) (E. L. Earle, Words E. M. Dunaway) pp. 660–1
The Master of Sedgewick Hall Ch. 2* pp. 662–3
Some New Patriotic Music (Mary Augusta Salmond) p. 667

Number 1074 (28 July 1900)
The Master of Sedgewick Hall Ch. 3 pp. 682–4

Number 1075 (4 August 1900)
Varieties (For Pianoforte Students) p. 691
The Soul's Awakening (poem) (Heper J. Miles) p. 696
Answers to Correspondents (Study and Studio heading) pp. 703–4
  Minnie M. Shaw (repertoire), Apple Blossom (guitar, mandolin, choosing instrument), Lois (violin, health)

Number 1076 (11 August 1900)
Some New Vocal Duets (Mary Augusta Salmond) p. 708
Music Students and Their Work (Florence Sophie Dawson) pp. 710–11

Offers details of scholarships and musical training available at the Royal Academy of Music, Royal College of Music and Guildhall School of Music and closes with a brief list of scholarships and diplomas awarded at Trinity College, Mandeville Place.
Illustration 'Music Students Leaving the Paris Conservatoire After the Day's Work' (from Jean Beraud painting) plate facing p. 710

Number 1077 (18 August 1900)
Some New Pianoforte Music (Mary Augusta Salmond) p. 727
Question and Answer p. 734
    Winifred asks the meaning of the refrain to 'The Bonnie, Bonnie Banks o' Loch Lomond'.
Answers to Correspondents (Study and Studio heading) p. 735
    RAM scholarship notice, Nanette (zither, repertoire)

Number 1078 (25 August 1900)
Answers to Correspondents (Study and Studio heading) p. 752
    A Lover of Mendelssohn (France) (repertoire), Milly (repertoire), Ellen (repertoire)

Number 1080 (8 September 1900)
The Invitation (music score) (Myles B. Foster, Words Charles Peters) pp. 772–5
A Washing-Day Song (poem) (Mary Rowles Jarvis) p. 777

Number 1081 (15 September 1900)
Answers to Correspondents p. 800
    Blighted Peach Blossom (voice, health, practising)

Number 1082 (22 September 1900)
Royal Musicians Part 5 pp. 809–11
    Includes music score 'The Vain Lament' for voice and piano composed by Hortense, Queen of Holland with English translation by Elsa D'Esterre-Keeling.

Number 1083 (29 September 1900)
Answers to Correspondents p. 827
    A Lover of Singing (voice, health)

Glory of the Snow
Extra Christmas Part for Volume 21 (1899)
The Dream of Theodora (Lily Watson) pp. 1–13
    Sister Monica interrupts Theodora Hamilton's dreams of attending Girton to request that she join in the family's entertainment for Christmas Eve. Lettice sings, Theodora plays her accompaniments and Maud plays 'those dreadful school-girl pieces we know by heart' (p. 7).
    Illustration 'Come here child; don't be afraid, I sha'n't eat you' shows Aunt Monica talking to Theodora in front of a piano p. 9
The Ingle-nook: A New Song (music score) (Suchet Champion, Words Augusta Hancock) pp. 17–19
'Brown Bess': A Story in Seven Chapters (Marian Findlay) pp. 20, 22–3, 25–8, 30–1
    To Bessie, with talent for singing but no means to cultivate it as a daughter of a clergyman of limited means, music is a passion and 'would never be a mere pastime or accomplishment' but rather 'an art to be reverenced and worshipped, and into which she threw her whole heart and soul' (p. 22).
Some Pretty New Mandoline Music (Mary Augusta Salmond) p. 37

224   Catalogue of musical content

A Christmas Message pp. 38–9, 41
   Miss Gabriella Tyrrell is alone in the world and poor, so takes a holiday engagement at Startens – light duties and lessons for an eight-year-old boy. The clergyman driving her mentions the Christmas anthem 'Rejoice in the Lord Alway' and asks if she is musical. Her employer's son, a misshapen young man who finds happiness in his music making as an organist, teaches Gabriella lessons about happiness and rejoicing.

Summer Songs
Extra Summer Part for Volume 21 (1900)
The Rajah's Daughter: Eastern Song (music score) (Theo. Marzials) pp. 44–6
John Field: The Pioneer of the Romantic School of Music (Eleonore D'Esterre-Keeling) pp. 54–5, 57

Volume 22 (6 October 1900–28 September 1901)

Number 1084 (6 October 1900)
A Houseful of Girls (Mrs George de Horne Vaizey) Ch. 1* pp. 1–2
  Two of the six Rendell daughters are musical. Maud spends two hours daily practising scales before returning to the piano for at least two more hours of sonatas and fugues. Elsie plays the violin. But the author's reference to 'the wail of a violin' and 'the jingle of the piano' through the open door of the house implies that music making is not a serious topic of the story in which engagements are marital, not musical (p. 2).
  Illustration 'The wails of her violin came floating downstairs' p. 1
The Organist at St. Olaf's (Eglanton Thorne) Ch. 1 pp. 9–11
  When the new rector of St. Olaf's asks organist Daniel Nankivell to step down from his post after almost 30 years to make way for a younger, professionally trained musician, the former organist's daughter, who eventually marries the new organist, helps ease the awkward transition.

Number 1085 (13 October 1900)
Margaret Hetherton Ch. 1* pp. 17–18
  The eponymous heroine likely is the least musical of her family – her father, a violinist, ekes out a living as a parish organist; her brother, also a violinist, composes. To help with family finances, Margaret, whose life revolves around 'her books, her music, her painting, her scribbling', leaves home to serve as a governess in Germany where her piano accompaniments for violinist Oskar König are the prelude to a betrothal (p.188).
The Organist at St. Olaf's Ch. 2 pp. 22–3
A Houseful of Girls Ch. 2 pp. 29–31

Number 1086 (20 October 1900)
A Houseful of Girls Ch. 3 pp. 33–6
Some Singers I Have Met (A Professional Vocalist) pp. 40–3
  Illustrations: photographs of Madame Albani, Miss Clara Butt, Madame Belle Cole, Miss Ada Crossley, Mr. Edward Lloyd, Madame Patti and Mr Kennerley Rumford
The Organist at St. Olaf's Ch. 3 pp. 43–5
Margaret Hetherton Ch. 2 pp. 45–7
Answers to Correspondents p. 47
  May (composition)

Number 1087 (27 October 1900)
A Houseful of Girls Ch. 4 pp. 50–1
Stories in Music (Eleonore D'Esterre-Keeling) Part 1 Three Caprices by Mendelssohn, Op. 16 pp. 52–4
Margaret Hetherton Ch. 3* pp. 61–3

Number 1088 (3 November 1900)
A Houseful of Girls Ch. 5 pp. 65–9
Margaret Hetherton Ch. 4* pp. 77–9
Answers to Correspondents (Study and Studio heading) p. 80
  Sissie and others for Miss E. Gardiner (repertoire)

Number 1089 (10 November 1900)
A Houseful of Girls Ch. 6 pp. 82–5
Three Minstrels (poem) (Clara Thwaites) p. 89

226   *Catalogue of musical content*

Margaret Hetherton Ch. 5* pp. 93–5
Answers to Correspondents p. 96
   Singing (violin, health, performance nerves), Peggy Pickle (music history and appreciation)

Number 1090 (17 November 1900)
Voices of the Night (poem) (William T. Saward) p. 97
A Houseful of Girls Ch. 7 pp. 104–7
Margaret Hetherton Ch. 6 pp. 110–11

Number 1091 (24 November 1900)
Anne Beale, Governess and Writer: Extracts from her Diary Part 4 pp. 118–19
   Popular Welsh novelist, poet and *TGOP* contributor Anne Beale was also a talented singer. An extract from her diary recounts a drawing-room concert in which she sang.
A Houseful of Girls Ch. 8 pp. 122–3
Margaret Hetherton Ch. 7 pp. 126–7

Number 1092 (1 December 1900)
The Cello Player (illustration) plate facing p. 129
   A man plays the cello with his music open on the floor in front of him.
A Houseful of Girls Ch. 9 pp. 129–32
Margaret Hetherton Ch. 8* pp. 134–5
Business *Versus* Art pp. 136–9
   At his fiancé Hope's urging, Paul Moncrieff quits his job clerking at her father's business in order to pursue his talent as a composer of symphonies and sonatas. Yet he does not succeed as a musician. Now married, the couple learns a hard, bitter lesson about 'business *versus* art', namely, that possessing talent does not assure an adequate income.
   Illustration 'The sweet sympathy of his wife' shows Hope comforting her discouraged composer husband p. 137
Answers to Correspondents pp. 143–4
   A Player on the Violin (violin)

Number 1093 (8 December 1900)
The Angel's Gift (Sarah Doudney) pp. 145–9
   Only John Rayne, one of a trio of young men with the 'angel's gift' of song, uses his talent wisely when he becomes a cathedral chorister; the other two seek fame and fortune and eventually lose their voices. John's sister Avice, who accompanies the singers on the organ, reminds them gently 'that a divine gift should be used only for divine ends' (p. 146).
   Illustration 'While Avice played the opening chords, he stood motionless' p. 145
On Christmas Eve: Rondeau (poem) (G. D. Lynch) p. 153
A Houseful of Girls Ch. 10 pp. 153–5
Margaret Hetherton Ch. 9* pp. 155, 157
Answers to Correspondents (Study and Studio heading) p. 160
   M.M.A. (composition)

Number 1094 (15 December 1900)
A Houseful of Girls Ch. 11 pp. 161–4
Stories in Music Part 2 Chopin's Two Nocturnes, Op. pp. 171–2
Margaret Hetherton Ch. 10* pp. 173–5
Answers to Correspondents (Study and Studio heading) pp. 175–6
   Lucie (repertoire), Viola (music education)

Number 1095 (22 December 1900)
A Houseful of Girls Ch. 12 pp. 178–80
More Chit-Chat About Singers (A Professional Vocalist) pp. 181–2
　　Illustrations: photographs of Madame Albani, Mr Andrew Black, the late Signor Foli, Miss Liza Lehmann, Miss Ella Russell, Mr. H. Gregory Hast and Mr. Charles Santley
Varieties (A Famous Composer – *H. H. Stratham*) p. 181
Margaret Hetherton Ch. 11* pp. 187–8
Answers to Correspondents (Study and Studio heading) p. 191
　　A Reader of the 'G.O.P.' and others for Nerina (repertoire), Mother's Pearl for Milly (repertoire), An Old Reader of the 'G.O.P.' (repertoire)

Number 1096 (29 December 1900)
A Houseful of Girls Ch. 13 pp. 194–5
Margaret Hetherton Ch. 12 pp. 202–3

Number 1097 (5 January 1901)
Joy After Sorrow: An Old-World Romance (Patrick Crossmichael) Chs 1, 2 pp. 209–11
　　After the recent death of both parents, Mary St Paul travels from London to Helmsbury Grange to stay with her aunt Frances, who asks for music after dinner. Not a brilliant musician, Mary nonetheless plays airs of bygone days on the piano and accompanies her aunt, once a refined singer, in Dowland's 'Now, oh now I needs must part'.
Girls of Fifty Years Ago and Now (Emma Brewer) pp. 212–13
　　Fifty years ago, 'the three R's, as they are called, a little French, and sufficient music to play the "Battle of Prague" ' comprised a girl's education (p. 212).
Margaret Hetherton Ch. 13 pp. 214–16
Great Tom of Oxford: A Song of the Bell (poem) (Sarah Doudney) p. 216
A Houseful of Girls Ch. 14 pp. 218–21
Varieties (Musical Neighbours) p. 222
Answers to Correspondents (Study and Studio heading) pp. 222–3
　　Jennie A.R.A. (repertoire), E. R. Red Anemone and others to Nerina (repertoire), E. R. Red Anemone and others to E.K.W. (repertoire)

Number 1098 (12 January 1901)
Joy After Sorrow Ch. 3* pp. 225–6
A Houseful of Girls Ch. 15 pp. 229–31
Margaret Hetherton Ch. 14* pp. 238–9
Answers to Correspondents (Study and Studio heading) pp. 239–40
　　Augharudderhah (reading music)

Number 1099 (19 January 1901)
Joy After Sorrow Ch. 4 pp. 241–3
A Houseful of Girls Ch. 16 pp. 244–7
Margaret Hetherton Ch. 15 pp. 252–4

Number 1100 (26 January 1901)
Joy After Sorrow Ch. 5 pp. 257–8
Margaret Hetherton Ch. 16* p. 261
A Houseful of Girls Ch. 17 pp. 266–8

Number 1101 (2 February 1901)
A Houseful of Girls Ch. 18 pp. 273–6
Music in the Royal Family (Frederick J. Crowest) pp. 276–9

228 Catalogue of musical content

Illustration 'The Prince Consort playing to Mendelssohn' p. 277
Margaret Hetherton Ch. 17 pp. 286–8

Number 1102 (9 February 1901)
Varieties (A Musical Critic) p. 294
A Houseful of Girls Ch. 19 pp. 297–9
Margaret Hetherton Ch. 18 pp. 302–4
Answers to Correspondents (Study and Studio heading) p. 304
    Evy (violin), Jeanie Hallam (general), Natalie Gorainoff (composition), Twenty (piano, voice), Alice A. Milner (composition), Miss Isabel E. Kent (practising society), Aileen and others for Nerina (repertoire)

Number 1103 (16 February 1901)
Margaret Hetherton Ch. 19 pp. 314–15
Stories in Music Part 3 Schumann's Novelettes Prelude, I, II, III pp. 316–18
A Houseful of Girls Ch. 20 pp. 318–20

Number 1104 (23 February 1901)
A Houseful of Girls Ch. 21 pp. 321–4
Margaret Hetherton Ch. 20* p. 327
Answers to Correspondents (Study and Studio heading) p. 336
    M. Priscilla Cunningham for A Lover of Music (repertoire), F.D.W. for Irene (repertoire), Emily Frank and others for Heartsease (repertoire)

Number 1105 (2 March 1901)
Margaret Hetherton Ch. 21* pp. 347–8
A Houseful of Girls Ch. 22 pp. 351–2

Number 1106 (9 March 1901)
Golden Strings (illustration) (from J. M. Strudwick painting) plate facing p. 353
Margaret Hetherton Ch. 22 pp. 354–6
A Lavender Song (poem) (Nora Hopper) p. 361
A Houseful of Girls Ch. 23 pp. 365–7
Answers to Correspondents (Study and Studio heading) p. 368
    RAM scholarship notice, A Quaver (organ, music education)

Number 1107 (16 March 1901)
A Houseful of Girls Ch. 24 pp. 369–72
Margaret Hetherton Ch. 23 pp. 378–9

Number 1108 (23 March 1901)
A Houseful of Girls Ch. 25 pp. 386–7
Varieties (Two Musical Epitaphs) p. 395
Margaret Hetherton Ch. 24 pp. 398–400

Number 1109 (30 March 1901)
A Houseful of Girls Ch. 26 pp. 402–5
Margaret Hetherton Ch. 25 p. 415
Answers to Correspondents (Study and Studio heading) p. 416
    Gerda (composition)

Number 1110 (6 April 1901)
A Houseful of Girls Ch. 27 pp. 417–20
The Failures of the Business Girl (Flora Klickmann) Part 2 In Music and Art pp. 427–8

Warns readers about overestimating their talent and underestimating the difficulties of the works they hear 'performed by those musicians who have "already arrived"' (p. 427).
Margaret Hetherton Ch. 26 pp. 428–9
Stories in Music Part 4 Schumann's Novelettes IV, V pp. 430–1

Number 1111 (13 April 1901)
A Scots Thistle (Leslie Keith) Ch. 1 pp. 433–6
>   After Beth Bethune's mother dies, her father marries a woman with two daughters, Jane and Clare. Clare is musical, and Mr Bethune bought her 'a very fine Bechstein' on which she rewards him with Chopin and Grieg. She offers to play 'a little sweet music' for Beth after a recent argument, but Beth scarcely listens to the brilliant playing or to her stepmother's murmuring. 'Mrs. Bethune could never be made to understand that music was not invented to encourage talk.' (p. 540)
>   Illustration 'Writing the reply' shows Beth Bethune sitting at a table with a piano in the background p. 433

Margaret Hetherton Ch. 27 p. 438
How Our Brothers May Earn Their Schooling (Flora Klickmann) pp. 440–2
>   It is easier for a boy to earn school fees than for a girl, for a boy with a fair voice can receive a general education and learn music as a chorister in one of England's cathedrals and royal and collegiate chapels.
>   Illustrations 'Choristers at the Funeral of Mandell, Bishop of London' p. 440; 'The Senior Chorister, Westminster Abbey' p. 441

Number 1112 (20 April 1901)
Margaret Hetherton Ch. 28 pp. 449–52
An Easter Song (poem) (Helen Marion Burnside) p. 455
A Scots Thistle Ch. 2 pp. 456, 458–9

Number 1113 (27 April 1901)
The Mother and the Wonder-Child: An Australian Story (Ethel Turner) Ch. 1 pp. 465–8
>   Australia discovers a 'wonder-child' in eight-year-old piano prodigy Challis Cameron. With the financial backing of supporters, Challis travels with her mother to Europe to build her music career while the rest of the cash-strapped family stays home. When she returns at age 15, Challis becomes the breadwinner for the family, and her concerts enable the family to return to England, where fortune at last comes their way.

A Scots Thistle (Leslie Keith) Ch. 3 pp. 474–6

Number 1114 (4 May 1901)
The Mother and the Wonder-Child Ch. 2 pp. 482–4
A Scots Thistle Ch. 4 pp. 494–5

Number 1115 (11 May 1901)
The Mother and the Wonder-Child Ch. 3 pp. 498–500
A Scots Thistle Ch. 5 pp. 508–10
Answers to Correspondents (Study and Studio heading) p. 510
>   Eva (piano, music teaching)

Number 1116 (18 May 1901)
The Mother and the Wonder-Child Ch. 4 pp. 521–3
A Scots Thistle Ch. 6 pp. 524–5

230   *Catalogue of musical content*

Number 1117 (25 May 1901)
The Mother and the Wonder-Child Ch. 5 pp. 529–31
Varieties (A Tenor Solo) p. 537
A Scots Thistle Ch. 7* pp. 538–40

Number 1118 (1 June 1901)
The Mother and the Wonder-Child Ch. 6 pp. 553–5
A Scots Thistle Ch. 8 pp. 556–8
Answers to Correspondents (Study and Studio heading) pp. 559–60
   Mrs Elinor Davis for E.K.W. (repertoire), E.M.L. (national anthem)

Number 1119 (8 June 1901)
The Mother and the Wonder-Child Ch. 7 pp. 562–3
A Scots Thistle Ch. 9 pp. 570–2
Answers to Correspondents (Study and Studio heading) pp. 575–6
   A Student of Music (violin)

Number 1120 (15 June 1901)
A Scots Thistle Ch. 10 pp. 578–80
The Mother and the Wonder-Child Ch. 8 pp. 584, 586–8
Answers to Correspondents (Study and Studio heading) p. 592
   Au Désespoir (terms), Lady Constance Coote and others for Miss Mabel Collier James (repertoire)

Number 1121 (22 June 1901)
The Mother and the Wonder-Child Ch. 9 pp. 600–3
A Scots Thistle Ch. 11 pp. 605–7

Number 1122 (29 June 1901)
Stories in Music Part 5 Schumann's Novelettes VI, VII, VIII pp. 613–14
The Mother and the Wonder-Child Ch. 10 pp. 618–20
A Scots Thistle Ch. 12 pp. 621–3
Answers to Correspondents (Study and Studio heading) p. 624
   Tatiana (repertoire), X. Y. (applied music), H.H.W. (repertoire)

Number 1123 (6 July 1901)
The Mother and the Wonder-Child Ch. 11 pp. 626–7
Deb's Enterprise; or, The Will and the Way (Mary Rowles Jarvis) Ch.1* p. 633
   Deborah Dean's sister Phoebe obtains a post as junior music mistress at Hedley Hall school and spends her time listening to long successions of scales and five-finger exercises.
Harmony (poem) (Isabella Fyvie Mayo) p. 636
A Scots Thistle Ch. 13 pp. 638–40

Number 1124 (13 July 1901)
Deb's Enterprise Ch. 2 pp. 641–2
A Scots Thistle Ch. 14 pp. 645–7
The Mother and the Wonder-Child Ch. 12 pp. 648–50

Number 1125 (20 July 1901)
Further Gossip About Musicians (A Professional Singer) pp. 657–9
   Illustrations: photographs of Anna Williams, Marian Mackenzie, Alice Esty, Mrs Helen Trust, Coleridge Taylor, Lloyd Chandos, Edward Elgar, Plunket Greene and F. Dawson p. 657

The Mother and the Wonder-Child Ch. 13 pp. 660–2
Deb's Enterprise Ch. 3* pp. 665–7
A Scots Thistle Ch. 15 pp. 669–71
Answers to Correspondents (Study and Studio heading) p. 672
   RAM scholarship notice, Clorinda (voice), B.M.C.W. (general)

Number 1126 (27 July 1901)
Deb's Enterprise Ch. 4* pp. 673–5
The Mother and the Wonder-Child Ch. 14 pp. 677–9
A Scots Thistle Ch. 16 pp. 682–4

Number 1127 (3 August 1901)
The Mother and the Wonder-Child Ch. 15 pp. 689–91
A Scots Thistle Ch. 17 pp. 701–3
Answers to Correspondents (Study and Studio heading) p. 704
   H. G. Moysey (repertoire), M.F.S. (piano, instrument purchase)

Number 1128 (10 August 1901)
The Mother and the Wonder-Child Ch. 16 pp. 706–9
A Scots Thistle Ch. 18 pp. 717–19
Answers to Correspondents (Study and Studio heading) p. 720
   Captive Nilepta (guitar, repertoire), Muddled (theory), Dewdrop (repertoire)

Number 1129 (17 August 1901)
The Mother and the Wonder-Child Ch. 17 pp. 722–4
Solos and Song Accompaniments for Violoncello and Violin (Mary Augusta Salmond) p. 727
A Scots Thistle Ch. 19 pp. 733–5
Answers to Correspondents (Study and Studio heading) pp. 735–6
   E.A.S. (music teaching), Sweet Violet (general)

Number 1130 (24 August 1901)
The Mother and the Wonder-Child Ch. 18 pp. 741–2
The Harpsichord Revival (Frederick J. Crowest) pp. 744–6
   Illustrations 'Harpsichord', 'The Table Virginal' and 'Another Style of Table Virginal' p. 744; 'Clavichord or Clarichord', 'Spinet or Couched Harp', 'The Table Spinet' and 'Double Spinet for Two Performers' p. 745
Varieties (Music at Home) p. 747
A Scots Thistle Ch. 20 pp. 750–1

Number 1131 (31 August 1901)
The Mother and the Wonder-Child Ch. 19 pp. 754–6
Varieties (Impossible Music) p. 762
A Scots Thistle Ch. 21 pp. 765–7
Answers to Correspondents (Study and Studio heading) p. 768
   Music (applied music), A Brisbane Girl (music education), Post Boy (repertoire)

Number 1132 (7 September 1901)
The Mother and the Wonder-Child Ch. 20 pp. 773–5
Mary Robertson; or, The Power of Good Over Evil (E. Maude Marshallsay) Ch. 1* pp. 777–8
   The eponymous heroine speaks of nature as a great musical composition with man as the dissonance and all else consonant, in harmony.

A Scots Thistle Ch. 22 pp. 781–3
Answers to Correspondents (Study and Studio heading) p. 784
   L.B.X. (Denmark) (music history and appreciation)

Number 1133 (14 September 1901)
The Mother and the Wonder-Child Ch. 21 pp. 787–9
The Apple of My Eye (poem) (G.K.M.) p. 793
Mary Robertson Ch. 2* pp. 793–4
A Scots Thistle Ch. 23 pp. 794–6
Answers to Correspondents (Study and Studio heading) pp. 798–9
   Iris (terms), Eric (repertoire)

Number 1134 (21 September 1901)
The Mother and the Wonder-Child Ch. 22 pp. 801–3
Mary Robertson Ch. 3 pp. 806–7
About Harvest Music pp. 810–11
A Scot's Thistle Ch. 24 pp. 814–15
Answers to Correspondents p. 816
   Madeline (violin)

Number 1135 (28 September 1901)
Mary Robertson Chs 4, 5, 6 pp. 818–20

Extra Christmas Part
For Volume 22 (1900)
Emily Wardour's Opportunities (Harriet Hughes) pp. 1–27
   Emily Wardour, mathematical mistress at a London girls' high school, has a cottage piano in her rented rooms. When the maid-of-all-work compliments her singing, Emily sees an opportunity to help the young woman by inviting her to her room to sing hymns on Sundays and by teaching her to read music.
   Illustration 'That was a beautiful song, Miss' shows Emily at the piano p. 4
The Silver Side of the Shield pp. 35, 37–8
   When, to support her fragile mother and herself, Orsola Devereux decides to put her musical training to the test on the professional stage, friend Frank is dismayed: '*You*, earning your bread by standing on a public platform and letting anyone who likes to pay for it stare at you? . . . Think of the temptations, the difficulties, the publicity . . .' Orsola understands, however, that work need not change her character (p. 35).
The Story of a Christmas Carol (Helen Marion Burnside) pp. 41–4, 46–8, 50
   At age 17, Marion Neville falls in love with the French drawing-master at her British school, marries him and moves to France, all against her parent's objections. They disown her, and when she returns to England years later penniless and starving, her twins Neville and Maude sing on the town's High Street for money. Two days before Christmas, a passerby recognizes the carol as one she wrote and her long-lost sister set to music; she takes her niece and nephew home, and the sisters are reunited. Marion learns that her parents forgave her before they died and restored her fortune.
A Christmas Carol (illustration) p. 45
   A young woman violinist.
Girlhood's Benedicite: A Carol for Girls (poem) (C. P.) p. 50
Christmastide Music (Frederick J. Crowest) pp. 63–4

The Extra Summer Part
For Volume 22 (1901)
The Teacher's Holiday pp. 18–19
    Laura Sanderson dislikes music mistress Miss Harcourt because she had struck Laura for hitting a wrong note. Other students side with Laura, but Dollie takes the teacher's side, for she once deserved that temper for poor piano playing, and Miss Harcourt then hugged her and apologized.

Sir John Stainer: A Recollection (Lily Watson) pp. 20, 22

Our Café Chantant (M.F.T.) pp. 25–8
    To help Silas Burns, whose cottage burned down, sisters Sybil and Laura set up a variety entertainment. Rose Amberly will sing and play banjo, Anne Babicombe will play violin, refreshments will be served and the evening will end with 'God Save the Queen'.

Something About Wedding Music (Frederick J. Crowest) pp. 29–31
    Illustration 'The Wedding March' shows a woman and girl playing a piano duet p. 31

Her Old Dears (L. G. Moberly) 32–5
    Joyce Lacy first meets the 'old dears' Jane and Maryanne Brinton at a Richter concert when she is a music student. When Joyce becomes 'the greatest singer of her day', the sisters are unaware of her fame, which she keeps secret until she invites them to a performance of *Lohengrin* – their first opera and Joyce's debut (p. 34).

Common Errors of Speech (Elsa D'Esterre-Keeling) pp. 50–3
    Includes correct pronunciation of a dozen composers' names.

The Timbrel-Player (illustration) p. 57
    A young woman is playing the timbrel.

The Evening Song (illustration) p. 61
    A young woman stands in field holding a violin and a music score.

Volume 23 (5 October 1901–28 September 1902)

Number 1136 (5 October 1901)
Silent Strings (Sarah Doudney) Ch. 1 pp. 1–3
> When their father dies, the four Wilmer siblings have to split up the family. Brother Drew's solution to raise their spirits is to sing a tune with a rousing chorus, which he accompanies on his banjo. After this last song, however, Drew leaves the banjo behind. The instrument's silent strings are a metaphor for the silent strings in many lives that are, as sister Kate muses, 'full of music that has never been called out of them' (pp. 30–1).
> Illustration 'The four young voices sang it lustily' p. 1

Pixie O'Shaughnessy (Mrs George de Horne Vaizey) Ch. 1 pp. 12–15
> Twelve-year-old Patricia Monica de Vere (Pixie) leaves Ireland to attend school in London. When she returns home to visit her ailing father, her sweetly sung hymn 'Come unto Me, ye weary, And I will give you rest!' brings tears to his eyes.

Number 1137 (12 October 1901)
Pixie O'Shaughnessy Ch. 2 pp. 17–20
Mademoiselle Janotha and Her Cat: An Interview with 'White Heather' (Mary de G.) pp. 20–1
The Fidelio Club (Eleonore D'Esterre-Keeling) pp. 28–9
> A new column for musical readers.

Silent Strings Ch. 2* pp. 30–1
Answers to Correspondents (Study and Studio heading) p. 32
> Cleopatra (mandolin, violin, choosing instrument)

Number 1138 (19 October 1901)
Pixie O'Shaughnessy Ch. 3 pp. 33–6
Miss Kathleen Purcell: Solo Harpist (K. M. Cordeux / 'Daniel Dormer') pp. 37–8
> Illustration 'Miss Kathleen Purcell' p. 37

Silent Strings Ch. 3 pp. 44–6

Number 1139 (26 October 1901)
Pixie O'Shaughnessy Ch. 4 pp. 49–52
The Birthday Page: November (Frederick J. Crowest) pp. 60–1
> Monthly column with portraits and descriptions of notable women, past and present, some of whom are musicians. Includes Madame Albani 'A Queen of Song' p. 61
> Illustration: photograph of 'Madame Albani' p. 60

Silent Strings Ch. 4 pp. 62–4

Number 1140 (2 November 1901)
Pixie O'Shaughnessy Ch. 5 pp. 65–7
Silent Strings Ch. 5 pp. 77–9
Answers to Correspondents (Study and Studio heading) p. 80
> Andante (composition), Miss Emily Hartland (practising society), Miss Louise H. E. Gall and others for Dolly Varden (repertoire), Gertrude H. Parker and others for Auf Wiedersehen (repertoire), Auntie and others for Dolly Varden (repertoire), Auntie and others for B. Pearl (repertoire)

Number 1141 (9 November 1901)
Silent Strings Ch. 6 pp. 81–4
Pixie O'Shaughnessy Ch. 6 pp. 86–9

Catalogue of musical content 235

Answers to Correspondents (Study and Studio heading) pp. 95–6
   Miss Mabel Entwistle (circulating music)

Number 1142 (16 November 1901)
Pixie O'Shaughnessy Ch. 7 pp. 97–100
Silent Strings Ch. 7 pp. 102–4
Answers to Correspondents (Study and Studio heading) p. 111
   RAM scholarship notice, Fidelio (pronunciation)

Number 1143 (23 November 1901)
Silent Strings Ch. 8 pp. 113–16
New Songs for Girls (Mary Augusta Salmond) p. 120
Varieties (The National Anthem) p. 123
Pixie O'Shaughnessy Ch. 8 pp. 124–7
Answers to Correspondents p. 128
   Auricula (piano)

Number 1144 (30 November 1901)
The Fidelio Club (Eleanore D'Esterre-Keeling) pp. 132–5
Pixie O'Shaughnessy Ch. 9 pp. 140–3

Number 1145 (7 December 1901)
Pixie O'Shaughnessy Ch. 10 pp. 145–8
Silent Strings Ch. 9 pp. 157–9

Number 1146 (14 December 1901)
Silent Strings Ch. 10 pp. 162–3
A Kitchen Song (poem) (Mary Rowles Jarvis) p. 165
Varieties (Where the Brass Band Was) p. 167
Pixie O'Shaughnessy Ch. 11 pp. 173–5

Number 1147 (21 December 1901)
Pixie O'Shaughnessy Ch. 12 pp. 177–80
A Decorated Box-Seat or Music Coffer (Fred Miller) pp. 180–1
Varieties (Rival Musicians) p. 181
Some New Music (Mary Augusta Salmond) p. 183
Silent Strings Ch. 11 pp. 187–9

Number 1148 (28 December 1901)
Pixie O'Shaughnessy Ch. 13 pp. 193–4
A Specimen Page of Miss Kate Greenaway's Work (illustration) (from the 'Pied Piper of
   Hamelin') plate facing p. 196
The Fidelio Club (Eleanore D'Esterre-Keeling) pp. 198–9, 207
Answers to Correspondents p. 208
   Column includes Fidelio Club heading with music replies.

Number 1149 (4 January 1902)
Pixie O'Shaughnessy Ch. 14 pp. 209–11
Silent Strings Ch. 12 pp. 220–2

Number 1150 (11 January 1902)
Pixie O'Shaughnessy Ch. 15 pp. 225–9
Silent Strings Ch. 13 pp. 237–9
Answers to Correspondents (Study and Studio heading) pp. 239–40
   Marion H. (repertoire)

236 *Catalogue of musical content*

Number 1151 (18 January 1902)
Pixie O'Shaughnessy Ch. 16 pp. 242–3
Silent Strings Ch. 14 pp. 252–3

Number 1152 (25 January 1902)
Pixie O'Shaughnessy Ch. 17 pp. 257–9
The Fidelio Club (Eleonore D'Esterre-Keeling) pp. 261–3
The Birthday Page: February (Frederick J. Crowest) pp. 267–9
    Includes Madame Clara Butt, 'Renowned English Contralto' p. 267; Adelina Patti 'The Singer of the Century' p. 268
    Illustrations: photographs of 'Madame Clara Butt', 'Adelina Patti' p. 268
Silent Strings Ch. 15 pp. 270–1

Number 1153 (1 February 1902)
Silent Strings Ch. 16 pp. 273–5
Coronation Hymn (The Rev. W. T. Saward) p. 280
Pixie O'Shaughnessy Ch. 18 pp. 284–7

Number 1154 (8 February 1902)
Pixie O'Shaughnessy Ch. 19 pp. 289–92
Silent Strings Ch. 17 p. 295

Number 1155 (15 February 1902)
Pixie O'Shaughnessy Ch. 20 pp. 305–8
The Anchoress of Ste. Maxime (M.H. Cornwall Legh) Ch. 1 pp. 312, 314–15
    Alison Woodward asks artist Hugo Archibald for advice: What would he make out of her narrow life? 'I love music, but what's the good of that, with only the cracked old piano in the *salon* to practise on?' she asks (p. 445). Besides, she prefers singing. He suggests that she get to know the peasants and fisher-folk of the French village where she resides and teach their children to sing.

Number 1156 (22 February 1902)
Pixie O'Shaughnessy Ch. 21 pp. 321–4
The Anchoress of Ste. Maxime Ch. 2 pp. 333–5

Number 1157 (1 March 1902)
Pixie O'Shaughnessy Ch. 22 pp. 337–40
The Anchoress of Ste. Maxime Ch. 3 pp. 347–9
Age Forty Ch. 1 p. 351
    Out of financial necessity, at age 40 Margaret Ashton becomes companion to Mrs Wynford's two daughters. A talented musician, Margaret fills in for the ailing professional accompanist engaged for an informal 'At Home' and saves the day for her employer.

Number 1158 (8 March 1902)
Pixie O'Shaughnessy Ch. 23 pp. 353–7
Age Forty Ch. 2 pp. 365–6
The Anchoress of Ste. Maxime Ch. 4 pp. 366–7

Number 1159 (15 March 1902)
Pixie O'Shaughnessy Ch. 24 pp. 369–72
Age Forty Ch. 3* pp. 379–80
The Anchoress of Ste. Maxime Ch. 5 pp. 381–2

Answers to Correspondents p. 383
   Eppy and others for New Reader (repertoire)

Number 1160 (22 March 1902)
Pixie O'Shaughnessy Ch. 25 pp. 385–7
Age Forty Ch. 4 pp. 390–1
The Anchoress of Ste. Maxime Ch. 6 pp. 397–9

Number 1161 (29 March 1902)
Pixie O'Shaughnessy Ch. 26 pp. 401–3
Age Forty Ch. 5 pp. 404–6
The Birthday Page: April (Frederick J. Crowest) pp. 411–13
   Includes Blanche Marchesi, 'Celebrated Concert Singer' p. 411
   Illustration: photograph of 'Blanche Marchesi' p. 411
The Fidelio Club (Eleonore D'Esterre-Keeling) pp. 413–15

Number 1162 (5 April 1902)
Pixie O'Shaughnessy Ch. 27 pp. 421–3
The Anchoress of Ste. Maxime Ch. 7 pp. 429–31

Number 1163 (12 April 1902)
Pixie O'Shaughnessy Ch. 28 pp. 433–6
Some Violin Music p. 442
The Anchoress of Ste. Maxime Ch. 8* pp. 444–6

Number 1164 (19 April 1902)
Pixie O'Shaughnessy Ch. 29 pp. 453–5
The Anchoress of Ste. Maxime Ch. 9 pp. 460–2

Number 1165 (26 April 1902)
Pixie O'Shaughnessy Ch. 30 pp. 465–7
The Fidelio Club (Eleonore D'Esterre-Keeling) pp. 474–6
Answers to Correspondents (Study and Studio heading) p. 480
   Ivy for Miss Mabel Collier James (repertoire), Cabo di Bona Esperanza (repertoire)

Number 1166 (3 May 1902)
'Two Little Tiny Wings' (music score) (E. Markham Lee, Words S. T. Coleridge) pp. 486–7
The Anchoress of Ste. Maxime Chs 10, 11 pp. 493–5

Number 1167 (10 May 1902)
The Anchoress of Ste. Maxime Ch. 12 p. 511

Number 1168 (17 May 1902)
The Anchoress of Ste. Maxime Ch. 13 pp. 525–6
Answers to Correspondents (Study and Studio heading) p. 527
   Tabbie for Tibbie (repertoire)

Number 1169 (24 May 1902)
Answers to Correspondents p. 544
   Z.Y.X. (piano, musician work)

Number 1170 (31 May 1902)
The Fidelio Club (Eleonore D'Esterre-Keeling) pp. 554–6, 559–60

Number 1171 (7 June 1902)
Varieties (A Motto for a Fiddler) p. 571

Number 1172 (14 June 1902)
Answers to Correspondents (Study and Studio heading) p. 592
  Acknowledgement of *Clavier* copy, E. J. Wales (Australia) and Sedgemoor for New Reader (repertoire), Iona for Isabella Fountain (repertoire), Miss J. Facey for Miss Edith King (repertoire)

Number 1173 (21 June 1902)
Answers to Correspondents (Study and Studio heading) pp. 607–8
  Clematis (composition)

Number 1174 (28 June 1902)
The Fidelio Club (Eleonore D'Esterre-Keeling) pp. 619–20
The Birthday Page: July (Frederick J. Crowest) pp. 621–3
  Includes Miss Agnes Zimmerman 'Absolute Artist' p. 621; Madame Titiens 'A Noble Woman' p. 622
  Illustrations: photographs of 'Miss Agnes Zimmerman', 'Madame Titiens' p. 621

Number 1175 (5 July 1902)
Varieties ('In *The Story of Music*') p. 631

Number 1176 (12 July 1902)
Abendlied (poem) (Florence G. Attenborough / 'Crystabel') p. 649

Number 1178 (26 July 1902)
The Birthday Page: August (Frederick J. Crowest) pp. 685–6
  Includes Lady Thompson (Kate Loder) 'Past Day Pianist' p. 686
  Illustration: photograph of 'Lady Thompson' p. 685

Number 1179 (2 August 1902)
The Wren's Song (poem) (Nora Chesson) p. 696
Answers to Correspondents (Study and Studio heading) p. 704
  Walton (composition), Spring Flowers (composition), A.J.H. (composition, violin)

Number 1180 (9 August 1902)
Varieties (Have a Place Near the Music) p. 715
Answers to Correspondents (Study and Studio heading) p. 719
  Minerva Alicia (voice)

Number 1182 (23 August 1902)
A Song of the Sea-side (poem) (G. D. Lynch) p. 744

Number 1183 (30 August 1902)
The Birthday Page: September (Frederick J. Crowest) pp. 763–5
  Includes Madame Schumann 'She Struck the Keys' p. 764; Felicia Dorothea Hemans 'Sweet Lyric Singer' p. 765
  Illustrations: photographs of 'Madame Schumann', 'Mrs Hemans' p. 764

Number 1186 (20 September 1902)
An Enthusiastic Fidelian (illustration) p 808
  Young woman seated at the piano.

The Birthday Page: October (Frederick J. Crowest) pp. 812–13
  Includes Jenny Lind 'The Swedish Nightingale' p. 812
  Illustration 'Jenny Lind' p. 812
Answers to Correspondents (Study and Studio heading) p. 816
  Thekla (repertoire), Miss F. White (repertoire)

Extra Christmas Part
For Volume 23 (1901)
Melodies of a Bygone Day (illustration) p. 13
  A woman with sheet music in her hand listens to a male violinist.
An Eastern Beauty (illustration) p. 16
  Woman playing a type of lyre.
Varieties (For All Who Have to Do with Church Music) pp. 63–4

Volume 24 (4 October 1902–26 September 1903)

Number 1188 (4 October 1902)
More About Pixie (Mrs George de Horne Vaizey) Ch. 1 pp. 1–5
    While convalescing from typhoid fever and foot surgery, Sylvia Trevor, a talented musician, hobbles to the piano and sings Christmas hymns in a weak little voice that 'wavered suspiciously toward the close', because she misses her father (p. 130). After her father's death, Sylvia muses what she could do 'that a thousand other girls could not accomplish equally well?' She could play a little, sing a little, paint a little and trim a hat, but she could not boil a potato. 'She possessed, in fact, a smattering of many things, but had not really mastered one.' (p. 379) Sylvia is the author's mouthpiece for a lesson in making it in the world: Girls should learn to do one thing well and measure their progress not by amateur standards but rather by professional ones.
The Erl-King: A Schubert Fantasy (Arthur Foxton Ferguson from German of Ottfried) pp. 10–11

Number 1189 (11 October 1902)
'Sonny'; or, The Jilting of Bruce Heriot (Evelyn Everett-Green) Ch. 1 pp. 17–20
    Both Sonny – Roderick Duncan – and his cousin Florence Rivers are musical. Sonny becomes a chorister who leads the choir and sings 'as clear and true as a bird' (p. 334).
The Robin (poem) (Norman Gale) p. 24
    Illustration 'Could I but sing as thou!' p. 25
More About Pixie Ch. 2 pp. 28–32
Answers to Correspondents (Study and Studio heading) p. 32
    Stretto (composition)

Number 1190 (18 October 1902)
More About Pixie Ch. 3 pp. 33–6
A Very Old Song (poem) (Sarah Doudney) p. 37
'Sonny' Ch. 2 pp. 42–4
Answers to Correspondents (Study and Studio heading) pp. 46–7
    E.M.H. (composition), Trudie (repertoire)

Number 1191 (25 October 1902)
More About Pixie Ch. 4 pp. 49–51
A Writer for the Press: A True Story of Modern London Life (Flora Klickmann) Ch. 1 pp. 52–4
    Aspiring novelist Jenny Ingram moves to the city to pursue her career. Miss Priscilla King, a British Library patron, draws on music to deliver some hard facts about young women's literary aspirations: 'No girl with any sense would expect to make a living at dressmaking, for instance, without some preliminary lessons and without at least a sewing machine. Neither would one think to succeed as a pianist without previous study and the possession of an instrument. Yet the large majority of failures in literature are people who started out to conquer the world with no other stock-in-trade than some paper, pens and ink. And then they cannot understand that they never get any further!' (p. 690) A letter from Jenny's older sister Madge reports a musical failure on the home front, when their sister Essie developed 'the most abnormal bump for music you ever heard of' and tortures her family with excessive practice of a song 'that she can't leave well enough alone' (p. 731).
'Sonny' Ch. 3 pp. 59–61

Music Competition p. 63
> Noting a 'conspicuous dearth of suitable "Graces Before and After Meat" for use in schools', the editor offers prizes of three guineas, two guineas and one guinea for the three best settings of the words 'Thou, by Whose power this food was raised, / For evermore Thy name be praised. Amen'.

Number 1192 (1 November 1902)
A Writer for the Press Ch. 2 pp. 65–8
More About Pixie Ch. 5 pp. 73–4
'Sonny' Ch. 4 pp. 77–9
Answers to Correspondents (Study and Studio heading) p. 80
> Music (repertoire)

Number 1193 (8 November 1902)
More About Pixie Ch. 6 pp. 81–4
'Sonny' Ch. 5 pp. 92–4
Answers to Correspondents (Study and Studio heading) p. 96
> Di-Methyl-Amine (composition)

Number 1194 (15 November 1902)
More About Pixie Ch. 7 pp. 97–100
Varieties (William Black, the Novelist, and Music) p. 107
'Sonny' Ch. 6 pp. 108–10
A Writer for the Press Ch. 3 pp. 110–12

Number 1195 (22 November 1902)
More About Pixie Ch. 8 pp. 113–16
Varieties (The Prima Donna) p. 119
Girls Then and Now: Musical (Lily Watson) pp. 122–4
> Watson compares girls' music making 30 years ago, when trivial drawing-room pieces were the norm, with the present, higher expectations in which superficial brilliancy, *tours de force* and dexterity 'do not entitle her to be deemed a musician' (p. 124).

'Sonny' Ch. 7 pp. 125–7

Number 1196 (29 November 1902)
More About Pixie Ch. 9 pp. 129–32
A Writer for the Press Ch. 4 pp. 138–41
The Fidelio Club (Eleonore D'Esterre-Keeling) p. 141

Number 1197 (6 December 1902)
More About Pixie Ch. 10 pp. 145–7
> Illustration 'What has happened to worry ye, my dear?' shows Pixie questioning sister Bridgie in front of a piano with open sheet music p. 147

'Sonny' Ch. 8 pp. 158–60

Number 1198 (13 December 1902)
More About Pixie Ch. 11 pp. 161–5
A Writer for the Press Ch. 5 pp. 166–7
'Sonny' Ch. 9 pp. 172, 174–5
Answers to Correspondents p. 176
> Orange Wool (mandolin)

242 *Catalogue of musical content*

Number 1199 (20 December 1902)
More About Pixie Ch. 12 pp. 177–81
The Coalies' Baby, and How I Came to Adopt It (Walter Prentice) pp. 181–2
   A tiny bellows-operated portable organ that the author, a missionary to the coal porters of London's wharves and depots, carries with him to accompany the singing of gospel hymns.
   Illustration 'The Coalies' Baby' shows a young woman holding the coalies' baby instrument p. 180.
'Sonny' Ch. 10 pp. 188–91

Number 1200 (27 December 1902)
More About Pixie Ch. 13 pp. 193–6
The Fidelio Club (Eleonore D'Esterre-Keeling) pp. 196–8
A Writer for the Press Ch. 6 pp. 203–5
'Sonny' Ch. 11 pp. 205–7

Number 1201 (3 January 1903)
A Writer for the Press Ch. 7 pp. 209–12
The Human Voice (Lady Dunboyne) pp. 212–13
   Both the speaking and the singing voices can be improved and made harmonious.
   Illustration 'Her voice was ever soft, / Gentle and low – an excellent thing in woman' shows a woman holding a stringed instrument p. 212
The Organ-Grinder: A Schubert Fantasy, or The Story of a Song (A. Foxton Ferguson from German of Ottfried) Part 1 pp. 214–15
More About Pixie Ch. 14 pp. 218–19
'Sonny' Ch. 12 pp. 220–2

Number 1202 (10 January 1903)
More About Pixie Ch. 15 pp. 225–8
The Organ-Grinder Part 2 pp. 230–31
'Sonny' Ch. 13* pp. 236–8
Answers to Correspondents (Study and Studio heading) pp. 239–40
   Michaelmas Daisy (repertoire), Forget-Me-Not (piano)

Number 1203 (17 January 1903)
More About Pixie Ch. 16 pp. 243–4
A Writer for the Press Ch. 8 pp. 245–8
'Sonny' Ch. 14 pp. 252–4
Answers to Correspondents (Study and Studio heading) pp. 255–6
   Margaret (general)

Number 1204 (24 January 1903)
More About Pixie Ch. 17 pp. 257–9
A Picture and a Song (poem) (Sarah Doudney) p. 264
   Illustration 'A Picture and a Song' shows a young woman and girl at keyboard p. 265
'Sonny' Ch. 15 pp. 268–70
Answers to Correspondents (Study and Studio heading) pp. 271–2
   Annie Gough (repertoire)

Number 1205 (31 January 1903)
More About Pixie Ch. 18 pp. 273–6
A Writer for the Press Ch. 9 pp. 277–9

The Fidelio Club (Eleonore D'Esterre-Keeling) pp. 282–4
'Sonny' Ch. 16 pp. 286–7
Music Competition Result p. 287
   Examiners Myles B. Foster and the editor considered the musical settings submitted for 'Graces Before and After Meat' 'eminently satisfactory'. After narrowing the 548 entries down to 15 prize-worthy ones, they awarded first prize to Walter Brooks of Wilesden Green, second prize to W. White, of Hitchin, Hertfordshire and third prize to Margaret Hannah Roberts of Leicester.
Answers to Correspondents p. 288
   Tudor Rose (instrument maintenance, piano keys)

Number 1206 (7 February 1903)
More About Pixie Ch. 19 pp. 290–2
'Sonny' Ch. 17 302–3
Answers to Correspondents (Study and Studio heading) pp. 303–4
   Marcella (transposing songs), Enid L. (Ceylon) (piano, harmonium), Lif, Tif, or Zif (piano)

Number 1207 (14 February 1903)
More About Pixie Ch. 20 pp. 305–8
A Writer for the Press Ch. 10 pp. 309–11
'Sonny' Ch. 18 pp. 317–19

Number 1208 (21 February 1903)
More About Pixie Ch. 21 pp. 321–4
'Sonny' Ch. 19* pp. 333–5
Questions and Answers p. 335
   Editor advises Rose, who 'can play the piano fairly well and talk French' and wishes to choose a profession or occupation by which to earn her living, that 'Moderately good pianoforte playing is not worth much in actual money'. He suggests more suitable lines of work.
Answers to Correspondents (Study and Studio heading) p. 336
   Firenze (composition), B. M. (practising society), A Fifteen-Year-Old Reader (voice, health)

Number 1209 (28 February 1903)
'Sonny' Ch. 20 pp. 337–40
A Writer for the Press Ch. 11 pp. 342–3
The Fidelio Club (Eleonore D'Esterre-Keeling) pp. 346–8
More About Pixie Ch. 22 pp. 350–2

Number 1210 (7 March 1903)
More About Pixie Ch. 23 pp. 353–5
'Sonny' Ch. 21 pp. 365–7
Answers to Correspondents (Study and Studio heading) p. 367–8
   Charité (general), Jean Hunter (repertoire)

Number 1211 (14 March 1903)
A Writer for the Press Ch. 12 pp. 369–72
'Sonny' Ch. 22 pp. 373–5
The Chorus of Life (poem) (E.C.S.) p. 377
More About Pixie Ch. 24* pp. 376–80
Some New Music (Various) (Mary Augusta Salmond) p. 382
Answers to Correspondents (Study and Studio heading) pp. 383–4
   L. A. Klein (repertoire), E. Palmer for Trudie (repertoire)

Number 1212 (21 March 1903)
More About Pixie Ch. 25 pp. 385–7
Paula's Professor (E. Meredith Cartwright) Ch. 1 pp. 392–4
   When Herr Augarten selects young orphaned Paula Maxwell to fill in for a celebrated violinist who is ill, Paula's music career takes a propitious turn, aided by a handsome Englishman who generously gives her his Stradivari violin before the concert.
'Sonny' Ch. 23 pp. 396–8
Answers to Correspondents (Study and Studio heading) pp. 399–400
   Annie Gough (repertoire)

Number 1213 (28 March 1903)
More About Pixie Ch. 26 pp. 401–3
Paula's Professor Ch. 2 p. 404
A Writer for the Press Ch. 13 pp. 405–7
The Fidelio Club (Eleonore D'Esterre-Keeling) pp. 410–12
'Sonny' Ch. 24 pp. 412–15

Number 1214 (4 April 1903)
More About Pixie Ch. 27 pp. 417–18
'Sonny' Ch. 25 pp. 428–30

Number 1215 (11 April 1903)
More About Pixie Ch. 28 pp. 433–5
'Sonny' Ch. 26 pp. 441–3
A Writer for the Press Ch. 14 pp. 445–7

Number 1216 (18 April 1903)
More About Pixie Ch. 29 pp. 449–51
'Sonny' Ch. 27 pp. 460–3

Number 1217 (25 April 1903)
A Writer for the Press Ch. 15 pp. 469–71
The Fidelio Club (Eleonore D'Esterre-Keeling) pp. 474–6
More About Pixie Ch. 30 pp. 477–9
Answers to Correspondents (Study and Studio heading) pp. 479–80
   RAM violin faculty notice

Number 1218 (2 May 1903)
More About Pixie Ch. 31 pp. 481–2
A Chat with Miss Marie Hall (E. Meredith Cartwright) pp. 483–4
   Illustration 'Marie Hall' with her violin p. 483

Number 1219 (9 May 1903)
A Writer for the Press Ch. 16 pp. 502–4
More About Pixie Ch. 32 pp. 509–11

Number 1220 (16 May 1903)
The Chronicles of Sleepy Hollow II. The Village Concert pp. 517–18
   Describes how parishioners organize their festive winter entertainment to replenish funds for parochial charity. In one type of concert, 'London "stars" condescend to twinkle in our firmament', in the other, local talent takes the stage (p. 517).

The Journey's End (Dorothy Baird) Ch. 1 pp. 521–3
   Tenor Robin Gould was not cut out to work the land on his family's farm, but instead goes to London to take up a post as a church chorister. He hopes one day to marry Edna, who loves his voice but not him, and visits her the day before leaving. A cold he caught on that day leads to a critical illness that adversely affects his voice. Now a dying man, he returns home to visit Edna one last time, only to learn that she has a new man. Death came quickly to Robin the next day.
Varieties (A Well-Known Hymn Tune) p. 523
New Songs for Girls (Mary Augusta Salmond) p. 523

Number 1221 (23 May 1903)
Journey's End Ch. 2 pp. 538–40
A Writer for the Press Ch. 17 pp. 541–3
Answers to Correspondents (Study and Studio heading) p. 544
   Prosser (repertoire), Aspirant (composition)

Number 1222 (30 May 1903)
The Fidelio Club (Eleonore D'Esterre-Keeling) pp. 554–6
Answers to Correspondents (Study and Studio heading) p. 560
   Gabrielle (repertoire)

Number 1223 (6 June 1903)
Home Song (poem) (Longfellow) p. 561
Music (from A. W. Cooper painting) p. 568
   A young woman sits playing a keyboard instrument, while a man and boy, likely husband and son, listen.
The Story of a Bracelet (Sarah Doudney) Ch. 1* pp. 569–70
   Carry Lancaster, a rising star in her profession, has just returned from studying singing abroad. A valuable bracelet that Edmund de Warrenne intends to give governess Becky Selwood, whom he loves, finds its way first onto Carry's wrist after Edmund sells it for needed cash. She sends the bracelet to Becky on the latter's wedding day.
A Writer for the Press Ch. 18 pp. 573–5

Number 1224 (13 June 1903)
The Story of a Bracelet Ch. 2* pp. 577–9

Number 1225 (20 June 1903)
The Story of a Bracelet Ch. 3* pp. 593–5
A Writer for the Press Ch. 19 pp. 602–4
Answers to Correspondents (Study and Studio heading) p. 608
   A Constant Reader of the 'G.O.P.' for Many Years (repertoire)

Number 1226 (27 June 1903)
The Fidelio Club (Eleonore D'Esterre-Keeling) pp. 614–15
   The editor offers a two-guinea prize for the best 1000-word essay written by a Fidelio Club member over age 16 on 'Ideal Pianoforte Playing', and a one-guinea prize for the best 500-word essay written by a Fidelio Club member under age 16 on 'My Favourite Pianoforte Piece'.
The Story of a Bracelet Ch. 4 pp. 619–20

246 *Catalogue of musical content*

Number 1227 (4 July 1903)
Musical Odds and Ends (A Professional Vocalist) pp. 628–31
  After listing conductors who make her professional life a trial, the author acknowledges those who make her work a joy.
A Writer for the Press Ch. 20 pp. 634–6

Number 1228 (11 July 1903)
The Linden-Tree: A Schubert Fantasy (A. Foxton Ferguson from German of Ottfried) Part 1 pp. 649–50
Answers to Correspondence (Study and Studio heading) pp. 655–6
  Audrey E. (piano, practising)

Number 1229 (18 July 1903)
A Writer for the Press Ch. 21 pp. 661–3
The Linden-Tree Part 2 pp. 666–8

Number 1230 (25 July 1903)
The Fidelio Club (Eleonore D'Esterre-Keeling) pp. 678–9

Number 1231 (1 August 1903)
A Writer for the Press Ch. 22* pp. 689–92
Answers to Correspondents (Study and Studio heading) p. 704
  Molly (repertoire)

Number 1232 (8 August 1903)
The Rehearsal (illustration) p. 712
  A male organist accompanies female singers of a past century.

Number 1233 (15 August 1903)
A Writer for the Press Ch. 23* pp. 729–31
Answers to Correspondents (Study and Studio heading) p. 735
  Elvina (violin), Chanteuse (voice, music education), Ruby (music education)

Number 1234 (22 August 1903)
Conductors Continued (A Professional Vocalist) pp. 744–7
  Last in a series of articles sharing first-hand vignettes about musical celebrities with whom the author worked.
  Illustrations: photographs of the late Luigi Arditi, Dr Cowen, Sir Hubert Parry and H. J. Wood p. 745
Answers to Correspondents (Study and Studio heading) p. 752
  RAM scholarship notice

Number 1235 (29 August 1903)
A Writer for the Press Ch. 24 pp. 758–9
Answers to Correspondents p. 768
  M.W.B. (voice, music teaching)

Number 1236 (5 September 1903)
The Chronicles of Sleepy Hollow IV. The Harvest Festival pp. 772–3
  Describes the church service for the Harvest Festival at which the choir sings with lusty eagerness that makes one forgive occasional lapses from time and tune.
A Writer for the Press Ch. 25 pp. 774–5

Number 1237 (12 September 1903)
A Writer for the Press Ch. 26 pp. 785–8
Answers to Correspondents (Study and Studio heading) p. 800
    Ossian (composition), An Old-Time Fairy (terms), C.M.A. (repertoire)

Number 1238 (19 September 1903)
A Writer for the Press Ch. 27 pp. 805–7
Withered Flowers: A Schubert Fantasy (A. Foxton Ferguson from German of Ottfried) pp. 809–10

Number 1239 (26 September 1903)
The Fidelio Club (Eleonore D'Esterre-Keeling) p. 823

Extra Christmas Part
For Volume 24 (1902)
Saint Cecilia (illustration) p. 12
    Saint Cecila is at the organ, with angel musicians accompanying her.
Mara Cross pp. 18–19, 21–4
    The eponymous heroine, a young workhouse inmate with singing talent but a badly disfigured face, is rescued at age 16 by the organist of Wyecester Cathedral, who prepares her for a music career to earn her livelihood. Following her London debut at which she sings hidden behind a screen, Mara's marvelous voice becomes the talk of the town and attracts the dubious love of alcoholic Geoffrey Steyne, who talks Mara out of considerable sums of money. After his death, Mara loses her voice and never sings again.
A Te Deum (Cantatina for Girls' Voices) (music score) (Myles B. Foster, Words Helen Marion Burnside) pp. 35–9
A Tangled Web (Mary Bradford Whiting) pp. 49–51
    Karl Steinmann and Eva Northwick sing duets in the drawing room after dinner. When Eva suggests Mendelssohn's 'Oh, wert thou in the cauld blast?', Karl fears it would reveal his love for her too soon, so chooses 'Greeting' instead. Eventually, at another dinner party, they sing the first selection when he at last has the right to utter those cherished words.

Volume 25 (3 October 1903–24 September 1904)

Number 1240 (3 October 1903)
A Maiden of Dreams (Lily Watson) Ch. 1 pp. 1–4
> Rosemary Urquhart, a vicar's daughter, is sent to her distant relatives, the Colegraves, for her education. When the vicar visits at Christmas, Pamela and Clarissa Colegrave perform on the piano, after which Mr Colegrave informs the vicar that Rosemary, who takes music lessons, has no true musical ability.

A Girl Who Was Heir to the Throne: Some Incidents in the Life of Princess Charlotte Part 1 pp. 4–7
> Princess Charlotte, only child of George IV, was musical and composed a few simple airs; one is reproduced in the article.

Number 1241 (10 October 1903)
'Rebels' (Lady Margaret Majendie) Ch. 1 pp. 17–19
> Sir Eustace Mordaunt, on leave from India and guardian of Jack, Tom, Mollie and Baby Jane, comes to Ashton Hall to bring some order to the rebellious children who are without parents and have only a nurse tending them. Baby Jane is the first to capitulate when she climbs onto Audine Fitzjohn's knee at the piano and improvises a bass to her accompaniment. When Mordaunt leaves to receive the Victoria Cross, the household wakes up, and Audine opens the piano and sends 'the full volume of her beautiful powerful voice carolling throughout the rooms' (p. 138).

A Maiden of Dreams Ch. 2 pp. 30–2

Number 1242 (17 October 1903)
How to Enjoy Orchestral Concerts (H.A.J. Campbell and Myles B. Foster) Part 1 pp. 36–8
A Maiden of Dreams Ch. 3 pp. 41–3
'Rebels' Ch. 2 pp. 45–7

Number 1243 (24 October 1903)
A Maiden of Dreams Ch. 4 pp. 52–4
'Rebels' Ch. 3 pp. 61–3

Number 1244 (31 October 1903)
A Maiden of Dreams Ch. 5 pp. 66–8
Music as a Profession for Girls (A. Foxton Ferguson) Part 1 The Outer Glamour and the Inner Truth p. 69
> Multi-part series spells out problematic issues associated with a professional music career. Untitled Part 6 leaves readers with 'a real gift' and correct initial training a message of hope: 'The only things needed further are perpetual industry, calm courage, and dependence on oneself and not on others.' (p. 822)

Well Worth Taking Part In: A New Questions and Answers Competition for Girls of All Ages pp. 74–5
> The editor will ask 48 questions, in four series of 12, for readers to answer. Question 48 is about music.

'Rebels' Ch. 4 pp. 75–7
The Fidelio Club (Eleonore D'Esterre-Keeling / Mrs Hermann Stahl) pp. 78–9

Number 1245 (7 November 1903)
A Maiden of Dreams Ch. 6 pp. 81–4
Music as a Profession for Girls Part 2 Know Thyself and Thy Friends p. 87

'Rebels' Ch. 5 pp. 93–4
Answers to Correspondents (Study and Studio heading) p. 96
   Miss Eveline D. Connell (practising society)

Number 1246 (14 November 1903)
A Maiden of Dreams Ch. 7 pp. 99–101
A Concerto (from John Percival Girlish painting) p. 104
   Woman in a diaphanous dress plays a violin concerto with all-male orchestral accompaniment.
How to Enjoy Orchestral Concerts Part 2 p. 105
'Rebels' Ch. 6 pp. 108–10

Number 1247 (21 November 1903)
'Rebels' Ch. 7 pp. 113–15
A Maiden of Dreams Ch. 8 pp. 125–7
Answers to Correspondents pp. 127–8
   Would-Be Singer (voice)

Number 1248 (28 November 1903)
When My Gretchen Sings (poem) (S. B. McManus) p. 130
   Illustration 'When my Gretchen sings' p. 129
A Maiden of Dreams Ch. 9 pp. 130–2
'Rebels' Ch. 8* pp. 138–40
The Fidelio Club (Eleonore D'Esterre-Keeling / Mrs Hermann Stahl) pp. 142–3

Number 1249 (5 December 1903)
A Maiden of Dreams Ch. 10* pp. 145–7
'Rebels' Ch. 9 pp. 157–9
Answers to Correspondents (Study and Studio heading) pp. 159–60
   Essex (voice, choral singing)

Number 1250 (12 December 1903)
A Maiden of Dreams Ch. 11 pp. 162–3
'Rebels' Ch. 10 pp. 174–5
A New Questions and Answers Competition for Girls of All Ages p. 175
   Question 48. 'Who was the musical small coal man of whom the poet Prior wrote – "Though doomed to small coal, yet to arts allied, / Rich without wealth, and famous without pride, / Music's best patron, judge of books and men, / Beloved and honoured by Apollo's train"'. No answer printed.

Number 1251 (19 December 1903)
Kittens (illustration) (from Maud Goodman picture) p. 177
   A woman plays a keyboard instrument while a young girl plays with a kitten on the floor.
A Maiden of Dreams Ch. 12 pp. 178–80
How to Enjoy Orchestral Concerts Part 3 pp. 180–2
'Rebels' Ch. 11 pp. 190–1

Number 1252 (26 December 1903)
'Rebels' Chs 12, 13 pp. 193–5
Grey Skies and Blue (F.E.S.) pp. 198–9
   Elise Raymond, an impoverished musician, relies on her vocal talent to tide her brother Frank and herself over financially while he is disabled from an accident. That she is ill with a cold does not bode well for her suburban London chamber concert. But help

arrives when a lady in the audience who heard her sing sends her an unexpected £5 note. 'To make a merry Christmas for a brave little woman', reads the enclosed handwritten note (p. 199).
A Maiden of Dreams Ch. 13 pp. 202–3
The Fidelio Club (Eleonore D'Esterre-Keeling / Mrs Hermann Stahl) pp. 205–6

Number 1253 (2 January 1894)
A Reverie (from Frank Dicksee painting) plate facing p. 209
    A woman plays the piano oblivious to an apparition in her likeness that the man seated next to the piano sees.
How to Enjoy Orchestral Concerts Part 4 pp. 218–20
A Maiden of Dreams Ch. 14 pp. 221–3
Answers to Correspondents (Study and Studio heading) p. 224
    Mag (music education), Claudia (voice)

Number 1254 (9 January 1904)
A Maiden of Dreams Ch. 15 pp. 225–7

Number 1255 (16 January 1904)
An Occupation for Girls That Is Remunerative, Interesting and Not Over-Crowded (Anna) p. 243
    Healthy young women with a fair education, an aptitude for nursing and 'some knowledge of music and singing' should consider working in an asylum to earn their own living, Anna says. She explains the curious musical prerequisites in her follow-on article, 'The Duties of an Asylum Nurse' in the same volume p. 478.
Music as a Profession for Girls Part 3 Masters, Agents, Concert Giving, etc. p. 247
Sonnet (poem) (Rose Bowring) p. 248
Varieties (Singing Like a Bird) p. 252
A Maiden of Dreams Ch. 16* pp. 253–5

Number 1256 (23 January 1904)
A Maiden of Dreams Ch. 17 pp. 258–60
A Wild Flower Letter (A Welsh Spinster) pp. 260–2
    Describes winter flowers in South Wales in musical terms, comparing the music of a waterfall or rivulet to the perfection of a Wagner orchestra or an Albani, and the chorus of the sea 'echoing angelic songs' (p. 261).

Number 1257 (30 January 1904)
A Maiden of Dreams Ch. 18 pp. 274–6
The Fidelio Club (Eleonore D'Esterre-Keeling / Mrs Hermann Stahl) pp. 276–7
Answers to Correspondents p. 288
    D.E.S. for Rosemary (mandolin)

Number 1258 (6 February 1904)
How to Enjoy Orchestral Concerts Part 5 pp. 294–5
A Maiden of Dreams Ch. 19 pp. 301–3
Answers to Correspondents (Study and Studio heading) p. 304
    Lucy Myles (repertoire)

Number 1259 (13 February 1904)
A Maiden of Dreams Ch. 20 pp. 305–8

Number 1260 (20 February 1904)
A Maiden of Dreams Ch. 21 pp. 334–5

Number 1261 (27 February 1904)
The Fidelio Club (Eleonore D'Esterre-Keeling / Mrs Hermann Stahl) pp. 347–8
A Maiden of Dreams Ch. 22 pp. 350–1

Number 1262 (5 March 1904)
A Maiden of Dreams Ch. 23 pp. 354–6
'The Greatest of All' (Edith Prince-Snowden) Prologue, Ch. 1* pp. 360–2
    A cathedral chorister singing 'O rest in the Lord, wait patiently for Him, and He will give thee thy heart's desire' brings Elizabeth Athol an introspective moment: Frank Clavering is her heart's desire, but there is no love – it is a pretence – for *his* heart's desire is Sheila Beaumont.
How to Enjoy Orchestral Concerts Part 6 pp. 363–5

Number 1263 (12 March 1904)
'The Greatest of All' Ch. 2* pp. 374–5
A Maiden of Dreams Ch. 24 pp. 380–2

Number 1264 (19 March 1904)
A Maiden of Dreams Ch. 25 pp. 385–8
'The Greatest of All' Ch. 3 pp. 393–4
A Blind Girl Organist (Miss E. Lucas) pp. 395–7
    Having earned distinction as a Fellow of the Royal College of Organists, Emily Lucas, a clergyman's daughter blind since an early age, writes about the challenges and rewards of training a choir and playing for services at Saint Andrew Norwood when visually impaired. Illustration 'Miss Lucas, F.R.C.O., L.R.A.M. The blind girl organist in her Fellow's hood and gown' p. 397

Number 1265 (26 March 1904)
A Maiden of Dreams Ch. 26 pp. 402–3
'The Greatest of All' Ch. 4* pp. 406–7
The Fidelio Club (Eleonore D'Esterre-Keeling / Mrs Hermann Stahl) pp. 410–12

Number 1266 (2 April 1904)
A Girl's Dress in Japan (Norma Lorimer) pp. 417–19
    Illustration 'When will my lover come home from the war?' shows a Japanese woman in traditional dress playing a shamisen p. 417
Charity Concerts and 'At Homes' pp. 419–20
    Addressing the issue of remuneration, the unidentified author – A. Foxton Ferguson in Part 4 in his series 'Music as a Profession for Girls' – laments the current tendency for indiscriminate hostesses to exploit musicians at charity concerts and 'At Homes'. All musicians should have the right to accept or decline a request to perform and should be compensated accordingly.
A Maiden of Dreams Ch. 27 pp. 425–7

Number 1267 (9 April 1904)
Christianity and My Work (A. T. Schofield) pp. 440–3
    Illustration 'Piping songs of merry cheer' shows a young woman watching a young man playing shepherd's pipes in a meadow p. 441

252   Catalogue of musical content

How to Enjoy Orchestral Concerts Part 7 pp. 445–7
Answers to Correspondents p. 448
    Manx Heather (harpsichord), Baby Organ (coalies' baby instrument)

Number 1269 (23 April 1904)
A Spring Song (poem) (Helen Marion Burnside) p. 472
The Duties of an Asylum Nurse (Anna) p. 478
    Asylum chaplains who direct choirs for worship services are glad to have nurses with good voices as choir members. In addition, each ward has a piano, and the patients appreciate musical nurses. But the accomplishment is not a necessity, Anna explains, since some patients are professional musicians who sing and play exceptionally well.
New Books p. 479
    Reviews include *The Story of the Organ* by C. F. Abdy Williams, M. A., Mus. Bac.

Number 1270 (30 April 1904)
The Fidelio Club (Eleonore D'Esterre-Keeling / Mrs. Hermann Stahl) pp. 483–4
Answers to Correspondents (Study and Studio heading) pp. 495–6
    Mrs Collinson (repertoire), Millie Briscoe for Elvina (violin teaching), Moonshine (repertoire), Iris Gray (music teaching)

Number 1271 (7 May 1904)
A Club of Fair Women (Vera Stewart) Ch. 1 pp. 497–9
    Club member Florence Jeffries remembers an impossible marriage proposal while she and a suitor were trying over some new songs. She had to put the music stool between them and say 'No' a number of times.
The Girl-Poets of To-day (Henry Bernard) pp. 504–7
    Illustration 'Awake the lute' shows a young woman playing the lute in a meadow of flowers p. 505
Answers to Correspondents (Study and Studio heading) p. 511
    Wishaw (violin, instrument purchase)

Number 1272 (14 May 1904)
A Club of Fair Women Ch. 2 pp. 518–19

Number 1273 (21 May 1904)
How to Enjoy Orchestral Concerts Part 8 pp. 532–3
    A Club of Fair Women Ch. 3 pp. 543–4

Number 1274 (28 May 1904)
A Club of Fair Women Ch. 4* pp. 545–8
The Birthday Page: June pp. 549–50
    Includes 'Notable English Soprano' Clara Novello p. 549
    Illustration 'Madame Clara Novello' p. 549
The Fidelio Club (Eleonore D'Esterre-Keeling / Mrs Hermann Stahl) pp. 554–5

Number 1275 (4 June 1904)
Answers to Correspondents (Study and Studio heading) p. 576
    Prelude (writing musical fiction), Diana (practising, voice, health)

Number 1276 (11 June 1904)
Beethoven and the Muse (illustration) (after R. Eichstadt painting) p. 584
    A female harpist looks over Beethoven's shoulder as he sits at the piano.
How to Enjoy Orchestral Concerts Part 9 pp. 585–8

Number 1277 (18 June 1904)
Answers to Correspondents (Study and Studio heading) p. 608
  Fairy (music education)

Number 1278 (25 June 1904)
The Fidelio Club (Eleonore d'Esterre-Stahl) pp. 622–3

Number 1279 (2 July 1904)
The Battersea Polytechnic (Lily Watson) pp. 628–31
  The institution offers entertainments and organ recitals for the community.

Number 1280 (9 July 1904)
Professor Ševčík and His Pupils (Ludmia Marie Vojáčková) pp. 644–7
  Marie Hall's late accompanist writes about music making in Prague.
The Water-Sprite and the Violin (Florence Wilson) pp. 652–3
  A Scandinavian legend.
Answers to Correspondents (Study and Studio heading) p. 656
  Toby (repertoire)

Number 1281 (16 July 1904)
How to Enjoy Orchestral Concerts Part 10 pp. 660–2

Number 1283 (30 July 1904)
The Fidelio Club (The Editor) pp. 701–2

Number 1284 (6 August 1904)
A Rhapsody (illustration) p. 705
  A young woman playing the violin.
How to Enjoy Orchestral Concerts Part 11 pp. 710–11
How Helen Was Won (Arthur H. Henderson) Ch. 1* pp. 713–15
  That Helen Dunford, Harry Cartwright's dinner companion at his aunt's house, had rejected his marriage proposal six months earlier likely explains why, when asked to sing after dinner, he 'seriously disturbed the accompanist, in the middle of a pathetic ballad, by turning over two pages of the song at the same time' (p. 715).

Number 1285 (13 August 1904)
How Helen Was Won Ch. 2 pp. 730–1
Music as a Profession for Girls Part 5 Wealth and Music pp. 731–2

Number 1286 (20 August 1904)
How Helen Was Won Ch. 3 pp. 740–2
Answers to Correspondents p. 752
  Miss Lilie Milner for Judy (repertoire), Norah for Grace (repertoire)

Number 1287 (27 August 1904)
How Helen Was Won Ch. 4 pp. 756–8
The Fidelio Club (Eleonore D'Esterre-Keeling / Mrs. Hermann Stahl) pp. 762–3
Answers to Correspondent (Study and Studio heading) p. 768
  RAM scholarship notice

Number 1288 (3 September 1904)
A Greeting and a Song (poem) (Sarah Doudney) p. 782

Number (1291 (24 September 1904)
Music as a Profession for Girls Part 6 p. 822

The Extra Christmas Part
For Volume 25 (1903)

Grannie: A Christmas Adventure (Madge Wallace Ross) pp. 24–8, 30

    Neither Gladys May Swinburn, on her way to visit her unknown Scotch grandmother, nor schoolmate May Stainer, on her way to visit her British cousins, looks forward to her Christmas plans, so they switch places. May Stainer's violin playing exposes the switch, since the real May Swinburn is not musical.

Dost Thou Not Know? (music score) (The Rev. C. Pendock Banks, Words Ellen T. Fowler) pp. 33–5

Love or Lucre (Ruth Lamb) pp. 51–6, 58–60, 62–4

    Natalie Morrel and Peter Sanders are an oddly matched couple not only in height and age – she is tall, graceful and 22, he is shorter than his wife and 53 – but also in musical ability. Natalie has a delightful, well-cultivated voice. Peter, who enjoys but knows little about music, has a correct ear and tuneful, though uncultivated, voice. Natalie patiently trains her husband's voice so he can sing duets with her.

Volume 26 (1 October 1904–30 September 1905)

Number 1292 (1 October 1904)
The Heart of Una Sackville (Mrs George De Horne Vaizey) Ch. 1 pp. 1–3
    Una Sackville loves to sing and uses the charm of her sweet voice to break Wallace Forbes's heart 'for the sake of a little fun and excitement for myself, and as a sop to my wounded vanity!' To her credit, afterward Una 'felt utterly ashamed and despicable' (p. 274).
'My Neighbour' Ch. 1* pp. 9–10
    Katherine Lee, a music teacher lodging in a boarding house, befriends a young city clerk who sometimes amuses himself with one-finger performances of popular street melodies and favourite hymn tunes on the worn-out piano in the basement.

Number 1293 (8 October 1904)
'All Was for the Best!' (George Castellaine) Ch. 1 pp. 17–19
    Famous singer Anthony Jocelyn befriends substitute accompanist Gracie Banborough, an impoverished school piano teacher with an ill father, at a charity concert and saves her from a less than stellar performance. She eventually achieves 'a fair measure of success', earning about £100 a year by her school teaching, private pupils and concert engagements, but she 'had drifted into the profession of music' and was unlikely to earn more, for she was not a great executant. 'Her groove, moreover, was a narrow one.' (p. 462)
Evening (poem) (Adelaide Bush) p. 19
The Heart of Una Sackville Ch. 2 pp. 27–8
'My Neighbour' Ch. 2 pp. 30–1
Answers to Correspondents (Study and Studio heading) p. 32
    Rosemary (practising, music education), Miss A. Maud Jarrett (practising society)
A String Quartette (illustration) plate facing p. 32
    An all-women ensemble playing piano and stringed instruments.

Number 1294 (15 October 1904)
Varieties (Playing and Paying; Why Not Learn the Harp) p. 34
'My Neighbour' Ch. 3 p. 35
'All Was for the Best!' Ch. 2 pp. 43–4
The Heart of Una Sackville Ch. 3 pp. 46–8

Number 1295 (22 October 1904)
'All was for the Best!' Ch. 3 pp. 52–3
The Heart of Una Sackville Ch. 4 pp. 56, 58–9
Amateurs in Music (Myles B. Foster) pp. 61–2
    Author believes that a really good amateur is better than a mediocre professional musician and warns students 'against lukewarmness or half-heartedness in any undertaking, be it life's work or life's amusement' (p. 61). He then addresses amateurs who unfairly expect payment for their services and underbid professional musicians for whom remuneration is their livelihood.

Number 1296 (29 October 1904)
'All Was for the Best!' Ch. 4 pp. 66–8
The Heart of Una Sackville Ch. 5 pp. 76–7
The Fidelio Club (Eleonore D'Esterre-Stahl) pp. 78–9

Number 1297 (5 November 1904)
The Heart of Una Sackville Ch. 6 pp. 81–3
Varieties (What Became of C Flat?) p. 87
'All was for the Best!' Ch. 5 pp. 88, 90–1
Answers to Correspondents (Study and Studio heading) p. 96
   M. E. Calthrop for Sheila Loo (repertoire)

Number 1298 (12 November 1904)
'All Was for the Best!' Ch. 6 pp. 102–3
The Heart of Una Sackville Ch. 7* pp. 109–12

Number 1299 (19 November 1904)
'All Was for the Best!' Ch. 7 pp. 113–18
The Fidelio Club (Eleonore D'Esterre-Stahl) pp. 118–20
A New Portrait of Her Majesty the Queen of Romania (illustration) p. 121
   The Queen is playing a large pipe organ.
The Heart of Una Sackville Ch. 8 pp. 126–7

Number 1300 (26 November 1904)
The Heart of Una Sackville Ch. 9 pp. 130–2
'All Was for the Best!' Ch. 8 pp. 142–3

Number 1301 (3 December 1904)
The Heart of Una Sackville Ch. 10 pp. 145–7
Varieties (Practising as It Ought to Be; Advice to Singers) p. 157
'All Was for the Best!' Ch. 9 pp. 158–9
Answers to Correspondents p. 160
   Viloo Vakeel (India) (repertoire)

Number 1302 (10 December 1904)
'All Was for the Best!' Ch. 10 pp. 161–5
   Illustration 'We can't entertain each other; we must spend our evenings apart!' shows
   Bertha Carson at the piano talking to her father p. 161
The Heart of Una Sackville Ch. 11 pp. 170–2

Number 1303 (17 December 1904)
The Heart of Una Sackville Ch. 12 pp. 178–9
Aunt True (Olive Birrell) Ch. 1* p. 187
   In Miss Jenkinson's mind, orphan Gertrude (True) Beresford is selfless to a fault, for
   putting her siblings' needs consistently before her own and failing to cultivate the talent
   God had given her – a bird's throat. Now almost 30 years old, True never had learned
   to sing, even when family responsibilities let up. If True will not nurse her talent for
   herself, her adviser says, she should nurse it for others.
'All Was for the Best!' Ch. 11 p. 190
Answers to Correspondents pp. 191
   Andante (composition), Kangaroo (composition)

Number 1304 (24 December 1904)
'All Was for the Best!' Ch. 12 pp. 193–6
The Fidelio Club (Eleonore D'Esterre-Stahl) pp. 196–8
Aunt True Ch. 2* pp. 198–9

A Christmas Song (illustration) p. 200
   Girl singing with music book in hand.
Carol of Two Shepherds (poem) (Nora Chesson) p. 201
The Heart of Una Sackville Ch. 13 pp. 206–7

Number 1305 (31 December 1904)
A Village Choir Fifty Years Ago (illustration) p. 209
   Children and adults, singers and instrumentalists actively making music.
The Heart of Una Sackville Ch. 14 pp. 210–12
'All Was for the Best!' Ch. 13 pp. 218–20
Varieties (The Key is Fixed – *Emerson*) p. 220
Answers to Correspondents p. 224
   X.Y.X. (circulating music), Miss Lonsdale and others for Sursum (repertoire), Edward Osborne (repertoire)

Number 1306 (7 January 1905)
Come Back to Erin (illustration) plate facing p. 225
   A young woman plays an Irish harp.
The Heart of Una Sackville Ch. 15 pp. 225–8
'All Was for the Best!' Ch. 14 pp. 238–9
Answers to Correspondents p. 240
   T.A.S. (composition)

Number 1307 (14 January 1905)
The Heart of Una Sackville Ch. 16 pp. 242–3
'All Was for the Best!' Ch. 15 pp. 253–5

Number 1308 (21 January 1905)
The Heart of Una Sackville Ch. 17 pp. 258–9
The Fidelio Club (Eleonore D'Esterre-Stahl) pp. 267–8
'All Was for the Best!' Ch. 16 pp. 270–1

Number 1309 (28 January 1905)
The Heart of Una Sackville Ch. 18 pp. 273–6
'All Was for the Best!' Ch. 17 pp. 278–9

Number 1310 (4 February 1905)
The Heart of Una Sackville Ch. 19 pp. 290–1
How Musicians Live (A Professional Vocalist) Part 1 pp. 292–4
   Describes camaraderie, both social and professional, based on a shared faith in art in which musicians look after each other not unlike siblings in a family, especially when finances are tight.
'All Was for the Best!' Ch. 18 pp. 302–4

Number 1311 (11 February 1905)
'All Was for the Best!' Ch. 19 pp. 305–7
The Heart of Una Sackville Ch. 20 pp. 314–16

Number 1312 (18 February 1905)
The Heart of Una Sackville Ch. 21 pp. 322–3
Springtime (poem) p. 329

258 Catalogue of musical content

'All Was for the Best!' Ch. 20 p. 335
Answers to Correspondents p. 336
    M.A.B. (repertoire), Mrs Collinson (repertoire)

Number 1313 (25 February 1905)
The Heart of Una Sackville Ch. 22 pp. 340–1
Girls' Attire for March (Norma) pp. 344–6
    Illustration 'An evening gown in voile muslin on *crêpe de Chine* made in the rational style' shows a young woman sitting at the piano p. 345
The Fidelio Club (Eleonore D'Esterre-Stahl) pp. 348–9
'All Was for the Best!' Ch. 21 pp. 350–1

Number 1314 (4 March 1905)
The Heart of Una Sackville Ch. 23 pp. 358–9
The Critic's Dream (E. Meredith Cartwright) p. 361
    The dream illustrates performers who make music for the wrong and right reasons and an honest critic who knows the difference.
'All Was for the Best!' Ch. 22 pp. 363–7
Answers to Correspondents p. 368
    Miss Eveline D. Connell for X.Y.Z. (circulating music)

Number 1315 (11 March 1905)
Resignation (poem) (G. D. Lynch) p. 369
    Poem not musical but has a musical illustration.
    Illustration 'Grief' shows a young woman holding but not playing a guitar p. 369
Life (poem) (Constance E. Britton) p. 376
The Heart of Una Sackville Ch. 24 pp. 378–9
'All Was for the Best!' Ch. 23 pp. 382–3

Number 1316 (18 March 1905)
'All Was for the Best!' Ch. 24 pp. 385–8
Varieties (A Musical Conundrum) p. 391
How Musicians Live Part 2 pp. 393–5
The Erinna Club: A New Club for Literary Girls (Lily Watson) pp. 396–8
    TGOP reader 'Amethyst', who saw her verses on Paderewski's 'Nocturne' printed in the Erinna Club must have been pleased with conductor Lily Watson's remark that they showed 'power of musical understanding, and a fair command of form, so that we have read them with great pleasure' (p. 398).
The Heart of Una Sackville Ch. 25 pp. 398–400

Number 1317 (25 March 1905)
The Heart of Una Sackville Ch. 26 pp. 401–3
The Fidelio Club (Eleonore D'Esterre-Stahl) pp. 406–7
Varieties (Muscles and Piano-Playing) p. 412
'All Was for the Best!' Ch. 25 pp. 414–15

Number 1318 (1 April 1905)
A May Play (Frances Craig Houston) pp. 422–3
    Includes four songs and indicates tunes to which to sing them. No music scores.
'All Was for the Best!' Chs 26, 27 pp. 430–1
Varieties (Player and Instrument) p. 431

Answers to Correspondents p. 432
 Khan (repertoire), Lydia Whiting for Edward Osborne (repertoire), Music (repertoire)

Number 1319 (8 April 1905)
'All Was for the Best!' Ch. 28 pp. 444–7
Answers to Correspondents pp. 447–8
 East Coast (harp)

Number 1320 (15 April 1905)
Varieties (She Preferred Bridge) p. 455
Bringing Home the May (poem) (Helen Marion Burnside) p. 457
Sketch for the Pianoforte (music score) (Music B. Foster) pp. 459–61
'All Was for the Best!' Ch. 29 pp. 462–3
Answers to Correspondents p. 464
 E. L. Rawson-Ackroyd for Sursum (repertoire)

Number 1321 (22 April 1905)
The Fidelio Club (Eleonore D'Esterre-Stahl) pp. 468–9
'All Was for the Best!' Ch. 30 pp. 476–7

Number 1323 (6 May 1905)
Varieties (A Musical Success) p. 503
A Visit to Ireland (Olive Birrell) Ch. 1 pp. 505–6
 When visiting Waterford, Annabbel Forde, an English girl, coaxes Aunt Bride (Bridget O'Reilly) to sing some Irish ballads and offers to play piano to Aunt Bride's harp. With her beautiful, though sad and sweet, voice Annabel sings passionately, expressive of the history of the Irish people.

Number 1324 (13 May 1905)
A Visit to Ireland Ch. 2* pp. 516–18
Answers to Correspondents p. 528
 Lilian (repertoire)

Number 1325 (20 May 1905)
A Visit to Ireland Ch. 3 pp. 530–1

Number 1326 (27 May 1905)
The Fidelio Club (Eleonore D'Esterre-Stahl) pp. 554–5
A Visit to Ireland Ch. 4 p. 556–7

Number 1327 (3 June 1327)
Akin to Love (Ida Lemon) Ch. 1* pp. 569–71
 Miss Brown, who is 'hired help', plays Miss D'Arcy's accompaniments. Miss D'Arcy has a good, well-trained voice, but Miss Brown, though not a brilliant musician, has a soft touch and is a sympathetic accompanist, thinking not of herself but losing herself in the singer. That seemed to be her role in life in general – to accompany others 'and make them do their part well' (p. 571).

Number 1328 (10 June 1905)
Akin to Love Ch. 2 pp. 582–3
Answers to Correspondents p. 591
 Scottie (bagpipes)

260 *Catalogue of musical content*

Number 1329 (17 June 1905)
The Fidelio Club (Eleonore D'Esterre-Stahl) pp. 604–5
Answers to Correspondents p. 608
   Egypt (repertoire)

Number 1331 (1 July 1905)
The Doubting Heart (poem) (Augusta Hancock) p. 626

Number 1332 (8 July 1905)
Ladies' Bands and the Bâton (Lady William Lennox) pp. 644–5
   Noting that ladies bands 'seem springing up like mushrooms, and the cry is "still they come"', author seeks to dispel the notion that conducting means no more than simply waving a stick in time to the music (p. 644). As the outward expression of a composer's mind, the batôn helps interpret the music to its performers and in turn to its listeners.
Answers to Correspondents p. 655
   Musical Enthusiast (violin), Certificated Violinist (violin, ladies band)

Number 1334 (22 July 1905)
Water Music (Libretto for Cantata) (poem) (Helen Marion Burnside) pp. 681–2

Number 1338 (19 August 1905)
Correspondence p. 751
   G. B. Barnes and Miss Lilian Gore for Music (*The Vocalist*)

Number 1340 (2 September 1905)
Answers to Correspondents p. 784
   A French Young Girl (repertoire), Egypt (repertoire), Peggy Machree (repertoire), I. T. (Netherlands) for M.A.B. (repertoire), Montrose (repertoire), E. Maud Journeaux (Jersey) for Lilian (repertoire), Egypt (repertoire)

Number 1342 (16 September 1905)
House Music: Before Bed-time (illustration) p. 801
   One of two young girls appears to be playing a zither.

Number 1343 (23 September 1905)
A Harvest Song (poem) (Helen Marion Burnside) p. 825

Extra Christmas Part
For Volume 26 (1904)
A Song of Spring (illustration) (from Charles Jones painting) plate facing p. 32
   While not obviously musical, sheep in a meadow might be hearing their own song of spring.
A Lonely Christmas (Frances Lockwood Green) pp. 34–5, 37
   Raised in the workhouse, Mary Ann Smith is now a maid-of-all-work. Alone at Christmas when her employers depart suddenly, Mary Ann stumbles into a church, creeps into a pew and hears a woman playing and singing softly at the organ, joined by a tenor voice. Lulled to sleep, she is awakened by the vicar and his wife who invite her to their home on Christmas and later employ her as a trusted servant and friend.

Volume 27 (7 October 1905–29 September 1906)

Number 1345 (7 October 1905)
Odette: Soprano: A Story Taken from Life Chs 1, 2, 3, 4 pp. 8–11
   Eighteen-year-old Odette Gerard travels to Florence to study voice on a meagre £50. When at the end of two years her money has run out and she learns it will take two more years of training to make a credible debut, the discouraged singer marries a British physician who has been hovering in the background and returns to England to take up 'that other song, the song of love and home' (p. 451).

Number 1346 (14 October 1905)
Odette Chs 5, 6 p. 21
Margaret Dicksee, Painter (Jeanie Rose Brewer) pp. 24–6
   Illustration 'Handel discovered in the garret playing the piano' (from Margaret Dicksee painting) plate facing p. 25

Number 1347 (21 October 1905)
Odette Ch. 7 pp. 33–4
   Illustration 'I speak out of my soul, Maestro' p. 33
Musical Education in Germany and England (J. F. Rowbatham) pp. 43–5
   Begins with a comparative assessment of a Beethoven sonata played by two different pianists in two different styles. The first, a collection and succession of notes, reflects English training; the second, an intelligent rendering of the piece, reflects German training. Article continues with an outline of study in a German conservatorium. Because author includes no comparative outline of English musical training, the reader is left to conclude that music education in her own country is sorely lacking.

Number 1348 (28 October 1905)
The Fidelio Club (Eleonore D'Esterre-Stahl) pp. 59–60
Our New Prize Competitions p. 61
   Includes a Musical Research Competition outlined in the 'Prospectus' of the new volume.
Odette Ch. 8 p. 62
Answers to Correspondents p. 64
   Anxious Inquirer (music education), N. F. (repertoire), Lillian (repertoire)

Number 1349 (4 November 1905)
Odette Chs 9, 10 pp. 78–9

Number 1350 (11 November 1905)
Odette: Soprano Ch. 11 pp. 94–5

Number 1351 (18 November 1905)
Odette Chs 12, 13 pp. 104, 106

Number 1352 (25 November 1905)
The Fidelio Club (Eleonore D'Esterre-Stahl) pp. 116–17
Odette Ch. 14 p. 127

Number 1353 (2 December 1905)
Mother-Love (poem) (A. Mary R. Dobson) p. 137
Odette Ch. 15 pp. 140–1
Answers to Correspondents p. 144
   Orchestra (orchestra)

262 *Catalogue of musical content*

Number 1354 (9 December 1905)
Odette Ch. 16 pp. 158–9
Answers to Correspondents pp. 159–60
   A Hassan (instrument maintenance, piano keys)

Number 1355 (16 December 1905)
Odette Ch.17 pp. 161–2
   Illustration 'Sure, such merry voices never echoed before in that dismal ancient palace of the Vecciti' p. 161

Number 1356 (23 December 1905)
An Enthusiastic Fidelian (illustration) p. 184
   A girl plays the piano while a young woman listens, hands resting on the piano.
Odette Ch. 18 p. 190

Number 1357 (30 December 1905)
The Fidelio Club (Eleonore D'Esterre-Stahl) pp. 203–4
Odette Chs 19, 20 pp. 207–8
Answers to Correspondents p. 208
   Semper Fidelis (hymn text)

Number 1358 (6 January 1906)
On the Human Voice (Madame Norma Romano) p. 215
   About the singing voice.
Odette Chs 21, 22 p. 223

Number 1359 (13 January 1906)
Odette Chs 23, 24 pp. 238–9

Number 1360 (20 January 1906)
Odette Ch. 25 pp. 241–2
The Fidelio Club (Eleonore D'Esterre-Stahl) pp. 251–3

Number 1361 (27 January 1906)
Odette Ch. 26 pp. 257–9
   Illustration 'The applause increased, and she was obliged to go forward and bow a second time' p. 257
A Parisian School Eighty Years Ago pp. 259–60
   Madame Pascal, the music mistress at Madame Crosnier's school, 'did not seem to understand music very well, and she used to like heavy playing' (p. 260).
Answers to Correspondents pp. 271–2
   RAM scholarship notice, Mrs Collinson (repertoire), Day's Eve (repertoire), Lily Smith (repertoire)

Number 1362 (3 February 1906)
Odette: Soprano. A Story Taken from Life Ch. 27 p. 286

Number 1363 (10 February 1906)
Marconigrams (Annie M. Mann) pp. 300–1
   For spiritual Marconigrams to be successful, souls must be tuned to the same keynote.
Odette Ch. 28 pp. 301–2

Number 1364 (17 February 1906)
Odette Ch. 29 p. 319

Number 1365 (24 February 1906)
A Garden Lullaby (poem) (G. D. Lynch) p. 322
Odette Chs 30, 31 pp. 326–7
The Fidelio Club (Eleonore D'Esterre-Stahl) pp. 331–2
> Describes initial results of the 'Musical Research Competition' now renamed 'Music Quotation Competition'. The editor had offered a prize to subscribers who correctly named the pieces from which four musical quotations were taken, with their respective key signatures. When 20 subscribers submitted correct answers, the editor revised the contest and added eight more quotations. Entries had to mention key of the piece and of the passage.

Number 1366 (3 March 1906)
Odette Chs 32, 33 pp. 337–9
The Travelling Companions: A New Fairy Story (Adventure No. 197) (Lady Margaret Sackville) Ch. 1* pp. 340–2
> Of the six companions in search of adventure in a garden not their own, two are musical. Sèlysette is Orpheus-like when playing her violin named Thomaso. Benemerens, who comes from the sea, plays organs, water pipes, pianos and bugles.

Answers to Correspondents p. 352
> RAM scholarship notice, Mrs Lees and Mrs F. M. Sempore for Semper Fidelis (hymn text)

Number 1367 (10 March 1906)
The Traveling Companions Ch. 2* pp. 353–5
Extracts from Women's Writings p. 365
> Includes musical poetry of Anne Beale.

Odette Ch. 34 pp. 365–6

Number 1368 (17 March 1906)
Odette Ch. 35 pp. 382–3
Answers to Correspondents p. 384
> A Musical Inquirer (music education)

Number 1369 (24 March 1906)
Betty Trevor (Mrs George de Horne Vaizey) Ch. 1 pp. 385–7
> Eight-year-old Pam Trevor's heart surely is not in her music as she obediently but rebelliously wrestles with the 'Blue Bells of Scotland' while wishing she had never been born or had been born a boy. Pam's older sister Betty must have had similar thoughts when, at an evening drawing-room entertainment, she attempts to play Beethoven's 'Pathétique' with which she had 'wrestled' two hours daily for the past month. 'Poor Sonata! it really was rather pathetic, and it is to be feared that the audience was almost as relieved as was Betty herself, when it came to an end.' (p. 659)

The Fidelio Club (Eleonore D'Esterre-Stahl) pp. 396–8
Odette Ch. 36 pp. 398–9

Number 1370 (31 March 1906)
Odette Ch. 37 pp. 401–3
Betty Trevor Ch. 2 pp. 412–13

Number 1371 (7 April 1906)
Ruth Thornton's Wanderjahr; or, Two Girls and a Summer (Jean A. Owen) Ch. 1* pp. 417–20
> Ruth Thornton, a 16-year-old 'passionately fond of music' with 'a fine natural voice that could imitate the note of each song-bird', is sent to Chalky Hollow Farm in England

for school, where she meets Geraldine Maeburn (p. 418). When Ruth and 'Dina get lost after a picnic lunch, 15-year-old violinist Claud Merriweather walks them home. On half-holidays, Claud plays for farmers, cottagers and others to earn pocket money. Chapter 20 offers a commentary on the hard life of a music governess.

Extracts from Women's writings p. 421
    Includes musical poetry of Adelaide Anne Procter.
Odette Chs 38, 39 pp. 424–6
Betty Trevor Ch. 3 pp. 428–30

Number 1372 (14 April 1906)
Ruth Thornton's Wanderjahr Ch. 2 pp. 438–9
A Red Chrysanthemum Ch. 1 pp. 441–3
    Max, a pianist preparing for his debut recital at St James's Hall, mixes up two handwritten notes – one to his fiancé Evelyn Stewart, and one to his vocalist Isabel Merton – with nearly tragic results. A red chrysanthemum that Isabel wears to the recital saves the day.
Odette Ch. 40 p. 443
Betty Trevor Ch. 4 pp. 444–6

Number 1373 (21 April 1906)
Odette Chs 41, 42 pp. 449–51
The Fidelio Club (Eleonore D'Esterre-Stahl) pp. 451–2
Ruth Thornton's Wanderjahr Ch. 3 pp. 454–5
Betty Trevor Ch. 5 pp. 462–3
Answers to Correspondents p. 464
    Sapho (repertoire)

Number 1374 (28 April 1906)
Betty Trevor Ch. 6 pp. 468–9
A Red Chrysanthemum Ch. 2 pp. 470–1
Ruth Thornton's Wanderjahr Ch. 4 pp. 478–80

Number 1375 (5 May 1906)
Betty Trevor Ch. 7 pp. 485–7
Varieties (Those Street Bands) p. 487
Ruth Thornton's Wanderjahr Ch. 5* pp. 493–5

Number 1376 (12 May 1906)
Ruth Thornton's Wanderjahr Ch. 6* pp. 500–1
Betty Trevor Ch. 8* pp. 506–8

Number 1377 (19 May 1906)
Betty Trevor Ch. 9* pp. 520, 522
'Music and Poetry' (illustration) (from A. V. Thomas painting) plate facing p. 523
    Two of four Grecian maidens hold musical instruments.
Ruth Thornton's Wanderjahr Ch. 7 pp. 527–8

Number 1378 (26 May 1906)
Betty Trevor Ch. 10 pp. 529–32
The Fidelio Club (Eleonore D'Esterre-Stahl) pp. 532–3
Music Quotation Competition p. 541
    Results and Prize-Winners. Three papers correctly identified all 12 pieces, though none was perfect. The judges single out one of these papers by a 15-year-old as the most careful entry received and 'specially deserving of encouragement'.

Ruth Thornton's Wanderjahr Ch. 8 pp. 542–3
Answers to Correspondents p. 544
   J. S. (repertoire)

Number 1379 (2 June 1906)
Betty Trevor Ch. 11 pp. 545–8
Musical Queens (J. F. Rowbotham) Part 1 pp. 548–51
A Song of Roses (poem) (Gertrude H. Witherby) p. 553
Ruth Thornton's Wanderjahr Ch. 9 pp. 557–9

Number 1380 (9 June 1906)
Betty Trevor Ch. 12 pp. 566–7
Ruth Thornton's Wanderjahr Ch. 10 pp. 570–1
An Old Ballad: A Play in One Act (Patrick Kirwan) pp. 572–5
   Songs that characters Jasper Beuchamp and sisters Marjery and Hetty Dovely play and sing on the spinet reveal their true feelings in this eighteenth-century tale of love and loss.

Number 1381 (16 June 1906)
Betty Trevor Ch. 13 pp. 577–9
Absence (music score) (C. A. Lidgey, Words Anonymous) p. 583
Ruth Thornton's Wanderjahr Ch. 11 pp. 590–1
Answers to Correspondents p. 592
   Semper Fidelis (hymn text)

Number 1382 (23 June 1906)
Saint Cecilia (illustration) p. 593
   The saint is holding a portative organ.
The Fidelio Club (Eleonore D'Esterre-Stahl) pp. 594–5
Betty Trevor Ch. 14 pp. 597–9
Every-Day Pictures from the 'Simple Life' pp. 601–4
   British author, who lives in Switzerland with her professor husband, describes the 'Wald-concert' in the woods in which 'feathered songsters made every bush an orchestra and every tree a concert hall' (p. 603).
Ruth Thornton's Wanderjahr Ch. 12 pp. 606–8

Number 1383 (30 June 1906)
Ruth Thornton's Wanderjahr Ch. 13 pp. 609–11
Betty Trevor Ch. 15 pp. 613–15

Number 1384 (7 July 1906)
Betty Trevor Ch. 16 pp. 625–9
Ruth Thornton's Wanderjahr Ch. 14 pp. 638–9

Number 1385 (14 July 1906)
Betty Trevor Ch. 17 pp. 644–5
Ruth Thornton's Wanderjahr Ch. 15* pp. 653–4
Answers to Correspondents p. 655
   White Heather (music education), Alicia (repertoire)

Number 1386 (21 July 1906)
Betty Trevor Ch. 18* pp. 658–9
The Fidelio Club (Eleonore D'Esterre-Stahl) pp. 660–1
Ruth Thornton's Wanderjahr Ch. 16 pp. 670–1

266 *Catalogue of musical content*

Number 1387 (28 July 1906)
Ruth Thornton's Wanderjahr Ch. 17 pp. 673–5
Betty Trevor Ch. 19 pp. 685–6

Number 1388 (4 August 1906)
Betty Trevor Ch. 20* pp. 689–91
Varieties (Our Advertisers) p. 691
Norwegian Folklore (Alhed Schou) pp. 699–701
    Mentions violinist Ole Bull and relates a tale about the 'Fossegrim' with his fiddle. Music score for 'The Besseleik' – a 'Huldre-slaat' (or hill-lady's song) pp. 716–17
Ruth Thornton's Wanderjahr Ch. 18 pp. 701–3
Answers to Correspondents p. 704
    Valérie (composition), H.B.B. (repertoire)

Number 1389 (11 August 1906)
Betty Trevor Ch. 21 pp. 706–7
Norwegian Folklore Ch. 2 pp. 716–18
Ruth Thornton's Wanderjahr Ch. 19 pp. 718–20

Number 1390 (18 August 1906)
Norwegian Folklore Ch. 3 pp. 721–2
Betty Trevor Ch. 22 pp. 723–4
Musical Queens Part 2 pp. 724–7
The Fidelio Club (Eleonore D-Esterre-Stahl) pp. 728–30
    Illustration 'Beethoven' p. 729
Ruth Thornton's Wanderjahr Ch. 20* pp. 733–5

Number 1391 (25 August 1906)
    Ruth Thornton's Wanderjahr Ch. 21 pp. 737–9
    Betty Trevor Ch. 23 pp. 749–51

Number 1392 (1 September 1906)
Betty Trevor Ch. 24 pp. 753–6
How Ida's Loneliness Departed Ch. 1* pp. 758–9
    When at a health resort in Southchester, office worker Ida Coombes meets Austrian Marie Fischer, who plays zither. On return to London, Ida misses the music making and fellowship with other boarders at the resort, especially hymn singing around the piano, and eventually four of them set up housekeeping together.
The Travelling Companions: The Horrid Adventure (Lady Margaret Sackville) pp. 760–3
Ruth Thornton's Wanderjahr Ch. 22 pp. 766–8
Answers to Correspondents p. 768
    Bluebell (music education)

Number 1393 (8 September 1906)
How Ida's Loneliness Departed Ch. 2* pp. 769–70
Betty Trevor Ch. 25 pp. 773–5
Ruth Thornton's Wanderjahr Ch. 23 pp. 782–3

Number 1394 (15 September 1906)
Betty Trevor Ch. 26 pp. 786–8
A Few Words on Voice-Production (Anna Lynch) pp. 788–9
    Lynch, a pupil of M. Victor Maurel, speaks to those who sing and those who would like to sing.

A Song of Work (poem) (Adelaide Bush) pp. 792
The Fidelio Club (Eleonore D'Esterre-Stahl) pp. 794–5
How Ida's Loneliness Departed Ch. 3 pp. 796–7
Ruth Thornton's Wanderjahr Ch. 24 pp. 797–9

Number 1395 (22 September 1906)
Betty Trevor Ch. 27 pp. 802–4
Musical Queens Part 3 pp. 808, 810–11
Ruth Thornton's Wanderjahr Ch. 25 pp. 813–16
Answers to Correspondents p. 816
    Lynton (general)

Number 1396 (29 September 1906)
How Ida's Loneliness Departed Ch. 4* pp. 817–20

The Extra Christmas Part
For Volume 27 (1905)
An Averted Vengeance (Tracy Trevrew) pp. 1–16, 18–20, 22–3, 25–7
    In this tale of baby switching, Christopher Dennison whistles a popular air in a sweet true tenor voice' and Margaret Clitheroe, whom he wants to marry, sings gaily 'in a sweet, fresh voice', inherited from her mother, as she works about the house (pp. 6–7).
The Christmas Tree (Frances Forde) pp. 52–3
    On Christmas Eve in Germany the author, 'a poor lonely music student' shares her tree with others poorer and lonelier than herself (p. 52). Her violin master helps trim the tree and plays softly when the children are invited to see it.
    Illustration 'The Christmas Tree' p. 53
Nazareth (music score) (Charles Gounod) pp. 54–7

Volume 28 (6 October 1906–28 September 1907)

Number 1397 (6 October 1906)
Happiness: A Poetic Drama in One Act (Theodor Kirchner) pp. 12–16
   Libretto of German opera 'Das Gluck' by Rudolph Freiherr Prochazka with English translation by Ethel Moon.

Number 1398 (13 October 1906)
Pro and Con (Leslie Keith) Ch. 1 pp. 17–20
   Lacking a piano at the flat, Constantia Hereford has set her music aside, since her husband has no ear for music and would not miss her 'small performance'. But her father-in-law, who enjoys hearing her 'simple ditties', will not let her drop any of her few accomplishments, though Constantia doubts he even recognizes the tune 'God Save the Queen' (p. 323).
Happiness (cont.) pp. 30–1
Answers to Correspondents p. 32
   Mrs Collinson (repertoire), J. H. Cooksey, Esq. for J. S. (repertoire)

Number 1399 (20 October 1906)
How to See Rome in a Week and Apply Its Lessons (Douglas Sladen) Part 1 pp. 37–41
   Illustration 'Angels by Rafaelle' shows angels playing stringed instruments p. 45
The Fidelio Club (Eleonore D'Esterre-Stahl) pp. 41–3
Pro and Con Ch. 2 pp. 43, 46–7
Answers to Correspondents p. 48
   Miss S. J. Reilly for J.S. (repertoire)

Number 1400 (27 October 1906)
Pro and Con Ch. 3 pp. 54–5
The Work of a Professional Singer (Greta Williams) Part 1 p. 60
   Advises performers to 'leave all your troubles, anxieties and cares at home as soon as you enter the place where you are to sing' (p. 60).
   Illustration 'Greta Williams' p. 60

Number 1401 (3 November 1906)
Pro and Con Ch. 4 pp. 77–80

Number 1402 (10 November 1906)
Pro and Con Ch. 5 pp. 81–3
The Afterglow (F. E. Stevens) pp. 90–1
   Captain Macdonald, an elderly retired soldier, has lived in the Highland Hotel for 30 years. When Ethel, a visitor to the hotel, plays the piano in the drawing room where the old man sits, her Grieg, Beethoven and Chopin have little effect, but familiar old Scotch songs rouse him to request others. When she stops playing, the soldier sinks back into his chair, his head droops, and he once again enters his world of dreams.
Answers to Correspondents p. 96
   Mädchen (repertoire), L. Vaughan (hymn text), Music Mistress (music teaching)

Number 1403 (17 November 1906)
Pro and Con Ch. 6 pp. 105–7

Number 1404 (24 November 1906)
Pro and Con Ch. 7 pp. 114–16
The Fidelio Club (Eleonore D'Esterre-Stahl) pp. 122–3

Answers to Correspondents p. 128
  RAM scholarship notice

Number 1405 (1 December 1906)
Three Christmas Eves (May Lewis Smith) Scene 1* pp. 136, 138–9
  In a pleasant change from many accounts of governesses, 'teacher of music and daily governess' Maggie McDonald's employers are 'very kind friends' and her little pupils fill her days 'with the sunshine of their love' (p. 138).
Pro and Con Ch. 8 pp. 141–3
Answers to Correspondents pp. 143–4
  Winifred (harp)

Number 1406 (8 December 1906)
Pro and Con Ch. 9 pp. 145–7
A Christmas Carol (music score) (Mary Augusta Salmond, Words Helen Marion Burnside) pp. 148–9
Three Christmas Eves Scene 2 pp. 150–1
Answers to Correspondents p. 160
  Phyllis Clark (repertoire), Jonquil and others for Alicia (repertoire)

Number 1407 (15 December 1906)
Three Christmas Eves Scene 3 pp. 163–4
The Erinna Club: A Literary Club for Girls (Lily Watson) pp. 170–1
  Includes criticism of L'Artiste's poem 'Autumn Song', which Watson thought 'very pretty', showing a love of music (p. 170).
Pro and Con Ch. 10 pp. 171, 174–5

Number 1408 (22 December 1906)
Storm in Youghal Bay (poem) (Nora Chesson) p. 185
Pro and Con Ch. 11 pp. 190–2

Number 1409 (29 December 1906)
Pro and Con Ch. 12 pp. 194–5
The Fidelio Club (Eleonore D'Esterre-Stahl) pp. 196–7
Answers to Correspondents p. 208
  Florence (music education), A Reader of 'The Girl's Own Paper' Since Its Publication and others for Alicia (repertoire), Jean (correspondence course, orchestration)

Number 1410 (5 January 1907)
Moonlight Calm: For a Song (poem) (Ida Lemon) p. 209
Pro and Con Ch. 13 pp. 210–11
The Music of Jane Austen (Grace Hullah) p. 212

Number 1411 (12 January 1907)
Pro and Con Ch. 14 pp. 225–7

Number 1412 (19 January 1907)
Pro and Con Ch. 15 pp. 254–5

Number 1413 (26 January 1907)
The Fidelio Club (Eleonore D'Esterre-Stahl) pp. 266–7
The Work of a Professional Singer Part 2 p. 269
Pro and Con Ch. 16 pp. 270–1

Number 1414 (2 February 1907)
Pro and Con Ch. 17 pp. 278–9
Gavotte (music score) (Cécile Hartog) pp. 284–6

Number 1415 (9 February 1907)
Pro and Con Ch. 18 pp. 302–3
Answers to Correspondents p. 304
    Seagull (Belfast) (music education), Harold (repertoire), A Lover of Music (music student lodging)

Number 1416 (16 February 1907)
Pro and Con Ch. 19 pp. 305–8
Answers to Correspondents p. 319
    Fiddler (general)

Number 1417 (23 February 1907)
Pro and Con Ch. 20* pp. 322–3
The Fidelio Club (Eleonore D'Esterre-Stahl) pp. 330–1

Number 1418 (2 March 1907)
Pro and Con Ch. 21 pp. 338–9
Cold Potatoes, and What to Do with Them pp. 348–9
    A scientific housewife sings an amusing song about preparing meals the hygienic way.
Varieties ('A popular novel is like an organ') p. 351

Number 1419 (9 March 1907)
Concert Wrap of White Chiffon and Lace with a Hood (Jeanie Rose Brewer) p. 357
    Instructions for making the wrap include illustration of woman wearing the finished product.
Pro and Con Ch. 22 pp. 366–7

Number 1420 (16 March 1907)
Pro and Con Ch. 23 pp. 370–1
Answers to Correspondents pp. 383–4
    Miss Brunton (music teaching, voice), Emily (repertoire), J. S. (repertoire), Young Musician (music student lodging), C. McW. (general), Ernest (music education)

Number 1421 (23 March 1907)
Pro and Con Ch. 24 pp. 386–7

Number 1422 (30 March 1907)
Pro and Con Ch. 25 pp. 402–4
The Fidelio Club (Eleonore D'Esterre-Stahl) pp. 406–7
Answers to Correspondents p. 416
    M. C. (music selling), Fay (general)

Number 1423 (6 April 1907)
A Girl Without a Penny (Helen Marion Burnside) Ch. 1 pp. 417–20
    Orphan Ivy Hill, who has no money because of her deceased father's financial failure, comes to live with aunt, uncle and cousins Katie and Alice at Hillbrow. Because Ivy grew up in Brittany, her aunt assumes that she speaks French and plays the piano. She does and is very fond of music, including the violin, which she also plays. With Ivy's help, Alice, who is a beginning violinist with true musical feeling, becomes a better musician.
Pro and Con Ch. 26 pp. 430–1

Number 1424 (13 April 1907)
Pro and Con Ch. 27 pp. 433–4
A Girl Without a Penny Ch. 2 pp. 444–6

Number 1425 (20 April 1907)
A Girl Without a Penny Ch. 3 pp. 461–3

Number 1426 (27 April 1907)
The Fidelio Club (Eleonore D'Esterre-Stahl) pp. 470–1
A Girl Without a Penny Ch. 4* pp. 478–80
Answers to Correspondents p. 480
    Arpeggio (general), Miss W. P. for L. Vaughan (hymn text), Elizabeth (repertoire)

Number 1427 (4 May 1907)
A Girl Without a Penny Ch. 5* pp. 481–4

Number 1428 (11 May 1907)
Lovely May! A Song (poem) (Adelaide Bush) p. 497
A Girl Without a Penny Ch. 6 pp. 498–9

Number 1429 (18 May 1907)
The Fidelio Club (Eleonore D'Esterre-Stahl) pp. 518–19
A Girl Without a Penny Ch. 7* pp. 526–8

Number 1430 (25 May 1907)
A Girl Without a Penny Ch. 8 pp. 529–32

Number 1431 (1 June 1907)
A Girl Without a Penny Ch. 9 pp. 558–60
Answers to Correspondents p. 560
    Contralto (repertoire)

Number 1432 (8 June 1907)
A Girl Without a Penny Ch. 10 pp. 574–6

Number 1434 (22 June 1907)
Heather (Lilian Street) Ch. 1 pp. 593–6
    Eight-year-old orphan Heather Chesham is found by Harry Calder and raised by his family when her grandfather refuses to take her in. Her grandfather's eldest grandchild Lilllah Chesham, who plays piano, and Harry, who is intensely fond of music, attend a concert featuring Chopin's first Ballade for piano, and as he dreams, Harry's interpretation of the Ballade's meaning, reminiscent of programme notes, features a grown Heather, not Lillah whom his family wants him to marry.
Answers to Correspondents p. 608
    Musical (piano, musician work)

Number 1435 (29 June 1907)
How a Girl Should Dress (Norma) pp. 616–18
    Illustration 'An excellent example of a wide grey and white striped material' shows a woman pianist accompanying a female vocalist at a grand piano p. 617
The Fidelio Club (Eleonore D'Esterre-Stahl) pp. 620–1
Heather Ch. 2 pp. 621–3

Number 1436 (6 July 1907)
Heather Ch. 3* pp. 637–9
Answers to Correspondents p. 640
    The Rev. Prebendary F. Burd and others for Emily (repertoire)

Number 1437 (13 July 1907)
Heather Ch. 4 pp. 653–5

Number 1438 (20 July 1907)
Heather Ch. 5 pp. 657–9
'Well, perhaps you are right', said the spinet (Henry Bernard) p. 668
    The spinet and her fellow instruments reminisce in a neglected, melancholy music room in an old castle. The spinet remembers when they played for dances, until the young maiden and her cavalier fled from the castle, after which the instruments were silenced. To the violin, the joy of having carried the lovers away by a 'wild triumphant song' was worth the gathering dust, for, as he rhapsodizes, 'if it is good to cause their feet to dance, it is sublime if you can make their hearts to dance' (p. 668).
Answers to Correspondents p. 671
    Miss Payton for Emily (repertoire)

Number 1439 (27 July 1907)
Heather Ch. 6 pp. 674–5
The Fidelio Club (Eleonore D'Esterre-Stahl) pp. 682–3

Number 1440 (3 August 1907)
Heather Ch. 7 pp. 697–8
Three Girls and a Garden (Mary Rowles Jarvis) Ch. 1* pp. 702–3
    Orphans Rose, Violet and Lily inherit three 'freehold houses', live in one and rent the other two. Rose is a cashier, Violet, a daily governess, and Lily, who has spinal weakness, does their mending and provides music to cheer them in their tasks. Lily wants to give violin lessons to young children; the aunt with whom she lived previously did not think the 'fiddle' a respectable instrument for girls.

Number 1441 (10 August 1907)
Three Girls and a Garden Ch. 2 pp. 705–7
A Few Words on Voice-Production (A Singer) Part 2 pp. 713–14
    Author likely Anna Lynch, since articles of same title by her precede and follow this one.
Heather Ch. 8 pp. 718–19

Number 1442 (17 August 1907)
Three Girls and a Garden Ch. 3 pp. 721–3
Heather Ch. 9 pp. 734–5

Number 1443 (24 August 1907)
Three Girls and a Garden Ch. 4 pp. 738–9
The Fidelio Club (Eleonore D'Esterre-Stahl) pp. 745–6
    Illustrations 'The Rehearsal' (from L. Campbell Taylor painting) shows a woman pianist and two male string players p. 744; 'Intermezzo' (from E. Brack drawing) shows a young woman at the piano accompanying a male violinist while an older woman seated nearby looks on p. 745
Heather Ch. 10 pp. 750–1
Answers to Correspondents p. 752
    RAM scholarship notice

Number 1444 (31 August 1907)
Heather Ch. 11 pp. 762–3
To an Old Spinet (poem) (Christian Burke) p. 763

Number 1445 (7 September 1907)
Heather Ch. 12 pp. 769–71
The Chapel by the Sea (E. Tissington Tatlow) Ch. 1* pp. 776, 778
   Hearing 'the sweet sound of an organ in a church close by' makes Alec Hood feel sad, for he loves the organist, Laura Tressilian, and is afraid his past will make it impossible to win her (p. 776). An act of bravery for which a medal is earned, as well as his recently deceased father's estate, leads to Alec's marriage to Laura in the Chapel by the Sea.
Monday's Child (music score) (C. A. Macirone, Words Old Rhyme) pp. 780–2

Number 1446 (14 September 1907)
Heather Ch. 13 pp. 786–7
The Old Dove-cote (poem) (Helen Marion Burnside) p. 793
The Chapel by the Sea Ch. 2 pp. 794–5
Correspondence p. 800
   L. W. for Emily (repertoire)

Number 1447 (21 September 1907)
Heather Ch. 14 pp. 801–3

Number 1448 (28 September 1907)
The Fidelio Club (Eleonore D'Esterre-Stahl) pp. 819, 821
   Illustration 'Andante Expressivo' (from Stanhope A. Forbes painting) shows a woman playing the cello, with female violinist and male pianist in the background p. 820
Answers to Correspondents p. 827
   Roma (music teaching)

The Extra Christmas Part
For Volume 28 (1906)
The Making of Elsa (Lillian Street) pp. 1–20
   When Elsa Lindsay sings, her cousin Dan Wilton thinks surely her soul is as lovely as her face. 'It spoke through her voice, and permeated her presence.' (p. 6) At a concert at which Elsa accompanies singers, she compares Fred Powell's 'correct but thin tenor' unfavourably with Dan's 'rough, out-of-tune bass' (p. 7).
   Illustrations '"Kate's washing up," Dan said abruptly behind his book' shows Elsa standing at the piano p. 5; '"Why won't you sing?" Dan asked' p. 12
One Woman's Story (Pattie E. Varnam-Coggan) pp. 28, 30–2
   Anna Foster teaches music to her numerous young siblings. 'The worn piano tinkled out the strains of "The Maiden's Prayer" and "The Bird Waltz," varied by Czerny's five-finger exercises and stumbling scales.' (p. 30)
The Little Old Maid's Romance (Dorothy Baird) pp. 34–6
   Little old maid Aunt Caroline, 'flushed with pleasure' at the thought of attending the opera, sits 'in speechless delight, weeping softly' and wonders how the music does not awaken some feeling in her niece Carmiola's and hubby Hugh's cold hearts (p. 35).
Mrs. Deacon Brown (Lilian Gask) pp. 47–8
   Miss Clare, a dressmaker in Fordingbridge, sings in the choir on Sundays 'in a sweet and true soprano' and cherishes a reverent admiration for Deacon Brown, a widower with three small children, whom she marries.
Carol (poem) (Ida Lemon) p. 59

Volume 29 (5 October 1907–26 September 1908)

Number 1449 (5 October 1907)
Big Game (Jessie de Horne Vaizey) Ch. 1 pp. 1–4
  Margot Vane and her brother Ronald, a writer, travel to Scotland where Margot hopes the air will benefit her brother's health and writing. Nature had provided Margot 'with a sweet thrush-like voice'; she was not a talented pianist, 'but what she could play she played by heart'. When gloomy Mr Macalister, a guest at the inn, needs amusement, Margot plays on the parlour's 'wheezy old piano', then sings his favourite Scotch airs. As luck would have it, he is passionate about music and became 'quite genial and agreeable in the course of that musical hour' (p. 210).
A Sensitive Plant (C.E.C. Weigall) Ch. 1 pp. 10–13
  Clarissa St Aubyn is musical and sings simple ballads 'with verve and charm' (p. 119). As a nursery governess and then companion to Archie Hawkes, a crippled child, she finds comfort in the hymn 'O God, Our Help in Ages Past' and the anthem 'He Watching over Israel'.
Answers to Correspondents p. 16
  An Inquirer (general)

Number 1450 (12 October 1907)
A Sensitive Plant Ch. 2 pp. 17–20
Big Game Ch. 2 pp. 30–1
Answers to Correspondents p. 32
  Geranium (organ)

Number 1451 (19 October 1907)
Big Game Ch. 3 pp. 34–6
A Sensitive Plant Ch. 3 pp. 45–8

Number 1452 (26 October 1907)
Big Game Ch. 4 pp. 52–4
The Fidelio Club (Eleonore d'Esterre-Stahl) pp. 58–9
A Sensitive Plant Ch. 4 pp. 61–3

Number 1453 (2 November 1907)
A Sensitive Plant Ch. 5 pp. 65–8
Big Game Ch. 5 pp. 79–80

Number 1454 (9 November 1907)
Big Game Ch. 6 pp. 81–4
A Sensitive Plant Ch. 6* pp. 94–6
Answers to Correspondents p. 96
  M. E. (barrel organ, hurdy gurdy)

Number 1455 (16 November 1907)
A Sensitive Plant Ch. 7* pp. 102–3, 105
Big Game Ch. 7 pp. 110–11
Answers to Correspondents pp. 111–12
  C.S.S.M. (repertoire), Invidia Libera (repertoire)

Number 1456 (23 November 1907)
A Sensitive Plant Ch. 8* pp. 117–19
Big Game Ch. 8 pp. 126–7

Catalogue of musical content 275

Answers to Correspondents pp. 127–8
   Schoolgirl (piano)

Number 1457 (30 November 1907)
Big Game Ch. 9 pp. 132–5
The Fidelio Club (Eleonore D'Esterre-Stahl) pp. 138–40
A Sensitive Plant Ch. 9 pp. 141–3

Number 1458 (7 December 1907)
Big Game Ch. 10 pp. 145–8
Two Strong Wills (Ruth Lamb) Ch. 1 pp. 152, 154
   When younger, the Rowland children crept out of their beds to hear the 'weird Christmas music played by the dear old village folk in the kitchen' at Willowdene (p. 154).
A Sensitive Plant Ch. 10 pp. 156–9

Number 1459 (14 December 1907)
A Sensitive Plant Ch. 11* pp. 164–7
Expression in Music (Edgar Mills) pp. 169–70
   Speaking primarily to pianists, Mills, Inspector of Music in Schools for London University, emphasizes that one can attend to all directions printed in music and yet play without expression, resulting in 'nothing but dead manufacture' (p. 169).
Big Game Ch. 11 pp. 171–2
Two Strong Wills Ch. 2* pp. 173–4
   Illustration 'Christmas Eve in the Olden Times' shows five men playing musical instruments' p. 173
Answers to Correspondents p. 176
   Chorister (choral singing)

Number 1460 (21 December 1907)
A Sensitive Plant Ch. 12 pp. 178–80
Two Strong Wills Ch. 3 pp. 184, 186–7
The Fidelio Club (Eleonore D'Esterre-Stahl) pp. 187–8
Big Game Ch. 12 pp. 189–92

Number 1461 (28 December 1907)
A Sensitive Plant Ch. 13* pp. 193–6
Big Game Ch. 13 pp. 205–7

Number 1462 (4 January 1908)
Big Game Ch. 14 pp. 209–11
   Illustration 'Must carry me home to my north countrie' shows Margot singing at the piano p. 209
A Sensitive Plant Ch. 14 pp. 221–3

Number 1463 (11 January 1908)
A Sensitive Plant Ch. 15 pp. 230–1
Big Game Ch. 15 pp. 236–9

Number 1464 (18 January 1908)
A Sensitive Plant Ch. 16 pp. 245–7
Wrinkles, But Not Facial! (Yorkshire Woman) p. 252
   Tells how to whiten piano keys using nitric acid, soft water and a soft brush.
Big Game Ch. 16 pp. 253–5

276   *Catalogue of musical content*

Number 1465 (25 January 1908)
A Sensitive Plant Ch. 17 pp. 257–60
A Great Singer: Madame Tetrazzini pp. 261–2
  Illustration 'Madame Tetrazzini' p. 261
The Fidelio Club (Eleonore D'Esterre-Stahl) pp. 266–8
Big Game Ch. 17 pp. 269–71

Number 1466 (1 February 1908)
The Fisherman's Song (poem) (Neale) p. 273
A Sensitive Plant Ch. 18 pp. 274–6
Thomasina's Mission (Eleanor C. Saltmer) Ch. 1 pp. 278–9
  Thomasina Martyn's mission is to reunite her miserly maternal grandfather Thomas for whom she is named with her mother, whom he disinherited. When the grandfather is dying, he asks Thomasina to sing; 'in sweet tune and sweeter words'. She chooses the hymn 'The King of Love my Shepherd is' (p. 339).
Big Game Ch. 18 pp. 284–6

Number 1467 (8 February 1908)
Big Game Ch. 19 pp. 289–92
A Few Words on Voice-Production (Anna Lynch) pp. 297–8
Thomasina's Mission Ch. 2 pp. 300–1
A Sensitive Plant Ch. 19 pp. 302–4
G.O.P. Answers to Correspondents p. 304
  Bright Eye (music education)

Number 1468 (15 February 1908)
Big Game Ch. 20 pp. 306–7
Thomasina's Mission Ch. 3 pp. 312–14
A Sensitive Plant Ch. 20* pp. 316, 318–19

Number 1469 (22 February 1908)
A Sensitive Plant Ch. 21 pp. 321–3
  Illustration 'I have told Captain Wigram to come back again; I am going to marry him' shows Clarissa St Aubyn speaking to others in a room with a piano in the background p. 321
Thomasina's Mission Ch. 4 pp. 326–7
Big Game Ch. 21 pp. 331–2

Number 1470 (29 February 1908)
Thomasina's Mission Ch. 5* pp. 337–9
Big Game Ch. 22 pp. 341–3
The Fidelio Club (Eleonore d'Esterre-Stahl) pp. 346–7
A Sensitive Plant Ch. 22 pp. 348–50

Number 1471 (7 March 1908)
A Sensitive Plant Ch. 23 pp. 358–60
A Song of Hope (poem) (Lady William Lennox) p. 360
  Illustration 'A Song of Hope' shows a woman playing the harp p. 361
Big Game Ch. 23 pp. 362–3
Correspondence p. 368
  A.E.C. (repertoire)

Catalogue of musical content 277

Number 1472 (14 March 1908)
A Sensitive Plant Ch. 24 pp. 375–6
Big Game Ch. 24 pp. 378–9
Answers to Correspondents p. 384
   M.F.P. for C.S.S.M. (repertoire)

Number 1473 (21 March 1908)
A Sensitive Plant Ch. 25 pp. 390–1
Big Game Ch. 25 pp. 394–5

Number 1474 (28 March 1908)
Big Game Ch. 26 pp. 401–3
The Fidelio Club (Eleonore d'Esterre-Stahl) pp. 410–12
Answers to Correspondents p. 416
   Dorilee (repertoire)

Number 1475 (4 April 1908)
Chirp and Twitter (Bird's Song): Part Song for Girls' Voices (music score) (C. A. Macirone, Words trans. from Hans Andersen's Fairy Tales) pp. 423–6

Number 1476 (11 April 1908)
Answers to Correspondents p. 448
   Violet (repertoire), L. C. for C.S.S.M. (repertoire)

Number 1478 (25 April 1908)
The Fidelio Club (Eleonore d'Esterre-Stahl) pp. 476–7
Answers to Correspondents p. 480
   Francis Brotherton (general), Hopeful (voice, health)

Number 1480 (9 May 1908)
Answers to Correspondents p. 512
   Constance (musician work), Gracie (music education)

Number 1482 (23 May 1908)
The Fidelio Club (Eleonore d'Esterre-Stahl) pp. 535–6

Number 1483 (30 May 1908)
Chimes (poem) (Florence G. Attenborough) p. 551

Number 1484 (6 June 1908)
A Love Song (poem) (H. M. Trennant) p. 568
Answers to Correspondents p. 576
   A Worker (music teaching)

Number 1485 (13 June 1908)
Answers to Correspondents p. 592
   L. N. (music education), M. Edkins (general)

Number 1487 (27 June 1908)
The Fidelio Club (Eleonore D'Esterre-Stahl) pp. 620–1
Answers to Correspondents p. 624
   Musical (general)

278 *Catalogue of musical content*

Number 1488 (4 July 1908)
Diction and Phrasing in Song (Anna Lynch) pp. 631, 633

Number 1491 (25 July 1908)
Something about Hymns Written by Women Part 1 pp. 687–8

Number 1492 (1 August 1908)
Embellishments of Song (Anna Lynch) pp. 698–9
Answers to Correspondents p. 704
  Harold for C.S.S.M. (repertoire)

Number 1494 (15 August 1908)
Answers to Correspondents p. 736
  N. P. (music copying)

Number 1495 (22 August 1908)
Something about Hymns Written by Women Part 2 pp. 749–50

Number 1496 (29 August 1908)
The Fidelio Club (Eleonore d'Esterre-Stahl) pp. 765–6
Answers to Correspondents p. 768
Last music-related reply in the column.
  C.S.S.M. (repertoire)[1]

Number 1497 (5 September 1908)
An Orchard Song (poem) (Florence G. Attenborough) p. 770
Our Musical Lady-Help pp. 773–5
  Hetty Stannard, the Maitland's latest servant, is an accomplished pianist who saves the day when the accompanist scheduled for an 'At Home' has to cancel at the last minute.
  Illustration 'Everybody was charmed with the dainty young woman at the piano' (p. 775)

Number 1498 (12 September 1908)
My Friend Madge pp. 798–800
  Madge Lister, who studied singing in Florence, gives up her professional career for love and marriage to a Putney photographer, a decision that rich friend Dot Delaine, who thinks life on stage brings happiness enough, cannot understand until she is left orphaned and almost penniless and turns to Madge for help.

Number 1499 (19 September 1908)
The Fidelio Club (Eleonore D'Esterre-Stahl) pp. 805–6
The New Editor of the 'G.O.P.': An Interview with Miss Flora Klickmann (Mary H. Melville) pp. 810–13
  Klickmann turned to journalism when her health prevented a career as a concert pianist; she was also an organist. She already has articles about music, particularly the piano, planned for *TGOP*.
  Illustration 'Miss Flora Klickman: The New Editor of "The Girl's Own Paper," who assumes control of the Magazine with the November issue' plate facing p. 810

Number 1500 (26 September 1908)
Musical Queens (J. F. Rowbotham) pp. 819–20
Something about Hymns Written by Women Part 3 pp. 824–6

Granny's Fortune (Isabel Orman) pp. 826–8
  Mrs Carrington – Granny to 16-year-old Olive – will not let her granddaughter visit a fortune teller, for she herself had been misled by one. Granny, who was studying music at the Academy, gave it up when a fortune teller said it was not her talent.

Extra Christmas Part
For Volume 29 (1907)
Jack Frost and the Christmas Fairy: An Interlude (Sheila Braine) pp. 8–10
  A novel entertainment to distribute gifts at Christmas, with a song but no music score.
A Ring of Harmony (illustration) (by permission of Fred. Roe) p. 16
  Men, a woman and a boy are making music.
Little Sunbeam and Her Fairy Godmother: A Play for Female Characters Only (G. D. Lynch) pp. 18–20
  The play opens with Molly asking her mother if she heard the carolers collecting for the organ fund. Mom thinks rich parishioners could have raised the money without singing in the streets for it. The play ends with waits singing outside.
The Snares of the World (Ina K. Noel) pp. 24–7, 29
  When Claude Merrivale, the great London tenor, hears Nancy Poole singing in the village church on Christmas Day in pure, rich, bell-like, tones, he takes her to London for voice training and her concert debut. For Nancy, it is a dream come true until she learns that her benefactor has been 'playing' with her; she returns home disillusioned about fame and fortune.
The Nativity and Art (Lady Catherine Milnes Gaskell) pp. 48–51
  Illustration 'Nativité' shows a manger scene with musicians p. 51

Note
1 A correspondent thanks another for copying the hymn text about which she inquired.

Volume 30 (November 1908 – September 1909)

(November 1908)
When a Girl Becomes a Wife (Dean Hodges) pp. 21–3
   Article about maintaining domestic peace uses a musical example. When someone complained to Whistler that his 'Symphony in White' included a blue vase, the artist asked if a 'Symphony in F' is all in F. 'Life is best when lived on the symphonic, the orchestral principle; with many varying notes and instruments making a perfect harmony of delightful sound.' (p. 22)
The English Girl of To-morrow (Dr Emil Reich) Part 1 pp. 35–6
   Following his discourses on modern educational methods (Part 1) and the young girl as a pillar of the State (Part 2), Reich turns to her musical and physical education (Part 3).
Some Plans for the Immediate Future p. 41
   New *TGOP* editor Flora Klickmann plans to widen the scope of the Music Club to cater to vocalists, violinists, cellists and organists and welcomes correspondence requesting musical help. She also wants to help the 'thousands' of girls preparing for musical examinations, particularly those unable to study under a 'first-class' teacher. She is enlisting Mrs Eyre, senior professor of piano at Guildhall School of Music to 'conduct' a Music Club similar to the Fidelio Club of previous volumes. Plans are to include a list of pianoforte pieces on which readers can vote; Mrs Eyre then will analyze the two pieces most often requested.
How a Girl Should Study the Pianoforte (Moritz Moszkowski) pp. 42–3
   Writing especially for members of *TGOP*'s new Music Club, Moszkowski shares his views on technical standards in the days of classical versus modern-day composers.
   Illustration 'A recent portrait of Moritz Moszkowski', '*Whose compositions are dear to every pianist*' p. 40
A Gentlewoman's Pilgrimage (Lady Catherine Milnes Gaskell) pp. 44–6
   Fictional 18-year-old Annie Fairburn's preference for the music of Handel and Haydn brings laughter for being 'old-fashioned and out of date' (p. 45).

(December 1908)
When Love-Lamps in the Windows Hung (Zona Gale) pp. 92–6
   When newly engaged Lisa asks her 70-year-old Aunt Ettarre what a love-lamp is, the aunt decides to recreate the charming romantic tradition of a young man serenading his lady in her bower on a moonlit night when she has hung a love-lamp from her window. Aunt Ettarre enlists her husband Pelleas to mentor Lisa's fiancé Eric in the role. When the magical moment arrives that night, Aunt Ettarre discovers that the troubadour is not Eric, but Pelleas. 'Those young madcaps went off motoring with some friends, and I think the full moon asked me not to waste it,' he tells the love of his life (p. 96).
   Illustration 'He picked daintily at the strings in a thin, dipping melody' p. 95
A Bird-Song (poem) p. 96
How to Study my Compositions (Madame Cécile Chaminade) pp. 97–8
   Illustration 'Madame Chaminade' p. 98
What Money Is Really Good For (The Rev. Lyman Abbott) pp. 98–100
   Passionately fond of music, Abbott saved money to attend a *Messiah* performance at which Jenny Lind sang. After her aria 'Come unto Him', the silence was broken by an old sea captain's raspy snoring: 'He had money to buy a ticket, but no capacity to enjoy the music. And he could not buy capacity.' (p. 99)
The English Girl of To-morrow Part 2 pp. 111–12

Catalogue of musical content 281

Much German music that the world admires and loves such as Weber's *Invitation to the Dance* can be traced to young girls' *je ne sais quoi* that inspired idealistic sentiments in the composer.

(January 1909)
The Secrets of Good Pianoforte-Playing (Joseph Hoffman) pp. 217–18
    Illustrations 'The incorrect position of the little finger' and 'The correct position of the little finger' p. 217; 'The correct position of the thumb' and 'The incorrect position of the thumb' p. 218
The English Girl of To-morrow Part 3 pp. 228–9
    Proper singing is more effective than sports to develop the chest and healthier for women than piano or violin playing, which Reich considers harmful to woman's physique.

(February 1909)
The Editor's Page pp. 257–60
    Includes a picture of Mrs Eyre for members of the Musical Club, with whom she corresponds and feels as much interest in as she does in her private pupils.
    Illustration 'Mrs. Eyre' p. 258
Why So Many Students Fail in the Musical Profession (Madame Melba) pp. 261–4
    Practical advice concerning young women who flock to the Continent, lured by the glamour of a professional singing career, but who lack the true talent and adequate finances to sustain their vocal study.
Mr. Jackson, Advance Agent (Mabel L. Stearns) pp. 273–6
    While crippled Gabriel Newton delivers the message that his seriously ill father, a tenor, cannot not sing in that night's concert, the young boy gets a lucky break. A frantic organist/choirmaster enters the room with word that his solo chorister lost his voice and, on hearing Gabriel sing, offers him the position.

(March 1909)
Annie Fairburn Tries Parish Work (Lady Catherine Milnes Gaskell) pp. 342–3
    In another milestone in this gentlewoman's pilgrimage, Annie sings and plays for her Sunday-school class of 14- and 15-year-old mill girls and learns that teaching is harder than she thought.
The Use and Abuse of the Pedal (Joseph Hoffman) pp. 344–6
    Illustrations 'Mr. Hoffman illustrating the incorrect position of the feet when at the piano' p. 344; 'Mr. Hoffman illustrating the correct position of the feet on the pedal' p. 345

(April 1909)
How to play 'in Style' (Joseph Hoffman) pp. 416–17
An Old-Time Easter Carol (poem) p. 417
Hymns I Have Heard in Strange Surroundings (The Rev. John H. Ritson) pp. 418–21
    Christian hymns sung around the world sound sweeter in strange lands such as during the author's journey to the Far East.

(May 1909)
Her Psychological Moment (Fanny Heaslip Lea) pp. 449–53
    Miss Leonard and Miss Hayward have different opinions about *Lohengrin* and Melba.
How Rubenstein Taught Me to Play (Joseph Hoffman) pp. 485–7
    Hoffman reminisces about his two years as a private pupil of Anton Rubinstein.
    Illustration 'Whenever he wanted a special stress laid upon a certain note, his powerful fingers would press upon my left shoulder' p. 485

(August 1909)

How a Girl May Become a Professional Violinist (Marie Hall) pp. 647–9

At the editor's request, popular violinist Marie Hall offers practical suggestions to readers who are studying the violin.

Illustration 'Marie Hall' p. 648

(September 1909)

The Yielding of Elinor Grantly (Ernestine Winchell) pp. 718–22

For Gregory Fremont, singing songs – a bit of opera and rollicking college glees – at the piano is a prelude to his marriage proposal to Elinor Grantly, a widow with two young sons.

Illustration 'Come upstairs with me, Grandmother, and tell me about that silk patchwork quilt' spoken by Patricia Ellis, shows Gregory wooing Elinor, with the piano in the background p. 721

How Business Girls Are Housed in London pp. 726–7

At a 'living in' residence for female employees of Messrs Marshall and Shellgrove establishment, pianos in sitting rooms facilitate pleasant evening music making. Music and art students can stay at Alexandra House at Kensington Gore, which offers use of pianos and a concert room for residents.

The Failures (Pearl Wilkins) pp. 737–42

In this dreary picture of the life of businesswomen in a boarding house, the Girl from Ireland's repetitive playing of Schumann's 'Traumerei' on the piano represents the rut in which these aspiring authors find themselves when their talents do not match their dreams of success.

Volume 31 (October 1909 – September 1910)

(October 1909)
'Poor Little Helpless Thing' (Mary Heaton Vorse) pp. 11–16
  Six-week-old Louise Greatrax's parents must have wondered if she might be a child prodigy from the analysis her proud father John, who is fond of music, makes of her crying, which he likens to an unconventional song 'with its form, like any great musical composition' (p. 11).
Crown Princes at Play (illustration) two-sided plate facing pp. 32–3
  'Boys Who Are Heirs to Thrones' shows five photographs. In one, Princess Elizabeth of Bavaria is giving her son a violin lesson.
'Music – Not Money' (Sir Frederick Bridge) pp. 42–4
  Sir Frederick Bridge, then organist of Westminster Abbey, writes about the progress of music in England for those students wanting to enter the profession. Bridge is convinced that although studying abroad has its advantages, musical training in London is as good as that found anywhere else in the world.
  Illustration 'Sir Frederick Bridge in his robes' p. 42
The Editor's Page pp. 45–9
  Talks about Bridge's 'Music – Not Money' and gives biographical details about Bridge, 'probably the most popular of all musicians of England to-day' (p. 48).
  Illustrations 'The Lady Bridge Memorial Organ in Glass Parish Church' p. 45; 'Sir Frederick Bridge at the five-manual organ, Westminster Abbey' p. 47

(November 1909)
How to Make a Church Sing (Charles M. Alexander) pp. 106–8
  The American team of evangelistic minister Ruben A. Torrey and song leader Charles M. Alexander conducted revival services in Great Britain from 1903 to 1905, where Alexander later retired. Author gives pointers, such as simplicity in singing is cardinal; the song service must be made interesting; hymns should have a picture in every line; and a good choir is an organized choir.

(December 1909)
The Music of Poland (Ignaz Jan Paderewski with Comments by William Armstrong) pp. 135–7
The Repentance of the Smalleys (Jean K. Baird) pp. 153–4
  When Harry Smalley asks his sister to hem his trousers, she is at the piano playing over new music in an indifferent fashion.
  Illustration 'Can't you cut them off about two inches and a half and fix them up somehow?' shows Harry asking Edith, who is at the piano p. 153
The Editor's Page pp. 213–16
  Gives notice of an upcoming concert in Aeolian Hall given by Mrs Eyre's daughters – pianist Ruth, cellist Margery and violinist Phyllis – who 'are three of the most accomplished girls I know – and they are as modest and as charming as they are clever' (p. 216).
Preparing for the Musical Examinations (Mrs Eyre) pp. 249–50
  Analyses of List A, Advanced Grade, Local Examinations of the Associated Board are intended both for teachers and students.

(January 1910)
What a Piano-Player Can and Cannot Do (Josef Hofmann) pp. 274–6
  Covers the piano's possibilities and limitations. Precise knowledge of the possibilities and limitations of the instrument is important for anyone wanting 'to become a musicianly and artistic pianist' (p. 274).

284 Catalogue of musical content

Good Taste as a Guest (Lady Catherine Milnes Gaskell) pp. 288–90
  If a guest has a pretty voice, she should not refuse to sing if it will bring pleasure to others. Coyness is tiresome, as are an affected sore throat or a desire not to oblige.
How College Girls Arrange their Rooms (illustration) plate facing p. 288
  Six photographs subtitled 'Typical Students' Rooms at Lady Margaret Hall, Oxford', include one with caption 'The musical girl is constantly wrestling with the question how best to dispose of the piano. Do as this sensible student has done – place it flat against the wall.'

(February 1910)
The Portrait on the Wall (Harriet A. Nash) pp. 340–45
  The portrait of a Spanish ancestor serves a backdrop for change in musical tastes. The piano crowded out the guitar as the popular instrument for expression of sentiment, but the spinet purchased for Joseph's foreign bride still occupies its corner in the Prescott mansion.
Song (poem) (Alice Meynell) p. 366

(March 1910)
The King and Queen of the Belgians (John de Courcy Macdonnel) pp. 393–7
  King Albert and Queen Elizabeth have a passion for music and are enthusiastic Wagnerites.
Hymn (poem) (The Rev. George Matheson) p. 443

(April 1910)
The Minister's Boxes (Hetty Goldrick) pp. 459–62
  The five daughters on a plantation have no new clothes to wear to the 'all-day singing' at Squire Isham's house. Declaring themselves needy, they find suitable dresses to alter in the Ladies Working Society for Aiding Poor Ministers box. Fortunately, the new minister is a bachelor. The girls, who all have sweet voices, are expected to lead the singing.
The Easter Lilies in Church (Ellen Wyckoff) pp. 486–7
  Miss Barbara Allen last saw the Easter lilies on the Sunday she sang the anthem in her home church. Now older with failing eyesight and limited means, scraps of music drift her way from a different church across the way. Stopping in to see the lilies, she gets locked in and hears the organ and choir practising the Easter anthem 'Consider the lilies'. When a window closes on her arm as she tries that means of leaving, the vicar who finds her is her long-lost love.

(May 1910)
What Laura Realised (Mary Heaton Vorse) pp. 538–41
  Laura Andrews sings and plays and has 'something festal' about her; 'she came on as if a band were playing "See the Conquering Hero" for her to march by' (p. 538). She takes voice lessons in the nearest large town, and Laura's mother is saving up for her to study two years in London. But her voice is like her personality, 'a loud young voice with no more tenderness than a bugle' (p. 539).
Brothers Four (Grace S. Richmond) Ch. 1 pp. 549–51
  Anne Carey had planned to travel after her three years at a woman's college but instead moves in with her four brothers in their London flat. Brother Norm, a pianist, is the musician in the family, not Anne. When dusting, Anne sweeps sheets of Norman's loose music off the piano and onto the floor. Brother Walter picks them up, but Ann spends the rest of the night organizing them. 'It would never do to have Norman, invited to play for his guests after dinner, turn cross finding his music out of order.' (p. 679)

(June 1910)
The Love-Story of the Schumanns (Jeanie Rose Brewer) pp. 604–5
  Illustrations of young Robert and Young Clara p. 604; of older Robert and older Clara p. 605
A Note for Our Musical Readers p. 605
  Gives address of music publishers Messrs. Breitkopf and Hartel for readers who might want to order a catalogue of Schumann's compositions.
How an Artiste May Help Her Audience (Fannie Davies) pp. 615–16
  A pianist who has 'a wide and keen sympathy with all kinds of art' can give musical interpretations with 'artistic insight and conviction' that will touch the hearts of her listeners (p. 615).
Brothers Four Chs 2, 3 pp. 617–20

(July 1910)
How Girton Girls Arrange Their Rooms (illustration) p. 677
  In this series of six photographs, one has the caption, 'A musical girl has made the most of her limited quarters, and has packed the piano cleverly into a corner.'
Brothers Four Ch. 4* pp. 678–82
  Illustration 'The men all looked at her, to be sure – it would have been a blind man who would lose the chance' shows Norm at the piano, with music scattered about, and Anne nearby p. 679

(August 1910)
Brothers Four Chs 5, 6* pp. 718–23
A Reverie (illustration) (from P. Clarke painting) plate facing p. 720
  A woman is seated away from a keyboard instrument

(September 1910)
Brothers Four Ch. 7 pp. 802–8

Volume 32 (October 1910–September 1911)

(October 1910)
The Emotions of Martha (Mrs Maxwell Armfield Chs 1, 2* pp. 9–16
> Martha Spencer talks her parents into letting her go to London to study art. Sister Ruth, who is a musician, gives up her lessons to help with the expense. As Mrs Spencer justifies the sacrifice, 'the music lessons are only part of Ruth's interests, but this art school idea holds all Martha's future' (p. 15).

(November 1910)
The Peters Pudding (Annie Hamilton Douglas) pp. 65–8
> While her parents are weighing the merits of possible husbands for daughter Judith Peters, she walks in, having just returned from her singing lesson in the next town.

The Emotions of Martha Ch 3 pp. 69–76

(December 1910)
The Emotions of Martha Chs 4, 5 pp. 163–70
Retrospection (music score) (H.R.H. the Princess Beatrice – Princess Henry of Battenberg, Words Charlotte Elliott) pp. 178–81
> Reprint of piece that first appeared in the 3 October 1896 issue.

(January 1911)
The Emotions of Martha Chs 6, 7 pp. 196–205

(February 1911)
The Life-Story of Her Majesty Queen Mary (Jeanie Rose Brewer) Part 1 pp. 268–72
> Singing hymns was a feature of home life; Mary had 'a sweet, though not powerful, soprano', and 'The Lost Chord' was her favourite type of song (p. 271).

The Emotions of Martha Ch. 8 pp. 273–7
The Runaway Equator (Lilian Bell) Chs 1, 2 pp. 278–81
> When Mother gives Billy a geography lesson in the garden, she uses an orange, lemon stick and black rubber band to represent the earth on its axis. Her parting words, not to lose the equator, lead to dreams about the Geography Fairy and an adventure filled with songs.

(March 1911)
Begin Where You Are! (A London Woman) pp. 321–3
> Urges girls in country districts and provincial towns to use their musical talent, however small, in the service of their neighbourhoods by organizing glee clubs and village orchestras and assisting with temperance and religious musical activities.

The Emotions of Martha Ch. 9 pp. 325–9
The Runaway Equator) Chs 3, 4* pp. 329–33
The Making of a Useless Woman pp. 372–3
> Without the necessity to earn money, girls have spent time over music or perhaps painting because unwise parents wished to make them accomplished, an 'Old-Fashioned person' writes, but this fits them only 'to be the poorest wife a man ever had, a useless member of Society, or at the best the sure victim of disillusion and disappointment in life'. Why? Because 'Not one girl in ten thousand will ever be able to apply her knowledge of music or art to the earning of a penny or even to the entertainment or pleasure of her own family.' (p. 373)

(April 1911)
The Runaway Equator Chs. 5, 6, 7* pp. 388–91
The Emotions of Martha Ch. 10 pp. 395–400

(May 1911)
The Emotions of Martha Ch. 11 pp. 475–80
The Runaway Equator Chs 8, 9* pp. 500–4

(June 1911)
The Emotions of Martha Ch. 12 pp. 539–42
The Runaway Equator Chs 10, 11, 12 pp. 543–7

(July 1911)
The Emotions of Martha Ch. 13 pp. 596–600

(August 1911)
The Emotions of Martha Ch. 14 pp. 643–7
Things of This World (A London Woman) pp. 670–2
    The prejudice, meanness and smallness of snobbishness extends to music when having a piano and taking inexpensive fiddle lessons sets neighbours apart based on their material possessions.
Guarding Queens When on Their Holidays (Xavier Paoli) Part 1 pp. 673–7
    Queen Victoria and Prince Albert both adored music and used to sing duets to Mendelssohn's accompaniment. The Queen would ask Princess Henry of Battenberg, a skilled pianist, to play selections from her favourite composers.

(September 1911)
When Angel Sang (Mazo de la Roche) pp. 705–12
    David, an orphan called Angel because of his lovely singing voice, is asked after an audition to become a cathedral chorister. For his first important solo, instead of the one the organist taught him, Angel sings his dead mother's favourite song, a setting of 'God's in His Heaven, all's right with the world'.
    Illustration 'God's in His heaven – / All's right, all's right with the world' shows choristers singing in choir stalls p. 709

Topical listing of musical content: *The Girl's Own Paper*
Index to fiction

Musical heroines and heroes

'Acquired Abroad': A Christmas Story **6 Christmas** 1884
'All Was for the Best!' **26** (30 chs) 8 Oct – 22 Apr 1905
Angel's Gift, The **22** 8 Dec 1900
'Attraction': A Melody in Two Keys **11** (2 chs) 23 Nov 1889 (C Minor); 30 Nov 1889 (C Major)
Blanche Elmslie's Programme **6** (4 chs) 6–27 Jun 1885
Business *Versus* Art **22** 1 Dec 1900
Charity Begins at Home **5** (4 chs) 12–26 Jul 1884
Child of Genius, A **17** (24 chs) 18 Apr – 26 Sep 1896
Christmas Tree, The **27 Christmas** 1905
Critic's Dream, The **26** 4 Mar 1905
Forest Princess, The **20 Summer** 1899
Fortunate Exile, A: A Story of Swiss School Life **12** (12 chs) 4 Jul–19 Sep 1891
Grey Skies and Blue **25** 26 Dec 1903
Her Last Oratorio **19** (2 chs) 3, 10 Sep 1898
Her Old Dears **22 Summer** 1901
Her Own Way **16** (28 chs) 13 Oct 1894–20 Apr 1895
Her Violin: A Sketch in Sepia **5** (4 chs) 5–26 Jan 1884
His Heart's Desire **4** 30 Dec 1882
In the Days of Mozart: The Story of a Young Musician **8** (20 chs) 16 Apr–24 Sep 1887
Inheritance of a Good Name, The **8** (4 chs) 1–29 Jan 1887
Journey's End, The **24** (2 chs) 16, 23 May 1903
'Like a Worm i' the Bud' **15** (39 chs) 24 Mar–29 Sep 1894
'Little Miss Penny' **19** 27 Nov 1897
Love Out of Tune, A **17** (4 chs) 1–22 Feb 1896
Mademoiselle Merle: A Sketch **10** 17 Aug 1889
Malvolia **12** 20, 27 Jun 1891
Mara Cross **24 Christmas** 1902
Marsh Marigolds **16** (25 chs) 6 Oct 1894–23 Mar 1895
May Goldworthy **3** (4 chs) 1–29 Jul 1882
Midst Granite Hills: The Story of a Dartmoor Holiday **12** (5 chs) 1–29 Aug 1891
Mildred Austin's Two Christmas Eves **4 Christmas** 1882

Fiction 289

Miss Mignonette **3 Christmas** 1881
Mother and the Wonder-Child, The: An Australian Story **22** (22 chs) 27 Apr–21 Sep 1901
Mr. Jackson, Advance Agent **30** Feb 1909
Music **16** 8 Dec 1894
Music Hath Charms **12** (4 chs) 6–20 Dec 1890
Musical Romance, A **7 Christmas** 1885
My First Appearance **14** 6 May 1893
My Friend Madge **29** 12 Sep 1908
My Little Boy Blue **16 Summer** 1895
'My Neighbour' **26** (3 chs) 1–15 Oct 1904
Noël; or, Earned and Unearned **3 Christmas** 1891
Odd Girl Out, The **21** (4 chs) 7–28 Oct 1899
Odette: Soprano: A Story Taken from Real Life **27** (42 chs) 7 Oct 1905–21 Apr 1906
Organist at St. Olaf's, The **22** (3 chs) 6–20 Oct 1900
Organist's Daughter, The **14** (3 chs) 4–18 Mar 1893
Organist's Niece, The **6 Christmas** 1884
Our Musical Lady-Help **29** 5 Sep 1908
Our Patty's Victory; or, A White Hand **2** (4 chs) 7–28 May 1881
Paula's Professor **24** (2 chs) 21, 28 Mar 1903
Perilous Road, A **7** (4 chs) 6–27 Feb 1886
Queen o' the May, The **2** (27 chs) 9 Oct 1880–9 Apr 1881
Quite a Lady: A Story in Four Chapters **1** 10 Jul–21 Aug 1880
Red Chrysanthemum, A **27** (2 chs) 14, 28 Apr 1906
Result of a Song, The **18 Christmas** 1896
Ruling Passion, The **20** (2 chs) 7, 14 Jan 1899
Silence and Song **11 Christmas** 1889
Silver Side of the Shield, The **22 Christmas** 1900
Snares of the World, The **29 Christmas** 1907
Story of a Sorrow, The **9** 28 Jan 1888
Sudden Shadow, A **14** 8 Jul 1893
Teacher's Holiday, The **22 Summer** 1901
Tessa and Tonine **12** (10 chs) 5–19 Sep 1891
Twin-Houses, The **10** (4 parts) 2–23 Mar 1889
'Well, perhaps you are right', said the spinet **28** 20 Jul 1907
When Angel Sang **32** Sep 1911
When Love-Lamps in the Windows Hung **30** Dec 1908
White Rose of the Mountain, The **18** (36 chs) 10 Oct 1896–12 Jun 1897
Within Sight of the Snow: A Story of a Swiss Holiday **5** (6 chs) 3–31 May 1884
Zara; or, My Granddaughter's Money **1** (40 chs) 3 Jan–5 Jun 1880

Music in cameo appearances

'A Fateful Number': A Tale of Amalfi **14** (4 chs) 4–25 Feb 1893
About Peggy Saville **20** (27 chs) 8 Oct 1898–8 Apr 1899
Adelaide's Reward **16 Summer** 1895

Fiction

Afterglow, The **28** 10 Nov 1906
'Agatha's Choice' **18** (2 chs) 11, 18 Sep 1897
Age Forty **23** (5 chs) 1–29 Mar 1902
Akin to Love **26** (2 chs) 3, 10 Jun 1905
Aldyth's Inheritance **11** (32 chs) 8 Mar–29 Sep 1891
All From a Little Kindness **2** 25 Dec 1880
Anchoress of Ste. Maxime, The **23** (13 chs) 15 Feb–18 May 1902
Angel Unawares, An **6 Christmas** 1884
Annie Fairburn Tries Parish Work **30** Mar 1909
Aunt Diana **6** (24 chs) 21 Mar–26 Sep 1885
Aunt Lu's Legacy **14** (4 chs) 10–31 Dec 1892
Aunt True **26** (2 chs) 17, 24 Dec 1904
Averil **12** (24 chs) 4 Oct 1890–14 Mar 1891
Averted Vengeance, An **27 Christmas** 1905
Battle with Destiny, A **13** (35 chs) 19 Mar–24 Sep 1892
Belle of Birchwoods, The; or, The Uses of Adversity **6** (4 chs) 5–26 Sep 1885
Betty Trevor **27** (27 chs) 24 Mar–22 Sep 1906
Big Game **29** (26 chs) 5 Oct 1907–28 Mar 1908
Birdie; or, A Houseful of Girls **19 Christmas** 1897
Birds of a Feather **1** 5 Jun 1880
Both in the Wrong **2** (4 chs) 3–17 Sep 1881
Bound to Earth **4** (25 chs) 7 Oct 1882–21 Apr 1883
Brothers Four **31** (7 chs) May–Sep 1910
'Brown Bess': A Story in Seven Chapters **21 Christmas** 1899
Carved Umbrella, The **17 Christmas** 1895
Celia and Her Legacy **5** (7 chs) 5 Jul–27 Sep 1884
Chameleon, A **13** (7 chs) 2–23 Jan 1892
Chapel by the Sea, The **28** (2 chs) 7, 14 Sep 1907
'Charlie Is My Darling' **11** (25 chs) 12 Apr–27 Sep 1890
Christmas Message, A **21 Christmas** 1899
'Cis': A Short Story **19 Christmas** 1897
Clara's Christkind **10 Christmas** 1888
Clarice **18 Christmas** 1896
Club of Fair Women, A **25** (4 chs) 7–28 May 1904
Courtleroy **7** (52 chs) 26 Dec 1885–18 Sep 1886
Cousin Madeline **12 Summer** 1891
Cousin Mona **16** (24 chs) 30 Mar–21 Sep 1895
Crumpled Rose Leaves **11 Christmas** 1889
Daily Governess, A **13 Christmas** 1891
Dear Miss Meg **9 Summer** 1888
Deb's Enterprise; or, The Will and the Way **22** (4 chs) 6–27 Jul 1901
Dick Hartwell's Fortune **19** (4 chs) 5–26 Mar 1898
Disguised Blessing, A **13 Summer** 1892
Dream of Theodora, The **21 Christmas** 1899
Easter Lilies in Church, The **31** Apr 1910
Ella's Experiences **11** (4 chs) 3–24 May 1890
Emily Wardour's Opportunities **Christmas 22** 1900

Emotions of Martha, The **32** (14 chs) Oct 1910–Aug 1911
Esther **5** (23 chs) 6 Oct 1883–15 Mar 1884
Failures, The **30** Sep 1909
Five Letters **8 Christmas** 1886
Foster Sisters, The **7** (4 chs) 7–28 Apr 1883
From Strength to Strength: A Story of Two English Girls **2** (21 chs) 2 Apr–27 Aug 1881
Gentlewoman's Pilgrimage, A **30** Nov 1908
Girl Without a Penny, A **28** (10 chs) 6 Apr–8 Jun 1907
Girl's Patience, A **13 Summer** 1892
Grannie: A Christmas Adventure **25 Christmas** 1903
Granny's Fortune **29** 26 Sep 1908
Greyfriars: A Story for Girls **12** (24 chs) 11 Oct 1890–21 Mar 1891
Half-a-Dozen Sisters **17** (26 chs) 12 Oct 1895–5 Apr 1896
Heart of Una Sackville, The **26** (26 chs) 1 Oct 1904–25 Mar 1905
Heather (14 chs) **28** 22 Jun–21 Sep 1907
Her Psychological Moment **30** May 1909
High Failure: A Story in Three Scraps **12** 22 Nov 1890
Hill of Angels, The **10** (20 chs) 4 May–21 Sep 1889
His Great Reward **20** (4 chs) 4–25 Mar 1899
Honor Grant **3** 10 Jun 1882
Houseful of Girls, A **22** (27 chs) 6 Oct 1900–6 Apr 1901
How Helen Was Won **25** (4 chs) 6–27 Aug 1904
How Ida's Loneliness Departed **27** (4 chs) 1–29 Sep 1906
'If Loving Hearts Were Never Lonely – '; or, Madge Harcourt's Desolation **19** (28 chs) 2 Oct 1897–26 Mar 1898
In a Breton Castle **14 Summer** 1893
In Spite of All **19** (24 chs) 16 Apr–24 Sep 1898
Ivy Green, The: A Sequel to ''Twas in a Crowd' **4** (4 chs) 5–26 May 1883
Joy After Sorrow: An Old-World Romance **22** (5 chs) 5–26 Jan 1901
Kathleen's 'Handful' **11** (23 chs) 5 Oct 1889–8 Mar 1890
'La Génte Anglaise': A Sketch of Bohemian Life **8** (7 chs) 25 Jun–16 Jul 1887
Laura Leigh: A Tale of Highbridge Paper Mills **4** (17 chs) 7 Oct 1882–3 Mar 1883
Life's Trivial Round **21** (24 chs) 7 Oct 1899–17 Mar 1900
Little Country Maid, A **14 Christmas** 1892
Little Girl in Grey, The: A Story of Two Continents **14** (15 chs) 8 Oct 1892–21 Jan 1893
Little Miss Muffet **14** (24 chs) 1 Oct 1892–18 Mar 1893
Little Old Maid's Romance, The **28 Christmas** 1906
Lonely Christmas, A **26 Christmas** 1904
Lonely Lassie, A **13** (22 chs) 3 Oct 1891–12 Mar 1892
Long Lane with a Turning, A **4** (23 chs) 7 Apr–8 Sep 1883
Lost Flora, The **4 Summer** 1883
Love or Lucre **25 Christmas** 1903
Love Versus Money **10** (3 chs) 8–22 June 1889
Maiden of Dreams, A **25** (27 chs) 3 Oct 1903–2 Apr 1904

292   Fiction

Making of Elsa, The **28 Christmas** 1906
Margaret: A Sketch on Board Ship **1** 14 Feb 1880
Margaret Dane **7 Summer** 1886
Margaret Hetherton **22** (28 chs) 13 Oct 1900–20 Apr 1901
Margaret's Neighbours **4** (12 instalments) 21 Oct 1882–29 Sep 1883
Martin Spencer's Luck: A Story of Mendelssohn's Christmas Music **7 Christmas** 1885
Mary Robertson; or, The Power of Good over Evil **22** (6 chs) 7–28 Sep 1901
Master of Sedgewick Hall, The **21** (3 chs) 14–28 Jul 1900
Melany's Keepsake: A Story in Ten Chapters **14 Summer** 1893
Michaelmas Daisy **2** (21 chs) 7 May–24 Sep 1881
Mildred Ashcroft **3 Summer** 1882
Milly's Christmas Guest **11 Christmas** 1889
Minister's Boxes, The **31** Apr 1910
Miss Angel's Last Christmas **10 Christmas** 1888
Miss Brewson and Miss Smith **14** 29 Oct 1892
Miss Pringle's Pearls **9** (23 chs) 21 Apr–29 Sep 1888
Modern Martyr, A **13 Christmas** 1891
More About Peggy **21** (27 chs) 14 Oct 1899–14 Apr 1900
More About Pixie **24** (32 chs) 4 Oct 1902–9 May 1903
Mountain Idyl, A: An Episode from the Life of Ludwig II, King of Bavaria **13 Summer** 1892
Mountain Path, The **6** (24 chs) 4 Oct 1884–28 Mar 1885
Mrs. Deacon Brown **28 Christmas** 1906
My Father's Ward **14** (4 chs) 5–26 Nov 1892
My Godfather's Present **14** (3 chs) 2–16 Sep 1893
My Home in the Close **13** (4 chs) 7–28 Nov 1891
My Little Boy Blue **16 Summer** 1895
Next-Door Neighbours: A Story for Girls **14** (26 chs) 1 Apr–23 Sep 1893
Nobody's Holiday **10 Summer** 1889
'Not in Vain' **17** (4 chs) 4–25 Jan 1896
Old Dutch House, An **4** (4 chs) 2–30 Dec 1882
Old Maids' Christmas, The **20 Christmas** 1898
On the Cromer Cliffs **6 Summer** 1885
One Little Vein of Dross **9** (24 chs) 8 Oct 1887–21 Apr 1888
One Summer-Time **19 Summer** 1898
One Woman's Story **28 Christmas** 1906
Only a Commercial Traveller **15 Summer** 1894
Only a Girl-Wife **7** (25 chs) 3 Oct 1885–1 May 1886
'Only a Professional' **9 Summer** 1888
Other Peoples Stairs (New Serial Story) **17** (27 chs) 28 Mar–26 Sep 1896
Our Bessie **10** (24 chs) 6 Oct 1888–23 Mar 1889
Our Café Chantant **22 Summer** 1891
Our Connie **11 Christmas** 1889
'Our Little Genius' **15** (4 chs) 5–26 May 1889
Peters Pudding, The **32** Nov 1910
Pixie O'Shaughnessy **23** (30 chs) 5 Oct 1901–26 Apr 1902

'Poor Little Helpless Thing' **31** Oct 1909
Portrait on the Wall, The **31** Feb 1910
Pro and Con **28** (27 chs) 13 Oct 1906–13 Apr 1907
'Rebels' **25** (13 chs) 10 Oct–26 Dec 1903
Repentance of the Smalleys, The **31** Dec 1909
Romance of a Summer Night, A **3 Summer** 1882
Runaway Equator, The **32** (12 chs) Feb–Jun 1911
Ruth Thornton's Wanderjahr; or, Two Girls and a Summer **27** (25 chs) 7 Apr–22 Sep 1906
Sackcloth and Ashes **13** (26 chs) 9 Apr–24 Sep 1892
Scot's Thistle, A **22** (24 chs) 13 Apr–21 Sep 1901
Sensitive Plant, A **29** (25 chs) 5 Oct 1907–21 Mar 1908
Sheila: A Story for Girls **20** (8 chs) 8 Apr–27 May 1899
    Continues under 'Sheila's Cousin Effie: A Story for Girls'
Sheila's Cousin Effie: A Story for Girls **20** (18 chs) 3 Jun–30 Sep 1899
Silent Strings **23** (17 chs) 5 Oct 1901–8 Feb 1902
'Sister Warwick': A Story of Influence **20** (4 chs) 3–31 Dec 1898
Sisters Three **19** (27 chs) 2 Oct 1897–9 Apr 1898
'Sonny'; or, The Jilting of Bruce Heriot **24** (27 chs) 11 Oct 1902–11 Apr 1903
Story of a Bracelet, The **24** (4 chs) 6–27 Jun 1903
Story of a Christmas Carol, The **22 Christmas** 1900
Story of a Summer, The **11** (4 chs) 5–26 Jul 1890
Story of an Angle Window, A **8 Summer** 1887
Story of 1857, A **16** (2 chs) 1, 8 Jun 1895
Studio Mariano, The **13** (24 chs) 3 Oct 1891–2 Apr 1892
Sweet-Gale **15 Summer** 1894
Tangled Web, A **24 Christmas** 1902
Taught His Way: The Story of a Life's Purpose **6** (4 chs) 7–28 Feb 1885
That Horrid Boy Next Door **18** 6 Mar 1897
'That Peculiar Miss Artleton' **19** (4 chs) 7–28 May 1898
'The Greatest of All' **25** (4 chs) 5–26 Mar 1904
Thomasina's Mission **29** (5 chs) 1–29 Feb 1908
Three Christmas Eves **28** (3 scenes) 1–15 Dec 1906
Three Girls and a Garden **28** (4 chs) 3–24 Aug 1907
Three Old Maids of Leigh, The **17** (4 chs) 5–19 Oct 1895
Three Years of a Girl's Life **1** (17 chs) 5 Jun–25 Sep 1880
Tiny's Birthday **5 Summer** 1884
Toy Symphony, The **7 Christmas** 1885
Transformed: A New Serial Story **8** (9 chs) 23 Jul–17 Sep 1887
Travelling Companions, A: A New Fairy Story (Adventure No. 197) **27** (2 chs) 3, 10 Mar 1906
Two Christmas Days in a Girl's Life **20 Christmas** 1898
Two Strong Wills **29** (3 chs) 7–21 Dec 1907
Unattractive Girl, An **3** (3 chs) 1–22 Apr 1882
Uncle Caleb's Choice **17 Christmas** 1895
Up the Steep Hillside **13** (4 chs) 4–25 Jun 1892
Vera; or, A Good Match **8 Christmas** 1886

294 *Fiction*

Victory Is in Truth **9** (4 chs) 3–24 Dec 1887
Visit to Ireland, A **26** (4 chs) 6–27 May 1905
Wards of St. Margaret's, The **15** (26 chs) 24 Feb–18 Aug 1894
'Wandering Wings' **11 Summer** 1890
What Laura Realised **31** May 1910
Whisperer, The **4 Christmas** 1882
Wild Orchises **18 Summer** 1897
Wilful Ward, A **16** (23 chs) 27 Apr–28 Sep 1895
Winifred's Home **17** (6 chs) 18 Apr–5 Sep 1896
Work, Wait, Win **11** (27 chs) 12 Oct 1889–19 Apr 1900
Wrapped in the Robe of Mercy **1** 11 Sep 1880
Writer for the Press, A: A True Story of Modern London Life **24** (26 chs) 25 Oct 1902–12 Sep 1903
Wrong Colour, The: A Christmas Story **10 Christmas** 1888
Yielding of Elinor Grantly, The **30** Sep 1909

Stories about music compositions

Ballad Stories, Suggested by Popular Songs: Twickenham Ferry **1** 28 Feb 1880
Banbury Cross: A Ballad Story **2** 27 Nov 1880
Blue Alsatian Mountains, The **1** 20 Mar 1880
Charity: A Ballad Story **4** 25 Nov 1882
Children's Home, The: A Ballad Story **1** 17 Jul 1880
Child's Mission, The: A Ballad Story **2** 13 Aug 1881
Erl-King, The: A Schubert Fantasy **24** 4 Oct 1902
Lights of London Town, The: A Ballad Story **1** 26 Jun 1880
Linden-Tree, The: A Schubert Fantasy **24** (2 parts) 11, 18 Jul 1903
My Treasures: A Ballad Story **2** 2 Jul 1881
Once Again: A Ballad Story **1** 28 Aug 1880
Organ-Grinder, The: A Schubert Fantasy **24** (2 parts) 3, 10 Jan 1903
Songs Without Music: 'Darby and Joan' **2** 30 Oct 1880
Stories in Music **22** (5 parts) Part 1 Three Caprices by Mendelssohn, Op. 16 (27 Oct 1900); Part 2 Chopin's Two Nocturnes, Op. 37 (15 Dec 1900); Part 3 Schumann's Novelettes Prelude, I, II, III (16 Feb 1901); Part 4 Schumann's Novelettes IV, V (6 Apr 1901); Part 5 Schumann's Novelettes VI, VII, VIII (29 Jun 1901)
Stories of Famous Songs, The **9** 24 Dec 1887
Stories of Famous Songs, The: 'Auld Robin Gray' **9** 5 Nov 1887
Stories of Famous Songs, The: 'Home, Sweet Home', 'Sally in Our Alley' **9** 8 Sep 1888
Stories of Famous Songs, The: The American Marching Song, 'John Brown' **9** 12 May 1888
Stories of Famous Songs, The: The 'Marseillaise' **9** 14 Jan 1888
Stories of Famous Songs, The: 'The Village Blacksmith', 'Excelsior', 'The Old Clock on the Stairs **10** 3 Nov 1888

Stories of Famous Songs, The: 'The Watch on the Rhine', 'What Is the German's Fatherland?', 'The Sword Song' **10** 9 Feb 1889
Stories of Famous Songs, The: 'There's Nae Luck About the House' **9** 11 Feb 1888
Stream of Life, The: A Ballad Story **2** 19 Feb 1881
'The Children of the City' **2** 16 Apr 1881
Timothy's Welcome: A Ballad Story **1** 18 Sep 1880
Turnham Toll **1** 29 May 1880
Twenty-One **2** 19 Mar 1881
'When the Tide Comes In': A Ballad Story **2** 11 Dec 1880
Withered Flowers: A Schubert Fantasy **24** 19 Sep 1903
'Won't You Buy My Pretty Flowers?' **1** 24 Apr 1880
Worker, The: A Ballad Story **2** 22 Jan 1881
'Years Ago': A Ballad Story **2** 28 May 1881

Index to nonfiction

Biography

Artistic Life of Louisa Pyne, The **14** (6 chs) 15 Oct 1892–25 Mar 1893
Beethoven **15** (2 parts) 4 Nov, 9 Dec 1893
Blind Girl Organist, A **25** 19 Mar 1904
Cecil Frances Alexander **17** 18 Jan 1896
Chat with Miss Marie Hall, A **24** 2 May 1903
Christine Nilsson **13** 20 Aug 1892
Clara Schumann **4** 22 Sep 1883
Deborah: Poet and Musical Composer **9** 30 Jun 1888
Frances Ridley Havergal **9** 7 Jul 1888
Franz Schubert **19** 17 Sep 1898
Frau Dr. Clara Schumann: A Short Sketch of Her Life **13** 27 Feb 1892
From the Artistic World: The Diary of the Early Artistic Days of Natalie Janotha **11** (3 parts) 26 Apr–7 Jun 1890
Great Singer, A: Madame Tetrazzini **29** 25 Jan 1908
Handel **16** (2 parts) 13 Apr, 11 May 1895
Handel's Mother **9** 23 Jun 1888
Henry Purcell: The Pioneer of English Opera **20** 12 Nov 1898
In Memoriam [Mrs Meadows White] **6** 31 Jan 1885
Johann Sebastian Bach **19** 15 Jan 1898
John Field: The Pioneer of the Romantic School of Music **21 Summer** 1900
Love-Story of the Schumanns, The **31** Jun 1910
Madame Schumann **17** 27 Jun 1896
Mademoiselle Janotha and Her Cat: An Interview with 'White Heather' **23** 12 Oct 1901
Mendelssohn **15** (2 parts) 13 Jan, 10 Feb 1894
Miss Kathleen Purcell: Solo Harpist **23** 19 Oct 1901
Mozart: His Life and Influence on the Development of Pianoforte Literature **16** (2 parts) 10, 17 Aug 1895
Mrs. Hemans **10** 4 May 1889
New Violinist, The **1** 18 Sep 1880
Paderewski as a Composer **19** 19 Mar 1898
Romanticism of Beethoven, The **20** 9 Sep 1899

Signorina Teresina Tua **5** 12 Apr 1884
Sir John Stainer: A Recollection **22 Summer** 1901
Some Celebrated Musicians **13** (3 parts) St. Cecilia 16 Jan 1892, Sappho 23 Apr 1892, Jenny Lind 4 Jun 1892
'The Father of the Symphony': Joseph Haydn **19** 18 Jun 1898
Thomas Arne (The English Amphion) **20** 3 Jun 1899
Word About Herr Rosenthal the Pianist, A **17** 22 Feb 1896

Business

Charity Concerts and 'At Homes' **25** 2 Apr 1904
Conductors Continued **24** 22 Aug 1903
Failures of the Business Girl, The **22** (Part 2) 6 Apr 1901
Further Gossip About Musicians **22** 20 Jul 1901
How Musicians Live **26** (2 parts) 4 Feb, 18 Mar 1905
More Chit-Chat About Singers **22** 22 Dec 1900
Music as a Profession for Girls **25** (6 parts) 31 Oct 1903–24 Sep 1904
Musical Odds and Ends **24** 4 Jul 1903
Note for Our Musical Readers, A **31** Jun 1910
Some Singers I Have Met **22** 20 Oct 1900
Why So Many Students Fail in the Musical Profession **30** Feb 1909
Work of a Professional Singer, The **28** (2 parts) 27 Oct 1906, 26 Jan 1907

Church

Amateur Choir Teacher, The **8** 4 Dec 1886
Amateur Choirs; Their Organisation and Training **7** 5 Jun 1886
Amateur Church Organist, The **8** 2 Oct 1886
How Our Brothers May Earn Their Schooling **22** 13 Apr 1901
How to Make a Church Sing **31** Nov 1909
Hymns I Have Heard in Strange Surroundings **30** Apr 1909
Music and Scripture **6** 19 Sep 1885
On Part-Singing **2** 4 Dec 1880
On Singing Sacred Music **4** 18 Nov 1882
Singing in Church **5** 12 Apr 1884
Something About Hymns Written by Women **29** (3 parts) 25 Jul–26 Sep 1908
Women as Hymn Writers **6** 16 May 1885
Women as Hymn Writers, and What They Have Done **6** 28 Feb 1885

Competitions

Competition for Professional Girls, A **18** 24 Oct 1896
Competition for Professional Girls: The Five Prize Essays **18** 27 Mar 1897
Competition in Musical Composition, A **9** 15 Oct 1887
Fidelio Club, The **24** 27 Jun 1903
Fidelio Club, The **25** 31 Oct 1903
Fidelio Club, The **27** 24 Feb 1906

Girl's Own Questions and Answers Competition, The **20** 15 Oct, 12 Nov, 26 Nov, 10 Dec 1898
Girl's Own Questions and Answers, The: The Examiners Report on the First Twenty-Four Questions **20** 4 Mar 1899
Girl's Own Questions and Answers, The: The Examiners Report on the Second Twenty-Four Questions **20** 22 Apr 1899
Girl's Own Questions and Answers, The: The Examiners Report on the Third and Last Twenty-Four Questions **20** 13 May 1899
Music Competition **24** 25 Oct 1902
Music Competition Result **24** 31 Jan 1903
Music Quotation Competition **27** 26 May 1906
New Prize Competition, A: The Girl's Own Questions and Answers, Being Our Own School of Interesting Information **20** 1 Oct 1898
New Questions and Answers Competition for Girls of All Ages, A **25** 12 Dec 1903
Our Competition for Professional Girls **18** 27 Feb 1897
Our New Prize Competitions **27** 28 Oct 1905
Our Next Musical Composition **9** 24 Mar 1888
Report on the Musical Competition **10** 15 Sep 1888
Result of the Competition in Musical Composition, The: The Best Settings of Longfellow's Poem, 'The Rainy Day' **9** 24 Mar 1888
Well Worth Taking Part In: A New Questions and Answers Competition for Girls of All Ages **25** 31 Oct 1903

Concerts

Chronicles of Sleepy Hollow, The **24** II. The Village Concert 16 May 1903
For Listeners at Instrumental Concerts **6** (2 parts) The Strings of the Orchestra 11 Oct 1884, Wind and Percussion Instruments 9 May 1885
How to Enjoy Orchestral Concerts **25** (11 parts) 17 Oct 1903–6 Aug 1904
Music in Social Life **16** 6 Oct 1894
My 'At Home', and How I Managed It **5** 9 Feb 1884
Popular Concerts, The **11** 18 Jan 1890
Winter Entertainments in Villages **4** 3 Mar 1883

Crafts and needlework

Art Needlework **10** 6 Jul 1889
Decorated Box-Seat or Music Coffer, A **23** 21 Dec 1901
Embroidered Pianoforte Back, An **20** 11 Mar 1899
How I Painted a Tambourine **16** 22 Jun 1895
How to Drape **14** (Part 2) 8 Apr 1893
Marquetry Wood-Staining **14** 29 Oct 1892
My Work Basket **1** 17 Apr 1880
My Work Basket **2** 16 Oct 1880
My Work Basket **2** 11 Dec 1880
My Work Basket **2** 18 Jun 1881
My Work Basket **4** 9 Jun 1883

Nonfiction with music as a topic   299

My Work Basket **8** 13 Aug 1887
New Idea for Treating a Piano Back, A **19** 14 May 1898
Novelties for the Christmas Tree **8 Christmas** 1886
Outline Embroidery **1** 22 May 1880
Painted Silk or Satin Pianoforte Front, A **19** 2 Oct 1897
Pianoforte Fronts: And How to Decorate Them **6** 4 Jul 1885
Pincushions **13** 23 Jan 1892
Pretty Pianoforte Back, A **18** 7 Aug 1897
Use for Old Pianos, A **13** 31 Oct 1891
Wood Engraving as an Employment for Girls **7** (Part 3) 29 May 1886

Entertainments

'Christmas Festivity': A Musical Acrostic for Juvenile Parties **3** 3, 10 Dec 1881
Christmas Games for Young and Old **3 Christmas** 1881
Fairy Governess, The: A Musical Story **20** 10 Dec 1898
'Felix Mendelssohn': A Musically Illustrated Recitation **17** 2 May 1896
French and Swiss Rounds **15** 12 May 1894
Happiness: A Poetic Drama in One Act **28** 6, 13 Oct 1906
Jack Frost and the Christmas Fairy: An Interlude **29 Christmas** 1907
Little Sunbeam and Her Fairy Godmother: A Play for Female Characters Only
    29 Christmas 1907
May Play, A **26** 1 Apr 1905
Old Ballad, An **27** 9 Jun 1906
Old Daddy Christmas: A Musical Allegory **13 Christmas** 1891
Out-Door Games from Over the Sea **13** (5 parts) 24 Oct 1891–6 Feb 1892
Pedlar, The: A Pastoral **12 Christmas** 1890
Queen of Arcadee, The: Pastoral Operetta **11 Christmas** 1889
'The Frog Who Would a-Wooing Go' **20 Christmas** 1898

Fashion

Concert Wrap of White Chiffon and Lace with a Hood **28** 9 Mar 1907
Correct Clothing, and How It Should Be Made **4** 25 Nov 1882
Dress: in Season and in Reason **6** 26 Sep 1885
Dress: In Season and in Reason **7** 27 Feb 1886
Dress: In Season and in Reason **7** 29 May 1886
Dress: In Season and in Reason **7** 28 Aug 1886
Dress: In Season and in Reason **11** 26 Oct 1889
Dress of the Month, The **1** 27 Mar 1880
Dress of the Month, The **1** 15 May 1880
Dress of the Month, The **1** 24 Jul 1880
Girls' Attire for March **26** 25 Feb 1905
Girl's Dress in Japan, A **25** 2 Apr 1904
How a Girl Should Dress **28** 29 Jun 1907
My Clothes Month by Month **21** 30 Dec 1899
Seasonable Dress and How to Make It **2** 26 Mar 1881

300 *Nonfiction with music as a topic*

Fidelio Club

Fidelio Club, The **23** 12 Oct, 30 Nov, 28 Dec 1901; 25 Jan, 29 Mar, 26 Apr, 31 May, 28 Jun 1902¹

Fidelio Club, The **24** 29 Nov, 27 Dec 1902; 31 Jan, 28 Feb, 28 Mar, 18 Apr, 30 May, 27 Jun, 25 Jul, 26 Sep 1903

Fidelio Club, The **25** 31 Oct, 28 Nov, 26 Dec 1903; 30 Jan, 27 Feb, 26 Mar, 30 Apr, 28 May, 25 Jun, 30 Jul, 27 Aug 1904

Fidelio Club, The **26** 29 Oct, 19 Nov, 24 Dec 1904; 21 Jan, 25 Feb, 25 Mar, 22 Apr, 27 May, 17 Jun 1905

Fidelio Club, The **27** 28 Oct, 25 Nov, 30 Dec 1905; 20 Jan, 24 Feb, 24 Mar, 21 Apr, 26 May, 23 Jun, 21 Jul, 18 Aug, 15 Sep 1906

Fidelio Club, The **28** 20 Oct, 24 Nov, 29 Dec 1906; 26 Jan, 23 Feb, 30 Mar, 27 Apr, 18 May, 29 Jun, 27 Jul, 24 Aug, 28 Sep 1907

Fidelio Club, The **29** 26 Oct, 30 Nov, 21 Dec 1907; 25 Jan, 29 Feb, 28 Mar, 25 Apr, 23 May, 27 Jun, 29 Aug, 19 Sep 1908

Hints

Discoloured Pianoforte Keys **2** 30 Apr 1891

Instrument purchase, maintenance and construction

Girls as Pianoforte Tuners: A New Remunerative Employment **8** 23 Apr 1887

How to Choose a Pianoforte, and Keep It in Order **7** (4 parts) 17 Jul–18 Sep 1886

How to Purchase a Piano and Keep It in Good Order **2** 27 Aug 1881

How to Take Care of a Violin **8** 19 Feb 1887

On the Tuning of Stringed Instruments **5** 15 Aug 1884

Music education

How French Girls Are Employed **13** 7 Nov 1891

Music and Method at a German Conservatoire **6** 17 Jan 1885

Music Students and Their Work **21** 11 Aug 1900

Musical Art in Florence **18** (Letter 2) 5 Jun 1897

Musical Degrees for Our Girls **19** 19 Feb 1898

Musical Education in Germany and in England **27** 21 Oct 1905

My Musical Training; or, What I Did with a Hundred Pounds **9** (2 parts) 1, 8 Oct 1887

Preparing for the Musical Examinations **31** Dec 1909

Royal Conservatorium of Music at Leipzig, The **9 Summer** 1888

Student-Life in Florence **18** (letters 1, 3–7) 24 Apr–18 Sep 1897
   Letter 2 under 'Musical Art in Florence'

Violin, The – Its Pains and Pleasures **12** 1. Gradus ad Parnassum 7 Feb 1891

Music history and appreciation

Amateurs in Music **26** 22 Oct 1904

Anecdote of Haydn **2** 13 Aug 1881

Coalies' Baby, and How I Came to Adopt It, The **24** 20 Dec 1902
Edelweiss: Note on Mademoiselle Janotha's Pianoforte Piece **12** 7 Mar 1891
England's Musical Past **17** 8 Aug 1896
Girls Then and Now: Musical **24** 22 Nov 1902
Glee Maidens, The **13** 16 Jul 1892
Harpsichord Revival, The **22** 24 Aug 1901
Historical Sketches of Musical Forms **8** (5 sketches) 23 Oct 1886–23 Apr 1887
Historical Sketches of Musical Forms **9** 24 Dec 1887
How Rubenstein Taught Me to Play **30** May 1909
Jubilee Singers at Grosvenor House, The **6** 25 Jul 1885
Letter on Musical Rhythm, A **7** 19 Jun 1886
Mittenwald and Its Violins (8 chs) **10** 24 Nov 1888–8 Jun 1889
Modern Women Song-Writers **17** 2 Nov 1895
Music Among the Working Girls of London **11** 9 Aug 1890
Music of Jane Austen, The **28** 5 Jan 1907
Music of Poland, The **31** Dec 1909
Music of the Emerald Isle, The **14** 20 May 1893
Musical Composers **1** 8 May 1880
Musical Graces Before and After Meat **3** 22 Jul 1882
Musical Notes **5** 16 Aug 1884
Notes on Songs of Longfellow, and Some Musical Settings **15** 15 Sep 1894
Notes on Songs of Tennyson: with Reference to Their Musical Settings **13** 12 Mar 1892
Popular Christmas Festivities in Naples **17 Christmas** 1895
Professor Ševčík and His Pupils **25** 9 Jul 1904
Some Remarks on Modern Pianoforte Playing **12** 13 Jun 1891
Songs of Tyrol **11 Summer** 1890
St. Cecilia's Day at Rome **14 Christmas** 1892
Village Bands **6** 8 Nov 1884
Violin – Its Pains and Pleasures, The **12** II. Parnassus 14 Mar 1891
Violins and Mittenwald **10** (Ch. 1) 3 Oct 1888
    Continued under 'Mittenwald and Its Violins'
Water-Sprite and the Violin, The **25** 9 Jul 1904
Women and Music **2** 17 Sep 1881
Women Workers' Songs **16** 6 Apr 1895

Music mentioned in general nonfiction

Anne Beale, Governess and Writer: Extracts from Her Diary **22** (Part 4) 24 Nov 1900
Art of Packing, The **6 Summer** 1885
Bachelors in Central Italy, The **9** 2 Jun 1888
Band of Hope, The (Stay-at-Home Girls) **7** 11 Sep 1886
Battersea Polytechnic, The **25** 2 Jul 1904
Beatrice: A Study for Girls **16** (Part 1) 8 Jun 1895
Beauty of Evenness, The **12** 25 Apr 1891

302   *Nonfiction with music as a topic*

Begin Where You Are **32** Mar 1911
Bessie Gilbert **13** 14 Sep 1892
Birthday Page, The **23** 26 Oct 1901; 25 Jan, 29 Mar, 28 Jun, 26 Jul, 30 Aug, 20 Sep 1902
Birthday Page, The **25** 28 May 1904
Black and White Heroism: Stories from the Abolition Crusade **12** (Part 3) 13 Dec 1890
Care of the Voice, The **1** 17 Jul 1880
Christianity and My Work **25** 9 Apr 1904
Christmas Day in a London Hospital **11 Christmas** 1889
Chronicles of Sleepy Hollow, The IV. The Harvest Festival **24** 5 Sep 1903
Cold Potatoes, and What to Do with Them **28** 2 Mar 1907
Common Errors in Daily Life III. Errors in Taste **5** 5 Jan 1884
Common Errors of Speech **22 Summer** 1901
Daughter of the House, The **16** 6 Jul 1895
Duties of an Asylum Nurse, The **25** 23 Apr 1904
Editor's Page, The **30** Feb 1909
Editor's Page, The **31** Sep, Dec 1909
Educational Classes: Y.W.C.A. **9** 9 Jun 1888
Effie's Afternoon Tea **4** (2 chs) 21, 28 Jul 1883
Erinna Club, The: A New Club for Literary Girls **26** 18 Mar 1905
Erinna Club, The: A Literary Club for Girls **28** 15 Dec 1906
Etiquette for Ladies and Girls **1** 26 Jun 1880
Every-Day Pictures from the 'Simple Life' **27** 23 Jun 1906
Extracts from Women's Writings **27** 10 Mar, 7 Apr 1906
Fit of the Blues, A **14** 11 Feb 1893
Foundation of All Good Breeding, The **2** 30 Oct 1880
Four Periods, The: I. School-Life **3** 19 Nov 1881
French Girls **5** 17 Nov 1883
Genius or Perseverance **4** 6 Jan 1883
Girl Who Was Heir to the Throne, A: Some Incidents in the Life of Princess Charlotte (Part 1) **25** 3 Oct 1903
Girl-Poets of To-day, The **25** 7 May 1904
Girls and Their Pocket-Money **18** 3 Apr 1897
Girls as I Have Known Them **20** (6 parts) 29 Oct 1898–20 May 1899
Girls as Students **21** 30 Jun 1900
Girls' Friendships **8** (4 chs) 9 Oct 1886–5 Feb 1887
Girls of Fifty Years Ago and Now **22** 5 Jan 1901
Girls of Today, The **11** 21 Dec 1889
Girl's Own, The: An Occasional Page of Amateur Contributions **2** 3 Sep 1881
Girl's Own, The: An Occasional Page of Amateur Contributions **3** 31 Dec 1881, 8 Apr 1882
'Girl's Own' Musical Calendar for 1886, The **7 Christmas** 1885
Girton College **1** 31 Jul 1880
'Glorified' Workmen's Dwellings **19** (Part 2) 4 Jun 1898
Good Taste as a Guest **31** Jan 1910

Nonfiction with music as a topic 303

Guarding Queens When on Their Holiday **32** Aug 1911
Hour a Day, An **8 Christmas** 1886
Household Harmony **10 Christmas** 1888
How Business Girls are Housed **30** Sep 1909
How to Form a Small Library **2** (Part 2) **2** 20 Nov 1880
How to See Rome in a Week and Apply Its Lessons **28** 20 Oct 1906
Human Voice, The **24** 3 Jan 1903
'I Publish the Bans of Marriage'; or, My Sister's Wedding, and How We Organized It' **14** (2 parts) 15, 22 Apr 1893
King and Queen of the Belgians, The **31** Mar 1910
Life-Story of Her Majesty Queen Mary, The **32** Feb 1911
Little Kindnesses **12 Summer** 1891
Living in Lodgings **16** 27 Jul 1895
London Y.W.C.A. **11** 28 Dec 1889
Making of a Useless Woman, The **32** Mar 1911
Marconigrams **27** 10 Feb 1906
Margaret Dicksee, Painter **27** 14 Oct 1905
Mind and the Health, The **3** 19 Nov 1881
'My Long Life. By Mary Cowden Clarke' **18 Summer** 1897
Nativity and Art, The **29** Christmas 1907
New Books **25** 23 Apr 1904
New Editor of the 'G.O.P.', The: An Interview with Miss Flora Klickmann **29** 19 Sep 1908
New Employments for Girls **13** (2 parts) 10 Oct 1891, 5 Mar 1892
North London Collegiate School for Girls, The **3** 29 Apr 1882
Norwegian Folklore **27** (3 chs) 4–18 Aug 1906
Occupation for Girls That Is Remunerative, Interesting and Not Over-Crowded, An **25** 16 Jan 1904
On Making the Best of It **21** 12 May 1900
Our Ain Fireside **6 Christmas** 1884
Our Christmas Treat to the Poor **4 Christmas** 1882
Our Cooking Class: Roasting **1** 3 Jan 1880
Our Holiday in Quimper **5** (2 parts) 9, 30 Aug 1884
Our Life in a Country Village: An Actual Experience **14** 16 Sep 1893
Our Own Colleges **1** 7 Aug 1880
Our Poets' Corner: Reginald Heber (1783) **14** 12 Aug 1893
Our Poets' Corner: William Cowper **14** 1 Apr 1893
Parisian School Eighty Years Ago, A **27** 27 Jan 1906
Physical Education of Girls, The **5** 17 May 1884
Plain Words to Schoolgirls **13** 7 Nov 1891
Progress of Women's Work, The **15** (Part 2) 13 Jan 1894
Queen at Home, The **15** 3 Mar 1894
Quiver of Quotations, A **20** 10 Jun 1899
Rules of Society **20** (Part 2) 3 Dec 1898
School-Day Remembrances **12** 1 Aug 1891
Schoolgirl Troubles, and How to Cope with Them **11** 22 Mar 1890

304   *Nonfiction with music as a topic*

   Sloane Garden House **12** 16 May 1891
   'So Pleasant' **18 Christmas** 1896
   Some Plans for the Immediate Future **30** Nov 1908
   Some Types of Girlhood; or, Our Juvenile Spinsters **12** (3 parts) 4 Oct 1890–17 Jan 1891
   Some Words in Season **21** 21 Apr 1900
   Sorrows of Girlhood **19** (Part 4) 2 Apr 1898
   Stay-at-Home Girls: Our Y.W.C.A. Branch **7** 10 Apr 1886
   Three Social Evenings **7** 7 Nov 1885
   Thoughts on the Higher Education of Women **12** 8 Aug 1891
   ''Twas Johnnie's Favourite Song' **17** 16 May 1896
   Two of the Greatest Afflictions of Girlhood: Blushing and Nervousness **20** 21 Jan 1889
   What Girls Can Do to Hush 'The Bitter Cry' **5** 2 Aug 1884
   What Would You Like to Be? **3** 12 Nov 1891
   When a Girl Becomes a Wife **30** Nov 1908
   Wild Flower Letter, A **25** 23 Jan 1904
   Women of Intellect: Jane Austen **3** 11 Mar 1882
   Women's Clubs in London **11** (Part 2) 26 Jul 1890
   Work for All **5** I. Introductory, II. Teaching 13 Oct 1893; Music 1 Mar 1884
   Wrinkles, But Not Facial! **29** 18 Jan 1908

Odds and Ends

   [Harp, The] **16** 21 Sep 1895
   [Jenny Lind] **17** 9 Nov 1895
   [Organ Grinders] **17** 9 Nov 1895
   [Spiders and Music] **18** 20 Mar 1897
   [Ugliness of the Piano] **16** 18 May 1895

Opinion pieces

   Amateurs in Music **26** 22 Oct 1904
   Art of Accompanying, The: A Vocalist's Complaint **16** 5 Jan 1895
   English Girl of To-morrow, The **30** (3 parts) Nov 1908–Jan 1909
   Expression in Music **29** 14 Dec 1907
   Higher Thoughts on Girls' Occupations: Music **4** 29 Sep 1883
   Higher Thoughts on Housekeeping **5** 12 Jan 1884
   How a Girl should Study the Pianoforte **30** Nov 1908
   How an Artiste May Help Her Audience **31** Jun 1910
   How Music Speaks to Those Who Hear **21** 2 Dec 1899
   More About Accompaniments **16** 13 Apr 1895
   'Music–Not Money' **31** Oct 1909
   On Taste in the Choice of Songs **6** (4 letters) 21 Mar–1 Aug 1885
   On the Art of Accompanying Suggested by an Article in the 'G.O.P.' **16** 30 Mar 1895

Plea for Music, A **5** (letters 2–7) 26 Jan–19 Jul 1884
   Letter 1 under 'Power of Music'
Power of Music, The **5** (Letter 1) 15 Dec 1883
Singers and Singing **18** (2 parts) 24 Oct, 14 Nov 1896
Things of This World **32** Aug 1911
Touching the Pianoforte **8** 12 Mar 1887
What a Piano-Player Can and Cannot Do **31** Jan 1910
What Is 'a Correct Musical Taste'? **2** 6 Nov 1880
What Money Is Really Good For **30** Dec 1908
What Our Girls May Do **1** 17 Jul 1880

Primers for performance and teaching

Diction and Phrasing in Song **29** 4 Jul 1908
Embellishments of Song **29** 1 Aug 1908
Few Words on Musical Training, A **4** (2 parts) 31 Mar, 14 Apr 1883
Few Words on Voice-Production, A **27** (Part 1) 15 Sep 1906
Few Words on Voice-Production, A **28** (Part 2) 10 Aug 1907
Few Words on Voice-Production, A **29** (Part 3) 8 Feb 1908
Hints on Pianoforte Teaching **12** 1 Aug 1891
Hints on Practising Singing and Preserving the Voice **8** 22 Jan 1887
Hints on Practising the Voice **17** 12 Oct 1895
Home Accomplishments I. How to Sing a Song **1** 24 Jan 1880
How a Girl May Become a Professional Violinist **30** Aug 1909
How to Accompany a Song **1** 28 Aug 1880
How to Improve on the Violin **14** 1 Jul 1893
How to Improve the Voice **1** 26 Jun 1880
How to Improve Your Piano Playing **2** 2 Oct 1880
How to Make a Metronome **6** 4 Oct 1884
How to Play 'in Style' **30** Apr 1909
How to Play the Banjo **10** 1 Dec 1888
How to Play the Concertina **2** 30 Apr 1881
How to Play the Guitar **2** 26 Feb 1881
How to Play the Harmonium **1** 24 Jul 1880
How to Play the Harp **1** 25 Sep 1880
How to Play the Organ **1** 22 May 1880
How to Play the Piano **1** 13 Mar 1880
How to Play the Violin **1** 10 Apr 1880
How to Play the Zither **10** 1 Jun 1889
How to Sing at Sight **4** 2 Jun 1883
How to Sing in Oratorio **15** 7 Oct 1893
How to Sing in Public **2** 26 Mar 1881
How to Study My Compositions **30** Dec 1908
How to Teach the Elements of Music **10** 17 Aug 1889
Ladies' Bands and the Bâton **26** 8 Jul 1905

306 *Nonfiction with music as a topic*

    Mandolin, The **3** 14 Jan 1882
    Music at Home **7 Christmas** 1885
    Music-Copying as a Fine Art **18** 17 Oct 1896
    On Careful Treatment of the Voice (A Few Hints to Beginners) **11** 5 Oct 1889
    On Learning to Sing **8** 14 May, 17 Sep 1887
    On Method in Teaching the Pianoforte **2** 11 Jun 1881
    On Singing **8** 20 Aug 1887
    On Singing Sacred Music **4** 18 Nov 1882
    On Some Points of Deportment in Singing **20** 10 Jun 1899
    On the Human Voice **27** 6 Jan 1906
    On the Practice of Duet-Singing **11** 6 Sep 1890
    On the Technique of the Pianoforte: A Practical Talk to Earnest Students **12** 25 Oct 1890
    Pianoforte Fingering **15** 11 Aug 1894
    Pianoforte Practising **18** 10 Apr 1897
    Secrets of Good Pianoforte-Playing, The **30** Jan 1909
    Singing **5** (3 parts) 13 Oct–3 Nov 1883
    Study of Harmony, The **11** 14 Dec 1889
    'The Xylophone' **18** 13 Feb 1897
    Thoughts on Practising **3** 17 Jun 1882
    Use and Abuse of the Pedal, The **30** Mar 1909

Repertoire
    About Harvest Music **22** 21 Sep 1901
    Analysis of Beethoven's Sonata in G Minor, Op. 49, No. 1, An **8** 28 May 1887
    Art of Translating Verse for Music, The **10** 6 Oct 1888
    Beethoven's Sonata in E Flat, Op. 7: Analysis of Its Design and Harmony **9** 24 Mar 1888
    Christmastide Music **22 Christmas** 1900
    How to Play Beethoven's Sonatas **3** (4 parts) 8 Oct 1881–7 Jan 1882
    How to Play Mendelssohn's 'Songs Without Words' **2** (2 parts) 21, 28 May 1881
    Impressions of Celebrated Pianoforte Pieces **11** (2 parts) 12 Oct, 2 Nov 1889
    Mendelssohn's 'Song Without Words', in G, Op. 62, No. 4 **12** 11 Apr 1891
    Musical Design for Musical Babes: An Analysis of the Slow Movement of Beethoven's Sonata in D, Op. 28 **10** 20 Jul 1889
    Notes on Two Choral Works by Johannes Brahms I. German Requiem; II. A Song of Destiny **19** 20 Nov 1897
    Old Christmas Carols **4 Christmas** 1882
    Old Christmas Carols **6 Christmas** 1884
    On Taste in the Choice of Songs **6** (4 letters) 21 Mar–1 Aug 1885
    On the Choice of Pianoforte Pieces **9** (4 parts) 7 Jan–19 May 1888
    Pianoforte Duet Playing **10** 13 Oct 1888
    Pianoforte Duets and Pianoforte Duet Playing **10** (4 parts) 10 Nov 1888–9 Feb 1889

Something About Wedding Music **22 Summer** 1901
Winter Evening of Old English Music, A **9 Christmas** 1887

Reviews of printed music[2]

New Music **2** 29 Jan, 26 Feb, 26 Mar, 30 Apr, 28 May, 25 Jun, 30 Jul, 27 Aug, 10 Sep 1881
New Music **3** 22 Oct, 26 Nov, 10 Dec, 31 Dec 1881; 28 Jan, 18 Feb, 25 Feb, 18 Mar, 25 Mar, 8 Apr, 15 Apr, 22 Apr, 20 May, 3 Jun, 10 Jun, 24 Jun, 8 Jul, 15 Jul, 22 Jul, 5 Aug, 12 Aug, 19 Aug, 9 Sep, 23 Sep, 30 Sep 1882
New Music **4** 14 Oct, 21 Oct, 28 Oct, 18 Nov, 16 Dec, 30 Dec 1882; 6 Jan, 13 Jan, 3 Feb, 10 Feb, 17 Feb, 3 Mar, 17 Mar, 31 Mar, 14 Apr, 5 May, 19 May, 9 Jun, 14 Jul, 21 Jul, 11 Aug, 18 Aug, 8 Sep 1883
New Music **5** 13 Oct, 3 Nov 1883
Music **5** 17 Nov 1883
New Music **5** 8 Dec 1883; 12 Jan, 19 Jan, 2 Feb, 9 Feb, 8 Mar 1884
Music **5** 15 Mar 1884
New Music **5** 29 Mar, 12 Apr, 3 May, 17 May, 14 Jun, 21 Jun, 28 Jun, 5 Jul, 12 Jul, 26 Jul, 23 Aug 1884
New Music **6** 25 Oct, 1 Nov, 29 Nov, 13 Dec 1884; 10 Jan, 14 Feb, 21 Feb, 14 Mar, 25 Apr, 6 Jun, 11 Jul, 25 Jul, 15 Aug, 12 Sep 1885
New Music **7** 31 Oct, 12 Dec 1885; 9 Jan 1886
Music for the Month, The **7** 20 Feb, 27 Mar, 24 Apr, 22 May 1886
Notices of New Music **7** 26 Jun, 24 Jul 1886
Notices of New Music **8** 16 Oct, 20 Nov, 25 Dec 1886
New Music **8** 26 Feb 1887
Notices of New Music **8** 16 Apr, 28 May, 25 Jun, 16 Jul 1887
New Music **9** 22 Oct, 26 Nov 1887
Notices of New Music **9** 17 Dec, 31 Dec 1887; 28 Jan, 25 Feb, 24 Mar, 12 May, 23 Jun, 15 Sep 1888
Notices of New Music **10** 27 Oct, 24 Nov, 29 Dec 1888; 9 Feb 1889
New Music and Musical Events **10** 30 Mar 1889
New Music **10** 25 May 1889
New Music **11** 14 Dec 1889
Notices of New Music **11** 25 Jan, 29 Mar, 5 Apr, 13 Sep 1890
Notices of New Music **12** 25 Oct 1890; 28 Mar, 16 May, 11 Jul 1891
Notices of New Music **13** 29 Nov 1891; 18 Jun 1892
Notices of New Music **14** 29 Oct 1892; 28 Jan, 25 Mar 1893
Music **14** 17 Jun 1893
Notices of New Music **15** 21 Oct 1893; 3 Feb 1894
Notices of New Music **16** 3 Nov 1894
Some Soprano Songs for Girls **19** 27 Nov 1897
Some New Mezzo-Soprano Songs for Girls **19** 18 Dec 1897
Some Useful New Music **19** 9 Apr 1898
New Music: Some Pretty Vocal Duets and New Two-Part Songs for Girls **19** 23 Jul 1898
Some New Contralto Songs for Girls **19** 13 Aug 1898

308   *Nonfiction with music as a topic*

    Some New Sacred Songs **19** 20 Aug 1898
    New Helps to Music Study: For Younger Musicians **19** 10 Sep 1898
    Some New Guitar Music **20** 18 Mar 1899
    Some Holiday Music **20** 10 Jun 1899
    Useful Cantatas and Operettas for Girls **20** 2 Sep 1899
    Some New Light Pianoforte Pieces for Girls **21** 25 Nov 1899
    Some Pretty New Mandoline Music **21 Christmas** 1899
    Some Recent Violin and Violoncello Music **21** 20 Jan 1900
    New Songs for Sopranos **21** 21 Apr 1900
    Some New Contralto Songs for Girls **21** 5 May 1900
    Some New Patriotic Music **21** 21 Jul 1900
    Some New Vocal Duets **21** 11 Aug 1900
    Some New Pianoforte Music **21** 18 Aug 1900
    Solos and Song Accompaniments for Violoncello and Violin **22** 17 Aug 1901
    New Songs for Girls **23** 23 Nov 1901
    Some New Music **23** 21 Dec 1901
    Some Violin Music **23** 12 Apr 1902
    Some New Music (Various) **24** 14 Mar 1903
    New Songs for Girls **24** 16 May 1903

Royalty

    Music in the Royal Family **22** 2 Feb 1901
    Musical Queens **27** (3 parts) 2 Jun–22 Sep 1906
    Musical Queens **29** 26 Sep 1908
    Royal Musicians **21** (5 parts) 4 Nov 1899–22 Sep 1900

Self-improvement

    Between School and Marriage **7** 4 Sep 1886
    Evenings with Our Great Living Composers **4** (6 parts) 20 Jan–29 Sep 1993
    Girl's Outlook, The; or, What Is There to Talk About? **16** (10 parts) 24 Nov 1894–21 Sep 1895
    Girls' Year, The; or, January to December Spent with Pleasure and Profit **9** (12 parts) 29 Oct 1887–22 Sep 1888
    Hour a Day for a Year, An **8 Christmas** 1886
    How to Improve One's Education **2** (Part 2) 10 Sep 1881
    How We Sang Rounds and Catches **5 Summer** 1883
    'Just Out' **2** 20 Nov 1880

Varieties

    'A popular novel is like an organ' **28** 2 Mar 1907
    Advice to Lady Vocalists **4** 14 Oct 1882
    Advice to Musical Students **8** 2 Jul 1887
    Advice to Pianoforte Students **20 Summer** 1899
    Advice to Singers **26** 3 Dec 1904

Advice to Young Pianists **11** 7 Jun 1890
Alphabetical Note, An **4** 3 Feb 1883
Answer to Twelve Buried Musicians **21** 24 Mar 1900
Associations of Music, The **5** 29 Mar 1884
At an Evening Concert **4** 4 Nov 1882
'B.A. kindly sends us the following information' **17** 13 Jun 1896
Beethoven in Germany **8** 23 Oct 1886
Bird-Like **3** 4 Jun 1882
Black and White **6** 5 Sep 1885
Bridal Hymn **1** 22 May 1880
Classical Music **20** 1 Apr 1899
Composer and the Sea-Captain, The **8** 20 Nov 1886
Cottage Pianos **17** 12 Oct 1895
Cure for Deafness, A **11** 13 Sep 1890
Daughter's Criticism, A **7** 5 Dec 1885
Dawn of Genius, The **2** 11 Jun 1881
Delight in Praising **20** 1 Oct 1898
Diligent Practising **7** 6 Mar 1886
Divine Art of Music, The **14** 17 Jun 1893
Division of Time for the Musical, A **2** 5 Mar 1881
Dolls of a Musician, The **8** 20 Aug 1887
Early Start, An **21** 16 Dec 1899
Eccentric Organist, An **15** 8 Sep 1894
End of Music, The **4** 18 Nov 1882
Envying the Cats **14** 11 Mar 1893
Extraordinary Musical Feat, An **14** 24 Jun 1893
Famous Composer, A **22** 22 Dec 1900
Faults in Pianoforte Playing **8** 11 Jun 1887
Fifteen Minutes a Day **17** 18 Jan 1896
First-Rate Voices Are Rare **21** 11 Nov 1899
Foolish People **17** 23 May 1896
For All Who Have to Do with Church Music **23 Christmas** 1901
For Pianoforte Students **21** 4 Aug 1900
For the Musical **4** 16 Dec 1882
For Those Who Sing Out of Tune **2** 24 Sep 1881
From the Temple at Jerusalem **6** 11 Jul 1885
Girls and Singing **14** 13 May 1893
Good Musicians **16** 15 Dec 1894
Good Reasons for Learning Singing **8** 9 Mar 1887
Grave of Mozart, The **15 Summer** 1894
Greatest Effect in Music, The **2** 24 Sep 1881
Guitars in Fashion **6** 31 Jan 1885
Handel Made Simple **2** 20 Aug 1881
Have a Place Near the Music **23** 9 Aug 1902
Haydn in London **8** 16 Apr 1887
Haydn's Wife **8** 2 Jul 1887

310 *Nonfiction with music as a topic*

He Was Not Musical **15** 24 Mar 1894
'Her voice was sweet' **15** 26 May 1894
High and Low Notes **14** 25 Mar 1893
Highland Music **6** 13 Dec 1884
Hint for Singers, A **6** 18 Jul 1885
Hint to Singers, A **4** 7 Oct 1882
History of the Piano, The **7** 10 Oct 1885
How a Chinaman Described a Piano **16** 10 Aug 1895
How She Sang **18** 7 Aug 1897
How to Become an Intelligent Musician **1** 17 Jan 1880
How to Compose an Overture **3** 21 Jan 1882
How to Play at Sight **8** 19 Feb 1887
How to Practise Music **21** 21 Oct 1899
How Two Friends Parted **3** 15 Jul 1882
Hundred Guineas a Lesson, A **19** 21 May 1898
Impossible Music **22** 31 Aug 1901
In Dread of a Trumpet **11** 10 May 1890
In Praise of Good Music **3** 10 Dec 1881
In Praise of Music **8** 30 Jul 1887
'In the *Story of Music*' **23** 7 Jul 1902
Influence of Music, The **5** 5 Jul 1884
Intelligent Musician, An **1** 3 Jan 1880
Is It So? **17** 6 Jun 1896
Key is Fixed, The **26** 31 Dec 1904
Killed by Music **11** 30 Aug 1890
Left-Handed Compliment, A **18** 24 Jul 1897
Lesson for a Choir-Singer, A **20** 3 Dec 1898
Lesson in Music, A **8** 12 Mar 1887
Lover of Music, A **11** 11 Jan 1890
Lovers of Music **6** 11 Oct 1884
Making Melodies **1** 7 Feb 1880
Meaning in Music **20** 8 Jul 1899
Mendelssohn at the Piano **2** 20 Nov 1880
Modern Orpheus **6 Christmas** 1884
Moonlight Sonata, The **8** 2 Oct 1886
Motto for a Fiddler, A **23** 7 Jun 1902
Mozart as a Musical Prodigy **7** 1 May 1886
Mozart's Observations on a Lady's Pianoforte Playing **5** 19 Jul 1884
Murdering Music **7** 23 Jan 1886
Muscles and Piano-Playing **26** 25 Mar 1905
Music **12** 13 Dec 1890
Music **18** 15 May 1897
Music and Morals **5** 20 Sep 1884
Music as Medicine **11** 13 Sep 1890
Music at Home **22** 24 Aug 1901
Music Has Charms **17** 30 May 1896

Music, Heavenly Maid **18** 26 Dec 1896
Music in China **16** 9 Mar 1895
Music in Earnest **7** 24 Apr 1886
Music in Japan **17** 15 Aug 1896
Music in the Drawing-Room **2** 8 Jan 1881
Music in Type **6** 6 Dec 1884
Music of a Cheerful Heart, The **3** 11 Mar 1882
Music of a Cheerful Heart, The **12** 4 Jul 1891
Music of Rossini, The **6** 15 Aug 1885
Music of the Future, The **4 Summer** 1883
Music of the Future, The **10** 23 Mar 1889
Music of the Olden Time **17** 2 Nov 1895
Music Run Mad **8** 26 Feb 1887
Musical Advice **21** 18 Nov 1899
Musical Conundrum, A **26** 18 Mar 1905
Musical Critic, A **22** 9 Feb 1901
Musical Decoration **6** 20 Dec 1884
Musical Degree for Handel, A **12** 8 Nov 1890
Musical Enthusiasm **19** 20 Aug 1898
Musical Families **10** 6 Jul 1889
Musical Instruments **7** 20 Mar 1886
Musical Neighbours **22** 5 Jan 1901
Musical Performers **8** 12 Feb 1887
Musical Performers **20** 9 Sep 1899
Musical Progress **12** 15 Nov 1890
Musical Sister, A **19** 5 Feb 1898
Musical Success, A **26** 6 Mar 1905
Musical Surname, A **6** 5 Sep 1885
Musical Talent **6** 6 Jun 1885
Musicians, Take Note **17** 29 Aug 1896
National Anthem, The **23** 23 Nov 1901
New Church Organ, The **11** 7 Jun 1890
New Zealand Chants **6** 6 Dec 1884
No Pieces Sold Here **19** 6 Nov 1897
No Time to Play on It **20** 13 May 1899
Nonsense about Music **6** 4 Apr 1885
Not at All Musical **5** 2 Aug 1884
Note for Vocalists, A **7 Summer** 1886
Notes on the Bagpipes **8** 3 Sep 1887
Of What Use Is Music? **6** 4 Apr 1885
Old Air, An **6** 11 Jul 1885
On a Bad Singer **12** 4 Oct 1890
Ordinary Faults in Piano Playing **2** 24 Sep 1881
Our Advertisers **27** 4 Aug 1906
Out of Tune **17** 5 Oct 1895
Paying Music **15** 28 Oct 1893

Perfect Singing **7** 7 Nov 1885
Philosophic Musician, A **11** 11 Jan 1890
Piano, The **14** 1 Jul 1893
Piano Has Been Sold, The **20** 25 Feb 1899
Pianoforte, The **15** 15 Sep 1894
Pianoforte Practising **8** 20 Aug 1887
Player and Instrument **26** 1 Apr 1905
Playing and Paying **26** 15 Oct 1904
Playing the Piano by Machinery **6** 6 Jun 1885
Poverty at the Piano **13** 16 Jul 1892
Power of Music, The **11** 10 May 1890
Power of Music, The **13** 20 Aug 1892
Power of Music, The **20** 10 Jun 1899
Practising As It Ought To Be **26** 3 Dec 1904
Prima Donna, The **24** 22 Nov 1902
Printed Music in England **13** 27 Feb 1892
Profitable Music Lessons **14** 1 Jul 1893
Proud Musician, A **7** 15 May 1886
Rival Musicians **23** 21 Dec 1901
Rival Singers, The **12** 9 May 1891
Robert Schumann on Chopin's Playing His Own 'Etudes' **10 Summer** 1889
Saving a Violin **8** 13 Aug 1887
She Inherited It **17** 4 Apr 1896
She Preferred Bridge **26** 15 Apr 1905
She Refused to Sing **17 Summer** 1896
Singers and 'Wrapping Up' **4** 7 Oct 1882
Singers! Look to your Feet **5** 12 Apr 1884
Singer's Terms, A **8** 16 Jul 1887
Singer's Work, The **14** 25 Feb 1893
Singing **1** 28 Feb 1880
Singing Like a Bird **25** 16 Jan 1904
Singing of Jenny Lind, The **6** 29 Nov 1884
St. Cecilia **5** 20 Oct 1883
Starting Too High **7** 21 Nov 1885
Sweet Music **13** 12 Mar 1892
'Sweet the music of the step' **15** 26 May 1894
Tenor Solo, A **22** 25 May 1901
Those Street Bands **27** 5 May 1906
Three Things Needed **17** 5 Sep 1896
To Preserve the Throat in Singing **4** 14 Oct 1882
Tragic Chorus, A **11** 30 Aug 1890
Twelve Buried Musicians **21** 27 Jan 1900
Twenty-four Notes in One Bow **8** 16 Oct 1886
Two Musical Epitaphs **22** 23 Mar 1901
Useful Music **12** 30 May 1891

Violin-Playing Monarch, A **6** 15 Aug 1885
Voice Cultivation **6** 21 Feb 1885
Wagner Quizzed by Dumas **6** 4 Apr 1885
Well-Founded Belief, A **19** 24 Sep 1898
Well-Known Hymn Tune, A **24** 16 May 1903
What Became of C Flat? **26** 5 Nov 1904
What Her Voice Was Good For **18** 27 Feb 1897
What Music Can Do **11** 14 Jun 1890
When Oratorios Began **17** 12 Oct 1895
Where the Brass Band Was **23** 14 Dec 1901
Which Horn? **19** 27 Aug 1898
Whimsical Singer, A **11** 9 Nov 1889
Who Invented the Tuning Fork **11** 11 Jan 1890
Why Not Learn the Harp **26** 15 Oct 1904
William Black, the Novelist, and Music **24** 15 Nov 1902
Without Ears for Music **13** 13 Aug 1892
Woman's Work **6** 22 Nov 1884
Women in Music **7** 6 Mar 1886
Wonders of Pianoforte Playing **9** 7 July 1888
Words for Music **20** 6 May 1899

Notes

1 28 December 1901 Answers to Correspondent column includes Fidelio Club heading with music replies.
2 Chronological by volume with separate entry for each title variation.

Index to poetry[1]

Abendlied **23** 12 Jul 1902
Adelé **20 Christmas** 1898
Apple of My Eye, The **22** 14 Sep 1901
'Aspirations!' **2** 6 Nov 1880
Autumn **20** 1 Oct 1898
Bells of Spring, The **19** 26 Mar 1898
Bird-Song, A **30** Dec 1908
Birds Sing All the Year, The **14** 8 Jul 1893
'Blind' **16** 8 Jun 1895
Bridal Song, A **3** 25 Mar 1882
Bridal Song, A **20** 4 Feb 1899
Bringing Home the May **26** 15 Apr 1905
Broken Chord, The **5** 17 May 1894
Carol **28 Christmas** 1906
Carol of Footprints, A **20** 24 Dec 1898
Carol of Two Shepherds **26** 24 Dec 1904
Chimes **29** 30 May 1908
Chorus for May, A **6** 11 Apr 1885
Chorus for May, A **8** 16 Apr 1887
Chorus of Life, The **24** 14 Mar 1903
Christmas Bells **11 Christmas** 1889
Christmas Carol, A **13** 19 Dec 1891
Christmas Carol, A **17** 7 Dec 1895
Christmas Carol, A **20 Christmas** 1898
Christmas Guest, The **4 Christmas** 1882
Christmas Hymn **4** 23 Dec 1882
Christmas Melody, A **14 Christmas** 1892
Christmas Music **18 Christmas** 1896
Christmas Thoughts **7 Christmas** 1885
Cinderella, A **14** 9 Sep 1893
Come, Let Me Sing, Sweet Muse Sublime **15** 2 Dec 1893
'Come unto Me' **10** 9 Mar 1889
Coming of the King, The **15** 30 Dec 1893

'Consider the Lilies' **7 Summer** 1886
Coronation Hymn **23** 1 Feb 1902
Cradle Song, A **3** 4 Feb 1882
Crescendo, A **16** 9 Feb 1895
Doubting Heart, A **7** 6 Jan 1886
Doubting Heart, The **26** 1 Jul 1905
Dream of Heaven, A **4 Summer** 1883
Dream Within a Dream, A (Parable from the Divina Comedia) **15** 15 Sep 1894
Dreaming of Spring **8** 12 Feb 1887
Duetto **13** 30 Jan 1892
Easter Hymn, An **18** 17 Apr 1897
Easter Song, An **22** 20 Apr 1901
'Et in Arcadia, Ego' **18** 12 Jun 1897
Evening **26** 8 Oct 1904
Evening Hymn, An **19** 1 Jan 1898
Evening Recital, An – 'Prelude' and 'Symphony' **12** 19 Sep 1891
Evensong **8** 30 Jul 1887
Evensong **10** 17 Nov 1888
Exiled Rose, An **18** 21 Aug 1897
Fairies **19** 9 Apr 1898
Fairies, The **20** 13 May 1899
Ferry, The **22** 7 Sep 1901
Fisherman's Song, The **29** 1 Feb 1908
Flower Song **15 Summer** 1894
For a Little While **4** 6 Jan 1883
'For a Song' **2** 23 Apr 1881
Garden Lullaby, A **27** 24 Feb 1906
Gift of Song, The **3** 30 Sep 1882
Girlhood's Benedicite: A Carol for Girls **22 Christmas** 1900
Girl's Morning Hymn, A **4** 22 Sep 1883
Girl's Room, A **6** 15 Nov 1884
Grandest Love-Song, The **11** 21 Dec 1889
Great Tom of Oxford: A Song of the Bell **22** 5 Jan 1901
Greeting and a Song, A **25** 3 Sep 1904
Guitar Melody, A **11** 2 Aug 1890
Harmony **22** 6 Jul 1901
Harp of Life, The **6** 23 May 1885
Harvest Hymn **7 Summer** 1886
Harvest Song, A **26** 23 Sep 1905
Haymaking Song **10** 18 May 1889
Home Song **24** 6 Jun 1903
Homeward Bound: A Sailor's Song to His Wife **9** 24 Dec 1887
How to be Happy: A Poem for Girls **1** 17 Apr 1880
Hymn **31** Mar 1910
Hymn of the Night, A **11** 1 Feb 1890

I Love Old Songs **2** 2 Oct 1880
Inspirations **15** 2 Jun 1894
June Song, A **5** 10 May 1884
Kitchen Song, A **23** 14 Dec 1901
Lady Ella **9 Christmas** 1887
Lady to Her Musician, A **21** 6 Jan 1900
Lassie **15** 6 Jan 1894
Last Year's Roses **20** 1 Jul 1899
Lavender Song, A **22** 9 Mar 1901
Lesson from Nature, A **13** 2 Jul 1892
Letter to Mary, A **21** 7 Oct 1899
Life **26** 11 Mar 1905
Little Organ-Grinder, The **19** 21 May 1898
Love Song, A **29** 6 Jun 1908
Lovely May! A Song **28** 11 May 1907
Lullaby, A **17 Christmas** 1895
Maiden and the Poppy, The **3** 1 Jul 1882
May Song, A **9** 7 Apr 1888
Mental Melodies **18** 11 Sep 1897
Moonlight Calm: For a Song **28** 5 Jan 1907
Mother and the Child, The **3 Summer** 1882
Mother-Love **27** 2 Dec 1905
Mother's Deputy **17 Christmas** 1895
Music **2** 29 Jan 1881
Music **18** 3 Apr 1897
Music of the Past, The **17** 12 Sep 1896
Music's Empire **17** 21 Dec 1895
My Heart Is Like a Summer Sea **21** 14 Oct 1899
My Land of Memories **19** 16 Jul 1898
My Mother **4** 27 Jan 1883
My Music **14** 11 Mar 1893
My Song **12** 14 Mar 1891
'Nearer, My God, to Thee' **13 Christmas** 1891
Nightingale and the Robin, The: The Plea of a Minor Poet **18** 19 Dec 1896
Nightingale's Song, The **3** 22 Jul 1882
Nocturne **10** 27 Jul 1889
Old Court Dresses **3** 21 Jan 1882
Old Dove-cote, The **28** 14 Sep 1907
Old Pot-pourri Jar, The **2** 6 Aug 1881
Old Songs and the New, The **13** 3 Oct 1891
Old-Time Easter Carol, An **30** Apr 1909
On a Blackbird Singing During Divine Service **4** 17 Feb 1883
On a Very Old Piano: Lately Seen in a London Shop Window, and Labelled, 'Cash Price, Two Guineas' **20** 10 Jun 1899
On Christmas Eve: Rondeau **22** 8 Dec 1900
Only **15** 1 Sep 1894

Orchard Song, A **29** 15 Sep 1908
Organist, The **3** 19 Aug 1882
Orphan's Easter Hymn, The **11** 29 Mar 1890
Orpheus **20** 12 Nov 1898
Palace Wall, The **17** 8 Feb 1896
Parting Song **15** 7 Apr 1894
Piano and the Player, The **14** 17 Dec 1892
Piano-Player, The: A Life Picture **15** 3 Mar 1894
Picture and a Song, A **24** 24 Jan 1903
Resignation **26** 11 Mar 1905
Reverie in St. James's Hall, A **6** 10 Jan 1885
Rhyme of Songs, A **12** 8 Aug 1891
River Song, A **18** 10 Jul 1897
Robin, The **24** 4 Oct 1902
Saturday Afternoon **9** 22 Sep 1888
Sea of Life, The **15** 19 May 1894
Sea's Song, The **19** 20 Aug 1898
Seven Days **2** 4 Jun 1881
Signs and Tokens **7** 14 Aug 1886
Singers, The **2** 25 Dec 1880
Singing Lesson, A **12 Summer** 1891
Snowflake's Song, The **12** 13 Dec 1890
Sola **13** 30 Jan 1892
Solo **12** 22 Aug 1891
Song **11** 22 Mar 1890
Song **17** 19 Sep 1896
Song, A **19** 12 Mar 1898
Song **20** 7 Jan 1899
Song **21** 19 May 1900
Song **31** Feb 1908
Song for Julia, A **2** 9 Oct 1880
Song for the Old Year, A **8** 18 Dec 1886
Song of Briar Roses, A **13 Summer** 1892
Song of Hope, A **18** 6 Feb 1897
Song of Hope, A **29** 7 Mar 1908
Song of Love, A **15** 9 Jun 1894
Song of Roses **27** 2 Jun 1906
Song of Summer, The **3** 15 Jul 1882
Song of the City, The **21** 12 May 1900
Song of the Early Christians, Meeting in the Catacombs in Secret by Night **13** 19 Dec 1891
Song of the Fisherman's Wife **12** 15 Aug 1891
Song of the Moments, A **10** 5 Jan 1889
Song of the Needle, The; or, The Girl's Own Compass, The **1** 8 May 1880
Song of the Sea-side, A **23** 23 Aug 1902
Song of the Sewing Machine, The **1** 28 Feb 1880

Song of the Spring **10** 13 Apr 1889
Song of the Workers **12** 20 Jun 1891
Song of Work, A **27** 15 Sep 1906
Song: 'While Cuckoos Are Calling' **8** 21 May 1887
Song-Summer Days **10** 22 Jun 1889
Sonnet **25** 16 Jan 1904
Soul's Awakening, The **21** 4 Aug 1900
Spring Song **14** 15 Apr 1893
Spring Song **20** 22 Apr 1899
Spring Song, A **25** 23 Apr 1904
Springtime **26** 18 Feb 1905
Storm in Youghal Bay **28** 22 Dec 1906
Summer Days **13** 18 Jun 1892
Summer Hymn, A **13 Summer** 1892
Summer is y-comen in **18** 10 Apr 1897
Summer Song, A **8** 2 Jul 1887
Summer Song, A **11** 12 Jul 1890
Summer Spices (Flower Songs) **17 Summer** 1896
Sunbeams **5** 17 Nov 1883
Sweet Singer, A **4** 13 Jan 1883
Telegraph's Song, The **9** 14 Apr 1888
That Dear Old Song! **18** 19 Dec 1896
'The Song the Raindrops Sing' **20** 15 Apr 1899
There Are Ripples on the Ocean: Song **12** 14 Feb 1891
Thou Sing'st to Her: Old Song 1606 John Danvel **12** 11 Apr 1891
Three Minstrels **22** 10 Nov 1900
Time and the Maidens **18** 8 May 1897
To an Old Spinet **28** 31 Aug 1907
Tuner and the Tuning, The **13** 7 May 1892
Twilight Visions **6 Christmas** 1884
Two Sea Songs, 'Sixteen' and 'Sixty' **15 Summer** 1894
Very Old Song, A **24** 18 Oct 1902
Village Concert, A **9** 21 Jul 1888
Visions of the Departed **11** 4 Jan 1890
Voices of the Night **22** 17 Nov 1900
Voices on the River **19** 3 Sep 1898
Washing-Day Song, A **21** 8 Sep 1900
Water Music (Libretto for Cantata) **26** 22 Jul 1905
Way to Arcady, The **20** 30 Sep 1899
Wedding Song, A **9 Summer** 1888
When My Gretchen Sings **25** 28 Nov 1903
When Wilt Thou Come? Song **15** 3 Feb 1894
Winter Song, A **1** 3 Jan 1880
Worker's Song, A **16** 15 Dec 1894
Wren's Song, The **23** 2 Aug 1902

Youth **12** 4 Jul 1891
Yuletide **6 Christmas** 1884
Zither Player, The **7 Christmas** 1885

Note

1 Includes poetry with music in title, text or illustration.

Index to illustrations[1]

'A Good-Night Song in the Orphan School' **17 Summer** 1896
'A Reverie' **19** frontispiece
All Thy works shall praise Thy Name **14** 1 Oct 1892
Andante! **18** 17 Oct 1896
At a Concert **17** 21 Dec 1895
Bailiff's Daughter of Islington, The **9** 14, 21 Jan 1888
Beethoven and the Blind Girl – A Surprise Visit **17 Summer** 1896
Beethoven and the Muse **25** 11 Jun 1904
Cello Player, The **22** 1 Dec 1900 plate
Chloe **19** title page
Chopin **19 Christmas** 1897
Christmas Carol, A **Christmas 22** 1900
Christmas Mummers in Sweden **14** 24 Dec 1892
Christmas Song, A **26** 24 Dec 1904
Come Back to Erin **26** 7 Jan 1905
Concerto, A **25** 14 Nov 1903
Crown Princes at Play **31** Oct 1909 plate
Dream of Home, The **10** 20 Jul 1889
Early Summer **20** 13 May 1899
Eastern Beauty, An **23 Christmas** 1901
Enthusiastic Fidelian, An **23** 20 Sep 1902
Enthusiastic Fidelian, An **27** 23 Dec 1905
Evening Song, The **22 Summer** 1901
Girl's Own Carol, The **5** 22 Dec 1883 plate
Golden Strings **22** 9 Mar 1901 plate
Harvest Moon, The **6** 1 Aug 1885
'Heard melodies are sweet, but those unheard are sweeter' **14** 11 Mar 1893
House Music: Before Bed-time **26** 16 Sep 1905
How College Girls Arrange their Rooms **31** Jan 1910 plate
How Girton Girls Arrange their Rooms **31** Jul 1910
Hymn Pictures – I **17** 5 Oct 1895
Impromptu, An **7** 12 Dec 1885 plate
In the Garden **2** 23 Jul 1881
In the Gloaming – (Ballad Picture No. 1) **3** 5 Nov 1881

Jocund Spring **2** 2 Apr 1881 plate
Kittens **25** 19 Dec 1903
'Love Divine – All Love Excelling' **19** 2 Oct 1897
Melodies of a Bygone Day **23 Christmas** 1901
Memories **10** 4 May 1889
Merry Christmas to All, A **8 Christmas** 1886
Music **13** 2 Jan 1892
Music **24** 6 Jun 1903
'Music and Poetry' **27** 19 May 1906
New Portrait of Her Majesty the Queen of Romania, A **26** 19 Nov 1904
New Soprano, The **20** 12 Nov 1898
Old Song Ended, An **14** 25 Feb 1893 plate
Our Chief Composers **6 Christmas** 1884 plate
Pansies for Thought **14** 3 Jun 1893
Portrait Gallery of Contributors to 'The Girl's Own Paper' **20** 25 Feb 1899 multi-page foldout plate
Rehearsal, The **18** 14 Nov 1896 plate
Rehearsal, The **24** 8 Aug 1903
Reverie, A **25** 2 Jan 1904 plate
Reverie, A **31** Aug 1910 plate
Rhapsody, A **25** 6 Aug 1904
Ring of Harmony, A **29 Christmas** 1907
Roman Singer, The **14** 21 Jan 1893
Saint Cecilia **24 Christmas** 1902
Saint Cecilia **27** 23 Jun 1906
Shepherd with a Pipe, A **18** 5 Dec 1896 plate
Song of Olden Days, A **17** 12 Sep 1896
Song of Spring, A **16** 6 Apr 1895 plate
Song of Spring, A **26 Christmas** 1904 plate
Specimen Page of Miss Kate Greenaway's Work, A **23** 28 Dec 1901
String Quartette, A **26** 8 Oct 1904 plate
Sunday Evening **19** 20 Aug 1898
'The setting sun, and music at the close' **15** 8 Sep 1894
'The sweetest songs are those which tell of saddest thoughts' **20 Summer** 1899
'There is sweet music here that softer falls' **17** 11 Jan 1896
Timbrel-Player, The **22 Summer** 1901
Trio, A **17** 8 Aug 1896
Twilight Music **20** 8 Oct 1898
Village Choir Fifty Years Ago, A **26** 31 Dec 1904
Wandering Minstrel, A **14** 12 Aug 1893
Youthful Pianist, A **20** 11 Mar 1899
Zither Player, The **13 Summer** 1892

Note

1 Includes only full-page illustrations not part of other *TGOP* material.

Index to Answers to Correspondents

Music as separate heading

1   25 Sep 1880

   Topics: general, nuisance, performance nerves, piano, repertoire, terms, voice

2   26 Mar, 28 May, 2 Jul, 16 Jul, 20 Aug, 27 Aug, 10 Sep, 24 Sep 1881

   Topics: concertina, copyright, general, harmonium, health, instrument maintenance, music as profession, music copying, music education, music history and appreciation, organ, page turning, performance etiquette, piano, pronunciation, repertoire, terms, violin, voice

3   8 Oct, 15 Oct, 22 Oct, 29 Oct, 5 Nov, 12 Nov, 19 Nov, 3 Dec, 10 Dec, 31 Dec 1881; 7 Jan, 28 Jan, 11 Feb, 18 Feb, 25 Feb, 11 Mar, 18 Mar, 25 Mar, 1 Apr, 8 Apr, 22 Apr, 6 May, 20 May, 10 Jun, 1 Jul, 8 Jul, 15 Jul, 29 Jul, 12 Aug, 19 Aug, 26 Aug, 9 Sep, 16 Sep 1882

   Topics: applied music, choosing instrument, choral singing, composition, concertina, copyright, digitorium, general, guitar, harmonium, harp, health, instrument maintenance, mandolin, memory work, metronome, music education, music history and appreciation, music teaching, musician work, nuisance, organ, performance etiquette, piano, piano purchase, practising, pronunciation, reading music, repertoire, sight-reading, terms, theory, viola, violin, violoncello, voice, zither

4   21 Oct, 11 Nov, 2 Dec, 9 Dec, 16 Dec, 23 Dec 1882; 6 Jan, 13 Jan, 27 Jan, 24 Feb, 10 Mar, 17 Mar, 21 Apr, 28 Apr, 5 May, 26 May, 2 Jun, 16 Jun, 23 Jun, 30 Jun, 14 Jul, 28 Jul, 4 Aug, 1 Sep, 22 Sep, 29 Sep 1883

   Topics: applied music, choosing instrument, composition, copyright, general, guitar, harmonium, harp, health, instrument maintenance, mandolin, memory work, metronome, music education, music history and appreciation, music potential, music teaching, musician pension, nuisance, organ, piano, practising, practising society, pronunciation, repertoire, sight-reading, terms, theory, tonic sol-fa, violin, voice

Answers to Correspondents   323

5   6 Oct, 13 Oct, 20 Oct, 15 Dec 1883; 19 Jan, 26 Jan, 23 Feb, 1 Mar, 5 Apr, 26 Apr, 24 May, 31 May, 7 Jun, 21 Jun, 19 Jul, 26 Jul, 2 Aug, 9 Aug, 16 Aug, 23 Aug, 6 Sep, 27 Sep 1884

Topics: applied music, bagpipe, choosing instrument, copyright, flute, general, harmonium, harp, health, instrument maintenance, music copying, music education, music history and appreciation, music potential, music teaching, musician work, nuisance, organ, page turning, performance etiquette, performance nerves, piano, practising, practising society, publishing music, reading music, repertoire, sight-reading, terms, theory, tonic sol-fa, violin, voice

6   4 Oct, 11 Oct, 13 Dec 1883; 3 Jan (Correspondence Awaiting the Editor), 7 Feb, 7 Mar, 4 Apr, 18 Apr, 2 May, 9 May, 23 May, 30 May, 11 Jul, 25 Jul, 15 Aug, 19 Sep, 26 Sep 1885

Topics: applied music, banjo, choosing instrument, choral singing, composition, concertina, flageolet, flute, general, guitar, harp, health, instrument maintenance, Irish harp, mandolin, melodeon, military bands, music and Christianity, music copying, music education, music history and appreciation, music potential, music teaching, musician salary, national anthem, nuisance, organ, performance etiquette, performance nerves, piano, practising, practising society, pronunciation, repertoire, terms, theory, viola, violin, violoncello, voice, zither

7   17 Oct, 31 Oct, 7 Nov, 12 Dec 1885; 2 Jan, 9 Jan, 16 Jan, 6 Feb, 13 Feb, 13 Mar, 27 Mar, 1 May, 19 Jun, 3 Jul, 17 Jul, 24 Jul, 7 Aug, 21 Aug 1886

Topics: applied music, composition, copyright, dulcimer, general, harmonium, harp piano, health, instrument maintenance, lesson etiquette, metronome, music as accomplishment, music education, music history and appreciation, musical pitch, ocarina instrument, organ, performance etiquette, piano, practising, practising society, pronunciation, repertoire, terms, theory, tonic sol-fa, violin, voice, zither

8   13 Nov, 20 Nov, 11 Dec 1886; 5 Feb, 12 Feb, 5 Mar, 16 Apr, 7 May, 21 May, 30 Jul 1887

Topics: banjo, choosing instrument, clarionette, composition, flute, general, harmonium, health, mandolin, memory work, music copying, music education, music history and appreciation, musician pension, organ, performance etiquette, performance nerves, piano, practising, practising society, repertoire, theory, tonic sol-fa, voice, zither

9   1 Oct, 8 Oct, 15 Oct, 12 Nov, 26 Nov 1887; 18 Feb (Correspondence), 17 Mar, 31 Mar, 22 Sep 1888

Topics: general, guitar, harp, health, instrument maintenance, music as accomplishment, music education, music history and appreciation, music

324   *Answers to Correspondents*

potential, nuisance, performance, piano, practising, pronunciation, repertoire, terms, theory, violin, voice

10 27 Oct, 3 Nov, 15 Dec 1888; 12 Jan, 2 Feb, 2 Mar, 23 Mar, 6 Apr (Correspondence), 4 May, 7 Sep 1889

Topics: banjo, buglette, choosing instrument, general, health, instrument maintenance, lyre, mandolin, music education, music history and appreciation, music potential, music teaching, organ, piano, practising society, repertoire, terms, viola, violin, voice, whistling

11 5 Oct, 2 Nov, 23 Nov, 14 Dec 1889; 4 Jan, 25 Jan, 15 Feb, 5 Apr, 12 Apr, 19 Apr, 26 Apr, 3 May, 10 May, 14 Jun, 12 Jul, 19 Jul, 13 Sep 1890

Topics: applied music, banjo, composition, correspondence course, crwth instrument, general, guitar, harmonium, health, instrument maintenance, lesson etiquette, memory work, music education, music history and appreciation, music potential, music teaching, musician work, performance nerves, piano, practising, practising society, repertoire, sight-reading, terms, theory, tonic sol-fa, violin, violoncello, voice, zither

12 11 Oct, 25 Oct, 15 Nov, 22 Nov, 13 Dec 1890; 17 Jan, 14 Feb, 28 Mar, 16 May, 23 May, 13 Jun, 27 Jun, 8 Aug, 22 Aug, 29 Aug, 5 Sep, 12 Sep, 19 Sep 1891

Topics: applied music, charity entertainments, choosing instrument, composition, general, guitar, harmonium, health, instrument maintenance, mandolin, music education, music history and appreciation, music potential, music teaching, national anthem, nuisance, organ, piano, piano keys, practising, practising society, psaltery, reading music, repertoire, terms, theory, viol, violin, voice, wasted time

13 3 Oct, 10 Oct, 24 Oct, 31 Oct, 12 Dec, 19 Dec 1891; 16 Jan, 20 Feb, 5 Mar, 26 Mar, 2 Apr, 9 Apr, 23 Apr, 18 Jun, 25 Jun, 30 Jul, 27 Aug 1892

Topics: applied music, banjo, castanets, choosing instrument, choral singing, composition, concertina, copyright, dance music, digitorium, general, guitar, health, mandolin, music education, music history and appreciation, music lessons, music teaching, musician work, nuisance, organ, organ-accordion, organist salary, performance etiquette, piano, practising, practising society, pronunciation, repertoire, sight-reading, theory, violin, voice, zither

14 1 Oct, 19 Nov, 3 Dec, 17 Dec 1892; 4 Feb, 18 Feb, 11 Mar, 8 Apr, 13 May, 3 Jun, 8 Jul 1893

Topics: applied music, banjo, banjo-zither, choosing instrument, cithara, composition, correspondence course, dulcimer, general, guitar, harmonium, harp, health, music education, music history and appreciation, music potential, music student lodging, music teaching, nuisance, organ, piano, practising society, repertoire, terms, theory, voice, violin, zither

Answers to Correspondents 325

15 7 Oct, 14 Oct, 4 Nov, 11 Nov, 18 Nov, 25 Nov, 2 Dec, 23 Dec 1893; 6 Jan, 13 Jan, 20 Jan, 7 Apr, 14 Apr, 28 Apr, 19 May, 9 Jun, 16 Jun, 7 Jul, 28 Jul, 1 Sep 1894

Topics: applied music, banjo, barrel organ, choosing instrument, circulating music, composition, correspondence course, flute, general, guitar, harp, health, instrument maintenance, Irish harp, metronome, music education, music history and appreciation, music student lodging, music teaching, nuisance, organ, page turning, performance nerves, piano, practising, practising society, pronunciation, repertoire, sight-reading, terms, theory, violin, voice

16 13 Oct, 27 Oct, 10 Nov, 17 Nov, 15 Dec, 22 Dec 1894; 16 Feb, 23 Mar, 18 May, 8 Jun, 7 Sep, 14 Sep 1895

Topics: applied music, bagpipe, choosing instrument, choral singing, circulating music, composition, copyright, general, guitar, harp, health, instrument maintenance, mandolin, metronome, music education, music history and appreciation, music pension, music teaching, musician work, nuisance, organ, piano, practising society, repertoire, terms, theory, violin, violoncello, voice, wasted time, zither

17 2 Nov, 9 Nov, 23 Nov 1895; 11 Jan, 1 Feb, 15 Feb, 7 Mar, 9 May, 6 Jun, 1 Aug, 22 Aug 1896

Topics: applied music, banjo, circulating music, composition, copyright, correspondence clubs, general, guitar, harp, health, instrument tuner, mandolin, music education, music history and appreciation, music student lodging, music teaching, national anthem, nuisance, organ, performance nerves, piano, practising, practising society, pronunciation, psaltery, repertoire, terms, theory, violin, voice, wasted time, zither

18 17 Oct 1896

Topics: performance nerves, voice

Study and Studio heading with music replies

18 31 Oct, 5 Dec, 12 Dec, 26 Dec 1896; 2 Jan, 13 Feb, 6 Mar, 3 Apr, 10 Apr, 17 Apr, 24 Apr, 8 May, 15 May, 19 Jun, 3 Jul, 10 Jul, 24 Jul, 7 Aug, 20 Aug, 4 Sep, 18 Sep, 25 Sep 1897

Topics: applied music, composition, copyright, general, guitar, harpsichord, music copying, music education, music history and appreciation, performance nerves, piano, practising, practising society, pronunciation, reading music, repertoire, sight-reading, terms, theory, typewriting, violin, voice

19 23 Oct, 20 Nov, 4 Dec, 11 Dec 1897; 1 Jan, 8 Jan, 15 Jan, 5 Mar, 12 Mar, 19 Mar, 2 Apr, 9 Apr, 16 Apr, 7 May, 21 May, 4 Jun, 11 Jun, 25 Jun, 2 Jul, 23 Jul, 30 Jul, 6 Aug, 20 Aug, 3 Sep, 10 Sep, 17 Sep 1898

Topics: applied music, choosing instrument, choral singing, composition, correspondence course, general, guitar, health, Irish harp, mandolin, music education, music history and appreciation, music teaching, musician work, opera, organ, piano, practising society, repertoire, theory, violin, voice, Welsh harp

20 22 Oct, 29 Oct, 5 Nov, 12 Nov, 19 Nov, 31 Dec 1898; 7 Jan, 14 Jan, 21 Jan, 11 Feb, 18 Feb, 11 Mar, 8 Apr, 22 Apr, 3 Jun, 10 Jun, 17 Jun, 24 Jun, 15 Jul, 29 Jul, 5 Aug, 12 Aug, 19 Aug, 26 Aug, 16 Sep, 23 Sep, 30 Sep 1899

Topics: applied music, choral singing, clarionet, composition, flute, general, guitar, instrument maintenance, mandolin, memory work, metronome, music education, music history and appreciation, music teaching, musical stammering, nuisance, organ, piano, piano keys, practising, practising society, reading music, repertoire, Royal Academy of Music (RAM) scholarship notice, terms, violin, voice

21 7 Oct, 14 Oct, 21 Oct, 11 Nov, 18 Nov, 25 Nov, 23 Dec 1899; 6 Jan, 13 Jan, 3 Feb, 17 Feb, 17 Mar, 24 Mar, 7 Apr, 14 Apr, 21 Apr, 12 May, 2 Jun, 9 Jun, 23 Jun, 7 Jul, 4 Aug, 18 Aug, 25 Aug 1900

Topics: applied music, choosing instrument, choral singing, composition, general, guitar, health, hymn text, instrument maintenance, ladies orchestra, mandolin, music education, piano, practising society, pronunciation, RAM scholarship notice, repertoire, theory, violin, voice, zither

22 3 Nov, 8 Dec, 15 Dec, 22 Dec 1900; 5 Jan, 12 Jan, 9 Feb, 23 Feb, 9 Mar, 30 Mar, 11 May, 1 Jun, 8 Jun, 15 Jun, 29 Jun, 20 Jul, 3 Aug, 10 Aug, 17 Aug, 31 Aug, 7 Sep, 14 Sep 1901

Topics: applied music, composition, general, guitar, instrument purchase, music education, music history and appreciation, music teaching, national anthem, organ, piano, practising society, RAM scholarship notice, reading music, repertoire, terms, theory, violin, voice

23 12 Oct, 2 Nov, 9 Nov, 16 Nov 1901; 11 Jan, 26 Apr, 17 May, 14 Jun, 21 Jun, 2 Aug, 9 Aug, 20 Sep 1902

Topics: choosing instrument, choosing music, circulating music, *Clavier* copy, composition, mandolin, musician work, piano, practising society, pronunciation, RAM scholarship notice, repertoire, violin, voice

24 11 Oct, 18 Oct, 1 Nov, 8 Nov 1902; 17 Jan, 24 Jan, 7 Feb, 21 Feb, 18 Apr, 25 Apr, 23 May, 30 May, 20 Jun, 1 Aug, 15 Aug, 22 Aug, 12 Sep 1903

Topics: composition, general, harmonium, health, music education, piano, practising, practising society, RAM scholarship notice, RAM violin faculty notice, repertoire, terms, transposing songs, violin, voice

25 7 Nov, 5 Dec 1903; 2 Jan, 6 Feb, 30 Apr, 7 May, 4 Jun, 18 Jun, 9 Jul, 27 Aug 1904

Topics: choral singing, health, instrument purchase, music education, music teaching, practising, practising society, RAM scholarship notice, repertoire, violin, voice, writing musical fiction

26   8 Oct, 5 Nov 1904

Topics: music education, practising, practising society, repertoire

Music replies under other headings

1   14 Feb, 21 Feb, 28 Feb, 13 Mar, 20 Mar, 27 Mar, 3 Apr, 10 Apr, 17 Apr, 24 Apr, 1 May, 8 May, 15 May, 22 May, 29 May, 12 Jun, 19 Jun, 26 Jun, 3 Jul, 10 Jul, 17 Jul, 31 Jul, 7 Aug, 14 Aug, 21 Aug, 28 Aug, 11 Sep 1880

Topics: choosing instrument, flageolet, general, guitar, harmonium, harp, health, music education, music history and appreciation, music potential, nuisance, organ, performance etiquette, performance nerves, piano, practising, pronunciation, repertoire, terms, theory, violin, voice

2   2 Oct, 9 Oct, 16 Oct, 23 Oct, 30 Oct, 6 Nov, 13 Nov, 20 Nov, 27 Nov, 4 Dec, 11 Dec, 25 Dec 1880; 1 Jan, 8 Jan, 15 Jan, 22 Jan, 5 Feb, 12 Feb, 26 Feb, 12 Mar, 2 Apr, 9 Apr, 16 Apr, 23 Apr, 30 Apr, 7 May, 14 May, 21 May, 4 Jun, 11 Jun, 18 Jun, 25 Jun, 23 Jul, 30 Jul, 6 Aug, 13 Aug, 3 Sep, 17 Sep 1881

Topics: applied music, composition, concertina, copyright, flute, general, guitar, harmonium, health, instrument maintenance, memory work, music education, music potential, music publishing, music teaching, national anthem, nuisance, organ, page turning, performance etiquette, piano, piano front, practising, pronunciation, repertoire, terms, theory, violin, voice

3   1 Oct, 24 Dec 1881; 14 Jan, 21 Jan, 4 Feb, 4 Mar, 15 Apr, 13 May, 27 May, 3 Jun, 24 Jun, 23 Sep, 30 Sep 1882

Topics: general, instrument maintenance, music education, nuisance, performance etiquette, piano, practising, repertoire, terms, violin, voice, xylophone

4   7 Oct, 14 Oct, 4 Nov, 18 Nov, 25 Nov 1882; 10 Feb, 31 Mar, 7 Apr, 12 May, 19 May, 9 Jun, 7 Jul, 11 Aug, 18 Aug, 15 Sep 1883

Topics: choosing instrument, general, guitar, health, instrument maintenance, music education, music history and appreciation, piano keys, repertoire, terms, violin, voice

5   17 Nov, 1 Dec, 8 Dec, 22 Dec, 29 Dec 1883; 12 Jan, 2 Feb, 16 Feb, 15 Mar, 29 Mar, 19 Apr, 3 May, 10 May, 17 May, 28 Jun, 30 Aug 1884

Topics: instrument maintenance, memory work, music education, music history and appreciation, national anthem, nuisance, organ, page turning, piano, piano keys, practising, practising society, pronunciation, repertoire, terms, violin, violoncello, voice

6   25 Oct, 8 Nov, 15 Nov, 22 Nov, 6 Dec 1884; 21 Feb, 28 Feb, 28 Mar, 6 Jun, 22 Aug, 29 Aug, 5 Sep, 12 Sep 1885

Topics: applied music, choral singing, general, health, music education, music history and appreciation, music student lodging, nuisance, organ, piano, practising, practising society, pronunciation, terms, violin, voice

328   *Answers to Correspondents*

7   10 Oct, 24 Oct, 28 Nov 1885; 23 Jan, 24 Apr, 8 May, 5 Jun, 12 Jun 1886

Topics: general, music history and appreciation, nuisance, repertoire, voice

8   30 Oct, 6 Nov, 27 Nov, 4 Dec, 25 Dec 1886; 8 Jan, 15 Jan, 19 Feb, 26 Feb, 19 Mar, 25 Jun, 6 Aug, 27 Aug, 3 Sep 1887

Topics: applied music, choral singing, general, health, instrument maintenance, lesson etiquette, memory work, music as accomplishment, music education, music history and appreciation, music teaching, piano keys, practising, practising etiquette, pronunciation, repertoire, voice, violoncello

9   22 Oct, 5 Nov, 31 Dec 1887; 14 Jan, 28 Jan, 3 Mar, 10 Mar, 16 Jun, 23 Jun, 14 Jul, 4 Aug, 1 Sep, 8 Sep, 29 Sep 1888

Topics: composition, disability, general, instrument maintenance, instrument purchase, music as accomplishment, music history and appreciation, music potential, music teaching, piano, piano keys, practising society

10   6 Oct, 20 Oct, 17 Nov, 1 Dec, 8 Dec, 22 Dec 1888; 5 Jan, 9 Feb, 9 Mar, 16 Mar, 30 Mar, 18 May, 20 Jul, 17 Aug, 21 Sep, 28 Sep (Correspondence) 1889

Topics: accordion, concertina, general, harp, health, instrument maintenance, music as accomplishment, music education, music history and appreciation, nuisance, performance etiquette, piano, piano keys, practising society, repertoire, voice

11   12 Oct, 19 Oct 1889; 17 May, 24 May, 7 Jun, 28 Jun 1890

Topics: digitorium, health, musical confusion, repertoire, violin, voice

12   3 Jan, 10 Jan, 31 Jan, 21 Feb, 28 Feb, 7 Mar, 14 Mar, 21 Mar, 4 Apr, 11 Apr, 25 Apr, 2 May, 11 Jul, 18 Jul, 15 Aug 1891

Topics: banjo, choosing instrument, composition, mandolin, music education, music history and appreciation, music teaching, musician work, piano, practising, practising society, repertoire, terms, violoncello, voice, zither

13   14 Nov, 21 Nov 1891; 9 Jan, 23 Jan, 13 Feb, 30 Apr, 28 May, 2 Jul, 6 Aug, 20 Aug, 10 Sep, 17 Sep 1892

Topics: copyright, general, harmonium, lyre, music education, music history and appreciation, music potential, national anthem, nuisance, piano, practising, repertoire, terms, zither

14   8 Oct, 29 Oct 1892; 11 Feb, 25 Mar, 1 Jul, 12 Aug, 9 Sep, 30 Sep 1893

Topics: general, harmonium, music as accomplishment, music history and appreciation, performance etiquette, piano, practising society, violin

15   16 Dec 1893; 3 Feb, 24 Feb, 3 Mar, 24 Mar, 21 Apr, 5 May, 26 May, 2 Jun, 23 Jun, 18 Aug 1894

Topics: copyright, general, music history and appreciation, music teaching, nuisance, piano, practising, pronunciation, repertoire, voice

Answers to Correspondents 329

16   6 Oct, 29 Dec 1894; 12 Jan, 11 May, 13 Jul, 31 Aug 1895

Topics: general, instrument maintenance, music history and appreciation, piano keys, practising, repertoire, voice

17   19 Oct, 16 Nov, 7 Dec, 21 Dec 1895; 14 Mar, 21 Mar, 28 Mar, 4 Jul 1896

Topics: general, instrument maintenance, music education, music history and appreciation, terms, viola de gamba, violin, voice

18   7 Nov, 14 Nov, 28 Nov, 19 Dec 1896; 30 Jan, 6 Feb, 22 May, 31 Jul, 14 Aug 1897

Topics: general, health, instrument maintenance, music copying, music history and appreciation, organ, piano, piano keys, typewriter, voice

19   13 Nov 1897; 22 Jan, 26 Feb, 16 Apr, 9 Jul 1898

Topics: general, mandolin, music copying, musician work, nuisance, piano, practising society, repertoire

20   4 Mar, 6 May, 27 May 1899

Topics: accordion, choosing instrument, concertina, general, music teaching, practising society, pronunciation, repertoire, terms

21   15, 29 Sep 1900

Topics: health, hymn text, practising, voice

22   20 Oct, 10 Nov, 1 Dec 1900; 21 Sep 1901

Topics: composition, health, music history and appreciation, performance nerves, violin

23   23 Nov 1901; 18 Jan, 15 Mar, 24 May 1902

Topics: musician work, piano, repertoire

24   13 Dec 1902; 10 Jan, 31 Jan, 7 Mar, 29 Aug 1903

Topics: general, instrument maintenance, mandolin, music teaching, piano, piano keys, voice

25   21 Nov 1903; 30 Jan, 9 Apr, 20 Aug 1904

Topics: coalies' baby instrument, harpsichord, mandolin, repertoire, voice

26   3 Dec, 17 Dec, 31 Dec 1904; 7 Jan, 18 Feb, 4 Mar, 1 Apr, 8 Apr, 15 Apr, 13 May, 10 Jun, 17 Jun, 8 Jul, 19 Aug, 2 Sep 1905

Topics: bagpipes, circulating music, composition, harp, ladies bands, repertoire, violin

27   28 Oct, 2 Dec, 9 Dec 1905; 27 Jan, 3 Mar, 17 Mar, 21 Apr, 26 May, 16 Jun, 14 Jul, 4 Aug, 1 Sep, 22 Sep 1906

Topics: composition, general, hymn text, instrument maintenance, music education, orchestra, piano, piano keys, RAM scholarship notice, repertoire

330 *Answers to Correspondents*

28 13 Oct, 20 Oct, 10 Nov, 24 Nov, 1 Dec, 8 Dec, 29 Dec 1906; 9 Feb, 16 Feb, 16 Mar, 30 Mar, 27 Apr, 1 Jun, 22 Jun, 6 Jul, 20 Jul, 24 Aug, 14 Sep (Correspondence), 28 Sep 1907

Topics: accompaniment, correspondence course, general, harp, hymn text, music education, music selling, music student lodging, music teaching, musician work, orchestration, piano, RAM scholarship notice, repertoire

29 5 Oct, 12 Oct, 9 Nov, 16 Nov, 23 Nov, 14 Dec 1907; 8 Feb (G.O.P. Answers to Correspondents), 7 Mar, 14 Mar, 28 Mar, 11 Apr, 25 Apr, 9 May, 6 Jun, 13 Jun, 27 Jun, 1 Aug, 15 Aug, 29 Aug 1908

Topics: barrel organ, choral singing, general, health, hurdy gurdy, music copying, music education, music student lodging, music teaching, musician work, organ, piano, repertoire, voice

Other replies to correspondents' musical questions

17 Replies to Often-Asked Questions 9 May 1896

Topic: organ-playing

19 Questions and Answers: Our Open Letter-Box 11 Dec 1897

Topic: repertoire

21 Question and Answer 18 Aug 1900

Topic: repertoire

24 Questions and Answers 21 Feb 1903

Topic: music as profession or occupation

Index to music scores by instrument

Organ, harmonium

Adagio ma non Troppo (Myles B. Foster) (pianoforte or American organ)[1] **19** 10 Sep 1898

Allegretto Giojoso (Myles B. Foster) (pianoforte or American organ) **12** 12 Sep 1891

Allegro con Moto Agitato (Myles B. Foster) (pianoforte or American organ) **19** 22 Jan 1898

Andante Pastorale (Myles B. Foster) (pianoforte or American organ) **12** 31 Jan 1891

Chorale (Myles B. Foster) (pianoforte or American organ) **19** 11 Dec 1897

Crusaders' March (Myles B. Foster) (harmonium or American organ) **13** 27 Aug 1892

Elegy (Myles B. Foster) (harmonium or American organ) **13** 9 Apr 1892

Meditation (Myles B. Foster) (harmonium or American organ) **13** 24 Sep 1892

Postlude (Myles B. Foster) (pianoforte or American organ) **17** 12 Sep 1896

Rêverie (J. W. Hinton) (harmonium or American organ) **9** 4 Feb 1888

Supplication (Myles B. Foster) (harmonium or American organ) **14** 18 Mar 1893

Pianoforte

Albumblatt (E. Humperdinck) **17** 1 Feb 1896

Allegro (H.A.J. Campbell) **11** 1 Mar 1890

Andante: For the Pianoforte (H.R.H. Hereditary Grand Duke of Hesse) **16** 18 May 1895

Andante Scherzoso (Myles B. Foster) **5** 6 Sep 1884

Aubade (H.A.J. Campbell) **13** 9 Jul 1892

Barcarolle (from the 'Mountain Scenes') (Natalie Janotha, Op. 3) **17 Summer 1896**

Berceuse (Cécile S. Hartog) **7** 3 Apr 1886

Berceuse (J. W. Hinton) **8** 15 Jan 1887

Dernier Papillon, Le (Edwin M. Lott) **3** 29 Oct 1881

Edelweiss (Natalie Janotha) **12** 7 Mar 1891

Evening (Gordon Saunders) **7** 14 Aug 1886

Evening Clouds (Edwin M. Lott) **4** 4 Aug 1883

Fairies, The: Scherzo for the Pianoforte (Ernst Pauer) **6** 18 Oct 1884
Gathering Cowslips: Retrospect (Mrs Tom Taylor) **7 Summer** 1886
Gavotte (H.A.J. Campbell) **9** 10 Mar 1888
Gavotte (Myles B. Foster) (keyboard) **14** 19 Aug 1893
Gavotte (Cécile Hartog) **28** 2 Feb 1907
Impromptu (Albert W. Ketèlbey) **21** 17 Mar 1900
Intermezzo: Duet for Pianoforte (George J. Bennett) **14 Summer** 1893
L'Allegrezza (Annie E. Nash) **3** 4 Mar 1882
Little Mazourka, A: In Memory of Chopin (Born March 1, 1809) (Myles B. Foster) **7** 20 Feb 1886
Mille Amitiés (G. J. Bennett) **12** 1 Nov 1890
Mazourka in E Minor, Op. 6, No. 1 (Natalie Janotha) **15** 21 Jul 1894
Mazurka (Lady Thompson) **17** 23 May 1896
Mazurka in C Minor (Ethel M. Boyce) **10** 11 May 1889
Merrie England: 'Here's to the Maiden of Bashful Fifteen' (C. A. Macirone) **6** 6 Jun 1885
Merrie England: I. 'Oh, How Should I Your True Love Know?' (C. A. Macirone) **4 Summer** 1883
Minuet (Myles B. Foster) **14** 17 Dec 1892
Minuet and Musette (H.A.J. Campbell) **12** 20 Jun 1891
Minuet and Trio: From a Suite for Orchestra (Myles B. Foster) **6** 12 Sep 1885
Nocturne (H.A.J. Campbell) **9** 11 Aug 1888
Nocturne (Matthew Hale) **20** 1 Jul 1899
Norwegian Melody, A (Edvard Grieg) **6** 6 Dec 1884
Old-Fashioned Christmastide, An: A Reverie (Ruth S. Cove) **14 Christmas** 1892
Polish Melody, A (Gordon Saunders) **10 Summer** 1889
Prelude (H.A.J. Campbell) **10** 14 Sep 1889
Romance (Clara Schumann) **13** 17 Oct 1891
Rondino in G: For Pianoforte (C. A. Macirone) **8** 2 Apr 1887
Sketch for the Pianoforte, A (Arthur Carnall) **5** 24 May 1884
Sketch for the Pianoforte (Myles B. Foster) **26** 15 Apr 1905
'Sorrow' – 'Joy' (Fanny Scholfield Petrie) **11** 30 Aug 1890
Summer Song (Cécile Hartog) **12** 4 Jul 1891
'Tendresse' (Album Leaf) (Walter Macfarren) **6** 7 Feb 1885
Three 'Album Leaves': Solitude, Despair, Peace (Myles B. Foster) **11** 7 Dec 1889
To Dolly (C. Hubert H. Parry) **14** 12 Nov 1892
Under the Waves: A Pianoforte Piece (H.A.J. Campbell) **8** 2 Jul 1887
With the Tide: Holiday Duet for Pianoforte (Myles B. Foster) **12 Summer** 1891

Violin, cello

Andante: For Violin and Pianoforte (Arthur Bunnett) **4** 24 Mar 1883
'On Richmond Hill' (arr. C. A. Macirone) (piano, cello, violin) **14** 14 Jan 1893
Retrospect, A (Myles B. Foster) (1st, 2nd violins, piano) **11** 3 May 1890
Romance: For Violin and Piano (J. T. Field) **13** 7 May 1892
Romance: For Violin and Pianoforte (Professor Sir G. A. Macfarren) **8** 2 Oct 1886

Romance, for Violin and Pianoforte (G. A. Macfarren) **9** 12 Nov 1887
Romance for Violin: With Pianoforte Accompaniment (Myles B. Foster) **11 Summer** 1890
Sister's Lullaby, A: For Violin and Pianoforte (Lady Lindsay of Balcarres) **2** 9 Apr 1881

Voice, solo[2]

Afternoon in February (Mrs Tom Taylor, Words Longfellow) **4** 3 Feb 1883
Afternoon in February (E. Silas, Words Longfellow) **7** 16 Jan 1886
Absence (C. A. Lidgey, Words Anonymous) **27** 16 Jun 1906
Absent Friends (C. E. Rawstorne, Words Sarah Doudney from *Leisure Hour*) **3** 1 Apr 1882
All in Vain (Ballad) (Franz Abt, Words Edward Oxenford) **4** 1 Sep 1883
Antiphon: Daylight Fades Away (C. A. Macirone, Words George MacDonald) **13** 20 Feb 1892
Be Strong! (Myles B. Foster, Words Adelaide Procter) (keyboard acc.) **15** 16 Jun 1894
Because You Love Me (E. L. Earle, Words E. M. Dunaway) **21** 17 Mar 1900
Better Light, The (The Rev. W. J. Foxell, Words Mrs Payne-Smith) **10** 2 Mar 1889
Blackbird and the Choir, The (Edwin M. Lott, Words Alice King) **5** 23 Aug 1884
Blossom, The (Mary Carmichel, Words William Blake) **8** 5 Feb 1887
Blossom That Never Dies, A (Cécile Hartog, Words Caroline Radford) **10** 22 Jun 1889
Blue-Eyed Maiden's Song, The (H.R.H. Princess Beatrice – Princess Henry of Battenberg, Words The Earl of Beaconsfield) **16** 6 Oct 1894
Brook, The (Mrs Tom Taylor, Words Alfred Tennyson) **2** 9 Jul 1881
Brook and the Wave, The (Cécile S. Hartog, Words Longfellow) **6 Summer** 1885
Burden of the Wind, The (Ernst Helmer, Words Lady Elliot) **10** 2 Feb 1889
Canzonette (Walter Wesché, Words from *Measure for Measure*) **3** 13 May 1882
Changes: Song (Hamish MacCunn, Words Lady Lindsay of Balcarres) **15** 14 Oct 1893
Chimes of Evening (Franz Abt, Words Edward Oxenford) **3** 14 Jan 1882
Christmas (Ciro Pinsuti, Words S.E.G.) **3 Christmas** 1881
Christmas Angels, The (Elizabeth Philp, Words R. L. Gales) **5 Christmas** 1883
Christmas-tide Remembrance, A (C. A. Macirone, Words Mrs Norton) **9** 3 Dec 1887
Come Home Again (C. A. Macirone, Words *old MS*) **6** 3 Jan 1885
Constancy of Love, The (Alma Sanders, Words Anne Beale) **2** 3 Sep 1881
Cradle Song (Mrs Tom Taylor, Words from Blake's 'Song of Innocence') **11** 11 Jan 1890
Day of Rest, The (Cotsford Dick) **8** 21 May 1887
Dead Heart, The (Gordon Saunders) **2** 5 Feb 1881
Dost Thou Not Know? (The Rev. C. Pendock Banks, Words Ellen T. Fowler) **25 Christmas** 1903

Endymion: A New Song (Myles B. Foster, Words Longfellow) **18 Christmas** 1896
Eventide (J. W. Hinton, Words Augusta Hancock) **14** 23 Sep 1893
Eventide (Charles P. Banks, Words Adelina Fermi) **16** 29 Jun 1895
Exiles, The (Suchet Champion, Words Dora Gillespie) **11** 21 Jun 1890
Faithful (C. A. Macirone, Words Mary Cowden Clarke) **11** 1 Feb 1890
Father of Love: Hymn for a Wedding (Myles B. Foster, Words Henry Hamilton) (keyboard acc.) **18** 12 Jun 1897
Feeding the Deer (James Russell, Words John Huie) **1** 8 May 1880
'Forget Me Not!' (Alma Sanders) **1** 14 Aug 1880
For Old Sake's Sake (Lady William Lennox, Words Helen Marion Burnside) **6** 2 May 1885
Forgive and Forget (Madame Sainton-Dolby, Words S.E.G.) **3** 17 Dec 1881
Gladness of Nature, The (C. A. Macirone, Words Cullen Bryant) **9** 5 May 1888
Golden Thread, The (Mrs Tom Taylor) **3** 10 Jun 1882
Good Night (J. W. Hinton, Words Sarah Doudney) **1** 21 Feb 1880
'Good-bye!' (J. W. Hinton, Words from *The Sunday at Home*) **1** 4 Sep 1880
Good-Night! A Serenade (Myles B. Foster, Words Sarah Doudney) **10** 10 Aug 1899
Green Cavalier's Song, The (H.R.H. Princess Henry of Battenberg, Words The Earl of Beaconsfield) **17** 5 Oct 1895
Hail to the Chief! Boat Song (Mrs Tom Taylor, Words Sir Walter Scott) **8** 6 Aug 1887
Her Only Child (Louisa Gray, Words Fred. E. Weatherly) **4** 7 Jul 1883
Hidden Love (Edvard Greig, Words Björnson, English trans. F. Corder) **14** 22 Oct 1892
'I Love Old Songs' (J. W. Hinton, Words Anne Beale) **2** 20 Aug 1881
'I Need Some Music' (Song, introducing theme of Chopin's Nocturne in G Major) (Thomas Ely, Words Norman R. Gale) **20** 12 Aug 1899
Idyl, An (The Countess of Munster) **12** 18 Apr 1891
'In Autumn Days' (Charles P. Banks, Words E. Matheson) **15** 22 Sep 1894
In the Churchyard (Humphrey J. Stark, Words Knight Summers) **2** 1 Jan 1881
Ingle-nook, The: A New Song (Suchet Champion, Words Augusta Hancock) **21 Christmas** 1899
Invitation, The (Myles B. Foster, Words Charles Peters) **21** 8 Sep 1900
Jennie's Wooing (Cécile S, Hartog, Words Emma C. Dowd) **13 Summer** 1892
Kind Words (Cotsford Dick, Words Helen Marion Burnside) **3** 12 Nov 1881
'Leal' (Suchet Champion, Words Chas. J. Rowe) **9** 7 Jul 1888
Lessons of the Gorses (Alice Mary Smith [Mrs Meadows White], Words Elizabeth Browning) **4** 9 Dec 1882
Lo! the Herald (Franz Abt, Words Edward Oxenford) **8** 3 Sep 1887
Little While Ago, A (Charles P. Banks, Words Sarah Doudney) **15** 17 Mar 1894
Longing (Ethel L. Watson, Words Matthew Arnold) **18** 16 Jan 1897
Lord Is My Shepherd, The: A Sacred Song (C. E. Rawstorne) **5** 21 Jun 1884
Love and Laughter (C.H.H. Parry, Words Arthur Butler) **13** 19 Dec 1891
Love Is Ours (Louisa Bodda-Pyne, Words H. Barrington) **6** 8 Nov 1884

Music scores by instrument 335

Love's Summer Dream (Lady William Lennox, Words G. W. Gilbart Smith) **8** 12 Mar 1887
Lucy (Myles B. Foster, Words Wordsworth) **5** 16 Feb 1884
Lullaby, A (Joseph Barnby) **2** 9 Oct 1880
Margaret (Edwin M. Lott, Words Gertrude Moberly) **2** 7 May 1881
Mary Morison (George J. Bennett, Words Robert Burns) **11** 12 Jul 1890
Mona Spinning (Mary Carmichael, Words Alice Cary) **7** 10 Jul 1886
Morning (Gordon Saunders, Words Lewis Novra) **1** 17 Apr 1880
Mountaineer's Bride, The: Tyrolienne for the Voice (Sir Julius Benedict) **2** 5 Mar 1881
'Must We Part, and Part So Soon?'(Franz Abt, Words Edward Oxenford) **5 Summer** 1884
'My Little Knight' (Elizabeth Philp, Words Astley Baldwin) **7** 26 Jun 1886
'My Love' (Charles P. Banks) **14** 11 Feb 1893
My Love Is Dead (Mary Carmichael, Words P. B. Marston) **6** 11 Jul 1885
My Love Is Near! (Rosalind Frances Ellicott, Words Mabel Parsons) **11** 19 Oct 1889
Nazareth (Charles Gounod) **27 Christmas** 1905
Night Hymn at Sea (Natalie, Words Mrs Hemans) **3** 1 Jul 1882
O Yes! O Yes! O Yes! Part-Song for Mixed Voices (C. A. Macirone, Words from 'Roxburghe Ballads', 1500) (keyboard acc.) **7** 8 May 1886
Oh, Why Not Be Happy? 'A Quoi bon Entendre les Oiseaux' (A. C. Mackenzie, Words Victor Hugo, trans. Leopold Wray) **10** 20 Oct 1888
Old Memories (Charles Vincent, Words Arthur Burchett) **10** 13 Apr 1889
Old Songs (Suchet Champion, Words Anne Beale) **6** 8 Aug 1885
Old Times (Franz Abt, Words Edward Oxenford) **5** 3 Nov 1883
Out-bound Bark, The (Gordon Saunders, Words, Albert E. Drinkwater) **12** 8 Aug 1891
Rainy Day, The (Ethel Harraden, Words Longfellow) **9** 7 Apr 1888
Rainy Day, The (Amelia Corper, Words Longfellow) **9 Summer** 1888
Rajah's Daughter, The: Eastern Song (Theo. Marzials) **21 Summer** 1900
Reapers, The (Franz Abt, Words E. Oxenford) **3 Summer** 1882
Retrospection (H.R.H. the Princess Beatrice – Princess Henry of Battenberg, Words Charlotte Elliott) **18** 3 Oct 1896
Retrospection (H.R.H. the Princess Beatrice – Princess Henry of Battenberg, Words Charlotte Elliott) **32** Dec 1910
'Rise Up, My Love!' (The Countess of Munster, Words from 'The Song of Solomon') **7** 17 Oct 1885
Rose, The (The Rev. F. Peel, Words The Hon. C. F. Fox) **2** 18 Jun 1881
Rose and the Dewdrop, The (C. A. Macirone, Words from 'Pearls of Faith' by Edwin Arnold) **5** 5 Apr 1884
Sea Waves (Charles H. Bassett) **3** 11 Feb 1882
Sea-Boy's Song, The (Sir George C. Martin, Words The Rev. H. C. Shuttleworth) **19** 23 Apr 1898
See, the Dawn from Heaven Is Breaking! A Christmas Carol (W. C. Cusins, Words Thomas Moore) **7** 19 Dec 1885

336 *Music scores by instrument*

See! the Swallows Circle O'er Us (Franz Abt, Words Edward Oxenford) **11** 9 Nov 1889
Shine Out, Stars! (R. Thorley Brown, Words T. Moore) **11** 5 Apr 1890
'Since I Was Young' (Theo. Marzials, Words May Probyn) **16** 2 Feb 1895
Sing, Sweet Warblers (Franz Abt, Words Edward Oxenford) **14** 20 May 1893
Slumber Song, The (G. Feldstein, Words Maggie Macdonald) **4** 20 Jan 1883
Song (Frank Barât, Words Barham) **16** 17 Aug 1895
Song: – 'Come to Me, O Ye Children' (C. A. Macirone, Words W. H. [*sic*] Longfellow) **14** 10 Jun 1893
Song in a Dream, A (C. Villiers Stanford, Words N. Breton) **18** 19 Dec 1896
Spirit of Mine Eyes, The (John Gledhill) **4** 12 May 1883
Spring (Cotsford Dick, Words Sydney Grey) **4** 7 Apr 1883
Stay, Fleeting Hour (Franz Abt, Words Edward Oxenford) **7** 21 Nov 1885
Streamlet, The (The Rev. R. F. Dale, Words M. A. Stodart) **5** 19 Jul 1884
Success and Long Life to the 'G.O.P.' (M.B.F., Words Helen Marion Burnside) **20** 29 Apr 1899
Summer Morning, A (L. Meadows White, Words Edward Medland White) **15 Summer** 1894
Sunday Song: 'O Saviour, I Have Nought to Plead' (C. A. Macirone) **10** 13 Jul 1889
Sunset: A Lullaby (Ruth S. Cove) **17** 18 Jul 1896
'Sweet and Low' (Emily, Lady Tennyson, arr. Natalie Janotha, Words Alfred, Lord Tennyson) **16** 9 Mar 1895
Sweet Lavender (Mary Carmichael, Words Helen M. Burnside) **16 Summer** 1895
'The Lady I Love' (The Countess of Munster, Words Frederick Locker) **9** 8 Oct 1887
'They Say There Is Anguish' (Ernst Helmer, Words Everard Clive) **3** 5 Aug 1882
'Think Upon Me' (Sacred Air) (C. A. Macirone, Words Neh 5: 19) **12** 15 Nov 1890
Thistle, The: A Flower Ballad (C. A. Macirone, Words The Earl Lytton) **8** 4 Jun 1887
'Those Silv'ry Sounds' (Ethel Harraden, Words Gertrude Harraden) **10** 8 Dec 1888
Three Little Clouds, The (C. E. Rawstorne, Words Kate Kellog) **14** 29 Jul 1893
Time at the Ferry (Lady Benedict, Words Jetty Vogel) **4** 4 Nov 1882
To Chloris (George J. Bennett, Words Robert Burns) **9** 7 Jan 1888
True Love Never Dies (Annie Nash, Words William Gaspey) **5** 22 Mar 1884
Trust (Berthold Tours, Words C. A. Moberly) **2** 13 Nov 1880
Tryst, The (Mary Carmichael, Words W. Davies) **3** 2 Sep 1882
'Tuning Up' (Natalie Janotha, Words Charles Peters from '*The Quiver*') (soprano or tenor, organ acc.) **16** 15 Dec 1894
'Two Little Tiny Wings' (E. Markham Lee, Words S. T. Coleridge) **23** 3 May 1902

Under the Greenwood Tree (Myles B. Foster, Words William Shakespeare) **13** 19 Mar 1892
Under the Snow (John Farmer, Words Hannah F. Gould) **1** 31 Jan 1880
Vain Lament, The (Hortense, Queen of Holland, English trans. Elsa D'Esterre-Keeling) **21** 22 Sep 1900
Valley's Queen, The (Elizabeth Philp, Words F. B. Doveton) **6** 11 Apr 1885
Village Bells (Charles Bassett) **4** 23 Jun 1883
Weep No More (William Hayman Cummings, Words John Fletcher, A.D. 1647) **18** 14 Nov 1896
Whither? (Humphrey J. Stark, Words H. W. Longfellow from German of Muller) **1** (12 Jun 1880
Widow Bird Sate Mourning, A (Maude Valérie White, Words Shelley) **7** 6 Mar 1886
Wish, A (Mrs Tom Taylor) **6** 28 Mar 1885
Withered Flowers (H.A.J. Campbell, Words from German of W. Müller) **10** 10 Nov 1888
Wondrous Cross, The (Myles B. Foster, Words Dr Watts) **9** 16 Jun 1888

Voice, ensemble[3]

Angels of the Bells, The: A Cantatina for Two Sopranos and a Contralto (Myles B. Foster, Words Helen M. Burnside) **6 Christmas** 1884
Angels' Song, The (C. H. Purday, Words Frances Ridley Havergal) **4** 23 Dec 1882
Away to the Woodland Green: Two-Part Song (H.A.J. Campbell, Words H.G.F. Taylor) **21** 19 May 1900
Birds: Duet, The (C. A. Macirone, Words J. T. Coleridge) **8** 20 Nov 1886
Blest as the Immortal Gods: Duet for Mezzo-Soprano and Alto (C. A. Macirone, Words from Sappho, trans. Ambrose Phillips) **12** 2 May 1891
Carol for Female Voices (William H. Hunt, Refrain from Longfellow's 'Norman Baron') **5** 23 Dec 1893
Chirp and Twitter (Bird's Song): Part-Song for Girls' Voices (C. A. Macirone, Words Hans Andersen's Fairy Tales) **29** 4 Apr 1908
Christmas Carol, A (Cotsford Dick) **3** 31 Dec 1881
Christmas Carol, A (Aldred Scott Gatty) **4 Christmas** 1882
Christmas Carol, A (Mary Augusta Salmond, Words Helen Marion Burnside) **28** 8 Dec 1906
Christmas Rose, A: Cantatina for Girls' Voices (Myles B. Foster, Words Clara Thwaites) **7 Christmas** 1885
Coming of the King, The: A Cantatina for Two Sopranos and a Contralto (Myles B. Foster, Words Helen Marion Burnside) **16 Christmas** 1894
Evensong: Duet for Girls' Voices (C. A. Macirone, Words from an old Proverb) **9** 11 Aug 1888
Gipsies: Song and Chorus for Girls' Voices (Ethel Harraden, Words Gertrude Harraden) **20 Summer** 1899
Girl's Own Carol, The (Joseph Barnby) **5** 22 Dec 1883

'Give!' A Canon, with Intermezzo (Myles B. Foster, Words Adelaide Ann Procter) **9 Christmas** 1887

Gold, Frankincense, and Myrrh: Cantatina for Girls' Voices, in Three Parts (Myles B. Foster, Words Clara Thwaites) **8 Christmas** 1886

'Golden Bright on Hill and Valley': An Easter Carol (Myles B. Foster, Words Florence Hoare) **17** 21 Mar 1896

Hymn for the Girls, A (The Rev. Sir F. A. Gore Ouseley) **1** 3 Jul 1880

'In Vesture White': A Song and Chorale for Christmas-tide (Myles B. Foster, Words The Rev. Richard Wilton) **10 Christmas** 1888

'Joy Cometh in the Morning': A Short Cantata for Girls' Voices (Mary Augusta Salmond, Words Helen Marion Burnside) **17 Christmas** 1895

Love Having Once Flown (C. A. Macirone, Words Sir Philip Sydney) **4** 14 Oct 1882

Marching Tune: 'One Foot Up, and One Foot Down': Old Nursery Rhyme for Girls' Voices (C. A. Macirone) **17** 11 Apr 1896

Merry Harvest Time, The **4** 22 Sep 1883

Monday's Child (C. A. Macirone, Words Old Rhyme) **28** 7 Sep 1907

New Hymn Tune, A (C. A. Macirone) (organ acc.) **14** 29 Apr 1893

Old Christmas Carol, An **2** 25 Dec 1880

Parting: A Trio for Female Voices (C. H. Purday) **1** 20 Mar 1880

Te Deum, A (Cantatina for Girls' Voices) (Myles B. Foster, Words Helen Marion Burnside) **24 Christmas** 1902

'The Gladness of Winter' (Mary Augusta Salmond, Words Helen Marion Burnside) **20 Christmas** 1898

'The Old Refrain': Lines on the Death of a Chorister (The Rev. L. Meadows White, Words Edward Medland White) **18** 13 Mar 1897

Vocal Studies for Girls: For Solo, Duet, and Class Practice (Jacob Bradford) **15** 17 Feb 1894

Notes

1 Variations from the instrument heading included in parentheses after composer's name.
2 Scored for pianoforte accompaniment unless otherwise indicated.
3 Scored for pianoforte accompaniment unless otherwise indicated.

Index to music scores by composer

Abt, Franz

All in Vain (Ballad) **4** 1 Sep 1883
Chimes of Evening **3** 14 Jan 1882
Lo! the Herald **8** 3 Sep 1887
'Must We Part, and Part So Soon?' **5 Summer** 1884
Old Times **5** 3 Nov 1883
Reapers, The **3 Summer** 1882
See! the Swallows Circle O'er Us **11** 9 Nov 1889
Sing, Sweet Warblers **14** 20 May 1893
Stay, Fleeting Hour **7** 21 Nov 1885

Banks, Charles P.

Dost Thou Not Know? **25 Christmas** 1903
Eventide **16** 29 Jun 1895
'In Autumn Days' **15** 22 Sep 1894
Little While Ago, A **15** 17 Mar 1894
'My Love' **14** 11 Feb 1893

Barât, Frank

Song **16** 17 Aug 1895

Barnby, Joseph

Girl's Own Carol, The **5** 22 Dec 1883
Lullaby, A **2** 9 Oct 1880

Bassett, Charles H.

Sea Waves **3** 11 Feb 1882
Village Bells **4** 23 Jun 1883

H.R.H. Princess Beatrice (Princess Henry of Battenberg)

Blue-Eyed Maiden's Song, The **16** 6 Oct 1894
Green Cavalier's Song, The **17** 5 Oct 1895

Retrospection **18** 3 Oct 1896
Retrospection **32** Dec 1910

Benedict, Lady

Time at the Ferry **4** 4 Nov 1882

Benedict, Sir Julius

Mountaineer's Bride, The: Tyrolienne for the Voice **2** 5 Mar 1881

Bennett, George J.

Intermezzo: Duet for Pianoforte **14 Summer** 1893
Mary Morison **11** 12 Jul 1890
Mille Amitiés **12** 1 Nov 1890
To Chloris **9** 7 Jan 1888

Bodda-Pyne, Louisa

Love Is Ours **6** 8 Nov 1894

Boyce, Ethel M.

Mazurka in C Minor **10** 11 May 1889

Bradford, Jacob

Vocal Studies for Girls: For Solo, Duet, and Class Practice **15** 17 Feb 1894

Brown, R. Thorley

Shine Out, Stars! **11** 5 Apr 1890

Burnett, Arthur

Andante: For Violin and Pianoforte **4** 24 Mar 1883

Campbell, H.A.J.

Allegro **11** 1 Mar 1890
Aubade **13** 9 Jul 1892
Away to the Woodland Green: Two-Part Song **21** 19 May 1900
Gavotte **9** 10 Mar 1888
Minuet and Musette **12** 20 Jun 1891
Nocturne **9** 11 Aug 1888
Prelude **10** 14 Sep 1889
Under the Waves: A Pianoforte Piece **8** 2 Jul 1887
Withered Flowers **10** 10 Nov 1888

Carmichael, Mary

Blossom, The **8** 5 Feb 1887
Mona Spinning **7** 10 Jul 1886
My Love Is Dead **6** 11 Jul 1885
Sweet Lavender **16 Summer** 1895
Tryst, The **3** 2 Sep 1882

Carnall, Arthur

Sketch for the Pianoforte, A **5** 24 May 1884

Champion, Suchet

Exiles, The **11** 21 Jun 1890
Ingle-nook, The: A New Song **21 Christmas** 1899
'Leal' **9** 7 Jul 1888
Old Songs **6** 8 Aug 1895

Corper, Amelia

Rainy Day, The **9 Summer** 1888

The Countess of Munster

Idyl, An **12** 18 Apr 1891
'Rise Up, My Love!' **7** 17 Oct 1885
'The Lady I Love' **9** 8 Oct 1887

Cove, Ruth S.

Old-Fashioned Christmastide, An: A Reverie **14 Christmas** 1892
Sunset: A Lullaby **17** 18 Jul 1896

Cummings, William Hayman

Weep No More **18** 14 Nov 1896

Cusins, W. G.

See, the Dawn from Heaven Is Breaking! A Christmas Carol **7** 19 Dec 1885

Dale, The Rev. R. F.

Streamlet, The **5** 19 Jul 1884

Dick, Cotsford

Christmas Carol, A **3** 31 Dec 1881
Day of Rest, The **8** 21 May 1887

Kind Words **3** 12 Nov 1881
Spring **4** 7 Apr 1883

Earl, E. L.

Because You Love Me **21** 17 Mar 1900

Ellicott, Rosalind Frances

My Love Is Near! **11** 19 Oct 1889

Ely, Thomas

'I Need Some Music' (Song, introducing theme of Chopin's Nocturne in G Major) **20** 12 Aug 1899

Farmer, John

Under the Snow **1** 31 Jan 1880

Feldstein, G.

Slumber Song, The **4** 20 Jan 1883

Field, J. T.

Romance: For Violin and Piano **13** 7 May 1892

Foster, Myles B.

Adagio ma non Troppo: For the Pianoforte or American Organ **19** 10 Sep 1898
Allegretto Giojoso: For the Pianoforte or American Organ **12** 12 Sep 1891
Allegro con Moto Agitato: For Pianoforte or American Organ **19** 22 Jan 1898
Andante Pastorale: For the Pianoforte or American Organ **12** 31 Jan 1891
Andante Scherzoso: For the Pianoforte **5** 6 Sep 1884
Angels of the Bells, The: A Cantatina for Two Sopranos and a Contralto **6 Christmas** 1884
Be Strong! **15** 16 Jun 1894
Chorale: For Pianoforte or American Organ **19** 11 Dec 1897
Christmas Rose, A: Cantatina for Girls' Voices **7 Christmas** 1885
Coming of the King, The: A Cantatina for Two Sopranos and a Contralto **16 Christmas** 1894
Crusaders' March: For the Harmonium or American Organ **13** 27 Aug 1892
Elegy: For the Harmonium or American Organ **13** 9 Apr 1892
Endymion: A New Song **18 Christmas** 1896
Father of Love: Hymn for a Wedding **18** 12 Jun 1897
Gavotte **14** 19 Aug 1893
'Give!' A Canon, with Intermezzo **9 Christmas** 1887
Gold, Frankincense, and Myrrh: Cantatina for Girls' Voices, in Three Parts **8 Christmas** 1886

'Golden Bright on Hill and Valley': An Easter Carol **17** 21 Mar 1896
Good-Night! A Serenade **10** 10 Apr 1889
'In Vesture White': A Song and Chorale for Christmas-tide **10 Christmas** 1888
Invitation, The **21** 8 Sep 1900
Little Mazourka, A: In Memory of Chopin (Born March 1, 1809) **7** 20 Feb 1886
Lucy **5** 16 Feb 1884
Meditation: For the Harmonium or American Organ **13** 24 Sep 1892
Minuet **14** 17 Dec 1892
Minuet and Trio: From a Suite for Orchestra **6** 12 Sep 1885
Postlude: For Pianoforte or American Organ **17** 1896
Retrospect, A **11** 3 May 1890
Romance for Violin: With Pianoforte Accompaniment **11 Summer** 1890
Sketch for the Pianoforte **26** 15 Apr 1905
Success and Long Life to the 'G.O.P.' **20** 29 Apr 1899
Supplication: For Harmonium or American Organ **14** 18 Mar 1893
Te Deum (Cantatina for Girls' Voices) **24 Christmas** 1902
Three 'Album Leaves': Solitude, Despair, Peace **11** 7 Dec 1889
Under the Greenwood Tree **13** 19 Mar 1892
With the Tide: Holiday Duet for Pianoforte **12 Summer** 1891
Wondrous Cross, The **9** 16 Jun 1888

Foxell, The Rev. W. J.

Better Light, The **10** 2 Mar 1889

Gatty, Alfred Scott

Christmas Carol, A **4 Christmas** 1882

Gledhill, John

Spirit of Mine Eyes, The **4** 12 May 1883

Gounod, Charles

Nazareth **27 Christmas** 1905

Gray, Louisa

Her Only Child **4** 7 Jul 1883

Grieg, Edvard

Hidden Love **14** 22 Oct 1892
Norwegian Melody, A **6** 6 Dec 1884

Harraden, Ethel

Gipsies: Song and Chorus for Girls' Voices **20 Summer** 1899
Rainy Day, The **9** 7 Apr 1888
'Those Silv'ry Sounds' **10** 8 Dec 1888

Hale, Matthew

Nocturne: For Pianoforte **20** 1 Jul 1899

Hartog, Cécile S.

Berceuse **7** 3 Apr 1886
Blossom That Never Dies, A **10** 22 Jun 1889
Brook and the Wave, The **6 Summer** 1885
Gavotte **28** 2 Feb 1907
Jennie's Wooing **13 Summer** 1892
Summer Song **12** 4 Jul 1891

Helmer, Ernst

Burden of the Wind, The **10** 2 Feb 1889
'They Say There Is Anguish' **3** 5 Apr 1882

H.R.H. Hereditary Grand Duke of Hesse

Andante: For the Pianoforte **16** 18 May 1895

Hinton, J. W.

Berceuse **8** 15 Jan 1887
Eventide **14** 23 Sep 1893
Good Night **1** 21 Feb 1880
'Good-bye!' **1** 4 Sep 1880
'I Love Old Songs' **2** 20 Aug 1881
Rêverie: For the Harmonium or American Organ **9** 4 Feb 1888

Hortense, Queen of Holland

Vain Lament, The **21** 22 Sep 1900

Humperdinck, E.

Albumblatt **17** 1 Feb 1896

Hunt, William H.

Carol for Female Voices **15** 23 Dec 1893

Janotha, Natalie

Barcarolle (from the 'Mountain Scenes') **17 Summer** 1896
Edelweiss **12** 7 Mar 1891
Mazourka in E Minor, Op. 6 No. 1 **15** 21 July 1894
Night Hymn at Sea **3** 1 Jul 1882
'Tuning Up' **16** 15 Dec 1894

Ketèlbey, Albert W.

    Impromptu: For Pianoforte **21** 17 Mar 1900

Lee, E. Markham

    'Two Little Tiny Wings' **23** 3 May 1902

Lennox, Lady William

    For Old Sake's Sake **6** 2 May 1885
    Love's Summer Dream **8** 12 Mar 1887

Lidgey, C. A.

    Absence **27** 16 Jun 1906

Lindsay, Lady (of Balcarres)

    Sister's Lullaby, A: For Violin and Pianoforte **2** 9 Apr 1881

Lott, Edwin M.

    Blackbird and the Choir, The **5** 23 Aug 1884
    Dernier Papillon, Le **3** 29 Oct 1881
    Evening Clouds **4** 4 Aug 1883
    Margaret **2** 7 May 1881

MacCunn, Hamish

    Changes: Song **15** 14 Oct 1893

Macfarren, G. A.

    Romance: For Violin and Pianoforte **8** 2 Oct 1886
    Romance, for Violin and Pianoforte **9** 12 Nov 1887

Macfarren, Walter

    'Tendresse' (Album Leaf) **6** 7 Feb 1885

Macirone, C. A.

    Antiphon: Daylight Fades Away **13** 20 Feb 1892
    Birds, The: Duet **8** 20 Nov 1886
    Blest as the Immortal Gods: Duet for Mezzo-Soprano and Alto **12** 2 May 1891
    Chirp and Twitter (Bird's Song): Part-Song for Girls' Voices **29** 4 Apr 1908
    Christmas-tide Remembrance, A **9** 3 Dec 1887
    Come Home Again **6** 3 Jan 1885
    Evensong: Duet for Girls' Voices **9** 11 Aug 1888
    Faithful **11** 1 Feb 1890

Gladness of Nature, The **9** 5 May 1888
Love Having Once Flown **4** 14 Oct 1882
Marching Tune: 'One Foot Up, and One Foot Down': Old Nursery Rhyme for Girls' Voices **17** 11 Apr 1896
Merrie England: 'Here's to the Maiden of Bashful Fifteen' **6** 6 Jun 1885
Merrie England: I. 'Oh, How Should I Your True Love Know?' **4 Summer** 1883
Monday's Child **28** 7 Sep 1907
New Hymn Tune, A **14** 29 Apr 1893
O Yes! O Yes! O Yes! Part-Song for Mixed Voices **7** 8 May 1886
Oh, Why Not Be Happy? 'A Quoi bon Entendre les Oiseaux' **10** 20 Oct 1888
'On Richmond Hill' **14** 14 Jan 1893
Rondino in G: For Pianoforte **8** 2 Apr 1887
Rose and the Dewdrop, The **5** 5 Apr 1884
Song: – 'Come to Me, O Ye Children' **14** 10 Jun 1893
Sunday Song: 'O Saviour, I Have Nought to Plead' **10** 13 Jul 1889
'Think Upon Me' (Sacred Air) **12** 15 Nov 1890
Thistle, The: A Flower Ballad **8** 4 Jun 1887

Martin, Sir George C.

Sea-Boy's Song, The **19** 21 Apr 1898

Marzials, Theo.

Rajah's Daughter, The: Eastern Song **21 Summer** 1900
'Since I Was Young' **16** 2 Feb 1895

Nash, Annie E.

L'Allegrezza **3** 4 Mar 1882
True Love Never Dies **5** 22 Mar 1884

Ouseley, The Rev. Sir F. A. Gore

Hymn for the Girls, A **1** 3 Jul 1880

Parry, C. H. Hubert

Love and Laughter **13** 19 Dec 1891
To Dolly **14** 12 Nov 1892

Pauer, Ernst

Fairies, The: Scherzo for the Pianoforte **6** 18 Oct 1884

Peel, The Rev. F.

Rose, The **2** 18 Jun 1881

Petrie, Fanny Scholfield

'Sorrow' and 'Joy' **11** 30 Aug 1890

Philp, Elizabeth

Christmas Angels, The **5 Christmas** 1883
'My Little Knight' **7** 26 Jun 1886
Valley's Queen, The **6** 11 Apr 1885

Pinsuti, Ciro

Christmas **3 Christmas** 1881

Purday, C. H.

Angels' Song, The **4** 23 Dec 1882
Parting: A Trio for Female Voices **1** 20 Mar 1880

Rawstorne, C. E.

Absent Friends **3** 1 Apr 1882
Lord Is My Shepherd, The: A Sacred Song **5** 29 Jul 1894
Three Little Clouds, The **14** 29 Jul 1893

Russell, James

Feeding the Deer **1** 8 May 1880

Sainton-Dolby, Madame

Forgive and Forget **3** 17 Dec 1881

Salmond, Mary Augusta

Christmas Carol, A **28** 18 Dec 1906
'Joy Cometh in the Morning': A Short Cantata for Girls' Voices **17 Christmas** 1895
'The Gladness of Winter' **20 Christmas** 1898

Sanders, Alma

Constancy of Love, The **2** 3 Sep 1881
'Forget Me Not!' **1** 14 Aug 1880

Saunders, Gordon

Dead Heart, The **2** 5 Feb 1881
Evening **7** 14 Aug 1886
Morning **1** 17 Apr 1880
Out-bound Bark, The **12** 8 Aug 1891

Polish Melody, A **10 Summer** 1889

Schumann, Clara

Romance **13** 17 Oct 1891

Silas, E.

Afternoon in February **7** 16 Jan 1886

Smith, Alice Mary (Mrs Meadows White)

Lessons of the Gorses **4** 9 Dec 1882

Stanford, C. Villiers

Song in a Dream, A **18** 19 Dec 1896

Stark, Humphrey J.

In the Churchyard **2** 1 Jan 1881
Whither? **1** 12 Jun 1880

Taylor, Mrs Tom

Afternoon in February **4** 3 Feb 1883
Brook, The **2** 9 Jul 1881
Cradle Song **11** 11 Jan 1890
Gathering Cowslips: Retrospect **7 Summer** 1886
Golden Thread, The **3** 10 Jun 1882
Hail to the Chief! Boat Song **8** 6 Aug 1887
Wish, A **6** 28 Mar 1885

Tennyson, Lady Emily

'Sweet and Low' **16** 9 Mar 1895

Thompson, Lady (Kate Loder)

Mazurka **17** 23 May 1896

Tours, Berthold

Trust **2** 13 Nov 1880

Vincent, Charles

Old Memories **10** 13 Apr 1889

Watson, Ethel L.

Longing **18** 16 Jan 1897

Wesché, Walter

Canzonette **3** 13 May 1882

White, the Rev. L. Meadows

Summer Morning, A **15 Summer** 1894
'The Old Refrain': Lines on the Death of a Chorister **18** 13 Mar 1897

White, Maude Valérie

Widow Bird Sate Mourning, A **7** 6 Mar 1886

No composer given

Merry Harvest Time, The **4** 22 Sep 1883
Old Christmas Carol, An **2** 25 Dec 1880

Works cited

Excludes references to *The Girl's Own Paper* and *The Boy's Own Paper*, which may be found in the Introduction end notes.

'Are We a Musical People?' *Chambers's Journal of Popular Literature, Science, and Art* 4th ser. 18 (2 July 1881): 417–19.
Barger, Judith. *Elizabeth Stirling and the Musical Life of Female Organists in Nineteenth-Century England.* Aldershot and Burlington, VT: Ashgate, 2007.
Beetham, Margaret. *A Magazine of Her Own? Domesticity and Desire in the Woman's Magazine, 1800–1914.* London and New York: Routledge, 1996.
Burgan, Mary. 'Heroines at the Piano: Women and Music in Nineteenth-Century Fiction'. In *The Lost Chord: Essays on Victorian Music*, edited by Nicholas Temperley, 42–66. Bloomington and Indianapolis: Indiana University Press, 1989.
Cox, Jack. *Take a Cold Tub, Sir!: The Story of the* 'Boy's Own Paper'. Guildford: Lutterworth, 1982.
Doughty, Terri, ed. *Selections from* The Girl's Own Paper, *1880–1907*. Peterborough, ON and Orchard Park, NY: Broadview, 2004.
Drotner, Kirsten. *English Children and Their Magazines, 1751–1945.* New Haven, CT and London: Yale University Press, 1988.
Dunae, Patrick. '*Boy's Own Paper*: Origin and Editorial Policies'. *The Private Library* 2nd ser., 9/4 (1976): 125–58.
Ehrlich, Cyril. *The Music Profession in Britain since the Eighteenth Century: A Social History.* Oxford: Clarendon, 1985.
Ehrlich, Cyril. *The Piano: A History.* London: Dent, 1976.
The Eighty-First Annual Report of the Religious Tract Society. London: Religious Tract Society, 1880.
Forrester, Wendy. *Great-Grandmama's Weekly: A Celebration of* The Girl's Own Paper *1880–1901*. Guilford and London: Lutterworth, 1980.
Gaskell, Catherine Milnes. 'The Women of To-day'. *Nineteenth Century* 26 (November 1889): 776–84.
Gillett, Paula. *Musical Women in England, 1870–1914: 'Encroaching on All Man's Privileges'.* New York: St Martin's, 2000.
'The Girl's Own Annual'. *Musical Standard* 4th ser., 21 (17 September 1881): 192.
'The Girl's Own Annual'. *Musical Times* 22 (1 October 1881): 536.
Grace, June, ed. *Advice to Young Ladies from the Nineteenth-Century Correspondence Pages of* The Girl's Own Paper. N.p.: Author, 1997.

Green, Samuel G. *The Story of the Religious Tract Society for One Hundred Years*. London: Religious Tract Society, 1899.
Hindle, Roy, ed. *Oh, No Dear! Advice to Girls a Century Ago*. London: David and Charles, 1982.
Huneker, James. *Overtones: A Book of Temperaments*. New York: Scribner, 1904.
Klickmann, Flora. 'Moments with Modern Musicians: Famous Organists'. *The Windsor Magazine* 111 (January to June 1896): 665–78.
Lazell, David. *Flora Klickmann and Her Flower Patch: The Story of 'The Girl's Own Paper' and The Flower Patch Among the Hills*. Warmley: Flower Patch Magazine, n.d.
Ledbetter, Kathryn. *British Victorian Women's Periodicals: Beauty, Civilization, and Poetry*. New York: Palgrave Macmillan, 2009.
Leppert, Richard. *Music and Image: Domesticity, Ideology and Socio-Cultural Formation in Eighteenth-Century England*. Cambridge: Cambridge University Press, 1988.
'Literary Gossip'. *Athenaeum* no. 4184 (4 January 1908): 17.
Locke, John. *Some Thoughts Concerning Education* [1693]. Cambridge: University Press, 1895.
Loesser, Arthur. *Men, Women and Pianos: A Social History*. New York: Simon and Schuster, 1954.
Lustig, Jodi. 'The Piano's Progress: The Piano in Play in the Victorian Novel'. In *The Idea of Music in Victorian Fiction*, edited by Sophie Fuller and Nicky Losseff, 83–104. Aldershot and Burlington, VT: Ashgate, 2004.
Moruzi, Kristine. *Constructing Girlhood Through the Periodical Press, 1850–1915*. Farnham and Burlington, VT: Ashgate, 2012.
'No More Appropriate Christmas Present'. *Musical Times* 26 (1 December 1883): 740.
'The Pianoforte and Its Enemies'. *Musical Times* 37 (1 May 1896): 309.
Reynolds, Kimberly. *Girls Only? Gender and Popular Children's Fiction in Britain, 1880–1910*. Philadelphia: Temple University Press, 1990.
Rutland, Harold. *Trinity College of Music: The First Hundred Years*. London: Trinity College of Music, 1972.
Salmon, Edward. 'What Girls Read'. *Nineteenth Century* o.s. 116, n.s. 20 (1886): 515–29.
Skelding, Hilary. 'Every Girl's Best Friend? The *Girl's Own Paper* and its Readers'. In *Feminist Readings of Victorian Popular Texts: Divergent Femininities*, edited by Emma Liggins and Daniel Duffey, 35–52. Aldershot, Burlington, VT, Singapore and Sydney: Ashgate, 2001.
Stanhope, Philip Dormer. *Letters to His Son by the Earl of Chesterfield* [1749]. Vol. 1, Edited by Oliver H. G. Leigh. Washington and London: Dunne, 1901.
The Story of the House of Cassell. London, New York, Toronto and Melbourne: Cassell, 1922.
Tick, Judith. 'Passed Away Is the Piano Girl: Changes in American Musical Life, 1870–1900'. In *Women Making Music: The Western Art Tradition 1150–1950*, edited by Jane Bowers and Judith Tick, 325–48. Urbana: University of Illinois Press, 1986.
Trinity College, London: Calendar for the Academical Year 1877–1878. London: Reeves, 1877.
Turner, Michael, and Antony Miall, eds. *The Parlour Song Book: A Casquet of Vocal Gems*. London: Michael Joseph, 1972.
Weliver, Phyllis. *Women Musicians in Victorian Fiction, 1860–1900: Representations of Music, Science and Gender in the Leisured Home*. Aldershot and Burlington, VT: Ashgate, 2000.
Who's Who 1907: An Annual Biographical Dictionary. London: Adam and Charles Black; and New York: Macmillan, 1907.